WORLD'S FAIRS ITALIAN STYLE

The Great Exhibitions in Turin and Their Narratives, 1860–1915

According to conventional scholarship, Italy was not an influential participant in the nationalistic and imperialistic discourses that World's Fairs produced in Western nations in the late nineteenth and early twentieth centuries. However, during that period Italy hosted numerous national and international exhibitions expounding notions of national identity, imperial expansion, technological progress, and capitalist growth.

World's Fairs Italian Style explores the significance of World's Fairs in Italy at the turn of the twentieth century and compares them to their more famous counterparts in France, England, and the United States. Cristina Della Coletta demonstrates that, because of its social fragmentation and hybrid history, Italy was a site of both hegemony and subordination – an aspiring imperial power whose colonization started from within. She focuses on two best-selling authors, Emilio Salgari and Guido Gozzano, and illustrates how they interpreted their age's 'exposition mentality.' Salgari and Gozzano's narratives, Della Coletta argues, reveal Italy's uncertainties about its own sense of nationhood and its belated commitment to Western imperialism.

A fascinating glimpse into a hitherto unexplored area of study, *World's Fairs Italian Style* brings to light a cultural phenomenon that played a major role in shaping Italy's national identity.

(Toronto Italian Studies)

CRISTINA DELLA COLETTA is an associate professor in the Department of Spanish, Italian, and Portuguese at the University of Virginia.

D0813638

CRISTINA DELLA COLETTA

World's Fairs Italian Style

The Great Exhibitions in Turin and Their Narratives, 1860–1915

UNIVERSITY OF TORONTO PRESS
Toronto Buffalo London

© University of Toronto Press 2006
Toronto Buffalo London
www.utpublishing.com
Printed in the U.S.A.

Reprinted in paperback 2016

ISBN 978- 0-8020-9115-4 (cloth)   ISBN 978-1-4875-2056-4 (paper)

Printed on acid-free, 100% post-consumer recycled paper.

Toronto Italian Studies

Library and Archives Canada Cataloguing in Publication

Della Coletta, Cristina, 1962–
World's fairs, Italian style : the great exhibitions in Turin and their narratives,
1860–1915 / Cristina Della Coletta.

(Toronto Italian studies)
Includes bibliographical references and index.
ISBN 978-0-8020-9115-4 (bound). – ISBN 978-1-4875-2056-4 (paperback)

1. Exhibitions – Italy – Turin – History – 19th century. 2. Salgari, Emilio, 1862–
1911 – Criticism and interpretation. 3. Gozzano, Guido, 1883–1916 – Criticism
and interpretation. 4. Esposizione internazionale di Torino (1911). 5. Nationalism
– Italy – History – 19th century. 6. Nationalism – Italy – History – 20th century.
7. Literature and society – Italy – History – 19th century. 8. Literature and society
– Italy – History – 20th century. I. Title. II. Series: Toronto Italian studies.

T395.5.I8D45 2006   907.4'4512   C2006-903828-7

This book has been published with the assistance of a grant from the Dean of
the College of Arts and Sciences and the Vice President for Research and
Graduate Studies at the University of Virginia.

University of Toronto Press acknowledges the financial assistance to its
publishing program of the Canada Council for the Arts and the Ontario Arts
Council, an agency of the Goverment of Ontario.

 Canada Council
for the Arts   Conseil des Arts
du Canada

 ONTARIO ARTS COUNCIL
CONSEIL DES ARTS DE L'ONTARIO
an Ontario government agency
un organisme du gouvernement de l'Ontario

Funded by the   Financé par le
Government   gouvernement
of Canada   du Canada  Canadä

To Mike Thrift

Contents

Acknowledgments ix

Introduction The Spectacle of Inventing a Nation: World's Fairs and Their Narratives in Italy, 1860–1915 3

1 Prologues to World's Fairs: National Expositions and Nation Building in Turin 15
Turin, (Former) Capital of the Nineteenth Century 15
National Exhibits, Collective Identity, and the Ideology of
    Progress 19
Dreaming a Collective Dream: Civilization as Leisure 23
Of Maps and Towers: A Stroll along the Fairgrounds 33
Pro Aris et Foci: The King, the People, and the Nation 44
All the City's a Stage: The Exposition of Hegemonic
    Topographies in De Amicis's *Torino 1880* 52
Exhibition Mania on Stage: The Ballet *Excelsior* 65

2 Turin 1911: The 'Fabulous Exposition' 79
Ephemeral Architecture and the Invention of a National Style 79
Building Imperial Consensus: Italy's *Quarta Sponda* on
    the Po River 89
Italy and the Imperial Paradigm 102
Blazoned Pilots, Modern Media, and Vicarious Travels 110
Polar Explorers, 'Instant Books,' and the Politics of Travel 117

3 Emilio Salgari: Writing Exposition Style   123
    Salgari's Novels as Exposition Narratives   123
    Salgari and the Adventure-Tale Formula   136
    A Life Exposed: The Man, the Myth, and the Nation   150
    The Fall of a Crystal Palace: *Le meraviglie del Duemila*   166

4 Guido Gozzano's Imperial Ambiguities   176
    Reclaiming the Context: On Gozzano *gazzettiere* and the Archaeology
        of *Verso la cuna del mondo*   176
    The 'Compendium of the World': Gozzano's India as
        World's Fair Exhibit   184
    Of Mazes and Masks: India as Counter-Exposition   192
    Beyond the Exotic Surface: Gozzano's *Letters* as Hermeneutical
        Objects   202
    Historiography as Assemblage: Intertextual Montages in
        'L'Olocausto di Cawnepore' and 'Goa: "La Dourada"'   205
    Meddling with the Sex of Angels: Gozzano's Readings of Albrecht
        Dürer's *Melancholia I*   248
    Production for Profit and Creation for Pleasure: Beauty, Truth, and
        the Role of the Artist in the World of Universal Expositions   259

Conclusion   269

Notes   273

Bibliography   317

Index   339

Acknowledgments

In the course of writing this book, I received support and advice from many colleagues. Among those who read chapters and offered feedback on the manuscript, I would like to thank David T. Gies, Massimo Lollini, Stefania Lucamante, John Lyons, Randolph Pope, and Donald Shaw. I am indebted to my colleagues in the Italian program, Enrico Cesaretti and Adrienne Ward, for their collegiality in sharing work in progress, thoughtful critique, and affectionate encouragement. Lucia Re remains the model of intellectual clarity and innovative thinking that shaped my early academic career and continues to inspire it today. Zygmunt Barański, Andrea Ciccarelli, Pier Massimo Forni, Millicent Marcus, Barbara Spackman, and Rebecca West have my gratitude for their generous support and professional advice. I have also benefited from discussions with many friends, among whom I thank Christina Ball, for introducing me to the concept of the technological sublime, and my former student and now valued colleague, Letizia Modena, for intervening with sharp editing scissors when it was too painful to do the cutting on my own. I am grateful to all my students – past and present – for sharing their passion for my native culture and for continuing to renew my intellectual curiosity about all things Italian.

Numerous other people and institutions provided assistance with this project. I thank John F. Miller for giving me the opportunity to participate in the University of Virginia – Terza Università di Roma exchange program, which allowed me to pursue archival research at the Biblioteca di storia moderna e contemporanea in Rome. The Biblioteca di storia e cultura del Piemonte, in Turin, Italy, was a treasure trove of crucial materials related to the Italian World's Fairs. To the director Monica Cuffia and her staff goes my gratitude for making my stay in Turin so productive and pleasurable. I am also obliged for the research support provided by the Dean of the College of Arts and Sciences and the Vice President for Research and Graduate Studies of the University of Virginia. Several university fellowships for summer research allowed me to devote time to the completion of the manuscript. With the help of the University of Virginia's Small Grants Program, I was able to secure reproduction rights for the numerous images printed in this book.

I wrote *World's Fairs Italian Style* while I lived in one of the historic Pavilions on the University of Virginia Lawn. Though unrelated to the ephemeral and extravagant Pavilions of many World's Fairs, Thomas Jefferson's Pavilion VIII was as inspiring and spectacular as any of them. I owe thanks to the university for extending this fabulous opportunity to me, and to the Lawn community – Jeanette and Wade Lancaster and Charlotte and Carl Zeithaml especially – for making it such a unique academic experience. From them I learned what generous leadership is all about. The University of Virginia's Teaching Resource Center, its staff, and its director, Marva Barnett, in particular, have helped me tremendously. When I was getting absorbed in this book, the TRC enabled my discovery of the synergies between research, teaching, and service, without which my academic career would have remained hopelessly one-faceted.

At the University of Toronto Press, I am especially grateful to Ron Schoeffel who, with untiring patience and a great deal of expert guidance, helped me meet an unexpected deadline and navigate the publishing process. Anne Laughlin capably steered the manuscript through production, and Charles Stuart gave formal consistency to my rebellious style. Early versions of two sections in chapter 4, 'Historiography as Assemblage: Intertextual Montages in "L'Olocausto di Cawnepore"' and 'Goa: "*La Dourada*"' were published in the journal *Rivista di studi italiani* and the volume *Italian Modernism: Italian Culture between Decadentism and Avant-Garde*, respectively. I am obliged to the editors of these publications for their permission to incorporate the essays into this book.

I am indebted to my husband, Mike Thrift, for his patient editing, unflagging support, intellectual optimism and wit, and for generously taking on a lengthy commute to give me the time to write and teach in Charlottesville. To my parents and my aunt, I would like to express my gratitude and affection. Finally, I thank Alexander and Stephanie, for reading Salgari with me, and allowing me to experience, albeit vicariously, the wonders of a world of adventure seen though the bright eyes of curious and imaginative children.

WORLD'S FAIRS ITALIAN STYLE

Introduction

The Spectacle of Inventing a Nation: World's Fairs and Their Narratives in Italy, 1860–1915

Laboratories of modernity, inventories of the world, and shrines to progress, international and universal exhibitions (popularly known as World's Fairs) and their predecessors, national expositions, featured prominently during the nineteenth and twentieth centuries.[1] Since Walter Benjamin's scathing definition of World's Fairs as 'the sites of pilgrimages to the commodity fetish' ('Paris' 151), scholars have extensively discussed the role of national and international expositions in industrialized countries such as Great Britain, France, and the United States.[2] These studies consistently overlook Italy's role as both a participant in and sponsor of these events. The reasons for such an omission are evident: politically and economically, Italy was a latecomer as an independent and unified nation state and industrialized country. As late as 1880, industrialization was hardly a national phenomenon, the southern portion of the peninsula and the islands remaining extensively agricultural, and several of the central and northern regions of Italy still depended on pre-industrial modes of production in the leading textile-manufacturing businesses and the exploitation of natural resources. However, it would be a mistake to consider late-nineteenth- and early-twentieth-century Italy as a mere spectator in the shows of national pride and imperial might that the major Western powers staged in the arenas of World's Fairs. Without reaching the proportions, both in size and public attendance, of exhibitions in France, England, and the United States, national and international expositions in Italy were among the country's most successful mass-attended phenomena. By examining how Italian expositions masterminded Italy's process of nation formation from the margins of industrialized Europe yet within the ideological context of modern nationalism and imperialism, I offer ways to individualize and diversify what has often been constructed as the West's monolithic and univocal 'discourse of Empire.'

Because of the unprecedented impact of their social, political, economic, and aesthetic investments, World's Fairs are ideal case studies of how nationalistic and imperialistic discourses were produced, disseminated, and contested over time. In their totalizing ambitions, World's Fairs involved all types of human expression: numberless disciplines, such as architecture and the visual arts, science and technology, anthropology and history, journalism, literature, and the performing arts, all deployed their diverse semiotic codes to tell the fabulous tale of modern progress. By self-consciously exploiting these disciplines' varied representational techniques in order to reiterate a highly structured set of ideological notions, World's Fairs became catalysts of popular taste and promoters of mass culture. They gathered all social classes around bourgeois values and drew the lower social strata into modern market economies and consumption systems. Expositions shaped the relationship between technological development and free time and offered apparently simple solutions to social problems, political tensions, and economic and territorial competitions.[3] In the French Republic and the Unites States' industrial democracy, in Victorian England and the young Italian monarchy in search of recognition abroad, expositions were pliable instruments that expressed the aims and goals of the governments that supported them. As Eduardo Mendoza ironically pointed out in his novel *La ciudad de los prodigios* (The City of Marvels, 1986), devoted to the 1888 Barcelona World's Fair, expositions extracted a statement of universal peace from the show of military might, a testimonial of social harmony from the violent repression of workers' unrest, and a claim to universal brotherhood from the display of colonial subjects. The synthesizing and universalizing claims that Mendoza lampoons in *La ciudad de los prodigios* were nothing more than a rhetorical veneer aimed at concealing rather than resolving the antinomies on which the fairs' ideology was founded. The universal expositions' various semiotic codes thrived on the replication of the same binary logic. As Edward Said, Tzvetan Todorov, and Denys Hay (among many others) have eloquently argued, this oppositional logic allowed Western cultural imperialism to define cultures and national identities by means of binary opposites set in a fixed hierarchical structure: 'us' versus 'them,' 'superior' versus 'inferior,' 'active' versus 'passive,' and so on.

Without dismissing the extraordinary power of this logic, one should not overlook the fact that acts of resistance to the exposition mentality were often generated within the fairs' own ideological and cultural boundaries. Fairs inspired the development of subordinate discourses that challenged the absolute ideological unity and cultural hegemony that fairs relentlessly promoted. Here, I use the term *hegemony* in a self-consciously citational framework. While I borrow Antonio Gramsci's definition of hegemony as the cultural leadership that identifies Western identity as superior in comparison with other peripheral and subordinate cultures, I also argue that this powerful consensus-building force is never entirely homogeneous and standardized. That colonial subjects engaged in significant acts of cultural and ideological resistance during the time of the West's greatest control is a given in today's post-colonial studies. *World's Fairs Italian Style* carries this argument a step further and suggests that the imperial narrative contained its own currents of disruption and destabilization. As Italian World's Fairs and their narratives point out, these currents were neither ideologically coherent nor conceptually consistent. Some were politically militant and ideologically blunt, as the workers' unions' or women's rights associations' pronouncements often demonstrated. Other discourses were more nuanced, their ambiguities and dissonances reflecting the complex interplay of consent and opposition that the phenomenon of the World's Fairs inspired. By making discrepant and composite experiences coexist, these hybrid scripts criss-crossed the imperial divide, undermined the binary logic governing its ethos, and shattered the topographical duality implied in the notion of a fixed metropolitan centre governing a silent and subordinated periphery. The hybrid discourses produced in World's Fairs acknowledged and supported the business of empire while often obscuring and even opposing it, and it is precisely to these discourses, and to the inconsistencies, gaps, and mixed messages concealed within the World's Fairs' master narrative, that this book devotes special attention.

From guidebooks to exposition magazines and from popular narratives to 'high art,' literature was both a participant in and a producer of these discourses. My homological reading of the representational codes deployed in World's Fairs and the representational codes exploited by what I broadly term *exposition narratives* is inspired by the interrelated meanings of the term *exposition*. I consider an exposition a signifying practice that uses similar modes of representation across multiple semiotic systems. From a linguistic point of view, an exposition entails a rhetorical exercise that is both explanatory and descriptive, a use of language aimed at designating objects and conveying information: 'the art of expounding, setting forth, or explaining.' An exposition also involves a display of knowledge: 'the act of presenting to view,' thus implying the pre-eminence of the gaze.[4] This metaphorical chain brings us to another meaning of *exposition*: the visual and spatial arrangement of a series of collected objects. From this connotation derives the use of the term *exposition* to designate the institutional and social spaces where commercial, industrial, and artistic products are organized and displayed. Particularly in the context of national and international expositions, the term, in turn, suggests one of its most technical meanings: the notion of architectural *exposure*, that is, the 'art of positioning or turning a building in space' (Sieburth xi). An exposition is an ephemeral city laid out panoptically for the observer's visual appropriation, the symbolic space where societies offer a spectacular *mise en scène* of their beliefs, fashions, politics, economic systems, and power structures. Utopias of readability and absolute transitivity, expositions thus conjure up another common meaning of the term *to expose*: the act of revealing or uncovering something that was either concealed or publicly unknown. This connotation implies operations of laying open of meaning, of heuristic sleuthing (as in *exposing* an intention, a secret, or the 'truth').

In spite of these premises, the semiotic strategies that govern all exposition practices inevitably call into question their own claim of absolute epistemological transparency. Assembling the world into a verbal or ostensive machine is not a value-free enterprise. It implies acts of selection, systematization, spatial arrangement, and semiotic 'translation' that simultaneously point to the expositions' realistic accuracy and stylized spectacularity, to their truth-claims and self-conscious artifice. My reading of the *culture* of expositions, in all its interrelated meanings, aims at discussing the ideology of representation in its most important signifying practices, visual as well as textual, formal as well as thematic (these pairs being just sides of the same coin, as we shall see in the practice of *ekphrasis*). In *Culture and Imperialism*, Edward Said defined culture in two ways:

> First of all it means all those practices, like the arts of description, communication, and representation, that have relative autonomy from the economic, social, and political realms and that often exist in aesthetic forms, one of whose principal aims is pleasure. ...
>
> Second, and almost imperceptibly, culture is a concept that includes a refining and elevating element, each society's reservoir of the best that has been known and thought, as Matthew Arnold put it in the 1860s. Arnold

believed that culture palliates, if it does not altogether neutralize, the ravages of a modern, aggressive, mercantile, and brutalizing urban existence. (*Culture* xii–xiii)

My reading of expositions as hybrid domains that include socio-economic, political, and aesthetic practices (including high as well as popular art forms) questions Said's desire to somewhat divorce the aesthetic sphere from all other areas of human expression, and instead suggests that expositions provided the battleground where all these signifying practices engaged one another – where the literary domain (itself a heterogeneous space) was sometimes complicit with and sometimes critical of the 'aggressive [and] mercantile' ethos of the modern metropolis.

The expansive literary production by best-selling author Emilio Salgari and the refined exotic narratives and 'exposition pieces' by poet Guido Gozzano are ideal case studies in this context. Roughly contemporaries, Salgari and Gozzano both lived and wrote in Turin. Both authors enjoyed immediate and widespread success, and both paid curious and critical attention to the culture of World's Fairs. Yet, if we were to limit ourselves to information gathered in any history of Italian literature, we would be easily convinced that Salgari and Gozzano had precious little in common. Scholars have traditionally relegated Salgari's immense narrative output to the margins of the literary canon as an example of the adventure novel genre, mostly addressed to adolescent and casual adult readers, and bearing no connection with 'serious' art and engaged literature. A self-taught novelist with little formal schooling and a penchant for eccentric behaviour, Salgari emigrated from his native Verona to Turin in 1892 following his publishers' promises of literary recognition and financial reward.[5] In spite of these promises, Salgari lived as a literary outcast in Turin, his frequent relocations to cheaper and more peripheral areas of town reflecting as a perverse counter narrative the growing popularity of his novels among larger and larger sectors of the reading public.[6]

Guido Gozzano, on the other hand, was born into Turin's upper middle class, in a family boasting landowners, physicians, and senators among its most prominent members. A habitué of the Saturday literature classes that Arturo Graf, one of the leading literary figures in Italy, held at the University of Turin, Gozzano belonged to the clique of literati who included the poets Amalia Guglielminetti and Carlo Vallini and other distinguished names in Italian letters, such as Francesco Pastonchi, Enrico Thovez, Massimo Bontempelli, Attilio Momigliano, Salvator

Gotta, and Carlo Calcaterra. The laudatory reviews that internationally renowned critics bestowed upon Gozzano since the publication of his first volume of poetry, *La via del rifugio* (The Road to Shelter, 1907), granted him standing among the poetic and academic elites of his age. As the standard-bearer of the highly crafted, subtly ironical, and backward-looking poetic movement called *crepuscolarismo* (commonly translated into English as the Twilight School of Poetry), Gozzano's mental landscapes were at the antipodes of the modern cityscapes that marked all World's Fairs. By paying almost exclusive attention to his poetic works, critics have consistently disregarded Gozzano's exotic prose narratives and exposition pieces by considering them the journalistic, moneymaking efforts of a young poet whose more legitimate claim to literary fame they believed rested elsewhere.

Though they lived in the same town, Gozzano and Salgari never formally met, a fact that underscores the hermeticism of contemporary social formations as well as the strictly enforced division between high and popular literature. Undoubtedly, Gozzano and Salgari followed different generic models, the latter favouring the adventure novel and writing in the expansive manner of popular *feuilletons*, the former supplementing his poetry with chiseled prose works, including short travel narratives and elegant journalistic pieces. A close analysis of Gozzano's and Salgari's narrative works, however, shows how these barriers did not prevent the flow of similar cultural and ideological currents, thus inserting the two writers into the panorama of modernity of which the World's Fairs were such a defining element. By offering a wide-ranging analysis of the systems and processes of signification, representation, and communication underlying the World's Fairs phenomenon and their narratives, this book thus provides a revision of conventional interpretations of Salgari's and Gozzano's narrative works.

Chapter 1 introduces the process of nation formation in Italy by examining how Italy's industrialized northwestern region, and the city of Turin in particular, aggressively used the Fairs' universal language to build a sense of collective identity and impose it upon a still fragmented and heterogeneous country. Commenting on the political unification of Italy, Massimo D'Azeglio once famously quipped, 'Italy has been made, now we have to make Italians.'[7] My analysis differs from conventional historical approaches to modern Italy as, rather than focusing *post factum* on Rome as the bearer of Italy's national identity, I examine Turin's attempts to vie with Rome in the process of forging and controlling the process of nation formation around its own cultural, political, and administrative structures. Author of the Risorgimento foundational epic and the self-termed 'industrial capital' of Italy, Turin held the record of having sponsored the highest number of national and international expositions in Italy, with the other industrial leader, Milan, following closely behind. In spite of its being Italy's capital, Rome waited until 1911 to host an international exhibition; even then, it had to content itself with a purely representational and subordinate role. Italy was thus a significant departure from the countries that invented the World's Fair phenomenon, France and Great Britain, where the capital cities of Paris and London maintained the undisputed privilege of having hosted their respective countries' most significant expositions.[8]

Turin's national and international exhibitions constituted formidable tools to disseminate the values and ideas of the northern Italian bourgeoisie around a multi-pronged program of political integration, industrial hegemony, and cultural propaganda. In a significant merger, Turin's entrepreneurial elites engineered Italy's industrial take-off, monopolized posts of political leadership, and sponsored the city's numerous national and international expositions, thus initiating the powerful alliance between business, politics, and mass media that would characterize Italy up to the present day. With its many fairs, Turin constructed Italy's collective identity through the carefully choreographed display of its idealized past, its self-serving confrontation with stylized types of exotic otherness, and its wishful projections into a 'future perfect' dominated by scientific and technological advancement. The Italian people's new sense of entitlement to bourgeois leisure as the counterpart of profitable productivity found satisfaction in the many diversions that fairs provided. While engaging the collective pleasure principle, these diversions drew the picture of social harmony, institutional stability, and civilized well-being that Italy eagerly circulated in order to win international recognition.

The epic tale of Italy's industrial progress occurring under the aegis of its liberal and monarchic institutions expressed itself in numerous exposition narratives. This book identifies the representational techniques that these narratives utilized, paying special attention to their complex interplay of realist and spectacular codes. I study official exposition guides as well as 'auteurish' exposition pieces such as Edmondo De Amicis's *Torino 1880*. I investigate the semiotics of the fairs' topographic layouts and architectural designs to discuss the conceptual and representational conventions of the fairs' hegemonic discourses, and discuss how a wildly popular ballet such as Luigi Manzotti's *Excelsior* provided a spectacular synthesis of the fairs' mentality, capturing what was popularly defined the age's 'exhibition-mania.'

Chapter 2 focuses on what was, simultaneously, the first universal exposition in Italy and one of the last World's Fairs before the First World War.[9] The 'fabulous exposition' of 1911 celebrated the fiftieth anniversary of national unity with parallel exhibitions simultaneously held in the three cities that, at different times in Italy's history, had held the title of the nation's capital: Turin, Florence, and Rome. Turin 1911 both recapitulated the foundational tenets of the fairs' culture and, by bringing them to their spectacular apotheosis, carried them to a crisis point, revealing the contradictions and dissonances beneath these discourses' homogeneous ideological veneer.

In 1911, Turin carried out its most concerted effort to establish its own national and international leadership and build widespread consensus around Italy's colonial agenda. This leadership program was neither unilateral nor straightforward: while the exposition in Turin successfully competed to exceed in size, magnificence, and importance the exhibits held in Florence and Rome, the fair's tripartite location was obviously enough to challenge Turin's ambition of cultural and political centralization. Turin's plan to imbue the characteristic eclecticism of the World's Fairs with an overarching design to be endorsed as the *national* architectural style was perhaps the single most dramatic failure in Turin 1911, particularly if compared with the classical revival already under way in Rome. The erudite citation of the city's signature architectural style, the Turin baroque, failed to reactivate its original function, that of giving visible form to the spectacle of political hegemony. Unable to be collectively decoded, the revival of the Turin baroque did not give form to the collective idea of the nation, but remained marooned in an opaque and archaic regionalism, thus contradicting the very idea of national cohesion and historically sanctioned leadership that Turin 1911 otherwise aggressively proclaimed.

Italy's imperial agenda presented another cluster of contradictions in Turin 1911. In the year that preceded the exposition's official opening, Turin put forth a grand effort to organize the largest survey of Italy's colonial achievements that any fair had created to date. Chapter 2 surveys Turin 1911's colonial exhibits and connects them to other, less ephemeral projects, such as the publishing tour de force of the Biblioteca coloniale della direzione degli affari coloniali (Colonial Library of the Management Office of Colonial Affairs). The Biblioteca was a multivolume compilation on display at Turin 1911, aimed at outlining the history of Italy's colonizing feats from the beginning of the Roman Empire to the present. Though unfinished by the time of the exposition's inauguration, the Biblioteca witnessed the massive systematizing effort that was under way. I study the ostensive and rhetorical strategies of both colonial exhibits and colonial publications as concerted efforts to build a still shaky imperial consensus inside the nation, and discuss how these efforts strove to convince international public opinion that Italy was ready to become an equal player in the Western powers' competition for imperial dominance. Despite their commanding and synthesizing rhetoric, these ventures also revealed that, in 1911, Italy's colonial narrative was culturally dependent upon the age's imperial giants, France and Great Britain, and demonstrated all the incompletion of a work in progress, all the inconsistencies of an ideology still in its making.

Imperial desires and the advancement of modern technologies fuelled the myths of travel, exploration, and adventure. With its many forms of vicarious travel, ethnic and exotic displays, nation-specific pavilions, and the newly introduced automobile races and shows, Turin 1911 inaugurated novel imaginative routes. The fair's attempt to showcase and classify alien geographies and foreign peoples also served the purpose of self-definition in carrying out D'Azeglio's directive: 'We have to make Italians' implied constructing a static and unassailably self-evident notion of identity based on binary oppositions and clear-cut dichotomies. Not only were these dichotomies between 'us' (the 'Italians') and 'them' ('colonial subjects 'exotic tribes,' 'foreign nations,' et cetera), but, in a telling case of cultural elitism, also between a few intellectuals who (allegedly) were the repositories of the Italians' cultural identity and all the subordinate groups that needed to be instructed on who they ought to be. Undoubtedly, the culturally unifying success of Italian fairs demonstrated the extraordinary power of this simple dualistic and reductive epistemology. Nevertheless, the fairs' cultural discourse generated its own contradictions as well. Awareness of these often-silenced contradictions inspires what Said called a 'contrapuntal' reading of the imperial phenomenon (*Culture* 66–7). The fairs' 'making of the Italians' managed to marginalize, yet not eliminate, collective identities that, in their changeable and conflicting features, continued to challenge the expositions' compulsion to assign locations, labels, and roles to races, sexes, nations, and communities.

Chapter 3 presents the challenge of selecting a number of texts among Salgari's colossal literary production that would be interpretatively manageable yet suggestive of Salgari's eclectic inspiration and ideological complexity. Though I occasionally refer to other narratives, I concentrate on the four novels that comprise what critics identify as Salgari's first Ciclo della jungla (jungle cycle): *Le tigri di Mompracem* (The Tigers of Mompracem originally published as *La tigre della Malesia*), *I misteri della jungla nera* (The Mysteries of the Black Jungle), *I pirati della Malesia* (The Malayan Pirates), and *Le due tigri* (The Two Tigers). Published between 1883 and 1904, these novels underwent numerous editions, and critics unanimously consider them the most creatively original and artistically mature among Salgari's works. The 'jungle cycle' traced the exotic settings and developed the popular characters that became Salgari's signature traits for many generations of Italian and non-Italian readers. These readers enjoyed the suspenseful adventures of Sandokan, the Borneo-born avenger-pirate, and Yanez, his Portuguese first mate who embraces Sandokan's anti-imperial guerrilla warfare. They vicariously experienced Sandokan's melodramatic passion for Marianna Guillonk, and loathed James Brooke, the white rajah of Sarawak, and Sandokan's sworn enemy. These same readers enjoyed the echo effect created by Sandokan's alter ego, Tremal-Naik, and doubled their fictional pleasure by reading about his heroic feats with his faithful mate Kammamuri. They vicariously experienced Tremal-Naik's melodramatic passion for Ada Corishant, and loathed Sudoyana, the brutal leader of a bloodthirsty sect of Indian Thugs, and Tremal-Naik's sworn enemy.

As this synopsis points out, Salgari perfected the prefabricated, formulaic, and redundant plot lines of popular adventure/romance novels. However, rather than accepting the common critical wisdom that sees formula narratives as intellectually unchallenging in their flat subservience to mainstream ideologies and unoriginal recycling of conventional themes, I read Salgari's novels as highlighting the cultural dissonances and ideological conflicts of the society that inspired them. I examine how the formal and thematic features of Salgari's novels express the age's exposition mentality, with its categorizing ambitions, its nationalistic and imperialistic ideals, and progress-bound faith. I concentrate on the ways in which these novels swerved away from this mentality and estranged its intellectual presuppositions, forcing us to re-examine them with critical eyes. How did Salgari's audiences (implicitly Western, white, and Christian) deal with a 'positive hero' who is non-white, a Muslim, and by all contemporary standards, not reflective of the traits that the West associated with its 'higher' civilization (logic, reason, and bourgeois thrift in both moral and material economies)? How do we explain Salgari's tampering with the epic conventions typical of the adventure novel in his presentation of a hero who sees the sunset, rather than the dawn, of his world? In attempting to answer these questions, I contest the commonly held critical opinion that, precisely because Salgari was an ex-centric writer, isolated from his society and ignorant of literary tradition, he was able to create a character as exotic and as wildly original as Sandokan. I trace Sandokan's origins to a narrative, broadly read at the time but unfamiliar to non-specialists today: *Les mémoires de Garibaldi* (The memoirs of Garibaldi, 1860–1) by Alexandre Dumas. Rediscovering Garibaldi's corsair feats in Latin America as interpreted by the father of the French *feuilleton* not only strengthens the analogy between the young Garibaldi and Sandokan, but shows how the ideals of the Risorgimento, so fundamental in shaping Italy's national identity, were both confirmed and estranged in Salgari's novels by being forced into a difficult marriage with Italy's budding imperial aspirations.

The exotic and nostalgic atmosphere of the jungle cycle provides an uncanny contrast with the next novel I selected for my reading, *Le meraviglie del Duemila* (The Wonders of the Twenty-First Century, 1907). Set in New York City and devoted to the wonders of progress in a futuristic setting, *Le meraviglie* is a *unicum* in Salgari's production, and has consistently been either overlooked or interpreted as Salgari's token sacrifice at the altar of modernity. In *Le meraviglie*, Salgari estranges the representational codes of the natural sublime in his vision of a world ruled by sublime technologies. Salgari's 'technological sublime' does not create a science fiction utopia. I suggest that *Le meraviglie* constitutes Salgari's literary adaptation of the scientific notion of entropy – the principle of the second law of thermodynamics that defines the tendency of all systems to gradually degenerate into chaos and final stasis – to a society on the brink of self-destruction.

Chapter 4 repatriates the narratives that Gozzano wrote after his 1912 voyage to India and that Giuseppe Antonio Borgese collected in *Verso la cuna del mondo: Lettere dall'India* (Towards the Cradle of the World: Letters from India) to their original publication sites in several contemporary newspapers and periodicals. This archaeological move allows me to free Gozzano's heterogeneous and often extemporaneous compositions from the fetters of compositional unity and narrative consistency that Borgese imposed upon them, and see them in the magmatic context of contemporary popular culture. As components of Gozzano's prolific journalistic production, the letters from India intertwine with Gozzano's *reportages* on numerous current events, such as the 1911 international exposition in Turin. Viewed all together, these texts do not reveal, as Borgese would have wanted, a unitary picture. Instead, we perceive a montage of non-successive sketches, a Picasso-like coexistence of images seen simultaneously from multiple perspectives – a collage of citations, ready to be assembled in changing configurations from one composition to the next.

Like Salgari's, Gozzano's exotic and exposition narratives mirror the systematizing principles and the representational techniques typical of World's Fairs' displays. With an unmatched degree of aesthetic self-consciousness, Gozzano reveals these techniques' and principles' hermeneutical power, their ability, that is, to produce new knowledge, and, conversely, their tendency to confirm cultural expectations and validate ingrained intellectual presuppositions. At the same time, and not without contradiction, Gozzano's narratives also challenge the exposition mentality's ordering ambitions and totalizing hubris by exposing their conceptual discontinuities and logical inconsistencies, by thriving on the creative powers of paradox, and by experimenting with the non-linear processes of analogical thought. My reading of Gozzano does not attempt to smooth over his narratives' conflicting, uneven, and often redundant features. Gozzano's wavering between assertive thought based on linear logic and binary opposites, and his pained deconstruction of the intellectual presuppositions that founded this very thought mirrors the contradictions of a society in a state of transition. Borrowing Michel Foucault's terminology, we can say that Gozzano reflects a world on the threshold of an epistemic break, where the rules of formation of discursive rationality and the conventional configurations of knowledge are entering a state of crisis. These rules' intellectual presuppositions persist as new discursive systems are being elaborated. The dissonance between old and new systems produces conceptual ambiguity, a hybrid and liminal epistemology. While Gozzano never fully embraced the nomadic and 'rhizomatic' philosophies that haunted him, he nevertheless identified the limitations of deterministic thought and pointed to alternative ways to produce and disseminate knowledge, to establish both personal and collective identities, to negotiate power relations, and to define the role of the artist in the modern world.[10]

1 Prologues to World's Fairs: National Expositions and Nation Building in Turin

Turin, (Former) Capital of the Nineteenth Century

On 21 and 22 September 1864, among fierce popular unrest and a bloody military repression that killed more than two hundred protesters, Turin relinquished its role as Italy's capital city. In what they have labelled the long 'autumn of the Risorgimento,' numerous historians saw post-1864 Turin as the victim of a protracted period of political marginalization and identity crisis.[1]

These historians generally emphasize the decline of the Risorgimento ideals in post-unitary Italy, especially during the era of the 'famous deaths' between 1871 and 1882, when Italy lost it secular trinity: Giuseppe Mazzini, Giuseppe Garibaldi, and King Victor Emmanuel II. 'Una specie di vuoto' (a kind of emptiness) (Vernizzi 48) replaced the heroes whose deeds had nurtured the collective imagination during the Unification, and the former capital was often described as 'una città ripiegata su se stessa, come appassita d'un colpo, dall'aria vecchiotta e crepuscolare' (a city folded in upon itself, as if suddenly withered, an elderly city engulfed in a twilight atmosphere) (Castronovo, 'Da ex-capitale' 1204). Undoubtedly, with the transferral of the parliament, ministerial and governmental offices, the state mint, and numerous banks and businesses first to Florence and then to Rome, Turin underwent a sizable economic and demographic recession and lost political prominence on the European scene. The passions that had fuelled the unitary struggles were cooled by the reality of economic stagnation, political expediency, and cultural fragmentation. This is the Turin that Zino Zini described in his 'Appunti di vita torinese' as a 'città un po' tarda ... paradiso terrestre d'impiegati e pensionati, frequentatori di portici in inverno e di viali in estate' (somewhat slow city ... an earthly paradise for clerks and retirees, *habitués* of the arcades in the winter and the boulevards in the summer) (326).

In emphasizing this state of crisis, however, many historians have too quickly dismissed the role played by post-1864 Turin in the difficult process of forging a communal sense of national identity for the Italian people. Even after the trauma of losing its role as the country's capital, Turin challenged Rome in continuing to consider itself as Italy's moral and intellectual core, the keeper of the Risorgimento's legacy and the model for the unitary state. Proudly defending its mission of political leadership, Turin vied to control the process of national integration and strove to shape the country's institutional development according to its own political and administrative structures. As Valerio Castronovo points out: '[la] classe dirigente ... rivendicava al Piemonte un ruolo di mentore politico nei riguardi dell'Italia unita, una funzione di guida ... nel processo di sviluppo delle istituzioni civili e nei rapporti con l'Europa' (the ruling class [...] claimed for Piedmont a role of political mentorship with regard to united Italy, a function of guidance ... in the process of developing civil institutions and relationships with Europe) (*Storia* 16). Having shared the ideals of European liberalism and having hosted political exiles from all regions of Italy during the wars for independence, Turin claimed to be the most eclectically *Italian* of all Italian cities. Heartened by these cosmopolitan avowals, the elites that had led the unification process took on the daunting task of inventing a nation. Establishing a common denominator among the country's variety of customs, histories, dialects, and traditions was in many ways a utopian program, and the idea of building a universally shared sense of national identity rested on a *petitio principii*, as this alleged universality implied acts of exclusion and selection on cultural, political, geographic, and socio-economic levels. Moreover, constructing the Italian nation from the northwestern margins of the peninsula and, as often became the case, in opposition to and competition with Rome was both a problematic and an aggressively pursued endeavour.

Historically neither entirely French nor completely Italian, Piedmont itself had been what Vittorio Alfieri, in the second half of the eighteenth century, had called an amphibian country, and it was upon this reality of dualism and 'peripheralism' that the Savoy monarchy executed its program of political centralization. Between the first and the second halves of the eighteenth century, a capillary system of administrative and institutional control, managed by a class of functionaries and diplomats loyal to the cult of the king, created a homogeneous and hierarchically ordered nation state. In the top-down regulation of all collective relations, the nation state saw 'la massima garanzia di ... armonia fra le varie componenti del corpo sociale' (the highest assurance of ... harmony among the various components of the social corpus) (Castronovo, *Storia* 36). At the same time, an army of extraordinary proportions, if compared to the kingdom's size and demography, sustained a formidable military machine, adding the policy of territorial expansion to that of internal cohesiveness. The process of Italy's unification under the Savoy crown took shape from the point of view of this centralizing and colonizing mentality, a mentality that could only experience the events of 22 September 1864 as a traumatic challenge of unprecedented historical proportions.

In spite of conventional representations, between 1870 and 1911 Turin was not a moribund city, or a city in a state of shock after being relegated to the margins of a political reality now firmly controlled by Rome. On the contrary, if Rome as the new Italian capital was not built in a day, Turin did not fade into sudden oblivion, either. Just as all individual identities are not monolithic and invariable, the process of configuring the Italian nation's collective identity was neither linear nor univocal. It emerged out of multiple identity-formation sites, mirrored ideological power struggles and socio-cultural conflicts, and confronted regional fragmentation and inner divisiveness. It ultimately invented more than reflected a unitary national reality. Between 1870 and 1915, Turin vied to author the national autobiography – the great work-in-progress of the times, the authoritative *storied* Self of the Italian nation. Successfully striving to reinvent itself by negotiating its influential and traumatic past with its industrial future, Turin transformed its old agenda of direct political leadership into a more de-centred and multi-faceted program of economic, cultural, and ideological control of the rest of the nation.[2]

Today it may seem hard to imagine that a city that was so geographically peripheral and culturally extraneous to the rest of Italy could court the idea of governing it. For the leading classes of the time, however, the issue was not that of adapting to the common traits of the peninsula; the issue was to model the rest of the country's identity upon their own. Turin's intellectual elite played a central role in shaping Italy's myth of origins and disseminating the country's foundational images in order to counter what they saw as the immediate dangers of forgetfulness and inner fragmentation. Between 1870 and 1900, influential Turinese publishers such as Roux & Frassati and Fratelli Bocca issued numerous historiographic assessments of the Risorgimento, among which were Vittorio Bersezio's monumental *Il regno di Vittorio Emanuele II: Trent'anni di vita italiana* (The Reign of Victor Emmanuel II: Thirty Years of Italian Life, 1878–95) and Nicomede Bianchi's four-volume *Storia della monarchia piemontese dal 1773 al 1861* (A History of the Piedmont Monarchy from 1773 to 1861, 1877–85). The second half of the 1800s also saw the establishment of many national museums and national libraries, and Turin was the first Italian city to open a Museo del Risorgimento Nazionale in 1878. As the first museum of its kind, the Museo del Risorgimento transformed the events that led to Italy's independence into a heroic saga, organized around a display of emblematic objects that became the icons of the Risorgimento myth.

Integrity (as embodied by Victor Emmanuel II, 'the honourable king'), political pragmatism (Cavour), progress-bound idealism (Mazzini), and patriotic fervor (Garibaldi) became the legacy that Turin proudly bestowed upon a nation still searching for its moral identity. Garibaldi, in particular, became part of Turin's metropolitan landscape thanks to Edmondo De Amicis's best-selling novel *Cuore*. Conceived as a diary reporting the events occurring to a class of elementary school children during the 1881–2 school year (the year of Garibaldi's death), *Cuore* wove its daily urban narrative into its larger-than-life portrait of 'quello che affrancò dieci milioni d'Italiani' (he who liberated ten million Italians) (*Cuore* 337). Aware, as De Amicis was, of the identity-building power of all commemorative and celebratory endeavours, Turin's leaders accompanied the announcement of Garibaldi's death with the proposal to create a new Via Sacra in central Turin, a significant replacement of the Roman road in the Italian patriotic imagination.[3] Interestingly, these interpretations of the Risorgimento downplayed Mazzini's idealization of the 'eternal Rome' as the supreme goal of the national liberation process, and did nothing to foster the mythical rhetoric of *romanità* that doctrinaire patriots were energetically disseminating elsewhere in Italy. In Turin's pragmatic and self-serving perspective, the idea of transforming the Byzantine Rome of the popes into a modern and European capital, a centre of science and progress, would have been a dangerous proposition, had it not been considered a foolish utopia. For many, in fact, Rome remained the '"parasite city" of clerics, hotelkeepers, and beggars [whose] population existed on official handouts' that northern European popular literature conventionally portrayed (Mack Smith 86).

Given this massive and protracted effort of nation building, one should be cautious in arguing that, after 1864, Turin had to accept the fact that Cavour's plan of the *piedmontization* of Italy – the idea, that is, of turning the unified country into a greater Piedmont – had utterly failed. One should note, instead, that if *piemontesismo* had proven unsuccessful on a national scale, its founding values held fast in Turin. In the late 1860s and the 1870s, from the northwestern periphery, *piemontesismo* transformed itself and, from being the catalyst of national unity and political centralization, it became the banner of local autonomy and the paladin of regional economic and political interests. By 1880, the ideals that founded *piemontesismo* – efficiency, sound administration, moderate liberal reforms, and organic progress – slowly acquired a renewed national scope. They sustained, on the one hand, Giovanni Giolitti's liberal agenda in opposition to Agostino Depretis's politics of *trasformismo*. They identified, on the other hand, with Francesco Crispi's 'ritorno al Risorgimento' (back to the Risorgimento) political program. Self-styled heir to Mazzini and Garibaldi, Crispi favoured an authoritarian orientation of internal politics modelled on Bismark's Germany, and upheld a stricter alliance with the central empires. Between 1880 and 1915, the two sides of the liberal coin, one democratic and cosmopolitan, the other aggressive and imperial, successfully, if often contradictorily, came together in Turin as the city withstood the threat of political marginalization by wielding the weapons of industrial, commercial, and cultural leadership.

National Exhibits, Collective Identity, and the Ideology of Progress

After the extraordinary success of the 1851 exhibition at the Crystal Palace in London – the 'Great Exhibition of the Works of Industry of All Nations,' which was considered the 'founding spectacle of the world's fair genre' (Breckenridge 201) – and the Exposition universelle in Paris in 1855, Turin's political and industrial leaders paid close attention to the World's Fair phenomenon. The initial idea of an international exposition in Turin dates back to 1867, when city officials and sponsors selected the vast area of the Piazza d'Armi as the most appropriate site to deploy the products of over two thousand participants from Italy and several other countries in a fair scheduled to be held in 1872. In spite of the failure to bring this project to completion, the energy that had propelled the planning of the 1872 fair channelled itself into the creation of the Regio museo industriale di Torino in 1867, modelled upon the British South Kensington Museum. The Regio museo industriale was intended to facilitate scientific research, as well as form the nation's new entrepreneurial elites. During the ensuing decades, the museum's collections gathered materials purchased from various universal expositions, thus establishing an important, if very specialized, link between Turin and worldwide industrial production and scientific innovation.[4]

Publications such as *La grande esposizione di Londra* (issued by the Turinese Tipografia Subalpina between 24 May and 2 December 1851) and the catalogues of international fairs that the Milan-based publishers Sonzogno and Treves consistently issued reached a broader public beyond museum visitors. These publications' readership success demonstrates that the Piedmont-Lombardy regions were casting a far less provincial and more competitive gaze toward the European centres of industry, economy, and trade than one may today presume. They also show that fairs were a cultural phenomenon that quickly wove its way into Italian life. They involved ordinary people who had probably never attended a fair abroad, but who saw pictures and descriptions of products, inventions, and displays, and marvelled at, without yet partaking in, the culture of abundance, endless possibility, and unlimited self-fulfilment that these fairs promoted. Fairs were thus a formidable tool to build consensus regarding the values and ideals of the Northern Italian bourgeoisie, and to regulate all social classes according to the rules of capital and the demands of market consumption.

Although Turin had held its first Esposizione d'industria nazionale in 1829, with subsequent fairs regularly following at three- and, later, six-year intervals, the first modern national expositions should be considered those of 1850 and 1858.[5] These fairs were modern because they no longer exclusively featured objets d'art and artisans' products for the upper classes, but introduced mass-produced goods intended to invade foreign markets as well as local ones.[6] The 1850 and 1858 expositions brought the machine to the forefront, thus marking the beginning of Turin's industrial take-off. The program of industrial leadership that Piedmont's entrepreneurial elite staged with the 1850 exposition reaped significant international rewards in the great exhibitions of London (1851) and Paris (1855).[7] The fact that this same elite was drafting the political agenda for the newly unified country reveals the other claim to modernity of the 1850 fair, identifiable in the powerful alliance between politics and business that would mark all future expositions in Italy. As Pier Luigi Bassignana points out, in Turin expositions became part of the economic landscape and the political scene, and Turin developed 'una vera e propria cultura che vedrà nell'esposizione ... uno strumento utile a cementare l'alleanza tra monarchia e popolo' (a real culture that will see in the exposition ... a useful tool to cement the alliance between the king and the people) (*Le feste* 24).

Building upon these foundations, the 1858 exposition reflected the immense effort of technological innovation that, with the development of the railroad system and the great Alpine tunnels, would establish direct connections between the otherwise decentred Turin region and the bulk of Europe, and, more generally, alter the relationship between the Italian people and their geographical environment. While, by 1858, the Ferrovie dello Stato had become one of the largest employers in Italy, Piedmont's productive system had also reached a fair degree of diversification. Besides transportation, Turin's industries were at the international forefront in multiple sectors. They boasted successful entrepreneurs whose business talents and visionary skills carried their names into the twentieth and twenty-first centuries: for example, Cirio (food industry), Martini and Cinzano (wines and spirits), Talmone (confectionery industry), and UTET (the acronym for Unione Tipografico Editrice Torinese, then as now one of the leading printing houses in Italy). With the Fréjus tunnelling in 1871, Turin became the necessary transit point for all land-based international commerce from and to Italy, and the once-peripheral city celebrated the event with an exposition in which it presented itself as the 'vetrina industriale d'Italia' (Italy's industrial shop window) (Bassignana, *Le feste* 82).

It was with the 1884 exposition, proudly defined as 'la rivincita dei torinesi a vent'anni dal trasferimento della capitale a Firenze' (the revenge of the Turinese people twenty years after the transferral of the capital to Florence) (Marchis 98–100), that Turin confirmed its position as Italy's industrial capital. Turin 1884 also initiated the phenomenon of mass-attendance at fairs in Italy. If the 1881 census recorded that Turin and the Piedmont regions had, respectively, a population of approximately 253,000 and 3 million inhabitants, the 1884 fair reached the record number of 3 million total visitors. The daily average is calculated, depending on the sources, between eleven and twenty thousand people (Aimone, 'Nel segno' 147; Picone Petrusa 95). Reflecting popular enthusiasm, the Turinese publishers Roux e Favale issued a weekly paper, *Torino e l'esposizione italiana del 1884: cronaca illustrata della esposizione nazionale-industriale ed artistica del 1884* (Turin and the Italian Exhibition of 1884: An Illustrated Chronicle of the 1884 National Exposition of Arts and Industries), in which De Amicis recorded the energy and hope that the exhibition had generated with these words:

sulla riva sinistra [del Po], dal corso Dante al Valentino, tutto è mutato ...
una nuova città vi è sorta, la città dell'Esposizione, tutta brulicante d'operai
e sonante di lavoro, la quale spande intorno, lungo le due rive bellissime,
come un fremito d'aspettazione festosa e un soffio di gioventù e di speranza. (*Torino I: La città* 6)

(on the left bank [of the Po river] from Corso Dante to the park of Valentino [Castle] everything has changed ... a new city has been raised, the city
of the Exposition, all teeming with workers and resounding with labour.
This city spreads around itself and along the two gorgeous banks a sort of
quiver of festive anticipation and a fresh breath of youth and hope.)

Eager to participate in the discourse of modernity, Turin introduced the
crowds attending the exhibition to the wonders of the latest technological innovations and scientific discoveries. With a rhetoric that praised
the youthful vitality and driving optimism of these 'grandi Olimpiadi del
lavoro, [e] ... feste trionfali dell'industria' (Work's Great Olympic games
[and] ... Industry's triumphal celebrations) (Robustelli 1), Turin's bourgeois elite shaped collective dreams and instilled an awe-inspired faith
in civilization's unbound progress.[8] As the minister of agriculture, Luigi
Miceli, stated in his inauguration speech for the 1884 Turin fair:

Le esposizioni ... [sono] rassegna completa di tutto quanto le società incivi-
lite producono in ogni ramo del lavoro ... Non limitate alla mostra di
oggetti più o meno perfetti dell'arte e dell'industria, divengono la
riproduzione della vita sociale in tutte le sue manifestazioni, riflettendosi
in esse non solo l'intensità e l'estensione di tutte le forze produttive della
nazione, ma il grado di civiltà da essa raggiunto. (Sistri 1621)

(Expositions ... [are] complete reviews of all that civilized societies produce
in all branches of work ... As they are not limited to the display of more or
less perfect objects of art and industry, fairs become the reproduction of
social life in all its manifestations, and they reflect not only the intensity
and breadth of all national productive forces, but the degree of civilization
that a nation has achieved.)

Miceli's totalizing hubris is typical of the great exhibitions' mentality. It
constitutes the ultimate expression of the Enlightenment's encyclopedic
ardour for taxonomy, with its vocation to establish 'l'ordre et l'en-

chaînement des connaissances humaines' (the order and concatenation of human knowledge) according to reason's rigorously logical schemes (Diderot 20).[9] By providing the comprehensive inventory of Italian industrial resources, the fair's sponsors wanted to correct the image of Italy that northern European and North American travellers, particularly those writing in the Grand Tour tradition, had disseminated. When stating that they wished to convince 'l'Europa e il mondo a raddrizzare il concetto del paese del *dolce far niente*' (Europe and the world to correct the concept of the country of the *sweet idleness*) (Robustelli 82), these sponsors embraced what they perceived was the work ethic of continental rather than Mediterranean Europe. By portraying itself as the Italian capital of labour, Turin aspired to share Manchester's industrial might and Paris's cultural charisma, and as such expected recognition in Europe.

Dreaming a Collective Dream: Civilization as Leisure

The 1884 exposition attempted to paint this idealized self-portrait of its host city when it introduced two of the defining tropes of World's Fair culture: the display of work, productivity, and competitive achievement as visible signs of a nation's standing on civilization's ladder, and the celebration of leisure ('feste'), pleasure, and cultural diversion as marks of civilized well-being. The coexistence, without apparent break or contradiction, of these heterogeneous elements deserves further scrutiny. The *Guida illustrata del visitatore alla esposizione generale in Torino del 1884* (Illustrated Visitors' Guide to the 1884 General Exposition in Turin) reports how, in its organizers' minds, the 1884 fair was to be considered the 'prova generale' (dress rehearsal) for a future international exhibition. A city within a city, separated from everyday routine and strife in the charming park of Valentino Castle, the 1884 fair introduced a brilliant note into the sober arrangement of previous industrial expositions. One of the sponsors of the 1884 exhibition pinpointed the potential for entertainment and distraction that fairs had yet to exploit fully: 'Le esposizioni in generale per loro stesse sono monotone [e] ... Torino deve porvi riparo, facendo sì che i numerosi visitatori che v'interverranno ... trovino ... quelle distrazioni geniali d'ogni genere che sono indispensabili nelle epoche di grande concorso' (Expositions in general are tedious [and] ... Turin must devise a remedy for this problem by allowing the exposition's numerous visitors ... to find ... all those kinds of genial distractions that are indispensable in times of great public attendance) (Roccia 25). When selecting the park of Valentino Castle as the fair's site, organizers had in mind spectacular settings such as those of the 1851 Great Exhibition, held in an eighteen-acre plot in London's Hyde Park, or the 1876 Philadelphia Exhibition, hosted in Fairmount Park.[10] There were obvious logistical imperatives that guided the selection of a park as the most appropriate location for an exposition, but one should not overlook other, symbolic reasons as well.[11] The Valentino was an idealized, man-made 'zona di delizie' (place of delights) (Moriondo 6), which had the same relationship to real Turin (or the real world) as the small island on Po di Belvedere had to the Estensi Ferrara during the Renaissance. Arguably, the Crystal Palace's glass surfaces started this tendency by placing fairgoers more outside than inside reality (Baculo 35).[12] In the World Fairs' utopia, industrial objects were removed from their actual production sites. The crystal-clear surfaces of Joseph Paxton's palace replaced 'quell'atmosfera nebbiosa e affumicata in cui pallide masse si [muovono] febbrilmente di qua e di là' (that foggy and smoky atmosphere in which pallid masses feverishly scurry here and there), to cite Giacomo Arnaudon's chilly description of contemporary Manchester and Liverpool (111–12).[13]

'Fantastico giardino,' 'oasi fatale,' and 'asil di seduzion,' (fantastic garden, irresistible oasis, seductive haven) according to a popular poem (Roccia 20), the park of Valentino Castle appealed to the imagination of many mid- and late-nineteenth-century flâneurs in search of amusement and diversion. Similarly inspiring acts of 'diporto e sollazzo' (recreation and amusement), the peaceful waters of the river Po flowing through the Valentino offered themselves to wealthy youths who, like their British counterparts on the Thames, 'con leggieri e ben costruiti burchielli ... [solcano] le acque del fiume, che ... corrono limpide e tranquille, e mirabilmente si prestano al remeggiare' (with light and well-built rowing boats ... [plough] the water that ... flows clear and peaceful, and admirably lends itself to the act of rowing') (Baricco 566).[14] Solicitous to the demands of *loisir*-lovers, architects designed artificial sceneries that equally conjured up feelings of pastoral peace and evasion into the picturesque: 'un caffé, costrutto alla foggia degli *chalets* svizzeri, si discerne tra le ombrose piante; là si vede un piccolo poggio, a cui si sale per una scala scheggiosa, che richiama le salite alpestri' (Among the shady trees one can perceive a café built in the style of a Swiss chalet; up there one can see a small knoll, to which one climbs up through a jagged flight of steps reminiscent of an Alpine slope) (Covino 45). The exhibitions hosted at Valentino Park became parks within parks, promoting diversion in the second degree, and constructing grandiose *mises en abîme* of the principle of collective pleasure in the budding world of the capitalist market economy. Exposition planners exploited forms and images belonging to a collectively shared cultural archive, such as the century-long tradition that, from the Garden of Eden to Italian Renaissance literary gardens, British 'pleasure gardens,' and French *jardins de plaisir,* had associated gardens with picturesque and utopian spaces of wish-fulfilment and unlimited delight. Consider, for example, Vittorio Turletti's piece on Valentino Castle included in *Torino e l'esposizione italiana del 1884:*

> Prima che i tetti acuminati e plumbei del Castello del Valentino si specchiassero nelle acque del Po ... già esistevano su quelle amene sponde tradizioni di feste pubbliche e di concorso di popolo che l'Esposizione nazionale gloriosamente continua.
>
> Infatti, in riva al fiume ... esistevano fin dal 1400 viali e parchi ove i duchi di Savoja si recavano a caccia ed il popolo ad assistere a tornei, caroselli e giuochi pubblici medioevali.
>
> L'amenità del sito fece sorgere un luogo di delizie, ed il castello ... sorrise dalle sue cento finestre ai giardini che lo circondavano ... e parve subito trovarsi a suo agio in quell'ambiente d'armi, d'amori, di giostre e d'allegrezze. (Turletti 23)

(Traditions of public celebrations and popular gatherings were already taking place on the pleasant shores of the river Po ... even before the pointed and lead-coloured roofs of Valentino Castle reflected themselves in that river's waters. The National Exposition gloriously continues these traditions.

Since the 1400s, in fact, along the river banks ... there were boulevards and parks where the Savoy dukes hunted and people attended tournaments, carousels, and medieval public games.

The amenity of the location allowed the creation of a place of delight. Smiling ... from its hundreds of windows to the gardens that surrounded it, the castle appeared to immediately find itself at ease in that environment of arms, love, carousels, and merriment.)

In spite of these appeals to established cultural traditions, often debased to clichés ready for mass consumption, the organizers of the 1884 exposition understood that in an age of rapid transformation, the imperative of the *amusons-nous* demanded the engagement of the principle of novelty. As novelty was a feature of all that appeared as different and distant in either time or space, the escapist urge guiding the program of *divertissement* aptly fulfilled itself in the novelty of the exotic. In his descriptions of the numerous kiosks built for the 1884 fair, Giovanni Saragat especially admired '[il] grande chiosco del *Ristorante d'Europa* ... [una] costruzione in legno, civettuola per il suo stile mongolico ad archetti, a mensole, [e] ... lo stranissimo chiosco del *Ristorante Follis* che è una pagoda chinese a colori vivi, sormontati da una torretta alta ventidue metri e larga tanto da potervisi salire sino in cima, da dove si vede la gente che è giù' ([the] great kiosk of the *Ristorante d'Europa*, ... [a] wooden building, coquettish in its Mongolian style with its small arches and corbels, [and] ... the very strange kiosk of the *Follis Restaurant,* which is a Chinese pagoda painted in vivid colours, and surmounted by a slim tower, twenty-two metres in height and wide enough to allow people to climb to the top and look at the people below) ('I chioschi' 346; 378).

Besides the formal innovation that these exotic buildings introduced in Turin's symmetrical and severe architecture, the principle of novelty guided all that had the power of transforming everyday reality. The age's great protagonists, technology and applied science, cloaked themselves in magic. Prosaically familiar landscapes suddenly allowed for seductive encounters with the unknown and the fantastic. Fairs commonly featured the *Luftbahn,* or elevated railway, in which visitors travelled in charming 'vagoncini scoperti, veicoli bizzarri tra la barca e il paniere, con comodi sedili' (open little cable cars, bizarre vehicles half boats and half baskets, with comfortable seats) (Antonini 47). One of the standard features in today's amusement parks, the *montagne russe* (rollercoasters), allowed fairgoers to experience for the first time the thrill of that other great protagonist of modernity, speed. Mechanical tricks contributed to the estranging illusions in *La maison misterieuse,* or haunted house. Perhaps the most popular source of amusement was the *Tobogga* (or nautical railway), combining the appeals of the wild and the exotic, albeit harnessed by the iron devices of modern technology:

Gli Hawayani [sic] scelgono generalmente la sommità di uno scoglio che presenti un rapido declivio verso le acque: portano con loro una tavola larga un metro su tre di lunghezza appuntata all'estremità, vi si stendono sopra e con un leggiero movimento di mano spingono questo nuovo veicolo giù verso le acque ... Alla famosa esposizione di Chicago ... gli Americani hanno voluto offrire ai visitatori della loro Mostra la sensazione di questo gioco avainese: sensazione però mitigata dal progresso e dalla civiltà. L'idea è venuta al capitano Boyton, già celebre per la sua traversata della Manica. Un monticello prese il posto della roccia e alcune barche tennero luogo della tavola stretta e puntuta: esse però vennero munite di pattini perché potessero scivolare sulle guide di ferro fisse lungo i fianchi del monticello. Uno, due ... tre! Il dente che trattiene la barca l'abbandona: uno stridio prolungato riempie l'aria ... e la barca ... scende con rapidità vertiginosa sino alle acque sottostanti tra le quali salta levando dinanzi a sé, sotto la prua quadrata, un gran getto d'acqua. (Picone Petrusa 103)

(The Hawaiian people generally select the top of a cliff that falls sharply into the water: They carry a board one metre in width and three in length, pointed at one end. They lie face down on it and with a slight hand movement push this new vehicle into the water ... At the famous exposition in Chicago ... Americans decided to provide fairgoers with the sensation of this Hawaiian game, a sensation that was however mitigated by progress and civilization. Captain Boyton, already famous for his crossing of the British Channel, came up with the idea. A small hillock replaced the cliff and a few boats replaced the long pointed board. The boats were furnished with runners so they could slide on iron guides attached to the hillock's sides. One, two ... three! The hook that keeps the boat in place lets go: a prolonged screech fills the air ... and the boat ... lunges down with vertiginous speed into the water below. The boat leaps forward and an immense jet of water shoots in front of it from beneath the square prow.)

The fair's technicians both evoked and domesticated the sense of fright that the exotic practice inspired: the Hawaiian exercise maintained its adrenaline-induced edge, yet it was also bounded within iron guides and forced to stay within the limits of real material security. Thus, the European toboggan unsettled the bourgeoisie's spirits while safeguarding their bodies, the ride as suspenseful and the final splash as reassuring as the predictable plot and happy ending of a formulaic novel.

Another source of entertainment in 1884 Turin was the *ferrovia funicolare* (funicular railway) that linked Turin to the hill of Superga, overlooking the city and hosting the mausoleum of the Italian royal family. The *funicolare* did not limit itself to demonstrating the technological progress of the Turinese railroad industry or to providing a collective source of amusement. The trip on the *funicolare* became an ascent to the Crown, a pilgrimage and act of homage to the House of Savoy, with

Tobogga, Stigler Tower, and the ferrovia aerea. *Le esposizioni riunite di Milano 1894.*

which people strengthened their sense of collective identity and national pride. 'Poter salire senza fatica su quella deliziosissima vetta dove ... la bellezza della natura aggiung[e] attrattive al sentimento patriottico' (Being able to ascend with ease to that charming mountaintop where ... nature's beauty adds charm to patriotic feeling'), wrote reporter Nino Pettinati, corresponded to devoting 'un inno all'excelsior umano' (a hymn to human magnificence) (70).

Even before the advent of electricity and prior to its being fully exploited in its most common and utilitarian uses, the expositions' public illumination was intended to be admired as a wondrous spectacle, a visual display inspiring awe in the crowds of fairgoers. In 1881 Milan, for example, a certain Cavalier Giuseppe Ottino gained fame with his 'addobbi di illuminazione fantastica' (fanciful decorations of light), which illuminated the entire downtown area and attracted approximately three hundred thousand visitors (Picone Petrusa 90). Nineteenth-century writers often conjured up the enchanted atmosphere of fairyland to describe the fairs' night-time appearance.[15] Especially inspiring were the fountains with their light and water plays; these quickly became one of the defining visual topoi in all expositions ('Le

Ferrovia elettrica. Drawing by Matania. *Milano e l'esposizione italiana del 1881.*

fontane luminose' 226–7).[16] Besides devoting a large section to the International Electricity Exposition, the 1884 fair in Turin was the first Italian exposition that, in some areas, utilized one of the primary symbols of modernity, electric light. The beacons of light that from the top of the train station guided visitors down the main thoroughfare to downtown Turin anticipated the lights that would illuminate Paris from the Eiffel Tower, thus underscoring Turin's claim to modernity. In the passage below, the anonymous reporter gapes at the unprecedented assemblage of 'non meno di duecentomila persone' (more than two hundred thousand people) who wander along 'vie inondate di splendore' (streets basking in splendor) in what resembles a fairy-tale land ('L'illuminazione' 66). The very allusion to 'il regno d'una fata' (a fairy's realm) inspires imaginative flights while achieving a practical political goal. The writer succeeds in transposing what was, in a global perspective, the marginal and in many respects still fluid political reality of the Savoy monarchy – though evoked through its two most revered representatives, Vittorio Emanuele and Carlo Felice – to the space of fabled realms and grand, ever-lasting illusions: 'Il bel corso Vittorio Emanuele fu trasformato in un immenso porticato luminoso ... Anche il

Velocipede sospeso. Drawing by Dante Paolocci. *Milano e l'esposizione italiana del 1881.*

Displays of electric lights. Drawing by Chessa. *Torino e l'esposizione italiana del 1884*. By permission, Biblioteca di storia e cultura del Piemonte, Turin, Italy.

giardino di piazza Carlo Felice splendeva come il regno d'una fata' (The beautiful Vittorio Emanuele Boulevard was transformed into an immense glowing colonnade ... the garden of Carlo Felice Square was also shining like a fairy's kingdom) ('L'illuminazione' 66).[17]

By celebrating productivity while advertising leisure, and by fine-tuning the mechanisms that projected dream worlds while disseminating messages of ideological and political propaganda, the 1884 fair joined its European and North American counterparts in controlling a vast collective imagination. The classical dictum of *istruire divertendo* (instruct by amusing) – adopted as the motto for the 1900 World's Fair in Paris – became the mantra through which economic, political, and cultural powers imparted specific lessons to the growing crowds of fairgoers. The World's Fairs' 'inventor,' the man responsible for articulating the fairs' founding ideology that linked technological progress and the advance of Western civilization, was French engineer and economist Frédéric Le Play. Hired to direct the Paris 1855 exposition, Le Play was a social activist and an expert on European labour conditions who viewed fairs as didactic tools to help the working classes understand their role in the trajectory of progress. With this aim in mind, subsequent fair organizers combined philanthropy and paternalism and, with time, also a good deal of show-business savvy to design exhibition layouts, create specific exhibits such as those on the history of labour and colonial possessions, and organize special tours for working people.[18] Workers typically obtained free admission tickets and discounts on railroad and hotel fares to attend fairs and special events such as inauguration and closing ceremonies, prize allocations, concerts, and parades. Workers thus enjoyed as spectacle what they normally experienced as work, and pedagogy and ideology joined arms to emphasize a tale told for the sake of national prestige, industrial might, and interclass pacification.[19] Fairs were thus regarded as powerful consensus-building machines that, by amusement if not by instruction, would succeed in incorporating the lower classes in the growing bourgeois market economy.

This fairy tale of consensual pleasure did not fail to produce its own spectres. They haunted the exhibitions' precincts and materialized in the form of recurrent strikes and social revolts, as well as in the more structured organization of the first workers' movements.[20] The *fasci dei lavoratori*, or labour unions, in Sicily rose in rebellion during the Palermo national exposition (1891–2). The *fasci* were composed for the most part by peasants living below subsistence levels in an overpopulated countryside owned by a few absentee property owners. After the agricultural depression of the 1880s, nothing could have been more remote from these labourers' reality of quasi-starvation than the picture of industrial progress and universal civilization that fairs promoted. Conscious of their poverty and disaffected, these peasants took part in bloody agrarian uprisings, often marked by exemplary governmental repressions. Similarly, extensive worker strikes dotted the expositions in 1891 Palermo, 1894 Milan, and 1898 Turin. The *moti* of 6–7 May 1898 in Milan, which General Bava-Beccaris infamously quenched by turning cannon and grapeshot against an unarmed mob, occurred six days after the official opening of the Turin fair. The fair's organizers, who were members of a society called La Libertà (Freedom) devoted to the support and protection of factory workers, had originally proposed the fair as 'un'esposizione delle forze vive dell'operaio' (exhibition of factory workers' active strengths) ('Come nacque' 2). Fearing the danger of similar unrest in Turin, however, these same organizers felt it necessary to both distance themselves from the events in Milan and uphold the rule of order in a fair that 'aliena a ogni infecondo clamore' (extraneous to every unproductive clamour) (Villa 22) displayed the grand results of stable and efficient production. Yet, even a cursory look at contemporary newspapers reveals other stories, such as those of Rome's cab drivers on strike because the new streetcars, on display at many exhibitions, were depriving them of their jobs; of the mobs in Parma cutting telegraph wires and smashing electric lights, as emblems of a modernity that seemed to benefit only the privileged classes; of the fifty thousand soldiers sent to Sicily to put down what was portrayed as a socialist revolution rather than a protest against hunger; of martial law being proclaimed, constitutional rights abrogated, and 'dissident' parties dissolved, their leaders prosecuted.[21]

Of Maps and Towers: A Stroll along the Fairgrounds

As World's Fairs reached their maturity between 1880 and the turn of the century, their ordering principles became more exact. Organizers perfected the tools that allowed them to assemble and disassemble the world into a visual spectacle conveying carefully managed aesthetic and pedagogical messages. Fairgrounds' maps show how diverse spaces were structured in a unitary manner, so that the abundance of products would inevitably come under the visitors' methodically regulated observation. The transparent charts of the fairs' layouts, with their set directions, tapis roulants, glass architecture, and later even picture-taking vantage points, ordered heterogeneity into a geometrical formula. Fairs' fixed itineraries can be compared to closed narrative plots based on 'referential ostension and deictic display' (Sieburth x), triumphal epics of progress and eulogies of the powers in control of that progress. In the expositions' master narratives, the restoration points (cafés, bars, and restaurants), various attractions (such as prize ceremonies and sporting events), and numerous spectacles (such as fireworks, hot air balloon rides, dioramas, panoramas, and cinematic and photographic projections) constituted descriptive pauses or concise sub-plots, aimed at illustrating and replicating the fairs' progress-bound and universalistic message.

Utopias of readability, fairs empowered their visitors to play the part of universal interpreters when scouting, reconnoitring, and mapping these ordered compendia of the world. In 1881 Milan, for example, organizers arranged the exposition's materials 'secondo l'ordine naturale – cominciando dalle materie prime, procedendo alle trasformazioni che queste subiscono per opera dell'uomo, passando per gli strumenti e le macchine mercé cui tale trasformazione si compie e sal-

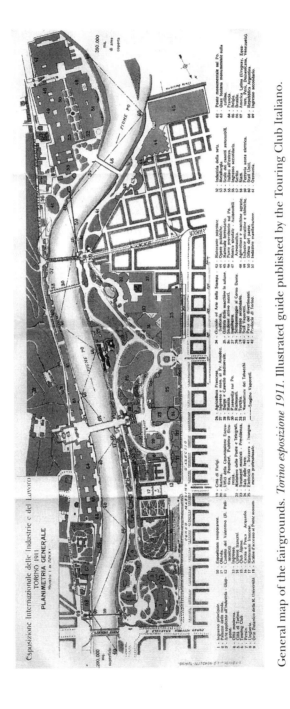

General map of the fairgrounds. *Torino esposizione 1911.* Illustrated guide published by the Touring Club Italiano.

endo gradatamente' (according to the natural order – starting from the raw materials, proceeding to the transformations that these materials undergo through the action of man, going by the tools and the machines that make these transformations possible, and gradually progressing upward) ('In che cosa la mostra' 10). Counting on the dramatic effect produced by displaying modern technologies first, 1884 Turin inverted, without otherwise altering, the Milanese ordering principle. One of the most visited spaces at the 1898 exposition in Turin was the gigantic Galleria del lavoro. Designed like a tunnel, the curved supporting beams of which impressed the sense of spatial advancement toward a brightly lit exit point, the Galleria treated fairgoers with a visual narrative of the progressive achievements of human labour.[22]

When entering these temples of science, technology, and production, fairgoers became unsuspecting cogs in a well-oiled and large-scale machine of representation. Fairs created what Roland Barthes would call a powerful 'reality-effect' ('The Reality Effect' 11–17) as they convinced fairgoers that they were watching a veritable compendium of the world, concentrated in a few square miles. As visitors strolled through the fairgrounds and stopped at designated vantage points, they participated in the codes regulating the exhibition, and felt the self-satisfying certainty that the object-world displayed was indeed knowable and willing to be intellectually appropriated. Several contemporary commentators noted the empowering effect produced on viewers by the ability to spread a totalizing gaze over the fairgrounds. The abstruse and apparently functionless frame of the Eiffel Tower had a key purpose. As Haussmann had done a few decades before, but with less human and architectural expenditure, the Eiffel Tower controlled the labyrinthine character of old Paris by allowing viewers to transform the city into an object that could be perused in a single encompassing gaze.[23] The elevator that carried forty people 185 feet up for a bird's-eye view of the 236 acres of the 1876 Philadelphia exposition, the Trocadéro Towers in 1878 Paris, and the Panoramic Tower of the Palermo 1891 National Exposition performed the same role. So did the gigantic Ferris Wheel of the 1893 Chicago exposition, which became a staple attraction in many subsequent fairs, as well as the forty-metre-high Stigler Tower, which was one of the main attractions at the 1894 Milan exposition.[24]

As early as 1855, the *Rapport sur l'Exposition universelle de 1855 présenté à l'Empereur par S.A.R. le prince Napoléon* (Report on the Universal Exposition of 1855 presented to the Emperor by HRH Prince Napoleon) stated that 'il faut ... qu'il y ait, pour la commodité du public et pour la

Galleria del lavoro. *L'esposizione nazionale del 1898*. By permission, Biblioteca di storia e cultura del Piemonte, Turin, Italy.

satisfaction du goût, des points d'où l'œil puisse embrasser l'ensemble' (for the visitors' comfort and the satisfaction of taste there must ... be some point where the eye can encompass the whole) (141–2).[25] New technological means such as those operating the gigantic elevators or the rotating platforms that oriented the viewers' points of view granted the power of this omniscient gaze. The technique of the bird's-eye view, so typical of all World's Fairs, afforded the illusion of omnipotence while provoking a state of awe.[26] This is what David Nye defines as the feeling afforded by the 'technological sublime': 'in a physical world that is increasingly desacralized, the sublime represents a way to reinvest the landscape and the works of men with transcendent significance' (xiii). The technological sublime so craftily exhibited at World's Fairs differed in significant ways from its Romantic predecessor, the natural sublime. Instead of emerging from the solitary wanderer's communion with a grandiose natural spectacle, the sublime became a collective experience organized for crowds of tourists looking at man-made artefacts. The individual feelings of immensity and awe persisted, but rather than translating themselves into hymns to the greatness of God, they turned into celebrations of human skill and of 'man's' own creations.

Exposition catalogues often furnished the verbal counterpart to this visual experience in their initial sections, typically titled 'Visione generale' (General View) or 'Veduta a volo d'uccello' (Bird's-Eye View) describing the 'colpo d'occhio' or the 'primo sguardo' (first glance) that the visitor could cast upon the fairgrounds from an elevated position, such as a terrace or the *ferrovia aerea*.[27] Often, the verbal description was accompanied by drawings of the fairgrounds as seen from above. Typically, while suggesting an itinerary through an exposition's main points of interest, these descriptions also provided the fair's time-constrained visitors with the gist of the fair's master narrative – the grand epic that, 'dalle prime industrie rudimentali a quelle più progredite ed organizzate' (from the first rudimentary industries to the more developed and organized ones), followed humanity's course toward modern 'progresso e ... benessere' (progress and ... well-being) (De Luca 195–6). Revealing a design 'ordinato con matematica precisione' (ordered with mathematic precision) (Lanza 6) and displaying a reality mastered by meticulous organization, the general view also dazzled the visitor with the grandeur and array of its many displays.

In the age of the 'world as exhibition,' to borrow Martin Heidegger's fortunate definition, the fairs' displays were asked to satisfy two mutually exclusive demands: they had to be realistic and they had to be spectacular. The realism of the representation assured the public that the models on display stood in perfect correspondence to something actually existing (or having existed) in the external world. As models of the real, fairs' exhibits became signifiers of objective truth, while their spectacularity elevated them from the banality of everyday life, and made them unique. Their sheer visual intensity marked, on the eve of the creation of the cinema industry in Turin, the dawn of a visual world. George Brown Goode, assistant secretary of the Smithsonian Institution and a well-known turn-of-the-century World's Fair authority, wrote:

> There is an Oriental saying that the distance between ear and eye is small, but the difference between hearing and seeing very great.
>
> More terse and not less forcible is our own proverb, 'To see is to know,' which expresses a growing tendency in the human mind.
>
> In this busy ... age each man is seeking to know all things, and life is too short for many words. The eye is used more and more ... and in the use of the eye, descriptive writing is set aside for pictures, and pictures in their turn are replaced by actual objects. In the schoolroom the diagram, the blackboard, and the object lesson, unknown thirty years ago, are universally employed. The public lecturer uses the stereopticon to reinforce his words, the editor illustrates his journals and magazines with engravings a hundred-fold more numerous and elaborate than his predecessors thought needful, and the merchant and manufacturer recommend their wares by means of vivid pictographs. The local fair of old has grown into the great exposition. (243)[28]

Through the impact of objectual concreteness, fairgoers felt the thrill of authenticity, that same *frisson* that inspired the great French Orientalist Sylvestre de Sacy to plan a museum that would function as

> [un] vaste dépôt d'objets de toute nature, de dessins, de livres originaux, de cartes, de relations de voyages, offert à tous ceux qui se livreront à l'étude de l'Asie; en sorte que chacun d'eux puisse se croire transporté, comme par enchantement, au milieu de telle tribu mongole ou de telle race chinoise. (Finot 5–6)

> ([a] large warehouse of objects of all kinds, of illustrations, of original books, maps and travel narratives, offered to all those who wish to give themselves to the study of Asia; in such a way that each of these students would be able to feel himself transported as if by enchantment into the midst of, say, a Mongolian tribe or Chinese race.)

As if by enchantment: as soon as it is stated, the plan of all-inclusive rational knowledge obtained through appropriation and classification gives way to its polar opposite: the uncanny pleasure that the imagination provides, the magic of the unquantifiable and the unknowable. As repositories of spectacular objects, fairs' displays open up the world of fantasy and escapism. It is not surprising that contemporary reviewers often described the illusory atmosphere of World's Fairs as a phantasmagoria, a term that is associated today with Benjamin's famous critique of universal expositions.[29] The concrete, material exposition of the 'object-world' was never an end in itself. The expositions' objects (or people, as we shall see) were *both* concrete models that could be touched and perused from all sides *and* signs pointing to something else – symbols relating to some larger meaning. In this function, these objects offered a paradoxical type of knowledge, one that at once familiarized and distanced. In their solid referential foundation, objects on display represented a knowable reality called, for example, Egypt. Yet these objects were also performing a metonymical gesture, as parts of a whole (Egypt) that they could not fully encompass. The show of objects both bound and accounted for Egypt and alluded to a broader, still mysterious reality, a reality that the imperial world was in the process of unveiling and appropriating.

A slightly different picture emerges from the expositions' practice of reproducing historical buildings and scenes, which created a time-bound rather than a space-bound exoticism. These reproductions were inspired by what was perceived as a canonized and concluded world, rather than by a colonial reality that was still somewhat fluid. The medieval castle and the medieval district that architect Alfredo D'Andrade built in the park of Valentino Castle for the 1884 exposition were such a success that, unlike all other exposition buildings, they were not demolished; instead, they became defining architectural features of the Turinese park. During exposition times, the castle was peopled by men and women in medieval costume, acting out a colourful slice of remote everyday life:

> Nelle varie botteghe sono i rispettivi artisti e negozianti in costumi varii e originali.
>
> I due farmacisti, dietro il loro banco popolato di svariate boccette, vendono i licori di lunga vita. Gli operai dell'Issel di Genova e del Farina di Faenza, vestiti in tela greggia, fanno i boccali in terra cotta mediante un tornio primitivo che fan girare col piede mentre altri operai dipingono i vasi con figure rozze, e una bionda e robusta borghigiana provvede alla vendita. ...
>
> In altra bottega sta dinanzi al suo telaio una brava tessitrice ...

> Il corteo [dei visitatori dell'esposizione] passa.
>
> È il mondo moderno che entra nel medioevo. È il secolo XIX che fa un ricorso fantastico nel XV. Quei due mondi destano un contrasto che non manca di una certa comicità. ('Al villaggio' 59)[30]

> (Artists and shopkeepers wearing varied and original costumes are found in their respective shops.
>
> Two pharmacists, behind their counter full of assorted little bottles, sell the elixirs of life ... Workers of the Issel factory from Genoa and the Farina factory from Faenza, dressed in rough cloth, make terracotta pitchers with a primitive wheel that they turn with their foot. At the same time, other workers paint vases with rough figures, and a blonde heavy-set female villager takes care of the sales ...
>
> In another shop a skilled weaver sits in front of her loom.
>
> The procession [of the exposition's visitors] passes by.
>
> This is the modern world that enters the Middle Ages. This is the nineteenth century that fantastically returns to the fifteenth. These two worlds create a contrast that does not lack a certain humour.)

The estranging, playful factor (in Turin's case the Middle Ages as a kind of *exotisme dans le temps*, and the shocking telescoping of the past into the present with the mixture of ancient and modern signs) coexisted with a pedagogical intent, the rediscovery of an embellished and idealized national past. Pedagogy, in turn, married ideology as the rediscovery of this 'national' past consisted in the re-evaluation of the Piedmontese late Middle Ages as a polemical alternative to the official Rome of Bramante. This local history thus acquired an emblematic and absolutized value. In a popular piece devoted to the medieval castle, Camillo Boito explained that D'Andrade had meticulously reproduced the real by copying and assembling elements pertaining to numerous Piedmontese castles.[31] However, Boito continued, as these separate elements combined into a whole, the resulting picture was one that was both more beautiful, more ordered, and therefore more fully decipherable than anything that the real Middle Ages had ever created:

> Comparisce rifatto in pochi mesi il lavoro di un secolo almeno; ma in modo più elevato e più bello. Il Villaggio risulta ben diverso dai villaggi del Medio Evo, una confusione di casupole e di catapecchie ... informi, [e presenta] all'incontro un ordinamento di edificii tutti importanti, degni di venire studiati dall'artista. (Boito 322)

(The work of at least a century is redone in a few months, though in a more elevated and beautiful manner. The Village differs greatly from the villages of the Middle Ages, with their confusion of ... formless huts and shacks. On the contrary, [this village presents] an ordered array of buildings, all important and worthy of being studied by the artist.)

While reproducing the real, the artist makes selective and ordering choices that allow his 'finzione del vero' (fiction of the real) (Boito 331) to disclose a deeper truth. If the relationship of a fair's exotic exhibit to the colonial reality was synecdochical or metonymical (a part for a whole still in the process of being surveyed), the relationship of a fair's historical reconstruction to its original was metaphorical (the essence for the accident). Boito argues that, by consolidating in one significant product the best that the Middle Ages had to offer, D'Andrade success-fully captured the essence of an otherwise remote and undecipherable era. Thus, Boito does not view the artist's idealizing and beautifying interventions as subjective interpretations, as individual constructs that are culturally bound and ideologically coloured. While reproducing the mysterious charms of a bygone era, these authorial interventions fur-nished the authoritative and absolute keys to the inner sanctum of the medieval mentality.

Overall, the expositions' success in the reproductive arts confirms the view held by Ludwig Feuerbach, who, in his 1881 edition of *The Essence of Christianity*, presented his contemporary age as one that favoured 'the sign to the thing signified, the copy to the original, fancy to reality, the appearance to the essence ... *illusion* only is *sacred*' (xiii). If the sacred is, by definition, the locus of original authenticity, Feuerbach's paradox – only *illusion* is *authentic* – captures one of the traits of modernity, as expressed by national and international expositions. From exotic repro-ductions to architectural revivals, expositions flaunted their citational nature, and invited fairgoers to become participants in their vicarious and ephemeral existence as replicas of wondrous and remote originals. While drawing itineraries in a second-degree reality, expositions also evoked, by sheer approximation, a first-degree reality of original models and authentic essences. Belated products of the Enlightenment's voca-tion to classify and order, fairs used their carefully arranged displays of *authentic reproductions* to create exhaustive and informative catalogues of the world. However, especially in the case of exotic displays, these cata-logues' discrete items also evoked an original reality out there, which remained charmingly mysterious to the common fairgoer and was still

Courtyard of the medieval castle. Drawing by A. Bonamore. *Torino e l'esposizione italiana del 1884.* By permission, Biblioteca di storia e cultura del Piemonte, Turin, Italy.

untouched by the proliferation of copies that modern technologies brought about. The full meaning of this reality gave itself up only to a few adepts: the scientist, the colonial functionary, the explorer, the archaeologist, the writer, the reporter, and ultimately also the various exhibits' organizers. These people were the mediators through whose authoritative perspective fairgoers experienced the world and its wonders. Thus, in the land of Cockaigne that were World's Fairs, eager audiences could taste the paradox of having their cake and eating it too. Through expert mediation reality-objects bestowed the pleasure of immediate contact and full disclosure, and through direct observation they evoked the phantasmic charms of unknown and exotic worlds still brimming with untapped potential and capable of yielding exciting new discoveries.[32]

This paradox, sustained by the careful balance between contradictory terms – reality and illusion, the aesthetics of realism and that of the spectacular – underwrote all World's Fair projects during the golden age of their existence. Arguably, this balance was a difficult one to maintain. While displaying, and thus asserting control over, the wondrous variety of the world, fairs also reflected and contributed to the process of global homogenization that resulted from the intersection of technological and political factors such as mass production and colonialism. The developments in transportation and the diffusion of new means of communication allowed unprecedented access to remote sites, unfamiliar objects, and diverse customs. Western culture imposed itself upon a progressively shrinking world, as Walter Benjamin's, Theodor Adorno's, and Max Horkheimer's entropic apocalypses in the 1940s, Claude Lévi-Strauss's attacks on monoculture in the 1950s, and Pier Paolo Pasolini's mourning over the loss of '*il sentimento dell'altrove*' (the sense of an elsewhere) (148) in the 1960s made all too clear.[33] Inspired by these critics' seminal arguments, influential sociologists, ethnographers, and philosophers read modernity as the site of loss and nostalgia: loss of cultural heterogeneity and alternative modes of life, nostalgia for a condition where wonder and discovery were still possible as human experiences. However, by becoming influential diagnoses of the modern condition, these interpretations perversely, if unwittingly, brought about what they were denouncing. The modern condition became a fixed and uniform state rather than a process, variable in time and across different social, national, and cultural formations. Reading World's Fairs as cultural phenomena offers a corrective to this interpretive danger, as fairs provide specific, nation-based examples for this itinerary of historical becoming that is the modern condition. The entropic stasis of global uniformity that Adorno and Benjamin saw as pervading the modern world was just the end point (real or dreaded) in the life narrative of universal expositions. The plot in its entirety spun a story based on affirmation as well as deferral: affirmation of Western might and the uniform cultural power of a 'Civilization' expanding to all corners of the world, and deferral of Western globalization in the name of the new, the exotic, and the spectacular on one hand, and of the ethnically and nationally specific on the other.

Pro Aris et Foci: The King, the People, and the Nation

In the world of universal expositions, the notion of national and ethnic distinctiveness counterbalanced the threat of homogenization and satisfied the fairgoer's desire to be provided with universal catalogues of the diverse and the heterogeneous. The 1867 Paris exhibition was the first to underscore the notion of nationhood by introducing several new features that became staples of all international expositions. Organizers invited participating nations to erect their individual buildings and introduced culturally based display techniques. The classification of exhibits was based on the country of origin. The fair's layout featured a central garden around which the displays were arranged 'in concentric bands' with the different nationalities intersecting the bands 'by transepts or avenues radiating from the centre' (Allwood 42). The centralizing and all-encompassing inspiration for the exposition resounds in Charles Boissay's ornate remarks regarding the main building in the Champ de Mars:

> 'L'Exposition embrasse et résume l'ensemble des connaissances humaines, exaltées à leur plus haut point actuel de perfection.
> Faire le tour de ce palais, circulaire comme l'équateur, c'est littéralement tourner autour du monde; tous les peuple sont venus; c'est un jubilé, les ennemis vivent en paix côté à côté. Ainsi qu'à l'origine des choses sur l'orbe des eaux, l'Esprit divin plane sur cet orbe de fer. (322)

> (The exposition embraces and summarizes the totality of human knowledge, elevating it to its highest point of current perfection.
> To tour this palace, circular, like the equator, is literally to go around the world. All peoples are here, it is a jubilee, and enemies live in peace side by side. As in the beginning of things, on the globe of waters, the divine spirit now floats over the globe of iron).

In the prototype for what would become the famed Rue des Nations at the 1878 Paris exposition, participating nations could express their individual specificity while being part of the communal journey of civilization's advancement.[34] The didactic display of each nation's contribution to civilization's progress blended with the fair's requirements for entertainment.[35] Joseph Wilson, the author of *The Masterpieces of the Centennial International Exhibition* (Philadelphia, 1876), detailed the pleasures afforded by the fair's numerous ethnic restaurants and cafés: 'Visitors were waited upon by young girls in the costumes of the different nationalities, and one met the blondes of Bavaria, the gay Austrian, the pretty Russian, crowned with a tinsel diadem, the Mulatto offering cocoa and guava, Greeks, Swiss, Neapolitans, Italians, Indians, and even the Chinese women, with their little tea shops. All languages mingled strangely together on this promenade, and all nationalities elbowed each other, from the elegant Parisian to the Bedouin in his burnous' (lxi)[36] In spite of this appreciation for ethnic diversity, fair sponsors never forgot that expositions were ideal sites for individual nations to assert themselves, satisfy their political ambitions, and express their will to power. Giant advertising machines, fairs offered the unique opportunity for the hosting cities to define their and their countries' collective identities, and display them for the rest of the world. According to Aram Yengoyan, 'Whether in France, England, or the United States, fairs became part of the "cultural ballast" of the nation and anchored the nation-state to values represented in world's fairs' displays' (5). The need for legitimization that Yengoyan identifies here was even more pressing for a country with a still hesitant and fragmented national identity, where, as demonstrated by Joseph Wilson's words, being Italian and Neapolitan were not consubstantial at all.

While manufacturing Italy's official image and promoting this culture of national self-assertiveness, Turin also aspired to be on equal terms with France, England, and the United States in shaping Western universalistic dreams and defining the role of 'civilization' in the rest of the world. Nation building demanded not only administrative and territorial unification, but also the construction of national loyalties in order to make citizens feel part of a common national episteme. Turin understood, better and earlier than anybody else in Italy, that fairs were ideal spaces to manufacture this very episteme – one that laid claim to a sense of nationality as well as universality. What Brad Epps points out regarding the Universal Exposition of 1888 in Barcelona can be applied to Turin as well: 'Barcelona [attempted] to fashion itself into a cosmopolitan site, a locus of universality. But this attempt, whatever its degree of success, is itself shot through with national aspirations. Like the connections between the country, the town, and the city, the connections between the national, the international, and the universal are as intense as they are multifarious' (175). Like Barcelona, Turin intended to give international credentials to its national particularities. Like Barcelona, Turin strove to place itself in a more continental than peninsular arena. But unlike the city in Catalonia that asserted itself as a recognized and respected alternative to Madrid, Turin had no pluralistic or secessionist aims: it simply wanted to *be* Rome. As loci of both displayed achievement and utopias of wish-fulfilment, expositions helped Turin reclaim the centrality it had lost. Even if only for the duration of a fair, Turin allowed itself to reappropriate what it felt was its own in the first place. By dint of cultural appeal and economic might, Turin replaced Rome on the exposition floor as the rightful leader of a (pseudo-) united country whose values it represented fully for the simple reason that it had imposed them upon what once was the periphery in the first place.

Tommaso Villa, a prominent political figure in Turin and the *grand patron* of many of its expositions, understood this dynamic well.[37] As early as 1884, he realized that the exposition was the occasion to reconfirm Turin's status as the cradle of the Risorgimento and initiator of the process of nation formation. He thus planned a Mostra del Risorgimento that would unite the various regions around the Turin hub. All the kingdom's provinces received a communication in which the exposition's organizers stated that they planned to 'raccogliere e ... presentare ordinati ed esposti come in un vasto quadro tutti i documenti di quel periodo della vita politica d'Italia che corre dai primordi della Rivoluzione fino al compimento della nostra unità' (gather and ... present, ordered and displayed as in a broad canvas, all the documents of that period of Italian political life that goes from the beginning of the Revolution to the achievement of our unity) (*L'esposizione del 1884*, 59). Besides the Risorgimento exhibit, Villa aimed at creating 'una biblioteca della Rivoluzione italiana, un museo illustrativo della nostra epopea nazionale' (a library of the Italian Revolution, an illustrative museum of our national epic) (*L'esposizione del 1884*, 62). The Italian regions' response exceeded all expectations, to the point that a special pavilion was built to host the various materials.[38] Villa paid close attention to this site's symbolic implications, and placed a reproduction of the Temple of Vesta just in front of the pavilion ('Il tempio' 81). Displaced from its original location in Rome, the temple devoted to the

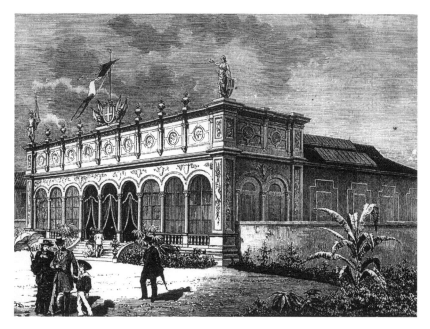

Padiglione del Risorgimento. *Album-ricordo dell'esposizione del 1884 in Torino.* By permission, Biblioteca di storia e cultura del Piemonte, Turin, Italy.

goddess of the domestic hearth linked Turin to the public worship of the state as the 'state-hearth,' thus creating an ideal continuity between Savoy past and present, and once again, challenging Rome's right to capitalhood.

By establishing closer ties between the state's apparatus and the fairs' bureaucracy, 'young' countries like Italy and the United States validated their presents with idealized images of their pasts. Significantly, these countries consistently associated their universal expositions with the celebration of political recurrences. The 1876 Centennial Exhibition in Philadelphia commemorated the one-hundredth anniversary of the birth of the United States, and meaningfully took place in the city-symbol of American political independence. The 1893 Chicago World's Columbian Exposition honoured the anniversary of the 'discovery' of America, and the Louisiana Purchase Exposition of 1904 celebrated the hundredth anniversary of the annexation of the Mississippi River territories to the United States. As we shall see in detail later, in 1911, Turin,

Florence, and Rome joined hands to honour the fiftieth anniversary of the birth of the Italian kingdom.

In this perspective, all these fairs represent an important yet rarely noted departure from the Great Exhibition of 1851 at the Crystal Palace, which in so many other ways defined the founding tropes of the World's Fairs' discourse. The Great Exhibition did not celebrate a political recurrence, but rather trumpeted the advantages of free enterprise and commerce, and thus promoted the abolition of custom tariffs in England and abroad. Many European and North American cities that hosted universal expositions shared London's original plan to establish advantageous international contacts and thus, especially in the case of Italy, emerge out of situations of commercial and economic isolation. However, in many universal expositions that followed the London archetype, the ties between politics and commerce became stronger, and their symbolic value more evident. Unlike the Great exhibition of 1851, which was financed by private enterprise, many subsequent fairs were funded by the hosting countries' governments. In Italy, in particular, the entrepreneurial class and the state combined financing efforts and thus cemented the alliance between political and industrial elites that marked the new country's collective identity. Italian expositions carefully combined political propaganda with the display of economic productivity, and their mass appeal had an extraordinary impact in creating a sense of national unity around the monarchic institution.[39]

Periodicals devoted to the expositions and popular magazines such as *L'illustrazione italiana* and *Margherita: giornale delle signore italiane* lavishly commented on the sovereigns' visits to the fairgrounds. Their rhetoric influenced the Italian people's sense of nationhood and nurtured their loyalty to a monarchy often presented in populistic and democratic overtones. The queen and king's exposition tours, frequently coordinated with parallel trips to hospitals, hospices, and orphanages, presented the genial side of the authoritarian coin, and exalted the monarchy's familiar and charitable traits. The Savoy royal family keenly exploited these modern venues of self-advertisement and consensus building. If in the pomp and magnificence of its celebrations the monarchy had traditionally presented itself to the masses as *spectacle*, the house of Savoy was particularly skilled in adapting the forms and the protagonists of the royal spectacle to the demands and needs of a rapidly changing world: 'Tutta la folla degli invitati, fra cui molte signore, si confuse alle autorità, circuì la famiglia reale, e pareva tutta una sola famiglia, e mai forse come allora ci siamo sentiti fratelli e abbiamo sen-

Exposition attire at the War Exhibit. Drawing by Dante Paolocci. *Torino e l'esposizione italiana del 1884.* By permission, Biblioteca di storia e cultura del Piemonte, Turin, Italy.

tito l'Italia' (All the invited people, among which there were many ladies, mingled with the authorities and encircled the Royal family, and they all looked like a single family, and perhaps never so much as in that occasion did we feel as brothers, did we feel as Italians) (*Milano e l'esposizione italiana del 1881,* 18). If middle-class women's taste in current fashion modelled itself upon these magazines' descriptions of the queen's exquisite 'exposition attires,' workingmen were invited to feel a sense of affinity for a king who consistently favoured the Machinery Hall over every other exhibit and knowingly discussed these machines' functioning as if they were indeed part of his daily experiences.

A direct consequence of the connection between politics and exhibitions was that fairs consistently aimed at presenting a somewhat self-serving and ideologically coloured portrait of the hosting nations. The 1853 New York fair, for example, celebrated the efficiency of Yankee industry in polemical opposition to the agrarian oligarchy of the South, therefore promoting Northern values as more befitting the States' official image and collective sense of identity. As festivals 'of national unity and progress' (Scobey 90), fairs spread a veil across political divisions and cultural anxieties. Thus, the 1855 Paris Exposition Universelle claimed to be 'a temple of peace, bringing all nations together in concord' in spite of the fighting in the Crimea (Allwood 33). In 1873, the twenty-fifth anniversary of Emperor Franz Joseph's reign was the pretext for Austria to reiterate the integrity of the Empire in spite of the serious military defeat of Sadowa in 1867, the unlucky alliance with France in the war against Prussia in 1870, the loss of the Veneto region to Italy, and the problems with Hungary. In 1878, Paris reaffirmed France's centrality in the world of liberal economies and politics in spite of the defeat of Sedan, the fall of Napoleon III, and the experiences of the Commune.

The 1898 National Exposition in Turin is perhaps one of the best cases in point, and one of the most ideologically complex. By celebrating the fiftieth anniversary of the statute that the king of Sardinia, Carlo Alberto, had granted in 1848, the exposition's planners traced a straight line connecting the end of absolutism, the advent of constitutional monarchy, the construction of the new nation state under Savoy's leadership, and the beginning of Italy's industrial take-off. As the first issue of *L'esposizione nazionale del 1898* proudly stated, 'Torino scrisse la pagina gloriosa dello Statuto; è giusto che dopo 50 anni si metta in festa; così si potrà dimostrare il cammino percorso in questo periodo grazie alle libertà sancite dallo Statuto' (Turin wrote the glorious page of the Statute; it is appropriate that we should celebrate it after fifty years to demonstrate the progress made during this time thanks to the liberties that the statute granted us) (2). For liberal thinkers, the celebration of the *Statuto Albertino* emphasized the end of absolutism, and the political as well as economic advantages of constitutional rule. The alliance between politics and industry, and between the power of progress and that of the nation state, constituted the main theme in the fair, as demonstrated in this list of the fair's objectives:

> dimostrare quali siano oggi le condizioni della nostra vita intellettuale, quale lo stato delle nostre industrie e delle arti, presentare alla nazione un inventario fedele delle svariate sue produzioni, rivelare al paese quanto valga in ogni espressione delle sua attività, è affermare nel modo più eloquente i benefici effetti di un regime che da cinquant'anni consacra la partecipazione di tutti i cittadini alla vita pubblica, la loro eguaglianza dinanzi alla legge, la libera esplicazione delle loro forze intellettuali e morali. (Villa, 'Discorso' 21)

(to demonstrate what is today the state of our intellectual life, and of our industries and arts, to present the nation with a faithful inventory of its various productions, and to reveal to the country how much she is worth in every expression of her activities means to affirm in the most eloquent manner the beneficial effects of a regime that for fifty years has been supporting the participation of all its citizens in public life, their equality before the law, and the free manifestation of their intellectual and moral qualities.)

However, for conservative politicians the same fair and the same celebrations offered the pretext to carry forward an antiparliamentarian program. A famous article by Sidney Sonnino that the prestigious journal *Nuova antologia* published in January 1897 argued for the abolition of Parliament and the full restoration of the original statute, which would invest the King, Umberto I, with much broader powers than those provided in a parliamentary system (Sonnino 575–97). This reactionary turn resulted from various events, including the consistent, if still clandestine, growth of the Socialist party, the rise of social disorders and workers' strikes, and the fall of Crispi's authoritarian leadership (1898), which many conservative politicians felt would open the doors to dangerous revolutionary strife.

Even before becoming shrines to mass entertainment and mass consumption – the '*Missa Solemnis* of traditional capitalist society' in Umberto Eco's words ('A Theory' 294) – expositions constituted grand efforts of recapitulation and provided comprehensive compendia of national production. Fairs' trumpeted 'universality' was not only geographical but also cultural: as the 1855 Paris exposition made clear, the analytical and ordered collection of *all* products of *all* sectors of human activity was meant to provide a synthesis capable of defining the type and degree of the civilization they represented. In spite of this urge for comprehensive nomenclature and encyclopedic inclusion, expositions presented a culling of the very best a nation had to offer through a process of selection and idealization. Thus, carefully assembled charts of political, economic, and cultural data homogenized national realities and inscribed them into the trajectory of progress marking the universal history of the 'civilized' world. Through these idealized representations, Turin vied for national leadership by promoting a public culture that would invest all Italians with a shared identity. These idealized representations also claimed Italy's right to play one of the leading roles in the master narrative of universal progress. With (and often against) France,

Great Britain, Germany, and the United States, Italy sought to portray itself as *the* paradigm of Western culture, while at the same time promoting the ideal of an international, cosmopolitan standard of culture. While catering to the will to power of individual nation states, this international standard of culture also expressed the 'unity, allure, and superiority of Western civilization,' which, in turn, imposed itself as a universal cultural value tout court (Gilbert 21).

Although in the plans and rhetoric of their organizers and upper-class underwriters expositions were born to promote and display a nation's productive machine, the Italian expositions – just like those of London, Paris, or Philadelphia – created a more complex system, where progress was subtly related to other strategies of persuasion and consensus building. Attracting larger and larger crowds, expositions became extraordinary tools to define public taste, influence mass psychology, and control national life. A small industrial and scientific elite thus controlled a grand *voyage d'instruction* that allowed fairgoers to assimilate the pride of an idealized and collectively shared past while admiring the functioning prototypes and the utopian designs that foreshadowed a future brimming with potential and abundant in possibilities. While building images of unified nation states by celebrating the myths and the heroes of the past, expositions traced new models of development and progress. Commercial and cultural spectacles of European nationalism and liberal thought, exhibitions thus validated a nation's past and deployed all the available resources for the ideological control of the future.[40]

All the City's a Stage: The Exposition of Hegemonic Topographies in De Amicis's *Torino 1880*

Perhaps no other work of literature mirrors the imaginative and ideological underpinnings of the World's Fairs so closely as the fashionable tour guide that Edmondo De Amicis entitled *Torino 1880*. Written as an elegant Baedeker for foreign travellers – whom we imagine visited Turin from one of the much-admired metropolises of Berlin, Paris, London, New York, or Philadelphia – *Torino 1880* was repeatedly featured as the pièce de résistance in many of the guides, magazines, and catalogues devoted to the numerous expositions held in Turin.[41] *Torino 1880* thus became the official portrait of the modern Italian metropolis, as De Amicis flatteringly associated Turin with the leading capitals of the nineteenth century. Widely read and widely quoted, *Torino 1880* is a classic 'exposition text,' as its formal configuration and descriptive strategies gave narrative form and writerly authority to the World's Fairs' popular epistemology.

In *Torino 1880* the city is presented as an efficient and well-planned site that flaunts the rationality of its design and the crystal-clear efficiency of its urban logic. Just as exposition guides provided detailed and comprehensive tours of the fairgrounds, so De Amicis's made the city legible by methodically displaying it according to a preordained pattern, neighbourhood by neighbourhood, boulevard by boulevard, and piazza by piazza. De Amicis's expository, or to use Philippe Hamon's terminology, 'dioramic,' narrative consists in fact of a series of sketches, with each sketch, scene, or tableaux framing a section of the city. Comparable to the articles in exposition guides usually titled 'Passeggiata per l'Esposizione' (A Walk through the Exposition) or 'A zonzo per l'Esposizione' (Strolling through the Exposition), *Torino 1880* functions as a metropolitan 'portrait gallery,' in which every urban sector is described with encyclopedic thoroughness. *Torino 1880* sports an entertaining and amusing style, although its intent was ultimately didactic. In spite of the leisurely connotations in their titles, exposition 'strolls' were never loosely structured, but emplotted the real according to evaluative and totalizing criteria, using effective, if repetitious, strategies of organization, hierarchization, and establishment of formal and thematic closure. Appropriately, De Amicis entrusted this organizational task to a knowledgeable native guide, charged with leading a newcomer through Turin's urban space. This guide depicts his habitat by displaying it in a disciplined manner before his visitor's inexperienced eyes. He gradually introduces his guest to an unfamiliar city by investing its various zones with increasing significance through 'ambulatory descriptions' (Hamon 107), or through exposition techniques comparable to the 'panoramic and processional' method of Henry James's 'pedestrian prowler,' as described in his preface to *The Princess Casamassima* (232).

Torino 1880 starts out as a panoramic text. De Amicis's guide and his guest linger on the imposing vista that they enjoy from the hill of Superga, dominating Turin. The opening expository paragraph functions as an affable, yet authoritative, overview of the real: it parades a totality by providing a sweeping, synthesizing assessment of what will be subsequently broken up into discrete elements and analysed, step-by-step, in closer detail. Thus, from the vantage point of that spectacular perch, the Superga belvedere, De Amicis exhibits, via the dependable gaze of his guide, the broad panorama of Turin:

Un Torinese che voglia far da guida a un Italiano il quale venga qui per la prima volta, dovrebbe, prima di lasciarlo entrare in Torino, condurlo diritto a Superga, per fargli provar subito un sentimento di meraviglia e di piacere ... Ci son degli spettacoli che sono per la vista degli occhi ciò che sono per la vista della mente le grandi intuizioni ... che abbracciano secoli di storia e migliaia di idee. Lo spettacolo che si gode da Superga è uno di questi ... Dalla sommità della cupola, con un solo giro dello sguardo, in tre secondi, si abbraccia tutto l'immenso cerchio dell'Apennino genovese e delle Alpi ...; sotto, tutti i colli di Torino, popolati di ville e di giardini, più in là i bei poggi del Monferrato, coronati di castella, le colline ubertose della sinistra del Tanaro, una successione di sterminati tappeti verdi, una campagna sconfinata, che si perde nelle pianure vaporose della Lombardia, argentata dalle mille curve del Po, seminata di centinaia di villaggi e di casali, rigata da strade innumerevoli, coperta d'una vegetazione lussureggiante di boschi, di vigneti e di messi: così rilevata e nettamente visibile fino alle più grandi distanze, così fresca e così italiana di forme e di colori, così grande e così terribile di antiche e di nuove memorie ... per cui l'immaginazione si slancia fino ai confini opposti d'Italia, che, dopo averla percorsa intera, a guardar giù la città di Torino ... viene spontaneo sulle labbra il *Te beata*, che gridò Ugo Foscolo a Firenze. (7–8)

(The citizen of Turin who wanted to act as guide to an Italian coming here for the first time, should, before letting his visitor enter Turin, take him straight to Superga, to make him feel right away a sense of wonder and pleasure ... There are spectacles that are for the eyes what great intuitions ... embracing centuries of history and thousands of ideas are for the mind. The spectacle that one enjoys from Superga is one ... From the dome's summit, with just one scan of the horizon, in three seconds, one embraces the whole immense circle of the Genoese Apennines and the Alps ...; below them, one sees all the hills of Turin, peopled with villas and gardens. Further ahead, the beautiful hills of the Monferrato region are crowned with castles, and the fertile hills on the left bank of the river Tanaro appear as a succession of immense green carpets. It is a boundless countryside, disappearing into Lombardy's hazy plains, which the thousand bends of the river Po streak with silver. Hundreds of villages and farmhouses dot this countryside, numberless roads line it, and a luxuriant vegetation of woods, vineyards and crops covers it. This countryside is so elevated and clearly visible even at the greatest distances, so fresh and so Italian in its forms and colors, and so great and terribly full of ancient and novel memories ... which make the imagination leap to the opposite borders of Italy, that, after surveying it all, the observer who gazes down upon the city of Turin ... feels the spontaneous desire to utter 'You Blessed One,' like Ugo Foscolo shouting to Florence.

In the early eighteenth century, in order to display its wealth and power, the Savoy family had commissioned court architect Filippo Juvarra to build a cathedral atop the Superga hill. By serving as the royal mausoleum from Vittorio Amedeo II to Carlo Alberto, the cathedral memorialized the Savoy dynasty, and became the site of innumerable patriotic pilgrimages. From this majestic and symbolically charged location, De Amicis's benevolent guide takes in the whole of the Turinese landscape, first framing it in a totalizing perspective, and then surveying it in the astounding variety of its parts.[42] He organizes the scenery's components in a hierarchical and disciplined order and extends the land metonymically to represent the whole of the Italian nation, all the while calculating the territory's aesthetic and economic worth and assessing its historical and patriotic appeal. The guide's appropriative and evaluative gaze corresponds to the gaze of authority and power: appropriately for its textual as well as referential location, it is symbolic of the ever-present eye of the king. Similar to the bird's-eye view descriptions typical of World's Fairs catalogues, De Amicis's inaugural paragraph has a controlling and pedagogical function: it furnishes an authoritative summary that prepares the reader's orderly journey through the expository narrative that is to follow.

De Amicis's commandeering description from Superga establishes the point of origin of a structured mechanism of power, a system of discipline. De Amicis organizes his tour through the city of Turin around the display of this power mechanism, which invests specific disciplinary networks and ultimately spreads across the social whole, assuring the infinitesimal distribution of power relations. In his analysis of the 'disciplinary society,' Michel Foucault famously extends the logic of Jeremy Bentham's Panopticon beyond the unique architectural form that Bentham designed to control inmates in a penitentiary, and defines it as a socially pervasive system whose driving concern is with 'individualizing observation, with characterization and classification, with the analytical arrangement of space' ('Panopticism' 203):

The Panopticon ... must be understood as a generalizable model of functioning; a way of defining power relations in terms of the everyday life of men ... The Panopticon must not be understood as a dream building: it is the diagram of a mechanism of power reduced to its ideal form; its functioning ... must be represented as a pure architectural and optical system: it is in fact a figure of political technology that may and must be detached from any specific use.

It is a type of location of bodies in space, of distributions of individuals in relation to one another, of hierarchical organization, of dispositions of centres and channels of power, of definition of the instruments and modes of intervention of power.

('Panopticism' 205)

In Foucault's interpretation, the figure of the king, with its looming material and symbolic presence, is the exact opposite of the physics of power represented by the panoptic scheme, which is disembodied and multiple in its sources, and pervasive in its applications. I would argue, rather, that panopticism evolves from the form of control that the king's authoritarian system exercises, refining it. Power is not only imposed upon a group of subjects from above, it also becomes a general function and inherent feature of the social body that this power intends to control. Power is thus and *at the same time* both hierarchical and diffused, and both imposed upon and shared by the social collectivity.

Descending from Superga – the symbolic origin of authority – tourist and guide enter Turin, where they see power at work as everyday praxis. Although apparently an aimless stroll, their tour is in fact organized according to the display of various centres of power and authority, with each stop or descriptive pause corresponding to the exposition of a different disciplinary site. First, they experience the most diffuse form of urban power: the all-embracing, democratically authoritarian, and plural gaze of 'the city,' a gaze that migrates from numerous sources of power and embraces the entire urban body, its aim 'to strengthen the social forces, to increase production, to develop the economy' (Foucault, 'Panopticism' 208): 'Qui c'è per tutto la città aperta, larga, pubblica, che vede tutto, che non si presta al crocchio, che interrompe le conversazioni intime, che dice continuamente, come il poliziotto inglese: "Circolate, lasciate passare, andate per i vostri affari"' (Here there is, everywhere, the open city, wide, public, that sees everything, that does not engage in idle gatherings, that interrupts private conversation, always saying, just like an English policeman: 'Move on, let people go by, go on with your business') (16–17). The metropolis's policing gaze is everywhere alert: it pierces and penetrates into the smallest aspects of everyday life, thus abolishing the juxtaposition between public and private spaces. In the city, as well as in De Amicis's controlled exposition, there are no gaps, no blind spots, and no discontinuities. Transparency dominates, both literally (the eye sees everything) and logically (everything is clearly understandable).

By making everything visible and open to inspection, the metropolis's gaze disciplines and controls the social whole. It regulates collective movements, eliminating idle chatter and waste of productive energy. It gets rid of the crowd as 'a compact mass, a locus of multiple exchanges, individualities merging together, a collective effect' as well as all spontaneous individual initiatives, replacing them with 'a collection of separate individualities,' easily isolable, easily controlled (Foucault, 'Panopticism' 201). Made up of a network of mechanisms that are ubiquitous and readily available, the city untiringly engages in the surveillance of all its parts, imposing order and bound motion upon its gears, efficiently eliminating all threats of coalition, sedition, and rebellious unrest. Turin's urban architecture reflects this disciplined social policy:

> Tutte le strade, a primo aspetto, si rassomigliano: tagliano tutte un lunghissimo rettangolo di cielo con due file di case color uniforme, su cui lo sguardo scivola dal cornicione al marciapiede, senza trovar nulla che l'arresti; allineate come lo erano i vecchi reggimenti piemontesi ... dopo un'ora di lavoro.
>
> Il color giallo impera, con tutte le sue sfumature ... [e] dà alla città un certo aspetto tranquillo di decoro ufficiale. Qua e là c'è un tentativo di ribellione d'una casa azzurra ... ma subito dopo si ristabilisce la disciplina di due lunghe file di case dalla solita tinta ... Percorse le prime strade, si comincia a notare qualche corrispondenza tra la forma della città e il carattere della popolazione ... Passando per quelle strade si ricorda involontariamente la disciplina dell'antico esercito sardo, le antiche abitudini disciplinari della popolazione (15–16)

(At first glance, all the streets look like each other: they all slice the sky into the shape of a very long rectangle, with two rows of houses of uniform colour. Making the gaze slide, without interruption, from their rooftops to the pavement, one sees that these houses are lined up like the old Piedmont armies ... after an hour's work.

The colour yellow rules, with all its hues ... [and] it gives the city a certain tranquil aspect of official decorum. Here and there, there is an attempt at rebellion with a light blue house ... but discipline soon re-establishes itself, with two long rows of houses of the usual colour. After passing through the first streets, one starts noticing some correspondence between the shape of the city and the character of the population. ... Going through those streets one is involuntarily reminded of the discipline of the ancient Sardinian army, and of the population's ancient disciplinary habits.)

Harmonious conglomerates where social groups allegedly enjoy contentment in a hierarchical setting, Turin's buildings reflect the overall urban physiognomy, and display the citizens' conformity to a common ethic and deference to a collective ideology. Turin's architectural and topographical design reproduces the formal structure of a power system organically built and rationally controlled from a single centre, the royal palace. This top-down discipline manifests itself in every detail of urban life. The vertical stratification of the palazzi, for example, prevents contrasts without erasing differences:

[Le] grandi case [sono] aperte ad angolo verso la strada, con cinque ordini di terrazzini, che mostrano mille piccoli particolari intimi della vita torinese, dal servitore che innaffia i fiori della contessa al primo piano, su su, scendendo per la scala sociale a misura che si sale per la scala della casa, fino all'impiegatuccio ... che legge il giornale sotto i tetti e alla moglie dell'operaio che stende i suoi cenci fuori della soffitta ...

L'archittettura è democratica ed eguagliatrice ... La divisione delle classi sociali a strati sovrapposti dal piano nobile ai tetti, toglie alla città quelle opposizioni visibili di magnificenza e di miseria. (20–1)

(With their five rows of balconies, [the] large buildings open their sides onto the street, and display the innumerable small and intimate details of Turin's life. Our gaze moves up, descending the social ladder in proportion as we climb the building's stairs, from the servant watering the Countess's flowers on the first floor, to the petty clerk ... who reads the newspaper under the roof, and the labourer's wife who hangs her rags outside of her attic ...

The architecture is democratic and egalitarian ... The subdivision of social classes into superimposed strata, from the main floor to the roofs, eliminates from the city all visible juxtapositions of magnificence and misery.)

Well on its way to purging itself of its slums, following a number of mid- to late-nineteenth-century urban-renewal projects, Turin – like

Haussmann's Paris – shows discipline in its straight boulevards, allowing unencumbered transit among all its neighbourhoods.[43] Turin's topographical layout, with its framework of rectilinear streets running parallel or perpendicular to one another, displays this dream of order, and reveals the city's original function as the core of Savoy's military might, an army town: 'la città par fabbricata sopra un immenso scacchiere' (the city seems built over an immense chess board) (15). The army is now in charge of the area of the Arsenal and the *Cittadella*, and De Amicis's guide describes 'una piccola Torino in armi ... nella quale s'incontra una sentinella a ogni passo' (a small Turin in arms ... in which you meet a sentry at every step) (40). The tour proceeds across other disciplinarian institutions, which control different neighbourhoods. Madhouses and hospices, poor people's hospitals and religious orphanages rule over the extreme periphery of town:

Il Ritiro del Buon Pastore, l'ospedale di San Luigi, il manicomio, lo stabilimento di Don Bosco, l'ospedale di Cottolengo [sono] edifizi chiusi e muti, dall'aspetto di conventi e di carceri, colle persiane rovesciate, coi finestrini ingraticolati, con porte ... sbarrate. (42–3)

(The Good Sheperd's Shelter, The Hospital of Saint Luigi, the mental hospital, Don Bosco's institute, and the Cottolengo hospital [are] closed and mute edifices that look like convents and prisons, with closed shutters, barred windows, locked ... doors.)

Enclosed institutions of discipline, heteropias set on the edges of society, these prison-like establishments separate and divide. They arrest communication, quarantine evil, and suspend time. They represent what Foucault calls the 'discipline-blockade,' the coarser form of a power mechanism that operates according to the violent logic of exclusion and expiation.

As De Amicis's guide leads us toward the centre of town, the urban landscape changes, together with the city's disciplinary mechanisms. Attached to the essential functions of the most important sectors of society, 'factory production, the transmission of knowledge, the diffusion of aptitudes and skills,' these mechanisms function increasingly as techniques for 'making useful individuals' rather than as mere places of alienation and exclusion (Foucault, 'Panopticism' 211). In De Amicis's Turin, for example, the gentle discipline of the university pervades the modest dwellings where 'tanti studenti ... martellano ostinatamente sui libri, menando una vita di sacrifizi, per procurarsi un avvenire onorato e lucroso' (many students ... stubbornly pore over their books, leading a life of sacrifice, to acquire an honourable and lucrative future) (20). By defining and systematizing knowledge, the university controls the intellectual disciplines. It establishes their norms, defines their content, and regulates their transmission.[44] As De Amicis's comments make clear, the university's apparatus not only orders knowledge, it also ranks individuals in relation to one another along a scale, depending on the quality of their adherence to the disciplinary norms. Ultimately, this apparatus either grants them the rights to prosperity *and* honour, or disqualifies them from a strictly controlled trajectory of moral and economic progress.

Discipline, Foucault insists, should not be identified solely with a single institution (a prison, a school), a unique apparatus (the medical or the legal systems), or an individual source of authority (the army or the police). Discipline is 'a type of power, a modality for its exercise, comprising a whole set of instruments, techniques, procedures, levels of applications, targets; it is a "physics" or an "anatomy" of power, a technology' ('Panopticism' 215). De Amicis's text reveals that there is an 'economy' of power as well. The economy of power is the disciplinary mechanism that governs acquisition and exchange; the power that, outside of the prison and the military academy, the university and the court of law, in the open space of the town square and in the traffic of the marketplace, controls the world of capital. In spite of the intensity of its exchanges and the freedom of its movements, the rule of the marketplace is as strictly structured as that of every other disciplinary institution.

At the periphery of town, De Amicis's guide and his guest find an economy of survival that feeds on the scraps and leftovers 'che il mare agitato della vita umana rigetta da sé, tutto quello che la mente può immaginare di più miserabile, di più inutile, di più spregevole, di più rifinito e di più snaturato dal tempo, dall'uso e dalla violenza' (that the stormy sea of human life rejects, the most miserable, useless, worthless, and patched-up stuff that the mind can imagine, stuff desecrated by time, usage, and violence) (51). A marginal society supports this marginal economy: bankrupt entrepreneurs, artists, junk dealers, the unemployed, the homeless, and the vagrants. Among all these individuals, De Amicis singles out a significant protagonist of modernity, the collector. 'In quello strano mercato ... ci va l'antiquario, il bibliomane ... [e] una processione di collettori' ('The antiquarian, the bibliophile ... [and] a procession of collectors ... visit that strange market') (51). Exceptional figures in this crowd, but typical of a disciplinary society devoted to categorizing, classifying, and displaying its objects, the collectors own the disciplinary tools and the specialized knowledge that allow them to bestow connoisseur value upon cast-off commodities.[45] Thus empowered to draw a profit out of this survival economy, collectors can transform discards into treasures. Recontextualized in the antique store, or housed in the bourgeois drawing room, the collector's item eventually celebrates itself as the opposite of what it was in the flea market: it is now rare, sensational, exotic and, therefore, costly.[46]

The main marketplace, in the Emanuele Filiberto square, draws a different economic picture. Initially, the picturesque intermingling of rich and poor, the blend of city and country types, and the promiscuous freedom of its carnival-like atmosphere set this space apart from the homogeneous decor of the rest of the city. Oppositions and differences coexist in joyful confusion, the discipline of work metamorphosing into the carefree mood of a country fair:

Tra il fumo delle castagne arrosto e delle pere cotte, gira e s'agita confusamente una folla fitta di contadini, di servitori, di sguatteri, di serve imbacuccate negli scialli, di signore massaie ... Passano delle signorine eleganti, dei grossi borghesi buongustai, dei cuochi tronfi e sprezzanti, delle cameriere padrone, dei curiosi allegri [e formano] una folla continuamente cangiante ... E non si può dire quant'è pittoresca e bizzarra quella confusione di gente e di cose, di lavoro e di festa, di città e di campagna, vista a traverso la nebbia della mattina. (44–8)

(Among the smoke of roasted chestnuts and cooked pears, a packed crowd of farmers, servants, dishwashers, maids wrapped in their shawls and stay-at-home-ladies mills about ... Young elegant women, hefty middle-class gourmets, pompous and contemptuous chefs, bossy maids, jolly and curious people pass by [and form] a constantly changing crowd ... It is impossible to say how picturesque and bizarre this confusion of people and things, of work and leisure, of city and country is, as seen through the morning mist.)

This intermixing, however, is only apparent and superficial, a spectacle for the eyes. Just like the rest of the city, the market square finds its deeper ordering principle in the rule of need on one end, the power of purchase on the other:

Da una parte c'è il mercato delle contadine ... e son là schierate ... colle loro derrate esposte ... strette le une alle altre come per tenersi calde, inzoccolate, ... con guanti di cenci ... In mezzo a loro passa la processione accalcata e lenta dei compratori. (44)

(On one side there is the peasant women's market ... lined up there ... with their products on display ... They wear clogs ... and gloves made of rags ... and huddle up one against the other as if to keep warm. A slow, close-packed procession of buyers passes among them.)

Finally, the upper bourgeoisie celebrates itself and its values in what De Amicis calls the most beautiful spectacle that Turin can offer: the promenade under the arcades and through the Galleria dell'Industria Subalpina. Inaugurated in 1874 as a temple to the new religion of commodities, the galleria represented the triumph of the bourgeois myth, a utopia of social pacification in a hierarchical setting:

Qui la folla è fitta ... come all'uscita da un teatro, tanto che nello spazio di tre braccia quadrate si ritrovano spesso un capitano d'artiglieria, una coppia matrimoniale, un prete, un accademista, una crestaia, un operaio, stretti in un mazzo, che paiono una famiglia sola. Qualche volta per pigliar spazio la folla è costretta a fermarsi, e tutti 'segnano il passo' come una colonna di soldati ... La gente gira tutt'intorno alla galleria Subalpina, a passi lenti, processionalmente, come nella sala d'un museo ... Par d'essere in una galleria d'un palazzo grandissimo, dove i convitati sfilino – rispettosamente ... C'è non so che idea d'intimità domestica in quel lento va e vieni di gente affollata sotto quegli archi, dinanzi a quelle vetrine splendide, che finiscono collo stamparsi nella memoria, ad una ad una, come i mobili della casa propria; c'è un'apparenza come di buon accordo universale, di affratellamento. (59–63)

(Here the crowd is thick ... like at the exit of a theatre. Within three square yards, one often finds an artillery captain, a married couple, a priest, an army cadet, a milliner, a worker, all bunched together like a single family. Sometimes, to make room, the crowd is forced to stop, and everybody 'marks time' like an army column ... People go all round the Galleria Subalpina with slow steps, like in a procession, as if they were in a museum room ... One has the impression of being in the gallery of an enormous palace, where guests parade respectfully ... There is a certain idea of domestic intimacy in that slow back-and-forth of people crowding those arcades, in front of those splendid windows that end up imprinting themselves in one's memory, one by one, like the furniture of one's own house; there appears to be a sense of fine universal accord, of brotherhood.)[47]

As Walter Benjamin reminds us, Fourier identified the architectonic canon of his phalanstery in the Paris arcades ('Paris' 148). However, if the arcades served strictly commercial purposes, Fourier made of his phalanstery a dwelling space. The Galleria Subalpina – the reign of luxury and leisure, where things of great price are displayed, admired, desired, and, when possible, purchased – is both a commercial site and the bourgeoisie's symbolic, collective dwelling. The utopian centre of Italy's first modern metropolis, the galleria's transparent glass and iron dome (fashionably modern, after Paxton's Crystal Palace design) and its stylish drawing-room interiors effortlessly combine public and private spheres. The galleria evokes the secure cosiness of an upper-class home while allowing its guests to engage in contented self-display in a stage-like setting. Its plush interiors offer a warm welcome to all social groups, as long as they respect class order, follow rules, act out their parts, and, at the end of the day, obediently cast off their Cinderella costumes and quietly return to wherever they came from.

Thus, just as all utopias conceal their dystopian traits, the galleria stages itself as an apparently unproblematic and seamless coexistence of opposites, a locus of 'reversibilities.' It is both a collective dwelling and a mere site of passage, a non-habitation. It is the quintessential locus of bourgeois leisure, as well as a place of repressive control, as exemplified by the gawking crowd parading in step like an army battalion. It is a centre of social homogenization (an interclass family) as well as an exhibit of 'worthy' objects and people (as evidenced by De Amicis's references to the museum and the palace's gallery); finally, like a vestibule and an arcade, it is both an interior and an exterior. Ultimately, as Turin's core, the galleria is the *punctum* (in Barthes's definition of this term) where the opposite signs of authenticity and forgery collapse into each other.[48] Surprisingly, and certainly unbeknownst to De Amicis, the transparent gallery becomes opaque, its significance rendered illegible by its interchangeable, yet contradictory, semiotics, and its commercial and material fullness unable to prevent it from turning into a non-space, the vaporous land of a collective dream.

As an interpreter of the modern metropolis, with its train stations, arcades, banks, boulevards, piazzas, crowds, markets, expositions, and public parks, De Amicis is an urban artist on equal terms with other bards of the industrial age such as Williams Carlos Williams and Walt Whitman. The stylistic exuberance of his Turin narrative matches Whitman's poetic enthusiasm for modernity's canonic spaces. Urban activity and the modern culture of work, with their exciting mixture of mechanical and human energies, are among the features that De Amicis identifies as the defining characteristics of metropolitan Turin.[49] The city's youthful delight with speed, its competitive mentality, and its unfaltering belief in the gospel of progress pair it with its northern European and North American counterparts: 'si vede, come nelle grandi città del Nord, una specie di gara a arrivare i primi' (one sees, like in the great Northern cities, a kind of race to be the ones to come in first) (55). According to De Amicis, Turin rivals Paris with its 'grande corso [Corso Vittorio Emanuele II] lungo quanto i Campi Elisi' (10) (great boulevard, as long as the Champs-Elysées), and mirrors that other centre of bourgeois productivity, London:

> Il Borgo San Salvario è una specie di piccola *city* di Torino, dalle grandi case annerite, velato dai nuvoli di fumo della grande stazione della strada ferrata, che lo riempie tutto del suo respiro affannoso, del frastuono metallico della sua vita rude, affrettata e senza riposo; una piccola città a parte, giovane di trent'anni, operosa, formicolante di operai lordi di polvere di carbone e di impiegati accigliati, che attraversano le strade a passi frettolosi, fra lo scalpitio dei cavalli colossali e lo strepito dei carri carichi di merci che fan tintinnare i vetri, barcollando fra gli omnibus, i tranvai e le carrette, sul ciottolato sonoro. L'aspetto del sobborgo è ancora torinese, ma arieggia la 'barriera' di Parigi. (35)

> (The San Salvario neighbourhood is a kind of little *City* in Turin, with its large blackened houses, veiled by the clouds of smoke of the great train station, which fills the entire neighbourhood with its laboured breathing, and with the metallic din of its rough life, hurried and without rest. This is a little city all by itself, thirty years young, industrious, swarming with labourers dirty with coal dust, and with frowning clerks who cross the streets with hurried steps, among the clatter of the colossal horses' hooves and the clamour of the carts full of wares that make the windowpanes rattle. They weave about among the buses, trams, and carts, on the resounding cobblestones. The look of the neighbourhood is still Turinese, but there is an air of the Parisian *banlieue*.)

Unlike Whitman, however, De Amicis's verbal topography is 'afraid of the merge' (Whitman 30), as the Italian writer replaces Whitman's famous syntactic accumulations with a compulsion to sort, categorize, and classify. If Whitman equalizes, De Amicis orders in harmonious hierarchies, and if Whitman's classless epic blots out differences, De Amicis's exposition narrative presents a picture of universal accord and social stability in a class-conscious society. The reader of *Torino 1880* is guided through a flowing yet layered urban landscape the discrete elements of which are arranged according to a vision of absolute rational control. The euphoric optimism and undaunted pleasure that characterize *Torino 1880* result from the sense of rational mastery exuding from all urban activities. From the symbolic height of monarchic authority to the closely interrelated networks that order social conduct, control and disseminate knowledge, and define the rules of economic exchange, Turin's pervasive disciplinary machinery guarantees social cohesiveness and political stability. Literally shaping the city's urban appearance, these power structures define the polis's collective identity. This collective identity, as it emerges from De Amicis's text, is ultimately the idealized self-portrait of the liberal bourgeoisie, the background design being a social idyll of public contentment, and the underlying master narrative a grand epic of balanced, strifeless, and communal progress.

Exhibition Mania on Stage: The Ballet *Excelsior*

Besides organizing the activities closely connected with the expositions, hosting cities often engaged in manifestations that reflected and expanded the expositions' aesthetics and ideology well beyond the fairs' precincts and duration. Sporting events such as bicycle and automobile races, and of course the Olympic Games, expressed the same competitive and patriotic drive that fuelled the national display of technological and scientific might (Bassignana, *Le feste* 122–3; Aimone 'Le esposizioni' 40).[50] With its spectacular and exotic atmosphere and highly structured performances, the circus offered a popular counterpart to many exhibitions. Theatrical and musical events also profited from the large audiences attending fairs, and there were people, such as renowned choreographer Luigi Manzotti, who developed an entire repertoire suited to the spirit of the expositions. Perhaps one of the most successful events connected with the exhibitions was Manzotti's *Ballo Excelsior*. 'Un'azione coreografica, storica, allegorica e fantastica in sei parti e undici quadri' (a choreographic, historical, allegorical and fantastic action in six parts and eleven scenes) (Manzotti 77), *Excelsior* premiered at Milan's prestigious Teatro alla Scala on 11 January 1881 for the Carnival-Lent season and in conjunction with the 1881 national exposition.[51] It was in Turin's Teatro Regio, however, that *Excelsior* received its most sumptuous staging thanks to Riccardo Fontana's splendid set designs and an extraordinary cast of first-rate dancers. Starting 7 January 1882, *Excelsior* was staged forty-five times in less than three months in Turin, becoming 'il colpo più clamoroso forse dell'intera storia del balletto al Regio' (perhaps the most clamorous hit of the entire history of ballet at the Regio) (Basso 400).[52] After making its way to the major Italian theatres, *Excelsior* gained unprecedented international approval as well, attracting mass audiences throughout Europe as well as the Americas.[53]

What is perhaps most astonishing in the history of *Excelsior* and of ballet in general is that *Excelsior's* popularity did not fade after a few seasons.[54] On the contrary, *Excelsior* is one of the few nineteenth-century ballets that, in revisions and reinterpretations that often responded to current events, has been consistently staged up to the present day. In 1919, the daily paper *Il Messaggero* commented on the recent performance of *Excelsior* at the Costanzi theatre in Rome by arguing that '*Excelsior* è forse il solo ballo degno di esistere e di resistere ... per la possibilità di essere aggiornato a ogni nuovo periodo del progresso e della civiltà' (*Excelsior* is perhaps the only ballet worthy of existing and resisting ... because it can be readily updated in each new period of progress and civilization) (Frajese 118).[55]

In its close relation with the cultural phenomenon of the expositions, *Excelsior* is an ideal case study for analysing how national-popular myths are created, disseminated, validated, and transformed over time. This analysis should begin by attempting to answer a few questions, specifically, what was *Excelsior* and what exactly were the myths it so successfully expressed? How did Manzotti's choreographic choices convey these myths? Why did *Excelsior* inspire such immediate favour and long-lasting admiration among culturally and socially diverse audiences?[56] Manzotti conceived of *Excelsior* as a 'kind of Jules Verne ballet' recording the heroes and achievements of modern science (Beaumont 520). More specifically, according to Manzotti's own testimony, it was the monument celebrating the 'portentoso traforo del Cenisio' (portentous tunnelling of Mont Cenis) (Manzotti 78) that gave him the idea for *Excelsior*.[57] This engineering feat, which had blasted open the most impenetrable natural environment for the development of commerce and transportation, became the ballet's founding metaphor to express the relentless march of Western civilization, with the triumph of 'man' over nature, and of technological progress over stagnation: 'la nuova vittoria del moto su di un colosso immobile' (the new victory of movement over a motionless colossus) (*Esposizione di Milano 1906* 4). Undoubtedly, Manzotti found inspiration also in contemporary expositions, with their much-visited replicas of the Alpine tunnels, which added one of the concluding chapters in the great nineteenth-century 'railroad narrative.'[58] These replicas provided accessible symbols that reiterated the age's leading ideals: the power of the applied sciences over nature's harshest environments, the notion of dynamic progress, and the consequent spread of Western civilization facilitating encounters among nations in the name of universal brotherhood.[59]

With musician Romualdo Marenco's engaging musical score and by anticipating the enormous casts and elaborate mises en scène of the first historical films (the so-called *colossals* such as *Gli ultimi giorni di Pompeii* by Luigi Maggi and *Cabiria* by Giovanni Pastrone), *Excelsior* initiated a new genre, aptly called '*ballo grande*' (grand ballet).[60] *Excelsior* was a grandiose spectacle employing over five hundred dancers, aiming at shocking its audiences with its rapid progression of scenes, its sudden juxtapositions of contrasting thematic and formal components, its breathtaking succession of elements of surprise, and its sheer, sustained splendour. In its ambition to methodically display the most impressive feats of modern civilization, *Excelsior* mimicked exposition books, as its successive, juxtaposed scenes provided a panoramic survey, an emblematic revue, and an 'object lesson' of Progress's achievements aimed at amusing and instructing its audiences. Like exposition books, *Excelsior* strove to provide the authoritative assessment of modernity's attainments, summarizing and judging an entire period via a structured overview of its most paradigmatic components.

In spite of all its formal complexity, *Excelsior* revolves around a strikingly trite allegory, juxtaposing the battles between the 'godmother of Progress,' called the Spirit of Light, and the 'Black spirit of Regression, Obscurantism,' or Spirit of Darkness (Manzotti 71). The first scene of act 1 opens on a sinister night in a Spanish town in ruins, with the Spirit of Darkness presiding over an Inquisition scene amidst people being tortured and burned at the stake. Toward the end of the scene, a beautiful young lady in chains rises from the ruins. In Manzotti's own words, 'È il Genio della Umanità, la Luce, il Progresso, direi quasi la sintesi del bene, della fratellanza dei popoli che ingigantisce agli occhi dell' Oscurantismo, dello spirito malefico delle tenebre' (It is the Genius of Humanity, Light, Progress, I might almost call it the synthesis of all

Good, of the brotherhood among peoples that rises to gigantic proportions in front of the very eyes of Obscurantism, the evil Spirit of Darkness) (*Excelsior* 79). As lightning flashes, the Spirit of Light slowly breaks free from her chains and foretells that the future will be freed from the Spirit of Darkness and achieve the fraternal unity among all the people of the world in the name of well-being and progress. In mystical tones, Light praises God's glory and His magnificent wonders, thus establishing the ballet's reiterated connection between positive science and mystical history: 'io ... m'innalzerò sulle ali della più ardente fantasia fino a Dio e numererò le sue glorie, i portenti suoi ... Scoperte sublimi, opre gigantesche ... meraviglieranno l'Universo' (I ... will rise to God on the wings of the most ardent fantasy and enumerate His glories and wonders ... Sublime discoveries and gigantic works ... will amaze the Universe) (Manzotti 79).

Scene 2 takes us to the Palace of Genius and Science, where a military-like parade of allegorical figures – Science, Power, Industry, Love, Perseverance, Union, Concord, Courage, Glory, Invention, and Commerce – march up to pay homage to Civilization, who is the prima ballerina. Civilization is surrounded by an extraordinary array of 314 allegorical figures wearing classical-style costumes and carrying national banners, flags, and shields. Act 1 ends with the triumphal encounter between the Spirit of Light and Civilization. The *gran ballabile del Risorgimento* concludes this section by allegorizing the foundational moment in the history of united Italy.

The next four acts include what Manzotti conceived as the ballet's 'historical' component. Under the aegis of the Spirit of Light and the impediments caused by that of Darkness, act 2, scene 1 presents Denis Papin's invention of the steamboat. The scene climaxes in the destruction of Papin's prototype caused by the oarsmen working on the river Weser, near Bremen, Germany, whom the Spirit of Darkness has misled into believing that the wondrous boat is a satanic creation. Once again, the confrontation between the Spirit of Light and the Spirit of Darkness allows the former to display her divination powers: 'Ecco la grande opra mia ... sappi, o iniquo, che il genio non si domina [e] ... che il duello da te meco impegnato ti sarà fatale' (Behold, here is my great work ... let it be known to you, oh wicked one, that genius cannot be vanquished [and] ... that the duel you have undertaken with me will be fatal to you) (Manzotti 84). Scene 2 shows the stage transformed into a 'grandiose *tableau vivant* of the steam power in all its glory' (Sinclair 75). Manzotti created a fanciful skyline of New York City and the Brooklyn Bridge ('a girdled iron bridge,' which in no way resembled the real thing, then under construction) with steam-powered trains crossing the bridge and steamboats in the water below (Manzotti 84).

Act 3, Scene 1 presents 'the Genius of Electricity,' Alessandro Volta, in his laboratory at Como, where he is trying to produce an electric spark from his newly constructed voltaic battery. The Spirit of Darkness unsuccessfully plots against Volta, while Light offers him inspiration. As the spark goes off, the stage is flooded with Light.[61] Obscurantism comically scurries offstage after receiving an electric shock from the battery he was trying to destroy. In a by-now familiar juxtaposition, the Spirit of Light reveals to Volta the future uses of his inventions. Scene 2 is set in Telegraph Square in Washington, DC., where the Spirit of Light, basking in the victory of technology and 'Divine Power,' surrounds herself with telegraph messengers who dance around her with small light bulbs that turn on and off as they move.

Act 4 brings us to an exotic North African desert setting, where a caravan of wealthy European merchants is making its way across the sand when a spectacular simoon, a desert sandstorm, rises and wreaks havoc among men and animals. Taking advantage of the situation, the Spirit of Darkness enlists a group of Arab robbers, who pillage and destroy the caravan of Western wayfarers. The curtain rises again to show a scene of progress: no more treacherous Arabs and shifting sand dunes, but a calm and shiny waterway, the Suez Canal, stretching across the desert toward the palaced city of Ismailia, the 'Venice of the Desert.' 'Tutta la civiltà europea è riunita come per incanto in quel punto dell'istmo, prima affatto deserto. Tutto è movimento tutto si prepara a solenni trionfi' (As if by enchantment, all European civilization is gathered at this point of the isthmus, which had earlier been entirely desert. There is great stirring, everything is being prepared for solemn triumphs) (Manzotti 86). Slowly, characters in colourful costumes and from all corners of the world convene to celebrate Ferdinand Marie de Lesseps's engineering feat. Here the character of 'Cosmopolitan Civilization,' with the word PAX embroidered on her bodice, dances playful duets with the representatives of four continents: a Turk, a Chinaman, a Mexican, and an Englishman. By mimicking the steps of each different partner, Civilization symbolizes the union and peace among all races. The climax of this much-admired section was the Oriental dance, which Flavia Pappacena describes thus: 'Un'avvenente Mora indiana, dalla lunga capigliatura corvina sciolta sulle spalle, danza su un tappeto orientale circondata da un suonatore indiano e 16 moretti, eseguendo sensuali ancheggiamenti e ripetuti rovesciamenti del busto indietro. L'atmosfera si fa altamente drammatica.' (A beautiful Indian woman, dark skinned and with long black hair loose on her shoulders, dances on an Oriental carpet, surrounded by an Indian player and sixteen Moorish children. She sensuously sways her hips and repeatedly throws out her bust. The atmosphere becomes highly dramatic) ('L'*Excelsior* di Luigi Manzotti' 15). At the end of the Oriental dance, a multitude of exotic dancers in 'native' costumes closes the scene: 'I neri del Sudan, gli Abissini e gli altri popoli dipendenti dal Kedivé ... danzano e giuocano caratteristica-mente' (Blacks from the Sudan, Abyssinians, and other people under Khedive rule ... perform characteristic games and dances), thus paying an exotic tribute to de Lesseps, who becomes the epitome of civilization and peace among all peoples of the world (Manzotti 87).[62]

The last historical episode (act 5, scenes 1 and 2) introduces the drill-ing of the Mont Cenis tunnel through the Alps between France and Italy. The setting was a familiar one, if one thinks that, for the Vienna Universal Exhibition of 1873, the Italian government had commis-sioned the construction of a huge model of the Italian entrance to the Mont Cenis tunnel, complete with railway lines, a full-size train, and even signalling devices. Widely publicized in magazines, guidebooks, and postcards, this exhibit expressed the power of applied science across political and geological boundaries, and in the service of civiliza-tion. On the stage of *Excelsior*, the tunnel's ominous atmosphere becomes the backdrop for the familiar skirmishes between the Spirit of Darkness, who spitefully attempts to halt the miners' work, and that of Light, who encourages it. When the 'last charge' explodes in an audi-ence-shaking thunder, French miners appear from the clouds of dust and debris and rush to embrace their Italian counterparts as the earth finally opens up and swallows the Spirit of Darkness. From the sombre initial scene of superstition and oppression to this display of engineer-ing might, *Excelsior* celebrated the memorable moments in the grand voyage of 'civilized progress,' each moment functioning as a brilliant billboard advertising 'European technology and those whose interest it served' (Sinclair 81).

In the ballet's grand finale ('The Harmony Among Nations,' act 6, scenes 1 and 2), all the nations of the world gather in the Palace of Civilization and a battalion of female dancers parades wearing 'a bal-letic version of the American, Russian, French, English and Italian army uniforms' (Poesio 152) and waving enormous flags to an acceler-ated adaptation of each country's national anthem, all in the name of cosmopolitan civilization and the celebration of 'Scienza, Progresso, Fratellanza, Amore' (Science, Progress, Brotherhood, and Love) (Manzotti 89). Thus, Manzotti created a secular Pantheon in which nationalism could marry cosmopolitanism, and the principles of Auguste Comte's positivist philosophy were translated into a wholehearted faith in a technological progress endowed with the inevitability of the supernatural.

Excelsior's extraordinary success derived from its appeal to the age's ambiguous mix of cosmopolitan and nationalistic feelings, allowing the simultaneous celebration of universal brotherhood, the supremacy of Western civilization, and the superiority of one's own national formation.[63] The first two elements – universal brotherhood and the superiority of Western civilization – could be logically reconciled under the assumption that the progress and well-being that Western culture was exporting to the 'backward' parts of the world would eventually promote peace and universal harmony. However, the third element – addressing the superiority of one's own national formation – revealed the vulnerability of this forced reconciliation and the chasm existing between utopian, if colonizing, thought and the complex network of political realities based on national interests and the increasing competition for the control of a shrinking world.

This contradiction became apparent in all foreign productions of *Excelsior*, where the flag of Civilization in the 'Harmony Among Nations' scene was consistently changed to bear the colours of the country in which the ballet was performed. When, in 1885, *Excelsior* was staged in Trieste, then part of the Austrian Empire, the standard-bearers in the scene of the 'Harmony Among Nations' were instructed to keep the Italian flag rolled up to avoid provoking demonstrations. The Italian royal anthem was replaced with the Austrian imperial anthem, alternating with some lines from the popular song 'Oh tu mia Austria, dov'io son nato!' ('Oh you my Austria, where I was born!') (Pappacena, 'The Transcription' 251–2). Conversely, and under a different political climate, the 1919 representation at the Costanzi theatre in Rome featured a large set depicting '[l']interminabile monumento a Vittorio Emanuele [e] ... l'apoteosi di Trento e Trieste' (the never-ending memorial to Victor Emmanuel [and] ... the apotheosis of Trento and Trieste) (Frajese 118).

Arguably, *Excelsior*'s blatant contradictions failed to inspire criticism because they simply reflected the broader contradictions of the age that produced the ballet. However, other elements facilitated the passive reception of the ballet's message. Paralleling what was happening at World's Fairs, Manzotti's application of the code of the spectacular left audiences gaping at *Excelsior*'s special effects and surprises. Reviewers often described audiences as riveted, chained to their seats, mesmerized, and amazed. *Excelsior* aimed at stunning its public, substituting insightful response with uncritical wonder and an addiction-like compulsion to repeat. In 1882, a Trieste newspaper discussed the innovative and enthralling nature of the ballet with these words:

> [*Excelsior* è un] ballo fenomeno – ballo che distrugge, annienta tutti gli altri balli ... dove il reale si accoppia col fantastico nel modo più ingegnoso, dove i colori, le linee, i ballabili, perfino le scene mimiche si succedono con tale armonia, con tale bellezza da incatenare lo spettatore al suo posto, sbalordito, confuso, per un'ora e mezza, e rimandarlo poi più voglioso che mai di ritornare. (*Corrispondenze* 8)

> ([*Excelsior* is a] phenomenal ballet – a ballet that destroys, annihilates all other ballets ... where the real combines itself with the fantastic in most ingenious ways, where colours, lines, dances, and even the mimes' scenes follow one another with such harmony and such beauty that spectators are chained to their seats, stunned and confused for one and a half hours, and sent home wishing more than ever to come back and watch it again.)

How did Manzotti achieve this theatrical enchantment? As was the case with World's Fairs, much depended on sheer visual accumulation, creating a veritable sensory overload, in what was defined as a 'tripudio fantasmagorico di persone, animali, cose' (joyful phantasmagoria of people, animals, objects) (Pagliasco 60).[64] *Excelsior* stood apart from more traditional ballets for its breathtaking pace, effective crescendos, dizzying scenic variety, and 'kaleidoscopic' juxtaposition of elements in motion. Another riveting effect depended on Manzotti's ability to coordinate, with the utmost precision, the movements of an unprecedented number of dancers (up to 450 people on stage at one single time). This precision inspired both military and mechanical analogies. According to a contemporary reviewer, 'la danza ch'egli [Manzotti] domanda alla sua piccola armata non consiste solamente nel gioco delle gambe; egli utilizza anche i movimenti del busto, della testa e delle braccia. Egli ha delle invenzioni da strategista, delle manovre impreviste che sono meravigliose' (the dance that he [Manzotti] requires of his small army does not entail only the use of the legs; he utilizes also the movement of the torso, head, and arms. He has inventions worthy of a strategist, unforeseen manoeuvres that are marvellous) ('L'*Excelsior* e la stampa francese' 7–8). Elena Cornalba, one of the prima ballerinas who performed in Paris, was said to have such mathematically exact steps that a reviewer likened them to the movements of a robot and the action of a chronometer. The mechanical regularity of her 'iron legs' also recalled the precision of those sewing machines that people admired at industrial exhibitions (Guest 40). Reflecting the mechanical accuracy of automatons and machines, or the martial discipline of a well-trained army, *Excelsior*'s corps de ballet expressed the age's infatuation with technological efficiency, military might, and the inexorable movement forward associated with the advancement of Western civilization.

In this context, it is worth noting that what appears today as the ballet's hackneyed metaphysical opposition between Light/Good and Darkness/Evil took on a novel meaning in the age of electricity. In 1881, Thomas Alva Edison had already invented the incandescent light bulb, but electric illumination in the major Italian cities such as Turin and Milan would not be available for over two years, and for a couple of decades electric lights would remain an exposition's wonder more than a reality for private households in European and North American towns. The model for all early electrical lighting systems, the Pearl Street Station of the Edison Electric Light Company, opened in the summer of 1881 in New York City, and, by the same late summer, many Italians would read ecstatic reports about the Exposition Internationale d'Électricité that was taking place in Paris. A dramatic source of spectacle, electricity was the visible 'correlative for the ideology of progress' (Nye 143).[65] *Excelsior*'s special effects involving the interplay of light and darkness directed the audience's stunned gaze into a future that was both technologically near and yet fantastically remote. Electricity had a theatrical and literary existence before having a practical one and therefore lent itself well to metaphorical and allegorical processes that recycled and renewed a broad and collectively shared baggage of conventional imagery.[66] As the fictional Edison creator of the *femme-machine* in Villers de l'Isle-Adam's *L'Ève future* claimed, 'quelle Schéhérazade que l'Électricité,' (146) thus emphasizing the exotic and textual existence of the electric power that had allowed Villers de l'Isle-Adam to conceive the prototype of an artificial generation of electro-human creatures. As *Excelsior* made clear, the electric light was, first and foremost, the 'great nineteenth-century medium of the spectacle ... In much social imagination, it was the premier mass-media of the future' (Marvin 6).[67]

By watching *Excelsior,* Italian audiences shared in the brilliant destinies of this excitingly modern world. The uncomplicated moral choices
that the ballet demanded of its public when juxtaposing Reason and Science against Ignorance and Superstition made everybody feel part of a
privileged and wholesome community. Collectively, audiences shared
the ballet's reiterated message that Italy was a rightful partner in that
international brotherhood destined to rule the world 'through applied
science' (Sinclair 74). In this perspective, *Excelsior* revealed Italy's effort
to assert itself before the other Western imperial powers. *Excelsior* translated Italy's hope in a successful colonial policy first in East Africa
(1880–90s) and then, in a significant concurrence with the fiftieth anniversary of the Unification in 1911, in Libya. If *Excelsior* emphasized the
glory deriving from Italy's colonial deeds, it concealed one of the reasons that made Italy's colonial policy particularly urgent, 'the thirst for
workable land, the illusion to escape in this way from the poverty that,
especially in the south, plagued hopelessly the majority of the population in rural areas' (Grillo 203). As Elena Grillo points out, the 1881
census revealed that only the regions of Lombardy, Piedmont, and Li-
guria had illiteracy levels less than 50 per cent. In the rural areas of central and southern Italy, often 90 per cent of the population was illiterate.
The public health picture was not any brighter. Pellagra, a disease deriving from malnutrition and vitamin deficiency, affected a hundred thousand individuals in 1881, and cholera and malaria were widespread,
especially among Southern peasants (Grillo 204). Arguably, Manzotti's
prophetic 'triumphalism' was particularly appealing to the Italian people because by championing the cause of progress it expressed the
country's underlying hope for a better tomorrow. While avid bourgeois
theatre-goers probably did not suffer either from malaria or pellagra,
neither had they benefited yet from the astonishing scientific conquests
that were represented on the stage. This urge for the future gained an
aura of inevitability as the new tenets of scientific positivism merged
with the rhetoric of metaphysical history to glorify the march of
progress and the expansion of Western civilization.

If the language of positivism was new, that of metaphysical history
belonged to a long and influential tradition. To stay relatively close to
the area explored in this study, one may consider, for example, the monumental *Storia universale di tutti i popoli, dal principio del mondo fino ai
giorni nostri* (Universal History of all the Peoples, From the Beginning of
the World to Our Days) that the Catholic historian Cesare Cantù published in Turin in 1838. Following the example of renowned Enlighten-

ment and Romantic philosophers such as Voltaire and Herder, Cantù saw historical facts as the manifestation of the providential plan announcing a future in which all people would become 'membri d'un associazione universale, diretta alla conquista della virtù, della dottrina, della felicità' (members of a universal association, aimed at the conquest of virtue, sound doctrine, and happiness) (2). According to Cantù, the present and the past have witnessed the existence of two historical configurations. On the one hand, there is the expansive history of the West, a history the ultimate goal of which is the progress and betterment of all of humankind. On the other hand, there is what we may as well term the negation of history-as-becoming, the Asian eternal present of stagnation and immobility. The future, Cantù argues, will achieve the completion of providential history, and the dichotomy of East versus West, with its century-long opposition of 'la razza immobile contro la progressiva' (the immobile race against the progressive race) (39), will resolve itself through the blending of all differences. In other words, in this great Christian epic, 'they' will simply turn into 'us':

> Chi in fatti trovò qual parte prendessero ai fatti più strepitosi della nostra civiltà i Chinesi, società patriarcale, immobile sulla base primitiva della domestica pietà; o gli Indiani che, petrificati in caste perpetuate da falsa interpretazione di tradizioni religiose, si direbbe che abbiano gettato l'àncora sul mare delle età; o tutte le popolazioni, non meno delle nostre numerose, che dietro immensi fiumi e gigantesche montagne, operano distintamente il loro incivilimento con moto sì tardo, che sta all'europeo come la processione degli equinozii alla rivoluzione annuale? ...
>
> Verrà giorno che anch'esse si confonderanno con noi per adempiere l'evangelica promessa; ed allora forse nel loro andamento comparirà un ordine della Provvidenza conforme al nostro. (34–5)

(Who has ever identified the role played in the most outstanding events of our civilization by the Chinese, a patriarchal society, motionless upon the primitive foundation of domestic piety, or by the Indians who, petrified in castes that perpetuated themselves through the false interpretation of religious traditions, appear to have cast anchor in the sea of time; or by all the populations which, as numerous as ours, behind immense rivers and gigantic mountains, distinctly carry on their civilizing process in such slow motion that, judged against the European [civilizing process] it looks like like the precession of the equinoxes as compared to the annual revolution of the earth? ...

The day will come when these populations will mingle themselves with our own in order to fulfil the evangelical promise, and then, perhaps, their course will reveal a providential order similar to our own.)

In Cantù's view, Western history is nothing other than Universal History proceeding to fulfil itself. This Eurocentric universalism prophesizes a unity to come resulting from the generalization of Western values and principles upon the rest of the world. These values and principles ultimately justify various forms of aggression, from political invasion to religious indoctrination and cultural conquest.

This quick detour into Cantù's philosophy of Universal History demonstrates that the late nineteenth century's belief in the advancement of the West and the progress of civilization was not a particularly original and novel idea. This idea, however, was granted remarkable momentum and renewed prestige thanks to the age's barrage of scientific discoveries and technological innovations that endowed the mystical language of providential history with the concreteness of science's positive facts and, in turn, gave the science that was being so often vulgarized at many World's Fairs' mass spectacles the allure and mystery of the sacred.[68] In this ideology of *secular miraculism*, the future was imminent, and as *Excelsior*'s final scene demonstrates, the prophecy of providential unity and 'Harmony Among People' seemed bound to fulfil itself, thanks to the powerful alliance between scientific positivism and Christian dogma.

A royalist and a patriot, religious but fascinated with the miracles of science and technology, Manzotti reflected common ideals and shared aspirations. With its neatly drawn binary oppositions and uncomplicated messages, *Excelsior*'s mythology was extraordinarily effective in evangelizing the masses of Italy's new industrial order. This mythology proved to be a strong coalescing factor in the creation of national-popular culture, as it contributed to the formation of Italy's national identity both through what it proclaimed and through what it left unsaid. While profoundly nationalistic, Manzotti's mythology clearly responded to the will to power of many Western nations. It has been argued that Manzotti was the 'inventor of the propaganda ballet' that was so profitably exported abroad. By 1900, the Alhambra Theatre in London – which had opened in 1854 as the Panopticon of the Arts and Sciences – was staging spectacles such as *Soldiers of the Queen*, aimed at capitalizing on popular sentiments aroused by the Boer War. Similarly, the Empire Theatre, also in London, hit the same patriotic and militaristic notes when it staged *Under One Flag* and *Our Crown*. The years of *Excelsior*'s most widespread

The ballet *Excelsior.* Drawing by Ettore Ximenes. *Milano e l'esposizione italiana del 1881.*

international success (1880–1910) were also, in the words of a lone and witty reviewer, 'the happy epoch of peace armed to the teeth' (D'Ormeville 2). This concise statement effectively unveils the core paradox that *Excelsior* both lavishly expressed and consistently repressed in front of massive audiences deployed to demand yet another encore.

2 Turin 1911: The 'Fabulous Exposition'

Ephemeral Architecture and the Invention of a National Style

Bianca fra il verde tenero delle giovani foglie, sfolgorante sotto un sole magnifico ... [è sorta] la nuova città fantastica tutta irta di cupole, di minareti, di antenne, tutta festante negli orifiammi che ondeggia[no] al vento primaverile. L'Esposizione internazionale di Torino ... col mostrare al popolo il progresso civile portato da mezzo secolo di pace, si è inaugurata alla presenza dei Sovrani e dei grandi dignitari italiani e stranieri. ('L'esposizione internazionale di Torino' 1)

(White among the soft green of the young leaves, shimmering under a magnificent sun ... the new fantastic city [has been raised], all spiked with steeples, minarets, and antennas, and all festive with flags wav[ing] in the spring wind. In the presence of the royal family and great dignitaries from Italy and abroad Turin's International Exposition ... was inaugurated by demonstrating to the people the civil progress brought by half a century of peace.)

L'Architettura italiana played a familiar tune in the spring of 1911, with this affected description of how Italy was celebrating the fiftieth anniversary of national unity. The 'fabulous exposition' of 1911 symbolically reunited the three capitals – Turin, Florence, and Rome – in what was proudly advertised as 'una delle maggiori esposizioni che il mondo [abbia] mai visto' (one of the most important expositions that the world [has] ever seen) (Moriondo 2). By 1911, Turin was the leading industrial metropolis in Italy, having surpassed Milan in terms of the number of factories built in its territory and the number of workers these factories employed. Between 1908 and 1910, more than 260 new industry associations were created in Turin, which in 1906 had become the seat of the prestigious Lega degli industriali and, a few years later, of the Confederazione italiana dell'industria. Perhaps more than any other Italian exposition, Turin 1911 recapitulated all the elements that had defined the culture of the World's Fairs. It showcased the expositions' didactic objectives concerning the working classes and their interclassist ideology, with their dream of achieving a great social reconciliation by generating consensus and creating political bonds. It portrayed the itinerary of the host city's political and industrial journey from 'cradle of the Risorgimento' to 'capital of labour,' and presented it as the main chapter in a broader narrative documenting 'lo sviluppo di tutta l'umanità' (the development of all humankind) (Moriondo 2).[1] Thus, Turin reiterated its message of national pre-eminence while claiming a leading role in the Western world's civilizing mission. Turin 1911 also perfected the expositions' plan to provide exhaustive catalogues of all the major achievements of the civilized world and to celebrate bourgeois initiative and enterprise by displaying the spectacles and wonders of science and technology. All-inclusive, eclectic, and, most of all, belated, the 1911 World's Fair reiterated the faith in the logic and organic development of labour's economic laws, and uttered the swan song of the magnificent and progressive destinies that the experiences of two world wars were about to radically question.[2]

Besides replicating the eulogizing formula of national greatness via the most recent developments in science and technology, the 1911 fair gave unprecedented supremacy to its spectacular side.[3] Exposition architects took advantage of the fair's ephemeral nature to put together an overabundant and eclectic repertoire of styles, 'novelties,' and eccentricities specifically geared at amazing, and amusing, the exposition's seven million visitors.[4] As Carlo Moriondo convincingly argues, there was the sense that Turin 1911 was to be the grand finale in the World's Fairs' spectacular season:[5]

gli architetti ... crearono sull'una e sull'altra riva del Po una città fantastica, uscita non si sa se da un sogno o da un delirio, di un biancore abbagliante, con scalinate, frontoni, cupole, colonnati sovraccarichi di fregi, con capitelli ridondanti quali mai si erano visti, fontane, cascate e *tapis roulants*, fastigi, portici, statue (tutte in purissimo gesso) di Vittorie con veli svolazzanti, aquile ad ali aperte, angeli che suonano trombe ... titani che lottano ... esseri giganteschi come Ercoli od Atlanti di entrambi i sessi, che rappresentavano, a piacimento, gli uni la Forza, la Fatica Umana, il Popolo Lavoratore; le altre, poco meno muscolate, l'Elettricità, la Prosperità, la Civiltà che avanza ... Qui, lungo le rive del Po, ai piedi della collina, ogni espediente fu esasperato, ogni trovata architettonica portata al limite estremo, come a dire che l'esposizione doveva segnare un *non plus ultra*, come se quella fosse l'occasione ultima per un certo tipo di spettacolo a grandissima scena. (Moriondo 2)

(the architects ... created a fantastic city on both banks of the Po river, a city emerging perhaps from a dream or hallucination, a city of dazzling whiteness, with staircases, pediments, steeples, and colonnades overburdened with friezes, with superfluous capitals as no one had ever seen before, with fountains, waterfalls, and *tapis roulants*, fastigia, porticos, statues (all made of pure plaster) of Victories with rustling veils, eagles with outstretched wings, angels playing trumpets ... Titans engaging in struggles ... gigantic beings like Hercules or Atlantis, of both genders, the former representing, according to one's own liking, Strength, Human Labour, or the Working Classes; the latter, which were a little less muscular, Electricity, Prosperity, or Advancing Civilization ... Here along the river Po's banks, at the bottom of the hill, every contrivance was exaggerated, every architectural idea brought to its extreme consequences, as if to say that the exposition had to signify a *non plus ultra*, as if that was the last chance for a certain type of grandly choreographed spectacle.)

Traditionally, the World's Fairs' cosmopolitan style, emphatically blending elements and decorations from all countries and ages, was meant to reflect the 'universality' of progress: in the fictive city of all people and all civilizations, there was to be space for every aesthetic expression.[6] This 'architectural delirium,' as Louis Hautecoeur ungenerously branded the style of all universal expositions, was not entirely unbounded (457). The fairs' eclecticism limited itself to a few recurring designs that by 1911 had become mannered and predictable. In the case of Italy, 'lo stile moresco e quello indiano, i più "festosi," [erano usati] per i saloni da ballo e per i padiglioni di svago, l'"imponente" barocco per gli edifici di esposizione più importanti, lo stile "severo" del Rinascimento per le amministrazioni e la direzione' (the Moorish and Indian styles, the most 'cheerful,' [were used] for the ballrooms and the entertainment pavilions, the 'imposing' baroque for the most important exhibit buildings, the 'stern' Renaissance style for the administration and management buildings) (Patetta 327).

Notwithstanding this eclectic imprint, fair organizers decided that the 1911 exposition in Turin required an overarching architectural style, and thus turned to the Turin baroque and, more specifically, to Juvarra's architectural designs.[7] Juvarra, who was a choreographer as well as an architect, had given architectural tangibility to the Savoy Dukes' absolute rule by capitalizing on what aesthetics-as-spectacle could do for the spectacle of politics. With the stage-like features of Turin's Piazza Castello and adjacent buildings, for example, Juvarra underscored the spectacular attributes of his Theatrum Sabaudiae, a stage-like space designed for state-sponsored military parades and army drills.[8] With the exquisitely ornaté *facciata-sipario* (curtain-like facade) of Palazzo Madama, Juvarra offered a peculiar rendition of the trompe-l'oeil effect typical of the baroque. The palazzo's large windows and its facade's formal consistency with the surrounding urban spaces appear to eliminate all separation between the inside and the outside: politics is indeed on stage, public, for everybody to see. With Palazzo Madama's facade, Juvarra devised an architectural semiosis whose visibility appeared to be a measure of its legibility. However, the expository ambition of this airy facade also conceals an extravagant stage, made with earlier architectural structures, including a medieval castle with its solid towers and fortress-like appearance. Thus, Juvarra's masterful rendition of the baroque duality and ultimate mixture of appearance and reality, the staged and the genuine, and open and closed architectural languages complicated the uniform message of mass-accessible propaganda that his patrons expected of him.[9]

The twentieth-century recreation of Juvarra's fantasies in the stage-like setting of Valentino Castle emphasized the inherent theatricality of the baroque and replicated the effect of grandiose mise en scène that characterized all World's Fairs. The very act of erecting an exposition's boundary defined a stage-like space separated from the rest of the metropolis.[10] Thus, the 'bounded domain' that, by definition, is the urban space created its own *monstrum*: another enclosed space as well as an *ou-topos* – a bourgeois utopia that displayed, in its ephemerality and staged fictiveness, the ambiguous cohabitation of the real with the spectacular.[11] Alberto Abruzzese convincingly discussed how the metropolis's formation process produced certain types of spectacle, such as national and international expositions, and how, in turn, these types of spectacle reproduced the metropolis, albeit in a fictionalized, that is, spectacular form:

La metropoli ottocentesca ... produsse forme di spettacolo come le grandi esposizioni: una città dentro un'altra città: la 'finzione' di una città ... che non fa che mettere in evidenza tutta la serie di meccanismi, di correlazioni, di spettacolazioni che la metropoli di fatto, di per se stessa produce, ma che esistono in forme o latenti o mascherate e che invece le grandi esposizioni mettono in scena. ('Sapere la tecnica' 97)

(The nineteenth-century metropolis ... produced forms of spectacle such as the great exhibitions: a city within another city: the 'fiction' of a city ... that emphasizes a whole series of mechanisms, of correlations, and of productions of spectacles that the metropolis de facto and by itself produces, but which exist in either latent or masked forms in the metropolis and which, instead, the great exhibitions put on stage.)

Abruzzese does not carry his analysis beyond this somewhat abstract and interchangeable *paesaggio metropolitano* (metropolitan landscape). However, if we hold his conceptual map up against that proto-metropolis that was late-nineteenth- and early-twentieth-century Turin, we can see that the ultimate self-portrait that the metropolis-as-spectacle produced was one that intended to generate the identity of the nation state as well. The metropolitan landscape of the House of Savoy aimed at extending itself well beyond the city walls, in accordance with the expansive politics of the Age of Nations and Empires that we have drawn so far.

Besides activating the semiotics of the theatre, in reproducing Juvarra's style Turin shared in the fashion of the architectural revival typical of many other expositions.[12] Unlike previous World's Fairs, however, by exclusively turning to Juvarra, Turin invested its revival with a consistent and homogeneous appearance, arguably with the intent to propose the Turin baroque as the model for a national architectural style. Prominent Italian politicians had repeatedly lamented the lack of a national style that would represent the values and ambitions of the unitary state, and a few zealots had gone so far as to draft a proposed law suggesting that all public buildings be executed in the baroque manner. As Paolo Boselli stated:

La terza Italia, l'Italia regia e popolare, ha un carattere che non solo nelle istituzioni, ma nei monumenti che la rappresentano dev'essere consacrato ... Il tempio, il foro, la basilica, il teatro attendono il loro riscontro, che narri nei poemi dell'architettura il grande sforzo e l'alto intento e l'audacia, e il lungo studio, per cui abbiamo fatto riconscere nel mondo il diritto nazionale. (Sistri 1636)[13]

(The Third Italy, the Italy of the King and the People, has a character that must be consecrated not only in its institutions, but in the monuments that represent it: ... The temple, the forum, the basilica, the theatre are awaiting the recognition that will narrate in architectural poems the great efforts and high goals, the bravery and extensive learning by which we have been able to have the world recognize our national right.)

By turning back to a momentous period of its history, Turin reaffirmed its own myth of origin, its own identification system and valued genealogy. As examples of the architectural culture of the revival, the buildings of the 1911 Turin fair were intended to inspire ideas of historical continuity and social stability. By linking a metropolitan-specific aesthetics to a political agenda related to the birth and rise of the nation state, Turin once again was proposing itself as the most legitimate representative of the Italian nation, or to quote Giovanni Robustelli's somewhat conceited definition, as 'il centro e il faro della nuova Italia' (the centre and the beacon of the new Italy) (4). Fair organizers demonstrated that they had fully assimilated Ralph N. Wornum's influential ideas, as expressed in his classic essay 'The Exhibition as a Lesson in Taste.' Wornum argued that exhibitions had to impose discipline on the popular gaze through the 'conveying of a distinct aesthetic expression.' This disciplining function was, Wornum concluded, paramount to advancing that specific 'national style' that would differentiate one nation from another (xxii).

The promotion of an architectural style worthy of representing the values of the nation state concealed the growing anxiety about the homogenizing power of modern civilization. Giulio Lavini expressed this fear eloquently in the pages of *L'architettura italiana*, where he argued that 'le più autentiche e costanti tradizioni non possono reggere alla inesorabile potenza livellatrice di ciò che si chiama la civiltà moderna colle sue formule igieniche ed umanitarie, colla sua gigantesca produzione industriale, che si propaga a colpi di concorrenza in ogni più remoto angolo del mondo' (the most authentic and durable traditions cannot withstand the inexorable levelling power of what we call modern civilization, with its hygienic and humanitarian formulas, and its gigantic industrial production that propagates itself by dint of competition in the remotest corners of the world) (13–14). Lavini argued that, in the absence of a specific national style, a country was bound to fall prey to either one of two opposing tendencies: the globalizing one that would eventually wipe away all national specificity, or the parochial one that would fragment a country into sets of proliferating and competing interests, multitudes of local traditions, and unrelated historical narratives. Italy seemed to be especially vulnerable to the latter. In spite of the 1911 exposition's attempt to establish the Turin baroque as the national style, the revival proved to be too obscure and esoteric a reference for too many Italians, and was ultimately unable to bear the weight of all the national symbols with which different political and cultural constituencies wanted to invest it.[14] Turin 1911, with its baroque exposition buildings, ultimately remained semiotically opaque, its symbolism made illegible by a lack of shared memories and commonly held emotional investments.

Interestingly, in Turin's arch-rival, Rome, host of the 1911 Esposizione internazionale d'arte, the architects Piacentini, Bazzani, and Venturi capitalized on the mass appeal that a more universally readable classic revival would provide. This classic revival, the three architects explained, was directly inspired by 'le pure forme' (the pure forms) of ancient Rome: 'l'anfiteatro, l'esedra ... la scalinata, le fontane, il colonnato' (the amphitheatre, the exedra, ... the flight of steps, the fountains, the colonnade) (Lancellotti 9). In other words, by avoiding the conventional detour into Renaissance adaptations and later contaminations of classical codes, Piacentini, Bazzani, and Venturi underscored that their revival resuscitated the *imperial* glories of a revered collective past. As Augusto Sistri points out:

Le colonne, le statue, i propilei, le esedre delle manifestazioni di Roma ... i frontoni recanti i versi del *carmen saeculare* sulla grandezza romana, sulla gloria italica, sul credito di civiltà nei confronti del mondo intero (era l'anno della guerra di Libia), fanno in un'esposizione le prove di cartapesta; [e costituiscono i] materiali già predestinati a futura memoria per una via imperiale all'architettura italiana. (1638)

(The columns, statues, propylaea, and exedrae of the Roman exhibits ... the pediments with the lines from the *carmen saeculare* about Roman greatness, Italic glory, and the debt that the entire world has to Roman civilization (it was the year of the Libyan war) are papier-mâché models in an exposition; [they constitute the] materials already predestined to future memory for the imperial course of Italian architecture.)

How this revival would eventually provide one of the most blatant and (at least temporarily) successful acts of political propaganda in modern history is part of the well-known narrative of the Fascist era in Italy. Conversely, the Turin baroque failed to reactivate its symbolic values in the present and thrust them forward into the future, and thus could not respond to the collective needs and appease the all-too-modern anxieties of united Italy. In other words, for the majority of people, the architectural script of the 1911 fair remained undecoded and relegated to a quaintly local urban past, thus contradicting universal expositions' globalizing and future-oriented agenda.

In spite of its original mandate (the celebration of the fiftieth anniversary of Italian unification), the 1911 exposition, divided as it was between Turin, Rome, and Florence, confirmed the country's ongoing fragmentation and the lasting divide between the North and the South. Consider, for example, the joint 'Proclama' made by the mayors of Turin and Rome, Secondo Frola and Ernesto Nathan:

> Alla metropoli del forte ed industre Piemonte [spetta] raccogliere in una Esposizione Internazionale industriale le manifestazioni varie della attività economica: a Roma, faro del pensiero italiano, [spetta] riassumere con le esposizioni patriottiche, storiche, artistiche, il concetto che a quelle attività economiche presiedette. (Nathan and Frola 4)

> (The metropolis of strong and industrious Piedmont [is charged with] gathering the various expressions of economic activity in an international industrial exposition; Rome, beacon of Italian thought [is charged with] summarizing the idea that inspired those economic activities in its historical, patriotic, and artistic exhibits.)

The 'idea' to which Nathan and Frola refer here is actually a heterogeneous entity, the crucible of paradoxes that constitutes the universal expositions' general episteme combining the notions of political unity, national identity, civilization's progress, and universal brotherhood. This idea, which is publicly discussed and disseminated in Rome, remains oddly separated from the action that necessarily derives from it, which takes place in Turin. If Turin is the motor of progress, Rome is the bearer of the very ideas initiating this progress. What remains unaddressed and unexplained, however, is why, if the idea *is* in Rome, it must travel to Turin to be set into practice. This meaningful silence eloquently tells the repressed story of the division between the northern and southern parts of the Italian peninsula.

In spite of their explicit rhetoric, national and international fairs contributed to broaden rather than fill the gap between the two Italies, and Turin 1911 was no exception. While trumpeting political unity, expositions held in the North consistently limited participation by the South. For example, the 1881 national exposition in Milan hosted over seven thousand exhibitors and, while over one and a half thousand exhibitors represented the city of Milan, only 157 came from Naples, and a mere two from the Basilicata region. Such a discrepancy is not realistic, even if we take into account the different rates of industrial development in the northern and southern regions. Beyond the rhetorical unitary facade, the Italy that was celebrating itself in the exhibitions was that of the northern entrepreneurial bourgeoisie: 'Tutta l'Alta Italia rappresenta nella mostra del 1881' (All of northern Italy is participating in the 1881 exposition) enthusiastically wrote Raffaele De Cesare, exalting 'il moto,' 'l'esuberanza,' and 'l'iniziativa' (the motion, the exuberance and the initiative) of this 'Italia superiore ... che gareggia coi paesi più industriali d'Europa' (superior Italy that competes with the most industrialized countries in Europe) (258). The implied contrast of course is with the other, southern Italy or, with meaningful wordplay, the 'inferior' Italy, the former Bourbon kingdom that Ferdinand II spitefully called the doorway to Africa, a land still waiting to be awakened from a century-long state of apathy and stagnation (De Cesare 258). This was precisely the bourgeoisie that, in 1911, belatedly invested Rome with a purely ceremonial and representative function. The arts' exhibits of the 1911 World's Fair carried out this function, thus emphasizing how art (just like history) was considered a didactic tool aimed at inspiring patriotic ideas and disseminating political propaganda.[15]

The driving force of the marketplace in both politics and culture explains why, in spite of various proposals, the Italian capital city failed to host a universal exposition in the second half of the nineteenth century and, even as late as 1911, had to content itself with what was regarded as an ancillary role. In the rest of the South, the situation was no different. The first national exposition of the Meridione occurred in Palermo in 1891–2. It was meant to strengthen 'i rapporti di scambio fra le regioni settentrionali e le meridionali d'Italia' (the trade relationships between northern and southern regions of Italy) (Marcora 2–3) and thus better the economic potential of the South. Unfortunately, this exposition demonstrated that the hopes that had prompted southern historians and economists such as Pasquale Villari and Giustino Fortunato to encourage northern industrialists to invest in the South had failed. The fair showed that the 1887 custom tariffs and the protectionist regime imposed by northern industrialists had seriously damaged the southern economy. The closure of foreign markets initiated a period of agrarian crisis that ravaged the South and resulted in massive emigration. What the fairs' electrifying narratives do not tell appears in much more sombre colours in the volumes of the *Annuario statistico*, which reported that by 1876 a hundred thousand people were leaving Italy each year, by 1901 half a million were leaving, and in the single year of 1913, 872,000 people left the country, one person in every forty. By 1914, thirty-five million people lived in Italy and five to six million Italians resided abroad (Mack Smith 214).

In spite of this crisis, at the Universal Exposition's grand opening in Turin on 29 April 1911, the king and queen of Italy, Prime Minister Giolitti, and the ambassadors of forty foreign countries attended a spectacle at the Palazzo delle feste, culminating in a cantata whose musical score was inspired by Wagner's *Lohengrin*. The cantata's trite rhetoric is worth mentioning because it blatantly flaunted the myths of progress and universal brotherhood that underwrote the imperial agendas of the Western powers that Italy wished to join:

Umanità redenta,
ogni discordia è spenta,
tutto che vive è Amor!

Amor! Pensier sovrano,
Scienza, Lavoro umano,
pacifico fervor!

...

La sacra via divina
– O Italia, pia Regina! –
scande all'Umanità. (Moriondo 25)[16]

(Redeemed humanity,
all discord is quenched,
all that lives is Love!

Love! Sovereign thought,
Science, Human labour,
Peaceful fervour!

...

The Sacred Divine way
– Our devout Queen, Italy! –
Shows to Humanity.)

In a by now familiar disjunction, the counterpoint to this cantata, with its praise of the ineluctable advance of progress through communal labour, was included in contemporary Turinese newspapers. These papers reported that massive police force and cavalry were employed to prevent the strike of five thousand construction workers from compromising the atmosphere of 'concordia e lavoro' (concord and work) (Moriondo 19) that the Universal Exposition's organizers were determined to have everybody enjoy. As for universal brotherhood, the crowds who, at the Valentino, gaped 'a quei modelli di navi, a quei cannoni, a quei fucili, a quelle tende, a quei traini, simbolo e saggio delle armi e degli ordigni [delle] valorose truppe di terra e di mare' (at those models of ships, those cannons and guns, those tents, those trailers, symbols and expression of the arms and weapons [of the] valorous troops of land and sea) (Moriondo 38) were the same who cheered the military trains departing from the Porta Nuova station directed to Libya.[17] The exposition that was inaugurated with the claim that all strife was quenched ended with the Italian troops disembarking at Tripoli and the Italian air force carrying out the first air strike in human history.

Building Imperial Consensus: Italy's *Quarta Sponda* on the Po River

Turin was one of the most vocal participants in the contemporary colonial debate. The liberal and progressive *La gazzetta piemontese* (renamed *La Stampa* in 1895) had historically opposed Italy's imperialistic adventures and promoted programs of social reform and political democratization over acts of colonial aggression (Castronovo, *La Stampa* 106–18). Yet, on 30 September 1911, when Italy declared war on Turkey, *La Stampa*, too, joined the unanimous chorus of patriotic fervour:

Cover illustration for the Turin 1911 exposition catalogue published by the Touring Club Italiano. By permission Archivio Storico della Città di Torino. Collezione Simeom (C 2027).

Ora il compito di dir l'ultima parola tocca alla nostra bella e forte armata, al nostro esercito glorioso: ad essi sono affidati il prestigio e l'onore del nome d'Italia nel mondo ... In quest'ora solenne tutti gl'Italiani, che hanno seguito con entusiasmo e concordia meravigliosi la preparazione, devono saper assistere all'atto risolutivo con cuore indomito ed animo sicuro. Mentre stiamo compiendo in questo glorioso cinquantenario un grande atto di forza, cui suffragano le ragioni del diritto storico e della civiltà, in quest'ora solenne per l'Italia come nessun'altra da quarant'anni in poi, il popolo italiano deve saper dare al mondo lo spettacolo di una coscienza nazionale salda ... Stiamo compiendo – sotto gli sguardi del mondo – un atto di forza e sia esso coronamento e consacrazione del cinquantenario della nostra redenzione ... Così e non altrimenti le nazioni civili si affermano e si espandono nel mondo ('L'Italia').

(Now our beautiful and strong army, our glorious military, must carry out the mission of saying the last word. To them are entrusted the prestige and honour associated with the Italian name in the world ... In this solemn hour, all Italians, who have followed with wonderful enthusiasm and agreement the preparation stages, must be able to view the decisive act with unvanquished hearts and confident spirits. On this glorious fiftieth anniversary, we are carrying out a great act of strength, supported by reasons of historical right and civilization. In this solemn hour for Italy, like no other in the last forty years, the Italian people must display their firm national consciousness to the world ... We are carrying out – before the eyes of the world – an act of strength. May it be the crowning and consecration of the fiftieth anniversary of our redemption ... In this way only, civilized nations affirm themselves in the world.

This wave of nationalistic pride swept the park of Valentino Castle as well, and several of the fair's exhibits played a leading role in shaping public opinion on the advantage of building Italy's 'quarta sponda' ('fourth shore') on the North African coast. Turin's pride in its technological and scientific advancements, its patriotic engagement in building a strong sense of national identity, and its traditional glorification of the army (it was the seat of the prestigious Military Academy) converged into a new myth of aggression. In spite of the burning defeats of the late nineteenth century, the economic prosperity and industrial growth of the early twentieth century favoured the renewed quest for markets and territories rich in raw materials to exploit. The Lombardy cotton manufacturers Mylius and Crespi had just started the Compagnia Commerciale del Benadir, and the company's promising economic prospects

translated into the explicit colonial messages conveyed at the 1911
Turin exposition:

> Sulla moltitudine che la sera sfollava dalle gallerie, con gli occhi stanchi
> di troppe meraviglie, corse, con i giornali che andavano a ruba, il fremito
> e la gioia di una vittoria. Al giusto compiacimento per l'affermazione data
> al mondo della propria attività economica si unì l'orgoglio legittimo di
> un'affermazione non meno lusinghiera di una nuova e più forte
> coscienza nazionale. E il nuovo senso si fuse armoniosamente col primo,
> perchè solo quella floridezza di commerci e di industrie consentì all'Ita-
> lia di impugnare le armi con la saldezza dei mezzi necessari al trionfo.
> (Moriondo 38)[18]

> (The quiver and joy of victory swept over the multitudes that streamed out
> of the galleries at evening time, their eyes tired with too many wonders,
> while newspapers were selling like hot cakes. Italy combined just satisfac-
> tion in showing its economic feats to the world with legitimate pride in the
> equally gratifying affirmation of a new and stronger national conscious-
> ness. This new sense harmoniously merged with the first, because only the
> prosperity of commerce and industry allowed Italy to take up its weapons
> with the reliable means necessary for triumph.)

A late arrival and minor player in the 'great game' that saw Western
powers vie for the partition of the world, Turin exploited its role as the
1911 international exhibition's host to engage in a rushed, unfinished,
yet massive effort to gather a vast array of materials pertaining to the
Italian colonies. Visitors to the 1911 World's Fair were treated to three
colonial exhibits: the Mostra della direzione centrale degli affari coloniali del ministero degli affari esteri, the Mostra della colonia eritrea,
and the Mostra della Somalia italiana. These exhibits were designed to
convince the Italian public that, in spite of previous failures (the defeats
of Dogali and Massaua were still in the minds of many), Italy's colonizing mission was successfully forging ahead with a pace that was both progressive and inevitable. The general report entitled *Le mostre coloniali
all'esposizione internazionale di Torino del 1911* set the 'timid' Eritrean
exhibits in 1903 Florence against the 'bold' colonial exhibits in 1911
Turin. *Le mostre coloniali* reveals the effort to cast a sense of natural
ineluctability to the process of civilization and to justify current acts of
aggression by dismissing past defeats as minor setbacks in an inevitably
progressive journey:

Chi visitò quell'Esposizione non ha più il diritto di parlare ... di tentativi di colonizzazione inesorabilmente falliti.

La necessità delle cose [e] ... l'opera civile che come buon seme fatalmente attecchisce e prospera, hanno determinato uno stato di fatto nelle nostre colonie d'Africa Orientale che non si può più oltre discutere. (*Le mostre* 5)

(The people who visited that exposition no longer have the right to talk about ... colonizing efforts that inexorably failed.

The necessity of things [and] ... the civilizing mission that, just like good seeds, inevitably take root and grow, have determined the current state in our East African colonies, which admits of no further debate.)

So pressing was the need to validate Italy's standing as a colonial power that the exposition's authorities corrected the ephemeral and transient nature of the fair's exhibits by promoting permanent recording strategies. The exhibition's specialists well understood the role that archives, libraries, museums, ethnographic agencies, publishers with their distribution agencies and advertisement departments, as well as the embryonic entertainment industry, held in shaping and disseminating imperial values. Besides disposable artefacts (posters, guides, postcards, but also keepsakes, souvenir albums, trinkets, and bric-a-brac), fair organizers planned to institutionalize the colonial exhibits with 'una biblioteca ... con un esteso catalogo ragionato, una ricca collezione di carte geografiche, corografiche e topografiche con un chiaro repertorio di riferimenti: altrettante guide o monografie illustrate quante le colonie di diretto dominio' (a library ... with an extensive catalogue raisonné, a rich collection of geographical, chorographical, and topographical maps and a clear inventory of references: as many guidebooks or illustrated monographs as there are colonies under Italy's direct control) (*Le mostre* 7).[19] Much has been written about the aims and effects of all these forms of generating, surveying, and controlling knowledge, particularly regarding the more established colonial powers, France and Great Britain. Suffice it to say here that exhibitions, museums, archives, and libraries cataloguing and circulating archaeological, topographical, geological, ethnographic, and anthropological surveys (just to name a few) contributed to the ever-renewed effort to secure the disorderly colony, to inventory obsessively and compulsively what Homi Bhabha famously called 'a fixed reality ... entirely knowable and visible' ('The Other' 156).[20]

This expansive and omnivorous impulse to classify the gargantuan body of colonial knowledge validates the ideology of imperial abundance. Imperial hunger feeds the dream of cognitive (moral and material) control over the colonized spaces. What is specific about Italy is that this attempt, which took the form of a multivolume publication entitled *Biblioteca coloniale delle direzione degli affari coloniali*, was only partially completed by the time the 1911 exposition began. Its first section, *Collezione di pubblicazioni coloniali italiane*, witnessed the rushed effort to lend status and credibility to current colonizing feats. In this volume, editors described the *Biblioteca coloniale delle direzione degli affari coloniali* project as providing a comprehensive history 'dell'esplorazione e del successivo sviluppo dell'idea della colonizzazione' (of the exploration and subsequent development of the idea of colonization) combined with the 'descrizione dello stato attuale dell'opera colonizzatrice in Italia' (description of the current state of Italy's colonizing activities) (*Le mostre coloniali* 7). This colonial narrative's progressive plotline was aimed at indoctrinating public opinion with the necessity of swift military intervention in North Africa.

Like all colonial narratives, Italy's had its set of 'native' characters, and they were subjected to the same piercing gaze and cataloguing zeal that were applied to industrial materials and technological innovations. At the 1884 exposition in Turin, for example, the 'villaggio Assabese' was one of the most visited 'attractions' (Saragat, 'Tipi umani' 219), and furnished a valuable way to poll Italian public opinion regarding the plan of colonial aggression that Prime Minister Agostino Depretis had just started to unveil.[21] In Palermo 1891–2, visitors were treated to the Eritrean village, which was praised in contemporary publications for its 'authenticity' because it had been built using tribal tools and construction methods. These were the years in which Italy celebrated the foundation of the Eritrean colony and the establishment of the protectorate over Abyssinia. Francesco Crispi had just signed the Treaty of Uccialli with Negus Menelik, and Italy's colonial future looked promising to many.

The colonial enthusiasm became much more controversial after the Dogali massacre of 26 January 1887, where five hundred Italian soldiers were killed, and especially the defeat at Adowa in 1896, which caused the fall of the second Crispi government. In the 1890s, national expositions addressed the colonial issue in a very cautious manner. In Turin 1898, for example, fair organizers deliberately blurred two different colonial discourses when they included the Eritrean village in a broader

Book displays. Drawing by Ettore Ximenes. *Milano e l'esposizione italiana del 1881.*

exhibit entitled 'Gli italiani all'estero' (Italians Abroad). This exhibit
was mostly devoted to Italian settlements in Argentina, Brazil, and Mex-
ico, which organizers termed the 'colonie libere' (free colonies) as
opposed to the 'colonie di diretto dominio' (colonies by direct domination), Eritrea and Somalia. Other exotic displays, such as the 'cinquan-
tina di Amazzoni del Dahomei accampate nei pressi del Ponte Isabella'
(fifty or so Dahomey Amazons camped in the vicinity of Ponte Isabella)
were considered more of an exposition prerequisite (emulating a similar 'show' in Paris 1889) than a statement of colonial power (Bassignana, *Le feste* 96). All of the other ethnic displays, such as those devoted
to the '"Indiani" d'Alaska e delle Montagne Rocciose ... indiani veri e
propri, cinesi, indigeni boliviani e palestinesi' ('Indians' from Alaska
and the Rocky Mountains ... real Indians, Chinese, natives from Bolivia
and Palestine) (Bassignana, *Le feste* 97), were included in the Mostra di
arte sacra e delle missioni cattoliche. This exhibit was situated near the
General Exposition grounds, to which it was linked by an overpass
named 'Ponte della Concordia' (The Bridge of Concord). Secular, positivistic, and often Masonic, and devoted to the lay values of the Risorgimento, the 1898 exposition organizers were pragmatistic enough to

understand that missionary action could lay the ground for colonial expansion. The 1898 exposition thus stated that, at least in distant lands and in light of spiritual or political expansionism, Church and State 'potranno completarsi a reciproca fortuna e reciproco splendore' (will be able to unite in mutual fortune and mutual splendour) (*Esposizione italiana 1898: Arte sacra* 3). Overall, however, the evangelizing and missionary tones prevailed over those of military aggression.

Turin's and Palermo's native villages were only small displays in both scope and size compared to what other countries were staging.[22] After 1883, when the Dutch held Europe's first international fair devoted primarily to colonialism, native villages and street scenes with native products and vendors and exotic dancing girls were routinely recreated for the amusement and entertainment of fairgoers.[23] The climax of this attempt to master the world and its inhabitants by means of affixing labels and, when appropriate, prices, was probably reached in the 1904 Louisiana Purchase Exposition in Saint Louis. The Saint Louis exposition hosted 'numerous types of many of the primitive races of the earth' and offered 'a complete exposition of the slow evolution of civilization' from the 'lowest known human stage' to the most 'enlightened' (Francis 522). Five different Filipino tribes, amounting to more than one thousand people, resided in villages on the grounds, the eleven-acre Jerusalem had one thousand natives, and a large encampment hosted two hundred American Indians.[24] There were vendors and belly-dancing women from the 'Streets of Cairo' and Eskimos from northern Canada. Fairgoers flocked to the Hall of Anthropology, on the fair's main grounds, to look at the Patagonian giants, African pygmies, Filipino Ilongots, and other aboriginal groups organized in what were regarded as evolutionary sequences, from the most 'primitive' to the more 'advanced.'[25]

Objects of visual consumption, elevated to the position of displaced commodities, and subjected to the logic of Western commercialism, the 'natives' re-enacted their everyday lives, thus playing a double role: they were both themselves and people *representing* themselves. This symmetrical mimic-world was both representational and self-refererential, thus fulfilling, once again, the fairs' double promise of authenticity and spectacle.[26] By detaching the 'natives' from the real domain of their traditions and by tearing them away from the fabric of their social existence, fairs transformed them into objects of entertainment and consumption, and exploited them for their 'exhibition value.' Comparable, perhaps, to the *curiosités* that De Amicis's collectors found at flea markets, the 'natives" authenticity was not in and of itself valuable: Europe's history of colonial aggression proves that it was in fact quite expendable. However, these human beings became valuable when estranged into 'authentic spectacles' for Western enjoyment, phantasmagorias of de-contextualized and disoriented commodities.[27]

The mechanical reproduction of exotic villages at World's Fairs deprived them of their contextual histories and resulted in the liquidation of their dwellers' heritage and their human aura. But was this not, after all, the very ideology of colonialism? In spite of all their nostalgic appeal to authenticity, fairs contributed to the erasure of alternative cultures and geopolitical sovereignties by the very act of systematically estranging and displaying these cultures within their own hegemonic boundaries. In the imperial master narrative that World's Fairs wrote, native displays constituted mere descriptive pauses, guided exercises in referential accuracy, and colourful quotations in an increasingly stilted foreign language.

Rather than offering what contemporary publications advertised as 'uno squarcio di vita vera' (a slice of real life) ('Villaggio somalico' 340), Turin 1911 joined its Western counterparts in staging ritualized representations 'starring' the imported natives from its colonies in Somalia and Benadir. Unlike the 'unclassified aggregation of many races' (Eastman 13) celebrating the lively confusion and imperial abundance of colonial life, the colonial villages in 1911 Turin inspired ideas of discipline and order. This was a substantial change from previous colonial displays that were made carefully haphazard and chaotic to mimic the 'native' lifestyle in contrast to the orderliness of the Western exhibits. With their lined-up huts and structured activities, the colonial subjects in 1911 Turin promoted the view that, far from being wastelands of sand and desert, their countries would become highly productive and commercially valuable, if properly exploited ('Il villaggio Eritreo' 293). Presented as 'ricca, ordinata e forte' (rich, orderly, and strong) ('Gli italiani all'estero' 525), the Somalian colony lured all those who had confidence in Italy's imperial destiny toward a mirage of imminent prosperity:

In tredici anni è forse questa la prima confessione esplicita ... che l'Italia ha due colonie; per molto tempo la secondogenita era stata occultata ... Qui, a Torino, il Benadir viene anch'esso alla luce del sole. È poco, di fronte alle altre nazioni. Ma è un bel segno che le timidità ufficiali davanti agli anti-africanismi accennano almeno a diminuire. E per la prima volta ... si dice

The Assabese village. Drawing by Ettore Ximenes. *Torino e l'esposizione italiana del 1884.* By permission, Biblioteca di storia e cultura del Piemonte, Turin, Italy.

The Somalian village at the 'Kermesse orientale.' *Le esposizioni del 1911 a Torino, Roma e Firenze*. By permission, Biblioteca di storia e cultura del Piemonte, Turin, Italy.

quel che per ora sussurravano soltanto le tariffe postali e le carte geografiche: accanto all'Eritrea ci è nata la Somalia. (Arcari 431)

(In thirteen years this is perhaps the first explicit confession ... that Italy has two colonies; and for a long time the second-born had been hidden ... Here in Turin, Benadir comes to the sunlight, too. It is little compared to the other nations. But it is a nice sign that official timidity in the face of anti-Africanism at least shows signs of diminishing. And for the first time ... people say what up to now only postage stamps and geographical maps whispered: Somalia is born beside Eritrea.)

Depicted as resource-rich and nature-bound, yet lacking the material tools that anthropologists equated with civilized people, colonial subjects offered themselves to the masters of technology as raw natural resources waiting to be exploited, developed, and refined. While Italy thus participated in the rhetoric of 'the white man's burden,' the Somalian presence at the exhibition validated the prophecy of a bountiful future, the prize that Italy's imperial prowess deserved.[28] As Robert W. Rydell aptly observes, 'fairs combined [the] principles of abundance with new principles of empire, rooted in the racist vocabulary of social

Darwinism and sanctioned by contemporary anthropologists' (*World* 35–6). This vocabulary is clear in the description that Paolo Arcari, a commentator at the 1911 Turin fair, devoted to the 'Mostra della guerra' ('War Exhibit'), craftily placed near the Somalian village. The War Exhibit displayed the Italian army's new equipment (especially that designed for use in Africa), together with mannequins showing the various uniforms of the colonial soldiers, as well as live 'gendarmi indigeni, ripuliti all'Europea' (indigenous policemen, all cleaned up European-style) (431). 'Ormai assorbiti in una vita superiore e più degna' (By now assimilated in a superior and more dignified lifestyle) (431), in Arcari's view, these policemen embodied the success of Italy's disciplining and civilizing feat. Arcari was pleased to point out that the Somalian village attracted numerous visitors, thus demonstrating that 'in questo spontaneo e giocondo interesse popolare ... c'è un principio di soddisfazione nazionale, c'è, in germe, il consenso al proposito d'espansione' (this spontaneous and happy popular interest ... expresses the birth of a sense of national pride; it expresses the germ of consent to the plan of [colonial] expansion) (431).

The mere fact that Arcari mentions the need to create a consensus around the budding program of colonial expansion reveals that, as late as 1911, the approval of Italy's colonizing 'mission' was far from unanimous and that, in spite of all its posturing, Italy was far from comfortable in its identity as a colonial power. Even expositions' magazines reported dissenting opinions. While far less frequent than the chorus of praise for 'la più grande Italia' (Greater Italy), these opinions were often virulent. A reporter by the nom de plume of Toga-Rasa, for example, compared the fair's '*Kermesse* orientale' (Eastern fairground) to Dante's Hell and dubbed it a 'saggio delle nostre miserie coloniali in Africa' (taste of our colonial poverty in Africa) (302). Toga-Rasa thus represented that segment of the Italian population who did not oppose colonialism out of respect for other peoples' rights of sovereignty, but because it deemed Italy unfit and unprepared to compete with France and England's imperial might.

Meaningfully, in Turin 1911, the organization of the fair's colonial 'attractions' was not an Italian accomplishment: it was rather entrusted to a French specialist, Ernest Pourtauborde, who had created the successful 'Oriental villages' at the 1900 Paris exhibition. Pourtauborde placed services and attractions such as bars, cafés, carousels, and menageries on the left bank of the river Po. He envisioned this area as a 'parco di attrattive meccaniche ... una Kermesse Occidentale [fatta di] ... vita turbinosa, chiasso, divertimenti, *bars*, caffé, giostre, tutto ciò insomma che ... corrisponde alla sete febbrile di movimento' (park of mechanical attractions ... a Western fairground, [consisting of] ... whirling life, noise, amusements, bars, cafés, rides, all that ... satisfies the restless thirst for motion) (Ferrettini, 'Un'ora' 246–7). On the right bank, he created the illusion of travel through exotic regions by presenting 'un campionario completo di gente d'ogni parte del globo' (an exhaustive catalogue of people from all over the globe) (Ferrettini, 'Un'ora' 247). More specifically, Pourtauborde provided fairgoers with 'una varia, pittoresca, interessantissima evocazione degli usi, dei costumi, dell'industrie, dell'arte, dei divertimenti, delle religioni, dei popoli orientali. L'Egitto, la Tunisia, l'Algeria, il Madagascar, il Congo, il Senegal, il Niger, la Colonia Eritrea, la Cina, il Siam, il Giappone e l'Indo-Cina vi saranno evocati con mirabile e impressionante fedeltà' (a varied, picturesque, and very interesting evocation of the usages, customs, industries, art, amusements, and religions of the Oriental peoples. Egypt, Tunisia, Algeria, Madagascar, Congo, Senegal, Niger, the Eritrean Colony, China, Siam, Japan, and Indochina will be evoked with admirable and impressive authenticity) (O.G.B. 107). Here Pourtauborde catered to the fairgoers' desire for novelty and surprise by emphasizing these countries' 'pittoreschi e caratteristici contrasti' (picturesque and typical contrasts) (Ferrettini, 'Un'ora' 247).[29] He also pacified potential anxieties about colonial aggression by offering carefully staged fictions of exotic life, where Western and non-Western values were fused 'in una armonia notevole' (in notable harmony) and where colonial people enjoyed the advantages of civilization without losing their 'carattere primitivo o fondamentale' (primitive or fundamental character) (Ferrettini, 'Un'ora' 247).

The river Po served to both separate and leisurely connect mass amusement and colonial exhibits. Besides its permanent bridges, the river was crossed by a specially built two-level bridge, complete with a *tapis roulant* on the lower level and an electrically driven aerial transporter on the upper one. Gondolas and conventional motor launches were also available. Pourtauborde thus suggested an unencumbered flow between mass entertainment and exoticism, and between the aesthetics of pleasure and the spectacle of the exotic. At the same time, while being readily available and easily accessible, the exotic display took place in a separate and circumscribed place which gathered all that did not fit into the main fairground's celebration of industry and technology, in sum into the apologia for Western values.[30]

Italy and the Imperial Paradigm

Hiring the Frenchman Pourtauborde to organize the colonial displays was not an entertainment coup alone. It also reflected the renewed effort to forge diplomatic and commercial bonds between Italy and France. Long before the opening of the exposition, the Consiglio Comunale di Torino had paid an official visit to Paris and, in turn, the French capital had sent its own delegation to Turin, to participate in the fair's inauguration ceremony. Besides the official French Pavilion, Paris also erected its own city pavilion, thus making France the most prominent presence among all participating countries.[31] Overall, France's massive involvement in the 1911 fair reflected a notable shift in the international political climate. While Italy still maintained its role in the Triple Alliance with Germany and Austria-Hungary, albeit in a strictly defensive key, the ties with France had become stronger, mainly because of their common colonial interests. Thus, while Italy did not intervene in the Moroccan crisis in 1911, France maintained a benevolent attitude when Italy engaged in the war with Libya.

Besides underscoring the important political transition that saw Italy distance itself from Germany and the Triple Alliance and nurture closer ties with France, the 1911 exhibition shows Italy's cultural indebtedness to the other great colonial power, Great Britain. The lavish descriptions of the *Palazzi* of France and Great Britain included in the Italian Touring Club's Guide to the 1911 Turin exposition reveal – if compared to the more cursory notes devoted, for example, to the United States, Belgium, and Germany – the cultural influence that these two countries exerted upon Italy.[32] References abound to the material, moral, and political importance of 'la forte Inghilterra' (strong England) (*Torino: esposizione 1911* 31) and to the 'magnifico slancio operoso' (magnificent industrious impulse) of France, 'nazione sorella' (sister nation) (*Torino: esposizione 1911* 37). Italian exposition magazines typically ran assessments of how the foreign press evaluated contemporary fairs, and it was British and French responses that invariably demanded the most attention. 'È un coro di lodi' (It is a chorus of praise), wrote the enthusiastic reporter for the 1881 National Exposition in Milan, quoting extensively from numerous British newspapers (*Milano e l'esposizione italiana del 1881*, 150). Pasquale De Luca, author of *Il giubileo della patria*, devoted to the 1911 International Exposition, particularly appreciated the comments from the *London Times*, as they helped redress current stereotypes:

L'Italia è il *pays de rêve* dell'inglese – e quand'egli è colà scopre che non è affatto un paese morto, ma una grande, energica, pratica realtà; non mero palazzo di Arte ma sede del più ardito pensiero scientifico e filosofico moderno, e il campo ancora, della più vigorosa e più illuminata attività sociale ed economica. (47)

(Italy is the *pays de rêve* for the English people – and when they get there, they find out that Italy is not a dead country, but a great, energetic, and practical reality. Italy is not a mere palace of Art, but the seat of the most daring and modern scientific and philosophical thought, and the field of the most vigorous and enlightened social and economic reality.)

De Luca elatedly reported that the unanimous 'hymn to modern Italy' was inspiring the French press to sustain the 'Latin alliance' against 'Teutonic pride' (55) and commended the socialist paper *L'Humanité* for placing Italy among the six major world powers (56). In a world shaped by evolutionary concepts, such approving comments became warranties of racial 'fitness' and culture. Italy was eager to prove that it was 'degna di star a fianco dei popoli più operosi e civili' (worthy of standing side by side with the most industrious and civilized peoples) (*L'esposizione di Torino 1911*, 3) and thus validate its standing on the Darwinian map of material and racial progress, a map where humanity arranged itself on a hierarchical continuum leading from 'savagery' to 'civilization.'[33]

The 1911 exposition thus shows how Italy strove to become part of the discursive space that we may call the imperial paradigm.[34] This unitary, though not uniform, paradigm, expressed by the cultural technologies of international fairs, created an imaginary community sharing similar values as part of a transnational imperial flow. Besides the native villages discussed earlier, the India that British colonial rulers designed for Western view following the famed India Pavilion at the Great Exhibition especially influenced the definition of the imperial paradigm. This India, whose 'material culture, denuded of social context and natural environment, was choreographed and displayed to impress the world with the talent, skill, and splendor of the subcontinent,' was lavishly reproduced at many subsequent colonial exhibits and had a lasting impact on Western popular consciousness, as we shall see in the case of Gozzano's Indian narratives (Breckenridge 205).[35]

A wishful participant in this discursive space, Italy worked on two fronts: on one, it was creating that sense of collective national identity

that would overcome its endemic regional, historical, and cultural fragmentation; on the other, it was proposing itself as a viable member of a
larger 'civilization' of which Great Britain and France constituted the
models. Understanding that 'the nation-state depended on this larger
ecumene for its cultural and political functioning' (Breckenridge 196)
was particularly pressing for Italy, a country striving to assert itself in
spite of its being a latecomer to and small player in the ideology and
pragmatics of the imperial partition of the world. In a society embracing
a notion of biological essentialism based on the idea that humanity was
composed of many races differing widely in terms of physical, moral,
and intellectual traits, being part of the leading group was not a matter
of economics and politics alone. It resulted from an extensive socio-
cultural and ideological project systematically pursued in all sectors of
knowledge.

One should briefly consider, in this context, the international success
of Cesare Lombroso's thought in the last decades of the nineteenth century. A follower of Charles Darwin, Lombroso established the new discipline of criminal anthropology at the University of Turin by combining
evolutionary and phrenological theories with the timely exploitation of
common beliefs based on the concepts of atavism and pauperism.[36] As is
well known, evolutionism proposed the existence of an uninterrupted
line linking the various degrees of human development, and anticipated
phrenological theories by establishing necessary correlations between
somatic and psychic features. Atavism proposed the regressive presence
in some aberrant human subjects of morphological and psychic features
that were considered innate traits of the primitive, the non-civilized, and
the criminal. In his analysis of criminal jargon, for example, Lombroso
argued that beyond individual variation there was a substratum 'che
rimane e sopravvive alle mutazioni che la moda, i tempi e le circostanze
sembrano arrecarvi continuamente' (that persists, surviving the changes
that trends, time, and circumstances seem to continually bring upon it),
and concluded that criminals 'parlano diversamente, perché diversamente sentono; parlano da selvaggi, perché sono selvaggi viventi in
mezzo alla fiorente civiltà europea' (speak differently because they feel
differently; they speak as savages because they are savages who live in the
midst of the flourishing civilization of Europe) (Portigliatti Barbos
1450). Finally, the culture of pauperism affirmed the biological and
moral inferiority of the 'dangerous classes,' and equated the poor, the
homeless, and the unemployed with the criminal.

Lombroso's thought had enormous influence on the definition of 'born criminals' as individuals who possess anatomical traits that signal psychic and moral aberration. These 'regressive' and 'abnormal' traits were considered as the morphological evidence showing that these individuals belonged to an inferior group. The Museo di antropologia criminale (Museum of Criminal Anthropology) that Lombroso created in Turin was a shrine to these theories as well as a peculiar manifestation of the culture of classification and display that characterized contemporary World's Fairs. The acts of gathering, ordering, measuring, documenting, and classifying heterogeneous materials – from the wax imprints of the faces of 'famous criminals' to the collection of tools documenting criminal modus operandi – were meant to bestow scientific accuracy on Lombroso's biological stereotyping in the Museo di antropologia criminale. Helped by the international attention that his research drew from scientists and common people alike, Lombroso gathered a substantial collection of criminal cases that he organized according to typologies of crimes and criminals. These typologies not only catalogued the anomalies, abnormalities, exceptions, and aberrations that constituted the criminals' stigmata but, by way of contrast, also sustained the implicit definition of what the 'norm' was supposed to be. If the 'civilized European man' constituted the 'norm' and if the 'normal' course of evolution was progressive rather than regressive, then the same logic that sustained Lombroso's identification of criminal personalities could be extended to define the physical and psychic traits of 'inferior' and 'superior' races. Lombroso's studies in the field of criminal anthropology not only sustained the belief in the superiority of civilized nations over the primitive, but also helped the development of eugenics, 'the science of the improvement of the human race by better breeding' (Rydell and Gwynn, *World* 46).

Another example of this program of human categorization emerges from the role that ethnology played in numerous national and international expositions in the latter part of the nineteenth century. While Italian fairs greatly contributed to disseminating the idea of national unity under the aegis of a univocal bourgeois identity, their ethnographic displays also created the conviction of the existence of fundamental differences among Italian regions. The display of regional differences was not intended as a form of equalization: 'una prima via verso l'unificazione attraverso la conoscenza della diversità' (an initial path toward unification through the understanding of diversity), as Mariantonietta Picone Petrusa optimistically claims (20). On the contrary, these displays applied to the study of ethnic groups in the field of ethnology the same Darwinian principles permeating the study of race in anthropology. The hierarchical dualism between civilized and primitive forms, centre and periphery, metropolis and rural areas, North and South, culture and nature, and present and past, governed all of these exhibits. Shepherds from Sardinia, villagers from the southern forests of Sila, and woodcutters and migrant workers from the frontier Alpine regions were scientific throwbacks, peoples in need of colonization, mere survivors soon to be replaced by more sophisticated prototypes, in sum, objects of spectacle. Their ethnological artefacts constituted quaint and folkloric remains. Looking at these people and their artefacts, fairgoers could adopt a limited set of responses. They could mimic the scientist's detached attitude before soon-to-be-extinct specimens, play the curious and appropriative role of the collector and the antiquarian, or display the nostalgic attitude of the *exote*, mourning, always from on high, the loss of primitive innocence.[37]

The similarities between the various expositions' approaches to colonial exoticism and regional folklore show that hierarchies without reflected hierarchies within. In spite of all official rhetoric, fair displays demonstrated that, if Italian unification had been a relatively simple act of annexation on the political end, a much more complex project of assimilation was still underway in the socio-cultural arena. The fact that bourgeois aggression continued to clash against what one could call a mentality of colonial resistance also reveals the ongoing opposition that constitutes the silent story of the other Italy. This Italy, which was not on display at any universal exposition, found one of its most eloquent expressions in the words of Don Fabrizio of Salina, the Sicilian prince protagonist of Giuseppe Tomasi di Lampedusa's *Il gattopardo*, who thus addresses the Piedmontese ambassador of united Italy, Aimone di Chevalley:

> Siamo vecchi, Chevalley, vecchissimi. Sono venticinque secoli almeno che portiamo sulle spalle il peso di magnifiche civiltà eterogenee, tutte venute da fuori ... Noi siamo dei bianchi quanto lo è lei, Chevalley, e quanto la regina d'Inghilterra; eppure da duemilacinquecento anni siamo colonia ... Lei mi parlava poco fa di una giovane Sicilia che si affaccia alle meraviglie del mondo moderno; per conto mio me sembra piuttosto una centenaria trascinata in carrozzino alla Esposizione Universale di Londra, che non comprende nulla, che s'impipa di tutto, delle acciaierie di Sheffield come delle filande di Manchester ...
>
> Crede davvero Lei, Chevalley, di essere il primo a sperare di incanalare la Sicilia nel flusso della storia universale? Chissà quanti imani mussulmani,

quanti cavalieri di re Ruggero, quanti scribi degli Svevi, quanti baroni angioini, quanti legisti del Cattolico hanno concepito la stessa bella follia; e quanti viceré spagnoli, quanti funzionari riformatori di Carlo III; e chi sa piú chi siano stati? (*Il gattopardo* 161–7)

(We are old, Chevalley, very old. For more than twenty-five centuries we've been bearing the weight of a superb and heterogeneous civilization, all from outside ... We're as white as you are, Chevalley, and as the Queen of England; and yet for two thousand and five hundred years we've been a colony ... You talked to me a short while ago about a young Sicily facing the marvels of the modern world; for my part I see instead a centenarian being dragged in a Bath chair around the Great Exhibition in London, understanding nothing and caring about nothing, whether it's the steel factories of Sheffield or the cotton spinners of Manchester ...

Do you really think, Chevalley, that you are the first who has hoped to canalize Sicily into the flow of universal history? Who knows how many Moslem imams, how many of King Roger's knights, how many Swabian scribes, how many Angevin barons, how many jurists of the Most Catholic King have conceived the same fine folly; and how many Spanish viceroys too, and how many of Charles III's reforming functionaries! And who knows now what happened to them all!) (*The Leopard* 182–9)

Needless to say, the official rhetoric of the 1911 exposition was quite different. Following a tradition that dated back to 1851, fair visitors could visit the Padiglione del giornale and see the exposition's magazine in its making. This magazine, *L'esposizione di Torino 1911: Giornale ufficiale illustrato dell'esposizione internazionale delle industrie del lavoro,* which was the official publication of the exposition's executive committee, displayed the exposition's triumphal facade. The magazine arrayed photographs of the foreign pavilions and contextualized them as architectural acts of homage to the hosting nation. Besides describing the various exhibits, the magazine also devoted a great amount of space (at least compared to the official magazines of previous expositions) to presenting the city of Turin itself, with its architectural treasures and natural beauties, its historical monuments and modern constructions, its factories and businesses. By encouraging the fair's visitors to expand their horizons beyond the exposition's precincts and explore a city that promised to be as fabulous as the exposition itself, Turin 1911 reiterated its civic pride while prompting unanimous admiration of its illustrious past and vibrant industrial present.

In carrozzella. Drawing by Dante Paolocci. *Milano e l'esposizione italiana del 1881.*

The pavilion of the Ville de Paris with the Monumental Bridge in Turin 1911. Drawing by Guerzoni. Author's private collection.

Blazoned Pilots, Modern Media, and Vicarious Travels

If the locomotive and the railroad were among the protagonists of nine-teenth-century expositions, the twentieth century's fairs opened new real and imaginative routes with their new star: the automobile. Fiat was born in Turin in 1899, followed, soon after, by Lancia, Itala, Diatto, and Isotta e Fraschini. Initially, automobile purchases were limited to soci-ety's upper echelons, and rather than being the utilitarian means of daily commutes, cars were the protagonists of shows, competitions, and adventures. Eager to display cutting-edge technologies and thus pro-mote national pride, Turin's expositions gave special emphasis to their automobile pavilions. Extolling competitiveness and flair for all things spectacular, the 1906 and 1911 fairs in Milan and Turin coincided with the first international automobile races in Italy.[38] With the assistance of enthusiastic press reports, these races created a new imaginative config-uration of space for the masses, and a fashionable hero was born: the racing driver. One of the guests of honour at the 1911 exposition in Turin was Prince Scipione Borghese, who had achieved national renown just a few years earlier after participating in the *raid* (as automobile races were called at the time) Beijing-Paris at the wheel of his fabled automobile, Itala. On 18 August 1907 *La Stampa* celebrated Borghese's arrival in Turin with a show of ornate and hyperbolic prose:

> La folla ... si stringe attorno alla macchina vittoriosa, si vuole contemplarla, palparla ... come se da ogni suo ordigno sudicio per la polvere e odorante di benzina dovessero emanare gli esotici profumi delle cento regioni attra-versate nella memorabile gita ...
>
> E così, gloriosamente, ha termine la grandiosa avventura, vissuta da tre uomini nostri, in terre estranee, fra popoli stranieri, in luoghi selvaggi e ... attraverso valli pietrose e fiumi gonfii, per montagne rudi e città sepolte nel fango. E [l'avventura] ha termine qui a Torino, donde prima è comin-ciata ... Questa di oggi è una vittoria torinese sopratutto, e Torino che ha accolto ... il *suo* glorioso vincitore, come una volta Roma accoglieva gli imperatori che avevano aggiunto una penna alle ali delle sue aquile ed una gemma alla sua splendente corona, non ha dato i suoi applausi che a se stessa. ('L'arrivo di Borghese')

> (The crowd ... gathers around the victorious car. People want to look at and touch it ... as if from every part of its mechanism, filthy with dust and reek-ing of gasoline, would waft the exotic perfumes of the hundreds of regions

Cover illustration for the *Guida Ufficiale dell'Esposizione di Torino 1911*. By permission, Archivio Storico della Città di Torino. Collezione Simeon (C 2022).

it had crossed during its memorable trip ... Thus, three of our own men gloriously carry out this grand adventure among foreign peoples, in unfamiliar
lands and wild places ... through rocky valleys and swollen rivers, across
rough mountains and cities buried in mud. And [the adventure] ends here
in Turin where it first began ... Today's victory belongs most of all to Turin,
and to herself alone Turin bestows her applause when she ... welcomes her
glorious champion, just as Rome once welcomed the emperors who added
a feather to her eagles' wings and a gem to her splendid crown.)

Borghese travelled approximately sixteen thousand kilometres across
two continents in sixty days from 10 June 1907 to 10 August 1907, arriv-
ing in Paris twenty days before all other participants. Luigi Barzini, one
of the most accomplished journalists of the time, accompanied Borghese on this trip. He was charged with the task of cabling his stories to
two of the leading newspapers in Europe, the Milanese *Corriere della sera*
and the London *Daily Telegraph*. The Parisian paper *Le Matin*, which
sponsored the race, had reporters in the field as well. In a communication media's feeding frenzy, the telegraph, the automobile, and the
press collaborated to disseminate 'i misteri del mondo esotico e sconosciuto' (the mysteries of the exotic and unknown world) among Western
readers (Barzini 8). In 1908, the Milanese publisher Urlico Hoepli
issued Barzini's reports in book form. *Da Pechino a Parigi in sessanta
giorni: La metà del mondo vista da un'automobile* (From Beijing to Paris in
Sixty Days: Half of the World as Seen From an Automobile) immediately
became a best-seller.

Barzini's fast-paced and impressionistic representation of extra-European realities constitutes the verbal equivalent of the colourfully exotic
scenes displayed in many World's Fairs. Writing in the age of motorized
travel and cable communication, Barzini gave novel emphasis to the
opposition between motionless East and progressive West: 'Vi è qualcosa
di talmente grande nella vittoria umana sul tempo e sullo spazio, otte-
nuta con dei fili e delle scintille' (There is something so great in the triumph of humankind over time and space, obtained with some cables
and some sparks), wrote Barzini, as he reported on Itala's progress from
Beijing, 'la superba capitale dell'immobilità' (the superb capital of
immobility) (34), toward the vibrant core of Western life, Paris:

Un colpo di manovella, e il motore rugge. Balziamo sulla macchina, e via!

Via, per il sentiero tortuoso e ineguale, senza curarci dei salti, degli
sbalzi, degli urti, pur di correre. L'automobile non è che alla seconda

velocità, ma ci par di volare ... È la voluttà d'una conquista, l'ebbrezza di un trionfo, e una sorpresa insieme, come un trasognamento per la singolarità fantastica di questa corsa in questo paese. Vediamo dei tetti di pagoda fra gli alberi. Ci pare d'interrompere una quiete millenaria, d'essere i primi a gettare fuggendo un segnale di risveglio ad un gran sonno. Sentiamo in noi l'orgoglio d'una civiltà e d'una razza, sentiamo di rappresentare qualche cosa di più di noi stessi: con noi è l'Europa che passa. Nella velocità si riassume tutto il significato della civiltà nostra. La grande brama dell'anima occidentale, la sua forza, il segreto vero d'ogni suo progresso, è espressa in due parole: 'più presto!' (74)

(A turn of the handle and the engine roars. We jump in the car and away we go!

Off we go along the winding and uneven road, careless of the leaps, jumps, and jolts, as long as we can speed. The automobile is only in second gear, but it seems that we are flying ... We feel the pleasure of conquest, the intoxication of triumph, and, at the same time, a sense of surprise, like a reverie, because of the fantastic exceptionality of this race in this country. We see some pagodas' roofs among the trees. We feel that we are interrupting a thousand-year long silence, being the first to issue, while fleeing away, the signal that awakens people from a long sleep. We feel the pride in our race and civilization, and we feel that we are here to represent something bigger than ourselves: Europe is moving along with us. The entire significance of our civilization is summarized by speed. The great desire of the Western soul, its strength, the real secret behind all its progress can be expressed in two words: 'go faster!')

If Itala, and with it the country that named it, symbolized the advance of Western technology, a blind old man, guarding a temple, became for Barzini the epitome of the whole of the Chinese race: 'Non era forse intorno a noi tutto un popolo che viveva solo del passato, e che assisteva senza vedere al poderoso irrompere d'un presente a lui ignoto?' (Were there not, all around us, peoples who lived only in the past, who looked at, without seeing it, the powerful advance of a present that was unknown to them?) (95). The ideological power of this rhetorical question lies in the affirmative reply it implies. With it, Barzini demands the complicity of a community of readers who expect to be titillated with new information about the exotic world while being reassured that Western 'innate ideas' about this very world remain true and need not be questioned.

Much has been written about the standardization of traditional exoticism and the consequent reinforcement of cultural stereotypes after the advent of the 'electronic, postmodern world' (Said, *Orientalism* 26). Barzini's cabled reports demonstrate that the late nineteenth and early twentieth centuries' new technologies and media resources had already mastered the forms of a cultural hegemony that saw in the World's Fairs one of its most formidable tools. All together, these technologies forced information 'into more and more standardized molds,' and intensified the hold of what Said called 'the nineteenth-century academic and imaginative demonology' of the mysterious and static Orient (Said, *Orientalism* 26). If, as we have seen, Barzini's reporting from the passenger seat of an automobile speeding through the Celestial Empire was an extraordinary means to renew consensus around the juxtaposition of Asian immobility and Western dynamism, in and of itself this hackneyed idea cannot explain the wild success of Barzini's reports any more than it could justify, for example, the *Excelsior* ballet's long-lived fame.[39] This success depends on what was constructed as a propitious concurrence of traditional epistemologies with modern discoveries. Specifically, contemporary interpreters saw the industrialized world's apology of *motion* – from the omnipresent dynamo pumping, driving, lighting, and setting gears into synchronized action to the various means of transportation and communication connecting previously isolated parts of the globe – as the practical confirmation of the opposition between progressive West and static East that we have seen theorized, for example, in Cantù's philosophy. Moreover, the combination of competitive sportsmanship and patriotism that Itala inspired, the aristocratic prestige that came with the name of the Borghese family, and Barzini's own journalistic fame after the *Daily Telegraph* purchased his articles, greatly contributed to the success of Barzini's reports. 'Era la prima volta che un giornale inglese si accorgeva delle cose nostre e di uno scrittore italiano' (It was the first time that a British newspaper became aware of our own things and of an Italian writer) (8), proudly wrote Barzini upon returning to Italy. His words demonstrate that, just like so many international expositions, the Beijing-to-Paris road journey ultimately was a political feat, one that proved Italy's ambition to compete with its imperial European neighbours, France and Great Britain. Last, but not least, trite as it was, *Da Pechino a Parigi*'s leading idea proved to be so successful because it helped appease widespread anxieties about an all-too-mobile China, after the Boxer Rebellion of 1900, the crisis of the Ch'ing dynasty, and the onset of the Chinese revolutionary movement.

The readers who eagerly followed the news about Scipione Borghese's *raid* were the same who enjoyed the technological sophistication of the Worlds' Fairs various forms of vicarious travel. At the 1898 national exposition in Turin, fairgoers who had probably never travelled beyond their own regional boundaries could row through Capri's Grotta azzurra and explore California's Montagne aurifere (Gold Mountains), scrambling through over half a kilometre of mine tunnels. Those who favoured more leisurely travel could board *Architetto* Giordano's Ferrovia-panorama (Panoramic Railway) and spend a few comfortable minutes crossing sunny valleys, chugging up to mountain tops, and racing along railway tunnels. The 'intera e perfettissima illusione' (complete and most perfect illusion) started in a building that reproduced a train station with its ticket office, waiting rooms, and railway platforms. The eager traveller who boarded the elegant, strictly first-class carriages experienced a trip to Naples from May to August, and one to Switzerland from September onwards. As *Architetto* Giordano explained, 'per mezzo di congegni meccanici, si otterranno le sensazioni tutte dell'accidentalità del terreno, le scosse, le oscillazioni, ecc.; sistemi di luce elettrica faranno passare lo spettatore dal giorno alla notte, ed infine non sarà trascurato il minimo particolare onde ottenere la più perfetta illusione del vero' (Mechanical devices will provide all the sensations of the roughness of the terrain, the jolting, the swaying, etc.; systems of electric lights will allow the spectator to go from day to nighttime. In sum, not the slightest detail will be overlooked in order to obtain the most perfect illusion of truth (Pavoni 19). A sophisticated system of rollers, levers, and pulleys operated the canvasses that reproduced the various sets that the passengers saw sliding past their windows, including 'il paesaggio incantato del golfo di Napoli, l'immensa città tutta bianca al sole, l'azzurra iridescente marina, il Vesuvio brullo e tormentato alle falde, fiammeggiante e fumoso alla vetta' (the enchanted landscape of the Gulf of Naples, the immense city all white in the sun, the iridescent blue marina, Vesuvius with its barren and tormented foot and its top aflame and full of smoke) (Antonini 50). Even the unfortunate event of the diorama's screen tearing up was taken into account and manipulated as to mimic a derailment. However, while powerfully evoked, this reality was also purged of any unpleasant connotation. A contemporary article reports:

Eccovi immense stazioni ferroviarie ... senza fumo e senza disordine, dove le rotaie corrono e si smorzano fra i tappeti: eccovi biblioteche senza pol-

vere; eccovi officine dove l'operaio lavora cogli abiti festivi ... ecco,
insomma, tutta quanta la vita civile depurata, fatta più semplice e più ricca
insieme, ecco il lavoro umano isolato e svincolato dalle asprezze e dalle vol-
garità della lotta economica. (Arcari 432)

(Here you have immense train stations ... without smoke and without confusion, with their rails running and smoothing themselves out among the
carpets. Here you have libraries without dust; workshops where the worker
works in his Sunday best ... Here, in sum, you have all of social life purified,
and made simpler and richer at the same time. Here is human labour
isolated and liberated from the harshness and vulgarity of the economic
struggle.)

By promoting fictions of universal satisfaction, fairs were 'magic mirrors' that reflected back beautified and purged images of the modern
world (Buel 1). Travel, in particular, which had been historically the
privilege of the aristocracy and the high bourgeoisie, became a mass
spectacle, readily available to all social classes, or at least those who
could afford the price of a fair's admission. Fairgoers could enjoy the
fascination of picturesque landscapes, unknown countries, and new and
unusual customs, without undergoing the financial strain and physical
exertion that travel normally demands. The visitors who, during the
Paris exposition of 1900, sat in the plush carriages of the Trans-Siberian
Railway model, and saw passing along the windows all the lands that lay
between Moscow and Beijing, enjoyed the pleasures of a tangible if temporary escape from the here and now of contemporary life. Furthermore, by participating in these spectacles of travel as leisure, they
experienced a form of social assertion, as they laid claim to a lifestyle
that, in reality, was far beyond their financial reach (Abruzzese, *Arte e
pubblico* 83).

The reconstruction of exotic locales, such as the Via del Cairo, the Via
di Costantinopoli, the Oriental Bazaar, and the many African villages
also provided some of the most successful means of vicarious travel and
geographic displacement that fairs all over the world continued to
exploit with undiminished popular satisfaction.[40] Similarly, the reproductions of polar environments responded to the age's fascination with
reaching the farthest limits of our planet. The 'viaggio all'estremo
Nord' (travel to the farthest North), a 'grandiose Pavilion' built for the
1906 exposition in Milan, featured stunning reproductions of the arctic

regions, with their 'rocce glaciali e [...] grandi orsi bianchi') (polar rocks and ... great white bears) (*Esposizione internazionale di Milano* 5).[41]

Polar Explorers, 'Instant Books,' and the Politics of Travel

As in other sectors, in that of travel and exploration Turin 1911 wished to provide a magnificent recapitulation and authoritative systematization of a world finally subjected to 'man's' control. In the Age of Empire's appropriative geography, the North Pole carried notable symbolic implications. Edge of the planet and ultimate exploitable space, *Ultima Thule* constituted the grand challenge to any modern Ulysses. Turin's extensive displays of the collections from the 1898 expedition to the North Pole accomplished by Luigi Amedeo, Duke of the Abruzzi and nephew of King Umberto, must be seen in this cultural context (De Luca 226). The duke's exhibits included his polar expedition's scientific materials, trekking equipment, utensils and gear, and extracts from numerous technical and popular reports about the journey, including contemporary newspaper articles, postcards, photographs, commemorative illustrations, posters, collector's cards, and almanacs featuring Luigi Amedeo, his first officer Umberto Cagni, and the rest of his crew. A place of honour was reserved for Luigi Amedeo's *La Stella Polare nel mare Artico* (The *Stella Polare* in the Arctic Ocean), the first-hand account of the expedition that, in spite of its often uninspiring style and technical jargon, had remained the most widely sold book in Italy for several years after its publication in 1903.[42]

Turin 1911 recapitulated a royal adventure that had started more than a decade before, and added an important chapter to the House of Savoy's shrewdly managed promotional and advertising campaigns regarding Luigi Amedeo's numerous expeditions.[43] Attuned as it was to the politics of travel in the imperial Zeitgeist and historically savvy about the power of self-advertisement, the House of Savoy capitalized on one of modernity's popular myths, that of the explorer.[44] When in 1897 twenty-four-year-old Luigi Amedeo planted the tricolour flag on top of Mount St Elias on the border between Canada and Alaska, the House of Savoy construed the young duke's first major climb to mean much more than a mere alpine success. Its popularity at an all-time low after the colonial defeat at Adowa and support of General Bava-Beccaris's use of violence in Milan, the royal house used Luigi Amedeo's ascent to lift the Savoy house's credibility after its political and diplomatic tumbles. Luigi Amedeo's expeditions allowed the diversion of public attention from the economic crisis, bank scandals, heavy taxation, growing poverty, and consequent popular unrest that were plaguing the nation.[45] They also created a renewed sense of national pride, and helped the post-Risorgimento generations coalesce around the young duke. As revealed by the caption of a first-page article in *La Stampa* of 7 September 1900 reporting on Luigi Amedeo's progress on the ice cap, 'Un Principe di Savoia più a Nord di Nansen') (A Savoy Prince More to the North than Nansen), Luigi Amedeo provided a heroic perspective to a country seeking new national heroes and competing for international acknowledgment.

The duke's expedition to the North Pole 'suscitò un clamore enorme' (made a huge splash) (Pozzo, 'Io terrei' xlvi). Numerous popular publications such as *La Stampa-Gazzetta piemontese, Il Corriere della sera* with *La Domenica del Corriere, Il Popolo, Il Fischietto,* and *Il Vittorioso* followed the expedition's lengthy preparation, building 'una campagna pubblicitaria perfetta, orchestrata con criteri modernissimi' (a perfect advertising campaign, orchestrated with very modern criteria) (Audisio and Mantovani xxix). Luigi Amedeo's collaborators groomed the public's curiosity about the duke's own expedition narrative by anticipating its publication as early as 1901 in the Italian Geographic Society's *Bollettino.* Over the next two years, publisher Urlico Hoepli staged a meticulous promotional campaign that, by previewing some of the book's contents, continued to raise public expectations for the duke's narrative. As early as 1900, Emilio Salgari accepted an invitation from the Genoese publisher Antonio Donath to write what was called, using the English expression, 'an instant book' in order to 'magnificare uno dei tanti ardimenti gloriosi dovuti ai figli di Casa Savoia' (exalt one of the many glorious acts of bravery that we owe to the children of the House of Savoy) (Viglongo, 'L'editore ai lettori: *La Stella*' ix).[46] In *La Stella Polare e il suo viaggio avventuroso* (The *Stella Polare* and Its Adventurous Voyage), Salgari liberally used information gathered from the Italian press, heavily borrowed from other published materials, and expanded his narrative by having several of his characters relate other famous polar adventures. Salgari used the conventional device of the story-within-a-story to flesh out a scant narrative, but also to let Luigi Amedeo of the wobbly House of Savoy share the ice with the likes of Nansen, Adrée, Payer, Peary, Cook, Amudsen, Wellman, Lerner, and Sverdrup.[47] The lawsuit that Luigi Amedeo was reported to be initiating against Salgari's alleged plagiarisms of his own polar report underscored the pitfalls of narrative practices based on rapid creation and production cycles. In Luigi

Amedeo's case, however, the lawsuit turned out to be a brilliant act of self-promotion, creating even more curiosity regarding the duke's polar adventure.[48]

Luigi Amedeo's return trip to Italy after the polar expedition was prepared with equal care, and his southbound pilgrimage through the peninsula's main cities to the mausoleum of King Umberto, whom the anarchist Gaetano Bresci had assassinated in July 1900, attracted 'un delirio di popolo quale da molto tempo non si vedeva' (a frenzy of crowds, such as had not been witnessed for a long time) (Audisio and Mantovani xxix). In the wake of this success, the International Exposition of Decorative Arts held in Turin in 1902 inaugurated one of its top attractions, the *cinematografo moderno*, with a short documentary entitled *L'arrivo della Stella Polare a La Spezia*.[49] The semiotics of the spectacle that underwrote national and international expositions magnified itself in the spectacular technology of the newborn cinema, which, in turn, was the most appropriate vehicle to display the triumphal conclusion of the age's most spectacular adventure.[50] Aggressively constructing the modern 'society of the spectacle,' the embryonic cultural industry, of which expositions and the cinema were powerful expressions, circulated cultural messages that were mutually reflective, endlessly reproducible, and easily accepted. The Duke of the Abruzzi's polar adventure thus became one of the first modern multimedia events, culminating in Turin 1911's comprehensive and celebratory hoopla.

The spectacle of travel was indeed one of the World's Fairs' founding tropes. The series of national pavilions with their distinctive architectural features, the succession of ethnic and colonial exhibits, and the many travel-based amusements allowed fairgoers one of the most powerful experiences of spatial estrangement that modernity could afford. Historical re-enactments and masked balls, reconstructed towns, neighbourhoods, and dwellings such as Albert Robida's trendsetting Vieux Paris and Village Suisse at the 1900 Paris World's Fair inspired journeys across all historical ages. Dreamlands such as the Padiglione della Moda (The Couture Pavilion) in 1911 Turin afforded excursions to worlds that were financially inaccessible and experientially remote to the great majority of people. Guided tours through the various stages of industrial production and scientific innovation narrated the journey of progress that underwrote all expositions. By inspiring feelings of novelty, wonder, diversion, and self-satisfaction, these itineraries provided fairgoers with well-engineered and sanitized adventures and safe returns home. One of the expositions' most popular images, a group of people floating in

Pallone Godard. *Album-ricordo dell'esposizione del 1884 in Torino.* By permission, Biblioteca di storia e cultura del Piemonte, Turin, Italy.

the air in a tethered balloon, eloquently captures the fairs' underlying design.[51] Note, for example, how a reporter described the coup d'oeil from the balloon's floating basket:

> Un'esposizione senza pallone frenato ormai non è possibile ... Pare che si abbia bisogno di elevarsi dalla folla che si riversa per le gallerie dell'Esposizione: ... [e che] si senta il bisogno d'un quarto d'ora di libertà, lassù all'aria vibrante, nella navicella che dondola ... senza pericolo, perchè la sua brava fune ci tiene legati alla madre antica, alla terra, dalla quale siamo scappati un momento, ma alla quale vogliamo ritornare fra poco perchè qui è il nostro paese, la nostra casa, la nostra Esposizione. (*Milano e l'esposizione italiana del 1881,* 71)[52]

(An exposition without a tethered balloon is by now impossible ... It seems that people need to elevate themselves above the crowds pouring into the exposition's galleries ... [and that] they need fifteen minutes of freedom up there in the vibrant air, in the swinging basket ... without any danger,

Padiglione della moda. Turin 1911. Author's private collection.

because its good old rope ties us to our ancient mother, our earth, from which we escaped for a moment, but to which we soon want to return because here is our country, our home, our exposition.)

In promoting travel without expenditure, adventure without danger, and escape without displacement, World's Fairs became formidable consensus-building machines. Shrines to material security and apologies for the bourgeois status quo, the fairs' ephemerality concealed the discipline of their recurrence, and their engagement with the diverse and the exotic confirmed the dominance of universalistic Western values. Similarly, their involvement with the historical past served to guarantee the order of the present, and their thrust toward the future to bolster the power of the current establishment. Beneath all their eclecticism and variety, and beyond all their investments with the myth of travel, Italian fairs traced the familiar architecture of the bourgeoisie's dwelling space, in its individual (the home) and collective (the homeland) components.

These apologies of equality and bourgeois contentment produced their own 'dialectical images' as well. The worker's delegations to the 1851 and 1862 exhibitions in London evolved into Marx's International Workingmen's Association. The 1855 Paris Exposition Universelle inspired Pierre-Joseph Proudhon's utopian *Projet d'une exposition perpétuelle* (Project for a Permanent Exposition). Participants in the 1886 International Workers' Congress in Paris insisted that the next congress be held in 1889, to coincide with the Universal Exposition celebrating the centennial of the French Revolution, in order to have the commemoration of the bourgeois revolution confront the proletarian struggle. National and international exhibitions were mobilizing grounds for Italian workers' movements as well and were instrumental in the creation of the Camere del lavoro, based upon the Parisian Bourse du travail and the British Trade Unions. Starting from 1878, fairs hosted congresses on the rights of women and organized exhibits devoted to women's occupations, arts, and skills, thus helping disseminate feminist principles on an international scale.

In re-proposing itself as the first home of the Italian nation and proud ambassador of the values of Western civilization, Turin 1911 exposed the utopian desires, political goals, ideological tensions, local ambitions, budding insecurities, and deep-seated nostalgia of a country still in its making in a world in rapid evolution. Belated partner in an ever-expanding imperial economy, Turin 1911 staged the last act of the grand drama of progress, the curtain closing on the 'favola bella' that enchanted millions of visitors in the charming setting of the park of Valentino Castle.

3 Emilio Salgari: Writing Exposition Style

Salgari's Novels as Exposition Narratives

On a September morning in 1883, the citizens of Verona awakened to see striking posters adorning the walls of the downtown buildings. The posters displayed a large tiger, its mouth open and its eyes glaring, but with no caption to explain its sudden and exotic appearance in the medieval district of this quiet northern Italian town. The townspeople assumed that a circus or a wild animal show was due to arrive. A couple of days later, *La nuova arena*, one of Verona's four daily papers, reported that a tiger had escaped from its cage in a neighbouring village. The Veronese people's puzzled curiosity turned into concern. Rumours, both in print and *in piazza*, ran rampant: it was a bear, not a tiger, which had escaped from a circus; it was indeed a tiger, but it was sighted in Milan, not Verona. A few days later, new posters appeared, this time with the cryptic caption 'La tigre sta per arrivare' (The tiger is about to get here). The suspense increased until the municipal bill-stickers put up a new set of posters announcing, in bold letters, 'La tigre della Malesia è arrivata: Leggete *La nuova arena*' (The Malayan tiger is here: read *La nuova arena*). It was 16 October 1883.

Perhaps unsurprisingly for a town renowned for having invented the balcony of Romeo and Juliet, thus cashing in on the curiosity of many romantically inclined Shakespearian travellers, the ferocious tiger turned out to be a harmless *être de papier*, a brilliantly orchestrated advertising trick.[1] The posters that had mystified the Veronese people became the birth announcements of one of the most beloved heroes of Italian popular culture: Sandokan, aka the Malayan Tiger, a dethroned Bornean prince turned formidable yet generous pirate. *La nuova arena's* publicity ploy paid off. The first instalment of Emilio Salgari's *La tigre della Malesia* was such a hit that *La nuova arena* achieved record sales, leaving the thrilled publisher unable to satisfy his readers' demands, and the prolific young writer eager to concoct new and wild adventures in the Borneo jungles, Indian Sundarbans, and Malay islands.

Underestimated and even ostracized by the literary elite, Salgari was the unrivalled champion of popular fiction in late-nineteenth- and early-twentieth-century Italy. His relentless narrative production spanned a twenty-five-year period and amounted to more than eighty novels and one hundred short stories. Financial need, unyielding contracts, and increasing demand from his ever-expanding readership forced him to produce adventure tales at an obsessive pace, often under different pseudonyms. Imitators were quick to take advantage of the Salgari fad, while fraudulent editions of his works circulated widely, creating a textual jungle that is difficult to explore even today.[2] In a country where illiteracy was still remarkably high and the reading public was mainly concentrated in urban centres, Salgari's record-breaking sales constituted a publishing triumph of unprecedented proportions.[3]

The 'Italian Jules Verne,' as Salgari was quickly labelled, was a fitting representative of the exposition mentality in Italian letters. In the age of modern imperialism, Salgari's extraordinary versatility and intellectual curiosity allowed him to depict every corner of the world on paper, as a random survey of some of his many titles attests: *Gli strangolatori del Gange, Le stragi delle Filippine, Gli orrori della Siberia, Sulle frontiere del Far West, I corsari delle Bermude, I predoni del Sahara, I pirati della Malesia, La regina dei Caraibi, Sull'Atlante, Il leone di Damasco, La capitana del Yucatan, Il bramino dell'Assam, I minatori dell'Alaska, Le pantere di Algeri, I naufragatori dell'Oregon, I cacciatori di foche nella baia di Baffin.* Translated into numerous languages, Salgari's adventure-filled yet often formulaic novels responded to widespread ideological and psychological needs and, as such, constituted one of the most interesting popular culture phenomena in early-twentieth-century Italy.

Critics partial to canonical 'high' literary genres argue that most popular fiction operates within standardized poetics and pre-established world views. Produced to replicate and confirm, rather than challenge, the ingrained beliefs of a specific socio-cultural environment, popular fiction, according to these critics, upholds the status quo by passively acquiescing to dominant ideologies. The archetypal struggle between virtue and vice typically engaged in popular plots always resolves itself with virtue's victory, virtue remaining defined within conventional ethi-

cal standards (Eco, 'Le lacrime' 13–24). Concluding, from these premises, that popular fiction lacks 'una originale tensione morale e in-
tellettuale' (an original moral and intellectual tension) (Petronio 17),
these critics define popular fiction in the negative, opposed to artistic
expressions that, instead, are thematically innovative, ideologically challenging, and formally experimental.

This Manichean approach imposes clear-cut distinctions between
high and low, elite and popular, innovative and formulaic, problematic
and demagogical, and, implicitly, good and bad art. While appealing on
an abstract organizational level, this classification system of binary opposition simplifies a literary reality whose elements are far more heterogeneous and interconnected. The difference between popular and non-
popular literary forms may be more a matter of shade and degree rather
than a simple case of black-and-white dichotomies. Moreover, if popular
novels such as Salgari's are worth examining as cultural phenomena,
that is, as representative examples of specific world views as shaped by
the conventions of precise generic models, one must not assume that
they entirely lack innovation or inner 'tension.' Within their conventional structures, these novels often echo the contradictions as well as
the assumptions of the culture that inspired them. By giving narrative
form to commonly held intellectual presuppositions, these novels
express precisely what normally remains *presumed* – that is, unformu-
lated and therefore uncriticized – in the cultural consciousness of a
given collectivity. In their blend of ideological assumptions, conceptual
dissonances, and epistemological ambiguities, these novels ultimately
invite readers to dispute the world views that they nevertheless helped to
promote and disseminate.

My analysis starts with a definition of literary modes and genres not
only as literary phenomena, but also as socio-historical constructs that
exist in a dialectic relationship with their extraliterary contexts. Like
social systems, genre systems are 'sediments of consensus' that represent
general models of thought and experience and can be thought of as
symptoms of the specific culture that creates and utilizes them.[4] In this
light, the ways in which Salgari exploited the conventions of exposition
narratives and worked both within and against the generic standards of
adventure novels acquire a significance that goes beyond the strictly aesthetic or literary sphere. If we agree with scholars such as Benedict
Anderson, Homi Bhabba, and Timothy Brennan, and see narratives as
the imaginative acts that help shape the communities that we call
nations, then we must ask ourselves how much Salgari's popular novels

of adventure expressed the aggressively nationalistic, expansionistic, and Eurocentric mentality of their time, and in which ways they diverged from this mentality. Discussing this interplay of similarities and differences helps delineate Italy's feelings about its status as nation state vis-à-vis its European neighbours. Salgari's adventure tales contributed to Italy's still fluid sense of nationhood by giving it shape as a cultural artefact – a popular narrative. This narrative, however, does not find its meaning in and of itself but together with, as well as against, the narrative acts of other imagined communities – France and Britain, primarily. Rather than emphasizing the escapist thrust of Salgari's novels, I suggest that the adventure genre was the ideal forum in which to give emotional legitimacy to the collective hopes and fears regarding Italy's national and international future, and to its still untold and non-manifest destiny.

In spite of his astounding declarations about his travels as a *capitano di gran cabotaggio*, Salgari, like many other literary adventurers, never journeyed far from home (his sole voyage, probably as a passenger, took him from Venice to the Dalmatian coast, then south to Brindisi, and back). Like his contemporary Karl May, Salgari constructed his vivid literary sets in the library. His main sources were the twenty-one volumes of Giulio Ferrario's *Il costume antico e moderno* (1817–34), Louis Rousselet's *L'Inde des Rajahs: voyage dans l'Inde centrale et dans les présidences de Bombay et du Bengale* (1875), Louis-Grégoire Domény De Rienzi's *Océanie, ou cinquième partie du monde: Revue géographique et ethnographique de la Malaisie, de la Micronésie, de la Polynésie et de la Mélanésie* (1836–8), Auguste Wahlen's *Mœurs, usages et costumes de tous les peuples du monde, d'après des documents authentiques et les voyages les plus récents* (1843–4), and Paolo Mantegazza's *India* (1884). He was also an avid reader of popular magazines such as *Il giornale illustrato dei viaggi e delle avventure di terra e di mare* (which Edoardo Sonzogno founded in 1879), *L'universo pittoresco*, *L'esploratore*, *Intorno al mondo*, *L'oceano*, *Il vascello*, *Il mare*, *Il giro del mondo* (the Italian version of the successful French magazine *Le tour du monde*), and *La valigia*, in which Salgari published his first novel, *I selvaggi della Papuasia* (The Savages of Papua) in 1883. Salgari himself was the director of *Per terra e per mare: Avventure e viaggi illustrati, scienza popolare e letture amene*, a weekly illustrated magazine issued by the Genoese publisher Antonio Donath. These texts were the informational archives from which Salgari borrowed – usually with little or no modification – many of the exotic descriptions, scientific data, and discipline-specific pieces that pepper all of his adventure tales.

Literary counterpart to the contemporary World's Fairs architects who were just beginning to exploit the functional advantages of prefabricated structures, Salgari used portions of these publications as textual blocks that were readily available, and could be easily collected, assembled, combined, and reused in different contexts. Arguably, like all *feuilletonistes*, Salgari could sustain his massive narrative production only by standardizing it. Not only did he recycle specific narrative themes from one novel to the next, but he also reproduced entire descriptive sequences. More often than not, Salgari was not the primary source for these descriptions, which he used according to montage-like techniques and to an implicit industrial-like subdivision of labour. In a way, the often-anonymous authors of travel and/or scientific reports in *Il giro del mondo* or *La valigia* worked as involuntary and unpaid ghostwriters for specific sections in Salgari's narratives. Moreover, by transposing entire passages from texts such as Rousselet's and Ferrario's into his own novels, Salgari redefined the notion of *plagiat* in a way that was similar to that of modernist collage artists. Producers of popular fiction – and as we shall see with Gozzano, up to a certain extent *Kunst* writers as well – came to consider the published word as a commodity available to be appropriated and reused. If this often sent authors and publishing houses headlong into thick legal quagmires, it also helped correct the concept of the art product as the absolutely original and unique creation of a single inspired individual, loftily detached from the rules of the marketplace and the influences of popular culture.

Salgari's success helped popularize a serially produced, highly standardized, and prefabricated literature that reflected the exposition mentality, systematizing hubris, and general modes of production of the industrial age. The volumes that provided the descriptive materials for Salgari's tales disseminated a discourse that was geared toward entertainment while carrying a message of authority, persuasion, and pedagogy. In Salgari's adventure tales, the omniscient narrator appropriates this discourse, acting as the ever-present yet unobtrusive source of encyclopedic *auctoritas*. Perhaps more than any other Italian writer of his age, Salgari assembled his textual world with extraordinary lexical virtuosity. Readers cannot but be impressed with the narrator's flaunting of knowledge, his absolute proficiency in the encyclopedia of the world, and the ease with which he switches from one idiolect to the next. A random perusal of Salgari's novels shows, for example, how the technical vocabulary of the botanist, brought to bear on the description of the jungle, gives way to the sailor's depiction of ships, the ethnologist's and zoologist's classification of peoples and animals, and the anthropologist's illustration of religious and cultural practices.

Like Jules Verne's, Salgari's inventories mirror the age's expository ambition to create comprehensive taxonomies of all of the types, species, and places of a bountiful yet knowable world. 'Gli invitati non erano più di cinquanta' (There were no more than fifty guests), Salgari writes in describing a reception at the home of the rajah of Sarawak in *I pirati della Malesia*, 'ma quanti costumi e quanti tipi diversi!' (but how many different outfits and types!), he exclaims, as he proceeds to account for all the invited parties:

> Vi erano quattro europei tutti vestiti di tela bianca, una quindicina di chinesi vestiti di seta e coi crani così pelati e così lucenti che sembravano zucche, dieci o dodici malesi dalla tinta verde oscura insaccati in lunghe zimarre indiane; cinque o sei capi dayachi colle loro donne, più nudi che vestiti ma adorni di centinaia di braccialetti, di collane di denti di tigre. Gli altri erano macassaresi, bughisi, tagali, [e] giavanesi. (*I pirati della Malesia* 93)

> (There were four Europeans, all dressed in white cloth; about fifteen Chinese dressed in silk, their heads so hairless and shiny that they looked like squashes; ten or twelve Malayans, dark green in complexion and all bundled up in long Indian robes; five or six Dayak chiefs with their women, more naked than dressed, but adorned with hundreds of bracelets and necklaces made of tiger teeth. All the others were Makassarese, Buginese, Tagalogs, [and] Javanese.)

Enumerative accuracy turns into numerical fastidiousness in Salgari's account of all the specific components of this scene. The white outfits of the four Europeans who open the ethnic parade constitute the evaluative degree zero that orients the Western viewer's assessing gaze upon the rest of the crowd. All the other groups define themselves via their difference – in skin colour, clothing or lack of it, amount and type of ornamentation – from this blank European paradigm. Moreover, the visually explanatory function of analogy subsumes difference to a lexical *sermo humilis* – the Chinese guests' heads are described as looking like squashes – that implicitly invites the readers to share a debasing value judgment toward the non-European groups. This passage, which is symptomatic of many other similar descriptions in Salgari's novels, reflects what in *On Human Diversity* Tzvetan Todorov defines as the ethnocentric bias: people are evaluated according to hierarchical criteria that place authors and readers at the top of the ethnic scale, as the gold standard against which all difference must perforce define itself.

Along with human beings, in Salgari's novels the natural environment offers itself as a spectacle. Salgari's toponymic precision and deictic profusion convey the impression of absolute spatial intelligibility:

> La foce del fiume, che forma una specie di porto riparato da banchi sabbiosi e da scogliere contro le quali rompesi la furia del mare, presentava un magnifico spettacolo. A destra, a sinistra e sulle due rive, stendevansi magnifiche boscaglie di *pisang* dalle gigantesche foglie e le frutta di un giallo dorato, di stupendi mangostani, di preziosi sagù dai cui tronchi si estrae una fecola assai nutritiva, di *gambir*, di *betel* e di colossali alberi della canfora, sui cui rami urlavano bande di scimmie di un bel color verde e cicalavano bande di tucani coi becchi enormi ...
>
> Sulle scogliere e sui banchi, si vedevano dei dayachi semi-nudi occupati a pescare e stormi di albatros, giganteschi volatili, forniti di un becco robustissimo che sfonda, senza fatica, il cranio di un uomo, e stormi di rapidissimi uccelli marini chiamati comunemente fregate. (*I pirati della Malesia* 46)

> (The mouth of the river offered a magnificent spectacle, as it forms a sort of harbour protected by sand dunes and cliffs against which dashes the fury of the ocean. On the right and left banks of the river there were wonderful forests of *pisang* trees, with enormous leaves and golden-yellow fruit, stupendous mangosteens, prized plants of sago, from whose trunks a very nutritious flour is extracted, and *gambir* and *betel* plants. On the branches of some colossal camphor trees, gangs of beautifully coloured green monkeys were screaming, and bands of huge-billed toucans chattered ...
>
> On the cliffs and sand dunes you could see semi-naked Dayaks occupied with their fishing, flocks of albatrosses, huge birds with a very strong beak that can easily crush a man's skull, and flocks of those very fast marine birds generally called frigates.)

The narrator's semiotic know-how – his mastery of numerous professional languages – funds his credibility and separates him from his average reader, who rarely matches his proficiency of such varied idiolects. Unless we are botanists, or have a dictionary at hand, we most likely would not know what *pisangs* and *gambirs* are any more than we would we be able to identify the boats in the following passage without the help of detailed descriptions or explanatory illustrations:

Piroscafi, barchi *brick*, brigantini, golette e *slopp*, s'incontrano dovunque lungo il ... corso [del fiume Hugly]. Non parliamo delle pinasse, dei *poular*, dei *bangle*, dei *mur-punky*, dei *fylt' sciarra*, dei *gonga* e di tutte quelle barche più o meno grandi, di costruzione indiana, che si contano a migliaia e che s'incrociano in tutti i versi. (*I misteri* 353)[5]

(All along [the Hugli river] ... one could meet steamboats, one-masted brigantines, brigs, schooners, and *sloops*, not to mention the pinnaces, *poular, bangle, mur-punky, fylt' sciarra*, and *gonga*, and the hundreds of big and small Indian-made boats that criss-cross the river in every direction.)

In cases like these, Salgari's technical precision obscures rather than explains the real, and what his readers perceive is not the represented world but, rather, the author's lexical virtuosity. Remote from the average reader's everyday experiences, referents turn into pure nouns, verbal abstractions, and free-floating signifiers. Faced with this sudden semantic opaqueness, readers cannot but defer to the narrator's scientific authority while succumbing to the mysterious charm of his lexical exoticism. Arguably, this is the way it should be: exoticism is indeed incompatible with knowledge. We cherish the exotic (as all that is different, strange, and remote from our everyday existence) precisely because of its unfathomable and mysterious qualities. The author is the authoritative mediator between us and this world of otherness, which (we trust) he has thoroughly unveiled and understood, before recloaking it in its *couleur locale*, for our enjoyment. The exotic strategy carries notable ideological implications because it cajoles the reader into accepting not only the author's descriptive competence, but also his evaluative statements:

Vi erano dei malesi di statura piuttosto bassa, vigorosi e agili come le scimmie, dalla faccia quadra e ossuta, dalla tinta fosca, uomini famosi per la loro audacia e ferocia; dei battias dalla tinta ancor più fosca, noti per la loro passione per la carne umana, quantunque dotati di una civiltà relativamente assai avanzata; dei dayachi della vicina isola di Borneo, di alta statura, dai lineamenti belli, celebri per le loro stragi che valsero loro il titolo di tagliatori di teste; dei siamesi, dal viso romboidale e gli occhi dai riflessi giallastri, dei cocincinesi dalla tinta gialla e il capo adorno di una coda smisurata e poi degli indiani, dei bughisi, dei giavanesi, dei tagali delle Filippine e infine dei *negritos* con delle testi enormi ed i lineamenti ributtanti. (*Le tigri di Mompracem* 11)

(There were some Malayans, rather short in size but as vigorous and agile as monkeys, their faces square and bony, dusky in colour. These men were famous for their daring and ferocity. There were some Bataks, their complexions even darker, and notorious for their appetite for human flesh in spite of their relatively quite advanced civilization. The Dayaks from the nearby island of Borneo were tall and handsome, and well known for the massacres that gave them the name of headhunters. The Siamese had diamond-shaped faces and eyes with yellowish reflections. Yellow in complexion, the people from Cochin China had extravagant ponytails adorning their heads. There were also Indians, Buginese, and Javanese, Tagalogs from the Philippine Islands and, lastly, some Negritos with enormous heads and revolting features.)

Salgari's inventorial technique provides an exhaustive exhibit, in one single time and space, of the most characteristic traits of an assorted ethnic milieu. Rather than merely amassing the variety of the world onto his pages with the omnivorous appetite of a modern Rabelais, Salgari carefully catalogues this world according to specific evaluative criteria. These criteria are the same that arranged humanity from its most 'primitive' to its most 'civilized' specimens in many World's Fairs' 'History of Humanity' exhibits. Indeed, evaluative inventories constitute the most frequent technique in Salgari's fiction. One may think of many other significant examples, such as the vivid description of Sandokan's ship, which gathers representatives of all the races of the Malay Archipelago, or the *kasbah* of *Le pantere di Algeri* (The Panthers of Algiers), which displays 'tutto il mondo musulmano' (all the Muslim world) (115) by parading through it a lively catalogue of human types, their physical and moral characteristics equally on full display:

Passavano gli snelli Cabili coi loro ampi mantelli di pelo di capra e le cinture riboccanti d'armi; i più fieri e bellicosi figli dell'Algeria, che dovevano, duecent'anni più tardi, dare tanto filo da torcere ai francesi e acquistarsi tanta rinomanza come guerrieri indomiti. Mori dall'aspetto maestoso, i nobili della Barberia, avvolti nei loro ricchi burnus bianchi e con le splendide fasce di seta variegata piene d'armi di gran valore; arabi dalla lunga barba, dai lineamenti vivi, gli occhi nerissimi e scintillanti, la pelle bruna, indossanti ampie camicie e con in capo colossali turbanti; Thuareg del Sahara, riconoscibili anche da lontano per il loro incedere cadenzato e i loro costumi neri; Fellah somiglianti a colossi di porfido, con la fronte bassa, gli occhi molto grandi e le sopracciglia folte; turchi risplendenti

d'oro e d'argento, poi negri di tutte le razze dell'interno, che schiamazza-
vano e ridevano allegramente, facendo brillare le loro due file di denti
bianchi, sgranando in modo curioso i loro occhi di porcellana. (116–17)

(Many were passing by: slim Kabyles, their flowing sheepskin cloaks and
belts loaded with weapons, Algeria's proudest and most belligerent sons,
who would become such a hard match for the French two hundred years
later, and gain much fame as indomitable warriors; Moors of majestic
appearance, the nobles of Barbary, wrapped in their rich white burnouses,
their splendid multicoloured silk sashes brimming with arms of great
worth; Arabs with long beards and lively features, shining black eyes and
brown skin, wearing wide shirts and colossal turbans; Saharian Tuaregs,
recognizable even from afar by their cadenced gait and black outfits; fell-
ahs resembling porphyry colossi, with low foreheads, enormous eyes and
thick eyebrows; Turks, all glittering in gold and silver; then blacks from all
the races of the interior, happily yelling and laughing, flashing their two
rows of white teeth and opening their porcelain eyes in an odd way.)

Salgari's syntactic choice to build his human pageant from the dynamic
imperfect tense of the verb 'passavano' gives visual immediacy and a cinematic mobility to this passage. We imagine a stationary observer positioned in a location favourable to surveying the scene, and for whose
entertainment the pageant is being staged. Physical location is the
objective correlative of the observer's ontological situation, a situation
that presupposed the centrality and stability of the Western self before
the processing of all other identities.

In spite of its lexical richness and its comprehensive ambition at com-
pleteness, Salgari's narratives structure the variety of the real according
to a restricted number of morphological paradigms. While evoking
mimetic accuracy, Salgari's exotic descriptions present a unitary and
consistent universe, the elements of which are systematized and
arranged as in a World's Fair exhibit. Having reached the fixity of the
map and the atlas, Salgari's exotic emporia reproduce the totalizing and
all-encompassing logic of the mind, and the unchanging closure of the
text. The citations above demonstrate how Salgari inserts human groups
into racial, ethnic, and religious categories that he defines by sets of predetermined and stable features. Consequently, the exoticism and difference evoked in Salgari's world do not compromise his intended
audience's understanding: just like botanical and animal species in a
manual of natural science, Salgari neatly packages complex and multi-

faceted human realities according to reductionist categories of European definition.

Salgari's narrative expositions exorcize all the dynamism, transformations, uncertainties, and incongruities of the world of historical becoming through a handful of fixed standards, static grids, and binary opposites. In *I misteri della jungla nera*, for example, Salgari justifies his protagonist's use of torture with a claim of moral and racial absolutism: 'far parlare il prigioniero [non è] cosa tanto facile essendo gli indiani più cocciuti delle pelli-rosse dell'America' (forcing the prisoner to talk [is not] very easy because the Indians are more stubborn than the American red-skins) (287). In *I predoni del Sahara* (The Raiders of the Sahara), Salgari displays a world in which each human being is a typical representative of one of two tribal groups, and thus excludes all that is casual, unexplainable, or merely randomly organized from the written page:

Due razze, egualmente feroci e ladre, si disputano l'impero del Sahara: I Tibbù ed i Tuareg.

I primi ... preferiscono ricorrere più all'astuzia che alla violenza per derubare i cammellieri ed i trafficanti ed in ciò non hanno rivali.

Dotati di agilità estrema, si nascondono delle giornate intere fra le sabbie, aspettando che qualche cammello si sbandi per alleggerirlo subito del suo carico e che i cammellieri si addormentino per saccheggiarli completamente.

I Tuareg ... sono tutti musulmani fanatici, che odiano ferocemente gli infedeli, anzi si fanno un merito a ucciderli, ma conoscono malamente il Corano ... Quando sanno che [una carovana] è in marcia, vi piombano addosso come uno stormo di avvoltoi e se non riescono ad ottenere un grosso diritto di passaggio, sterminano fino all'ultimo cammellieri e trafficanti. (129)

(Two equally ferocious and thieving races compete for the Saharan empire: the Tibbu and the Tuareg.

The Tibbu ... prefer to use cunning rather than violence in order to rob the camel drivers and traders, and, in doing so, they have no rivals. Endowed with exceptional agility, they hide among the sand dunes for days on end, waiting for some camel to break from the pack in order to quickly relieve it of its load, or for the camel drivers to fall asleep to rob them of everything.

All the Tuareg ... are fanatical Muslims who ferociously hate the infidels and take pride in murdering them, though they hardly know the Koran ...

When they know that [a caravan] is approaching, they descend upon it like
a flock of vultures and, if they are unable to obtain a huge right of passage,
they exterminate all the camel drivers and traders, down to the last one.)

By assertively dealing with both physical and moral characteristics in the
same passage, Salgari implies that the correlation between the two is
already established by universal agreement. He thus popularizes the
racialist-deterministic argument that the looks and behaviour of individuals depend on their 'group membership' as expounded in the scientific and philosophical works of Buffon, Renan, Taine, Gobineau, and
Le Bon.[6] Asked to explain his acts of courage in the face of certain
defeat, Kammamuri, the faithful servant of Sandokan's friend Tremal-
Naik, has only to state 'Sono maharatto' (I am a Mahratti) to have Yanez
conclude that Kammamuri could not have acted differently given that
he belongs to 'una razza che ha buon nome' (a race that has a good
name) (*I pirati* 14).

Salgari postulates a radical determinism when he implicitly equates
races with animal species. This does not merely mean that he believes
that there is the same distance between two races as between, say, horses
and donkeys. Salgari also supports the idea that the same unitary laws
govern both natural and human histories. He imaginatively engages
with this philosophical argument by creating a narrative world where
human beings are mirror images of animal species, and vice versa. Both
Sandokan and Tremal-Naik are compared to tigers, with which they
share keen instincts, ferocity, and power: '[Sandokan] si raccolse su se
stesso come una tigre che sta per lanciarsi sulla preda' ([Sandokan]
crouched down like a tiger preparing to jump on its prey) (*Le tigri* 20).
Darma, Tremal-Naik's tiger, has human traits and, like her master, is
faithful, cunning, and fearless. In Salgari's novels, men and animals
prowl liminal jungles and inhabit primeval oceans where men have the
murderous fierceness of wild beasts and animals are anthropomorphized in a context of predatory manliness, where only the fittest and
the bravest are bound to survive.

The recurring narratives of the premeditated and lethal struggles
between humanized animals (an orang-utan and a panther in *Le tigri di
Mompracem*, a tiger and a rhinoceros in *I misteri della jungla nera*, an elephant and a large crocodile in *Le due tigri*) create narrative sub-plots that
emphasize, by way of analogy, the sly strategies with which human foes
carry out their deadly battles. Obviously, these sequences display the
belated influence of a Darwinism tailored for entertainment and mass

consumption. More than that, however, Salgari creates a narrative universe in which the natural and human spheres are so interdependent that they consistently reflect and replicate each other. There is no place for ambiguity on Salgari's stage, where every prop and element of scenery serves to gloss his characters' feelings, which are thus theatrically externalized and enlarged to cosmic proportions. Sandokan's first appearance in *Le tigri di Mompracem* eloquently demonstrates this point:

> [Sandokan] aprì la porta, s'inoltrò con passo fermo fra le trincee che difendevano la capanna e si fermò sull'orlo della gran rupe, alla cui base ruggiva furiosamente il mare.
>
> Stette là alcuni minuti colle braccia incrociate, fermo come la rupe che lo reggeva, aspirando con voluttà i tremendi soffi della tempesta e spingendo lo sguardo sullo sconvolto mare, poi si ritirò lentamente, rientrò nella capanna. – Quale contrasto! – esclamò. –Al di fuori l'uragano e di qua io! Quale il più tremendo? (*Le tigri di Mompracem* 6)

> ([Sandokan] opened his door, walked with a steady pace across the trenches that protected his hut, and stopped on the edge of the great cliff, at the bottom of which the ocean furiously roared.
>
> He rested a few minutes, his arms crossed, immobile as the cliff upon which he was standing, eagerly breathing in the storm's tremendous gusts and peering into the distraught ocean. Then, he slowly moved back and returned to his hut. – What a contrast! – he exclaimed. – The storm outside and I right here. Which one is the most fearsome?)

The spectacle of the contrast between the power of man and that of nature illustrates Sandokan's awesome and combative character. This spectacle also conceals an underlying analogy, as Salgari conjures up all the clichés of the natural sublime (the stormy night, the cliffs, the raging ocean) in order to mirror the anthropological sublime embodied in his formidable hero.

Indeed, Salgari's narratives generate vacuum-sealed and self-reflective worlds. The islands in Sandokan's Malay archipelago, separated from one another by the ocean, and the unique environments of Tremal-Naik's Gangetic delta (islands, marshes, clearings, and jungles) provide variety within clear-cut boundaries. By thus affording both diversity and systemic closure, these environments allow their interpreters to categorize all their assorted yet numbered features, reduce them to a fixed formula, and thus explain them once and for all.

Salgari and the Adventure-Tale Formula

The systemic closure of Salgari's expositionary writing is both confirmed and challenged by the generic model that hosts it, that of the adventure tale. A latecomer to the great literary season of the adventure novel, Salgari capitalized on this narrative genre's standardized and predictable forms. Whether stressing the universality of the adventure novel's recurring archetypes or, rather, arguing for the cultural specificity of repeating story patterns, critics of popular fiction agree that the adventure tale's narrative formulas have the important function of providing their readers with a sense of literary déjà vu. The adventure novel, in other words, operates within a shared 'network of assumptions' that both responds to and helps define a certain culture's value system, its basic moods and concerns, and its dominant ideological beliefs. As Robert Warshow convincingly argues, 'conventions [impose] themselves upon the general consciousness and become the accepted vehicle of a particular set of attitudes and a particular aesthetic effect' (85). As they determine a community of readers' largely pre-established response to a text, the adventure tale's controlled and formulaic imaginative landscapes elicit escapism over engagement, passive gratification over systematic critical analysis, and devotion to time-hallowed narrative types over innovative ones. By providing relaxation, entertainment, and diversion, formulaic narratives constitute foolproof investments for audiences, writers, and publishers alike:

> Audiences find satisfaction and a basic emotional security in a familiar form; in addition, the audience's past experience with a formula gives it a sense of what to expect in new individual examples, thereby increasing its capacity for understanding and enjoying the details of a work. For creators, the formula provides a means for the rapid and efficient production of new works ... For publishers ... the production of formulaic works is a highly rationalized operation with a guaranteed minimal return as well as the possibility of large profits for particularly popular individual versions. (Cawelti 9)

If adventure novels depend on standardized structures and familiar themes, they demand novelty as well. Obviously, individual versions of an adventure formula must possess some unique and original features to inspire interest and curiosity: the vitality and resilience of the adventure tale rests on an individual author's ability to inject elements of novelty into the genre's airtight and formulaic structures. In particular, the destabilizing elements and forms of ambiguity that sneak into the adventure tale's prefabricated mould help to both renew the genre and inspire critical evaluation of what has been somewhat dismissively termed the adventure novel's 'artistry of escape' (Cawelti 14).

More importantly, as its etymology suggests, the term 'adventure' refers to all that is yet to come (*ad-venire*). By definition, the narrative time of adventure is that of an action-packed present rolling full steam ahead into an uncharted and open-ended future. Remote from everyday routines, adventurous feats conventionally thrive on suspense and elicit surprise, thwarting expectations, beating all odds, and reversing causal logic and deterministic closure. Arguably, the dynamics of suspense and surprise can undergo a process of standardization as well. Often the outcome of a suspenseful action provokes pleasure precisely because it confirms and conforms to a set of specific assumptions. 'Originality,' Warshow explains, 'is to be welcomed only in the degree that it intensifies the expected experience without altering it' (85). While we revel in the temporary sense of uncertainty and risk that all adventures entail, we trust that, in spite of all appearances, the machinery of salvation will work at just the right time, and the hero will ultimately triumph (Cawelti 17).

In his massive production, Salgari often turned generic conventions into stereotypes – transforming the typical into the clichéd. On the other hand, and equally often, Salgari skilfully spiced up the genre's conventional ingredients with new and exotic touches. He estranged familiar themes and narrative structures and also revitalized stereotypical characters by altering them in some meaningful way. Salgari's formulaic 'recycling' confirmed existing definitions of the world and, conversely, questioned the very ideological consensus it helped create. The notes of tension and the dissonant touches that Salgari interspersed in his narrative scores managed to upset the standard harmonies and predictable content of his otherwise formulaic plots.

Whether set in North Africa or India, the Far West or the South Pole, Salgari's adventures follow the genre's formulaic imperatives in that they emphasize action over thought. Salgari well knew that to be adventurous, actions must be exciting, unusual, risky, and violent; they must challenge or place themselves beyond the law and, often, on the very frontier of 'civilization.' As a cursory look at his titles demonstrates, Salgari's action-packed adventures occur in a world of men, and the values that Salgari expounds are tied to the ideology of masculinity typical of most adventure narratives. In his study of the adventure novel in Germany, Volker Klotz points out that adventure heroes are champions of the surface and protagonists of the body. In Salgari's adventures, as in Alexandre Dumas's *Les trois mousquetaires*, the focus is on bodies in action: bodies running, fighting, leaping, duelling, pursuing or being pursued, killing or being killed. Like most writers of adventure tales, Salgari arranges his narrative events so as to display the body's power as well as its vulnerability in conditions of extreme duress. Storms and other natural disasters, shipwrecks, mutinies, battles, and ambushes are the backdrops that emphasize the characters' heroics, their externalized actions, utterly devoid of psychological depth, irony, and introspection.

Besides being in physical motion, in adventure novels the hero's body constantly undergoes transformation and change. Wounded, starved, poisoned, tortured, tattooed, disfigured, disguised, concealed, and, eventually, revealed, this body governs the textual diegesis while maintaining an immobile core: the hero's absolute and undeveloping self. Like the grand epic protagonists of which they are the popular offspring, adventure heroes – as well as the spaces they inhabit – can be identified by a clear-cut and overarching quality: Sandokan is as 'formidable' as Ulysses was astute, and Yanez as cunning as Achilles was strong. Tremal-Naik is fearless, while his antagonist, Suyodhana, is wicked. Mompracem, Sandokan's island, is as wild as its ruler.

Psychological variety, albeit of the most superficial kind, is not an individual trait, but a collective one. The kind of male comradeship that flourishes on Sandokan's ship or among Dumas's musketeers identifies a group protagonist whose collective traits give variety to a complete and self-enclosed universe. Interdependent and mutually inclusive, these characters define a few essential archetypes: strength, astuteness, resilience, competitiveness, and brotherhood. In their individual exceptionality and collective wholeness they people an exotic and extraordinary realm, and are detached from the here and now of everyday life, as well as from the vagaries and uncertainties of historical becoming. They belong to the highly stylized world of legend and the completely actualized space of myth, fable, and romance. 'Piccolo, imperfetto ma inconfondibile maestro nell'arte di fondare l'unità del mondo nella parola' ('Small, imperfect, yet inimitable master in the art of creating the unity of the world in his writing') in Claudio Magris's affectionate words, Salgari was the last master of the epic absolute:

Il mito ... è un racconto delle origini che fonda una tradizione e dà forma al reale ... Sandokan fonda Mompracem, che prima di lui è amorfa ed anonima, Tremal-Naik costruisce la sua capanna di cacciatore, prima della quale nella Jungla Nera non c'è nulla ...

Il mondo di Salgari è ricco di peculiarità e di diversità pittoresche ed esotiche, ma ogni dettaglio convalida la legge e rimanda a una classe generale: il coraggio, la fedeltà, la viltà, l'amicizia. La sua epica ignora l'anomalia, la dissonanza, l'assurdità e ribadisce il noto sino all'iperbole: i *maharatti* sono sempre impavidi ... gli eroi sono alti più di sei piedi, Yanez fuma sempre l'ennesima sigaretta ...

Non c'è frattura, discontinuità, banalità, tutto è alto, sublime, eroico. [...] Ogni elemento ed ogni sentimento sono assoluti; non c'è pluralità di livelli stilistici ma un'unità di tono che esprime l'unità del mondo; l'epiteto esornativo, lo stereotipo omerico rassicura e conferma l'identità degli uomini e delle cose. (153–4)

(Myth ... is a narrative of origins that founds a tradition and gives shape to reality ... Sandokan founds Mompracem, which before him was formless and unnamed, Tremal-Naik builds his hunting hut, before which there was nothing in the Black Jungle ...

The world of Salgari is rich in picturesque diversity and exotic peculiarities, but each detail validates the law and leads back to a general category: courage, faithfulness, cowardice, friendship. His epic ignores anomalies, dissonance, and absurdity and repeats the known to a hyperbolic degree: the Maharatas are always courageous ... the heroes are more than six feet tall, Yanez is always smoking his next cigarette ...

There is no gap, discontinuity, banality. All is high, sublime, and heroic ... All details and all feelings are absolute; there is no plurality of stylistic registers, only a tonal unity that expresses the unity of the world. The essential epithet, the Homeric stereotype assures and confirms the identity of people and things.)

Magris's interpretation captures one of the essential features of Salgari's popular epic. However, in his own yearning for exegetical harmony, Magris neglects an equally important, albeit contradictory, facet of Salgari's fiction. What Magris fails to face is the formidable foe that besieges the absolute unity of Salgari's epic world, and this foe is historical change – the passing of time. The mythical founding of Mompracem belongs to the already said, the untold tale that precedes the first page of Salgari's jungle cycle. The narrative present thus alters formulaic conventions by choosing not to depict a bygone and self-enclosed world, but a transitional age, still brimming with epic grandeur yet already tarnished and unable to dispel the ravages of time:

> Tra un labirinto di trincee sfondate, di terrapieni cadenti, di stecconati divelti, di gabbioni sventrati presso i quali scorgevansi ancora armi infrante e ossa umane, una vasta e solida capanna s'innalzava, adorna sulla cima di una grande bandiera rossa con nel mezzo una testa di tigre.
>
> Una stanza di quell'abitazione è illuminata, le pareti sono coperte di pesanti tessuti rossi, di velluti e di broccati di gran pregio, ma qua e là sgualciti, strappati e macchiati, e il pavimento scompare sotto un alto strato di tappeti di Persia, sfolgoranti d'oro, ma anche questi lacerati e imbrattati.
>
> Nel mezzo sta un tavolo d'ebano intarsiato di madreperla e adorno di fregi d'argento, carico di bottiglie e di bicchieri del più puro cristallo; negli angoli si rizzano grandi scaffali in parte rovinati, zeppi di vasi riboccanti di braccialetti d'oro, di orecchini, di anelli, di medaglioni, di preziosi arredi sacri contorti o schiacciati ... In un canto sta un divano turco colle frange qua e là strappate, in un altro un *armonium* di ebano colla tastiera sfregiata. (*Le tigri di Mompracem* 4)

(A large and solid hut stood among a maze of smashed trenches, crumbling embankments, torn-up fences, and gutted earthworks, near which one could still see broken weapons and human bones. A large red flag with a tiger's head in the middle adorned the top of the hut.

A room in that hut is lit up. Heavy red draperies and valuable velvets and brocades cover the walls, but here and there they are creased, torn, and stained. The floor disappears under a thick layer of Persian rugs, ablaze with gold, but these too are torn and soiled.

In the middle there is an ebony table inlaid with mother-of-pearl and adorned with silver decorations. It is full of bottles and glasses of the purest crystal. In the corners there are large shelves, partly damaged, crowded with vases filled to the brim with gold bracelets, earrings, rings, medallions, and precious church ornaments, all twisted and crushed ... In a corner there is a Turkish divan, its fringes here and there torn off; in another corner there is an ebony harmonium with a badly scratched keyboard.)

If the great realist novelists, from Honoré de Balzac to Henry James, introduced meticulous expositions of chosen interiors as correlatives of both their protagonists' sensibilities and their purses, Salgari *exoticised* this bourgeois convention. Sandokan's living room mirrors its owner's violent and expansive soul – his bountiful yet wounded temperament. It also carries a melancholy undertone, and with its marred riches and broken objects it becomes the icon of a lost golden age. An injured and violated paradise, Sandokan's exotic world has indeed seen better days.

In this context, and in spite of its wildly imaginary plots, the chronology of Salgari's jungle cycle becomes historically meaningful. While there are no specific dates to situate the events occurring in the cycle's first volume, *Le tigri di Mompracem*, the fact that Salgari identifies Sandokan's arch-enemy in James Brooke, the British raja who historically ruled over Saravak between 1841 and 1863, allows us to place the narrated events within this time frame. Salgari becomes more explicit in *I misteri della jungla nera*, which starts on 16 May 1855 and narrates Tremal-Naik's efforts to liberate a beautiful maiden, Ada, from a sect of brutal Thugs. A caesura abruptly separates the first and the second parts of the novel. The second half of the novel introduces Ada's father, reporting his vain attempts to find his daughter following her kidnapping on 24 August 1853. Since he mentions that four years have gone by without his being able to recover his daughter, we infer that the caesura has covered two years, and that the narrative present is 1857. *I pirati della Malesia*, a sequel to *I misteri della jungla nera*, presents a chronological inconsistency, as it is set in 1856, one year before the events narrated in *I misteri*. *I pirati della Malesia* sheds light on the chronology of *Le tigri di Mompracem*, as it contains a summary of Sandokan's previous adventures that place the events of *Le tigri* in 1852. Finally, *Le due tigri* is set in 1857, another chronological discrepancy, since it recounts events that befall Ada and Tremal-Naik's own daughter, Darma, who is supposed to be four years old. However, this would place Darma's birth at a time that precedes Ada and Tremal-Naik's first encounter, as narrated in *I misteri della jungla nera*.

Salgari's chronological inconsistencies may in part be the result of his hurried writing style and of his oft-lamented inability to get access to his books' proofs to correct them. However, one should also consider how these temporal compressions effectively increase the action-packed atmosphere of Salgari's novels. Caught in this condensed chronology and the action-and-reaction of scenes of injustice and vengeance, capture and escape, and plot and counterplot, readers get the impression that numberless events are rushing to take place almost at the same time. Salgari indeed accelerates the motor of history in a world conventionally represented as following nature's slower and monotonous rhythms.

Salgari's narrative technique is particularly effective because, inconsistencies aside, the chronology of Salgari's jungle cycle refers to one of the tensest periods in the relationship between the British crown and its Indian colonies, and one of its most historically eventful. Although utterly imaginary, Sandokan's adventures partake of the historical turmoil that exploded in the Indian rebellion of 1857, and the first jungle cycle culminates in the bloody siege of Delhi, which Sandokan and his friends witness in *Le due tigri*. However, in spite of all his externalized heroics and adventurous hyperactivity, in this transitional age Sandokan is a spectator and victim rather than a maker of history. Comparable to other memorable protagonists in Italian letters, from Alessandro Manzoni's Count of Carmagnola to Giuseppe Tomasi di Lampedusa's Prince Fabrizio of Salina, Sandokan is not the typical hero of the epic adventure tale in that he does not engage in mythical, foundational acts. His continually renewed battle is indeed one of survival, as he musters all his skills to delay the impending end of the very world in which he lives:

> L'incrociatore si avanzava rapidamente mostrando il suo acuto sperone e rompendo le tenebre ed il silenzio con un furioso cannoneggiamento.
>
> Il *praho*, vero giuocattolo di fronte a quel gigante a cui bastava un solo urto per mandarlo a picco spaccato in due, con un'audacia incredibile assaliva pure, cannoneggiando meglio che poteva.
>
> La partita però, come aveva detto Sandokan, non era eguale, anzi era troppo disuguale. Nulla poteva tentare quel piccolo legno contro quella poderosa nave costruita in ferro, e armata potentemente.
>
> L'esito finale, malgrado il valore disperato delle tigri di Mompracem, non doveva essere difficile ad indovinare ... Due minuti dopo ... il loro legno, oppresso dai tiri delle artiglierie nemiche, non era altro che un rottame ... Sandokan comprese che l'ultima ora stava per suonare per le tigri di Mompracem. La sconfitta era completa. Non era più possibile far fronte a quel gigante che vomitava ogni istante nembi di proiettili. Non rimaneva che tentare l'abbordaggio, una pazzia poiché nemmeno sul ponte dell'incrociatore la vittoria poteva arridere a quei valorosi. (*Le tigri di Mompracem* 33–4)

> (The cruiser advanced rapidly displaying its sharp ram, and breaking the darkness and silence with its furious cannon fire.
>
> The *praho*, really just a toy before that giant, a single blow from which would have split it in half and sunk it, fought back with incredible daring, firing its cannons as best it could.
>
> As Sandokan had stated, the battle was not even, in fact it was very unbal-

anced. That little boat could do nothing against that heavily gunned iron ship.

The final outcome, in spite of the desperate valour of the tigers of Mompracem, would not have been difficult to guess ... Two minutes later ... the *praho*, overwhelmed by the shots of the enemy artillery, was nothing but a wreck ... Sandokan realized that the last hour was about to strike for the tigers of Mompracem. The defeat was total. It was no longer possible to withstand that giant that continued to spit out clouds of shots. All they could do was attempt to board it, a desperate act since even such brave men could not hope to win on the cruiser's deck either.)

The doomed struggle between Sandokan's *praho* and the British warship is a struggle between past and present, tribal craftsmanship and Western technology, hopeless human valour and contemptuous mechanical violence.

By sympathizing with the defeated outsiders – the people whom history will soon leave behind – Salgari situates his narrative space at the antipodes of canonic Western adventure tales, which had typically celebrated the triumphs of Western nationalism and imperialism. From *Robinson Crusoe* to the *Leatherstocking Tales*, adventure narratives gave imaginative consistency to what Martin Green defines as 'the empire-building explosion of the white race outward toward the rest of the world' (10) and recorded the 'experiences and the dreams of this race's adventurers and heroes – its explorers, engineers, army generals, and governors' (23). Green concludes that precisely that expansion has been *the* epic story of modern history, as seen from the eyes of white people. Green prefers to use the term 'white' when other authors use 'Western,' because he argues that it was 'precisely the whiteness that mattered to the adventure readers and to the other peoples who faced the thrust of Europe and its colonists' (10–11). Europe and North America, in particular, considered themselves as the bearers of the modern adventure spirit and consequently of the adventure tale as well.

One of the undisputed masterpieces in the genre of the adventure novel, Daniel Defoe's *Robinson Crusoe* perfected the archetypal theme of a solitary individual having to explore and master (and if possible profitably exploit) an alien environment.[7] If not as forcefully as Edward Said in his *Culture and Imperialism* (1993), critics have extensively argued that the story of Robinson's Protestant and Enlightenment values – his quiet efficiency, practical intelligence, adaptability, and thrift brought to fruitfully bear upon the wild new world of the deserted island – constitutes the imaginative rendition of England's ideology of overseas expansion.[8] Robinson Crusoe provided such a flexible imaginative template that a new sub-genre soon emerged, and, for over a century, the *Robinsonaden* reproposed familiar themes with changed details. After the international success of novels such as Johann David Wyss's *The Swiss Family Robinson* (1812) and Jules Verne's *The Mysterious Island* (1874), Salgari's *I Robinson italiani* (1896) was a somewhat tired attempt to apply the author's rich encyclopedic and expositionary writing to a topic of tested popular appeal.[9]

Complicating his own token acceptance of these 'imperialistic' literary paradigms, Salgari's jungle cycle estranges the master narrative of Western adventure by having non-Western eyes replace the perspective of the winners and the conquerors. The jungle cycle's most famous positive hero, Sandokan, is non-white and a Muslim. Twice-removed from Western models, Sandokan nevertheless demands assent from his Western readers, who admire his strange and darkly handsome looks and marvel at his extraordinary deeds:

> [Sandokan] è di statura alta, slanciata, dalla muscolatura potente, dai lineamenti energici, maschi, fieri e d'una bellezza strana. Lunghi capelli gli cadono sugli omeri: una barba nerissima gli incornicia il volto leggiermente abbronzato.
>
> ... Egli era il formidabile capo dei feroci pirati di Mompracem, era l'uomo che da dieci anni insanguinava le coste della Malesia, l'uomo che per ogni dove aveva dato terribili battaglie, l'uomo la cui straordinaria audacia, e il suo indomito coraggio gli avevano valso il nomignolo di Tigre della Malesia. (*Le tigri di Mompracem* 4–8).

> ([Sandokan] is tall and slim, with powerful muscles and vigorous, manly, and proud features, of strange beauty. Long hair falls on his shoulders and a jet-black beard frames his lightly tanned face.
>
> ... He was the formidable leader of the ferocious pirates of Mompracem. He was the man who for ten years had soaked the Malay coasts in blood; he who had engaged in dreadful battles everywhere. He was the man whose extraordinary daring and unvanquished courage had granted him the nickname of the Malayan Tiger.)

The conventional ethnocentrism evident in Salgari's novels appears to coexist with a full-fledged exoticism, in spite of the fact that the two ideologies are diametrically opposed. If the ethnocentrist argues that his or her values are superior to all others, the exoticist claims that the country with higher values is the one whose only significant characteristic is that it is not his or her own (Todorov 297). As an exoticist, Salgari asks his readers to admire Sandokan precisely because of his otherness, and this admiration implies a process of identification with a protagonist whose goals and beliefs are in sharp opposition to those of the imperial West. It is not surprising that Salgari's formulaic narrative world thrives on a notion of racial difference based on a crude moral binarism. Like other formulaic artists such as Ian Fleming, John Buchan, or Sax Rohmer, Salgari builds his plots around elementary conflicts and exploits race as a convenient way of channelling these conflicts. Unlike Fleming, Buchan, or Rohmer, however, Salgari's bogeyman does not have 'slanted eyes' or black skin. Salgari's despicable villain and Sandokan's arch-enemy is James Brooke, the man whose pale complexion and icy gaze condenses all of the evil, hypocrisy, and brutality of the West.

Though bound by the limitations of his formulaic representations of East and West as binary opposites, Salgari nevertheless rocked the West's moral boat by creating a non-European hero. Even when Salgari overcomes the racial divide – as is the case of the interracial brotherhood between Sandokan and his Portuguese companion, Yanez de Gomera – he does so by valuing Sandokan's otherness over Yanez's Europeanness. Undoubtedly, Sandokan and Yanez complement each other in a way that leaves racial stereotypes unaltered. Yanez represents logic and shrewdness; Sandokan stands for unbridled passion and brutal strength. Predictably, the two men's combined skills allow them to outwit their enemies and overcome all odds. Ultimately, however, it is the mind that submits itself to the heart, and narrative impasses often resolve themselves when Yanez's Western pragmatism gives way to Sandokan's idealized heroism and impulsive actions. If interracial duos are not rare in adventure novels (one thinks of Natty Bumppo and Chingachgook, Ishmael and Queequeg, and Huckleberry Finn and Jim), Salgari turns conventions upside down as he selects the non-white 'outsider' as the unquestioned leader, moral barometer, and pole of attraction in narratives intended for all-white bourgeois audiences. To sum up, while readers admire Yanez, there is no doubt that they wish to be Sandokan.

But how did Italian, and Western readers in general, comfortably identify with Sandokan, since this identification implies assent to Sandokan's virulent anti-imperial ideology and hatred of the West's white and Christian civilization? Salgari repeatedly reminds his readers that Sandokan's prime foe is England, and European aggression and colonialism are the ultimate wrongs that he and his people suffer. Predating the narrative time frame, this monumental offence crops up in summaries that, throughout the jungle cycle, Sandokan or other characters provide in narrative moments of great intensity:

> [Sandokan] aveva vent'anni quando salì sul trono di Muluder [sic], un regno che trovavasi presso le coste settentrionali del Borneo. Forte come un leone, fiero come un eroe dell'antichità, audace come una tigre, coraggioso fino alla pazzia, in poco volger di tempo vinse tutti i popoli vicino estendendo le proprie frontiere fino al regno di Varauni e al fiume Koti.
>
> Quelle imprese gli furono fatali. Inglesi e olandesi, gelosi di quella nuova potenza che pareva volesse soggiogare l'intera isola, si allearono al sultano di Borneo per fiaccare l'audace guerriero.
>
> L'oro dapprima e le armi più tardi, finirono per squarciare il nuovo reame. Dei traditori sollevarono i vari popoli, dei sicari prezzolati spensero la madre, i fratelli e le sorelle di Sandokan; delle bande potenti invasero il regno in vari luoghi corrompendo i capi, corrompendo le truppe, saccheggiando, trucidando, commettendo atrocità inaudite.
>
> Invano Sandokan lottò col furore della disperazione, battendo gli uni, schiacciando gli altri. I tradimenti lo raggiunsero nell'istesso suo palazzo, i suoi parenti caddero sotto il ferro degli assassini pagati dai bianchi, ed egli in una notte di fuoco e di stragi poté a malapena salvarsi con una piccola schiera di prodi. (*Le tigri di Mompracem* 152–3)

([Sandokan] was twenty years old when he seated himself on the throne of Malludu, a kingdom on the northern coast of Borneo. He was as strong as a lion, daring as a hero of antiquity, bold as a tiger, and courageous to the point of madness. In a short period, Sandokan had defeated all the neighbouring people and extended his territory's borders to the kingdom of Varauni and the river Koti.

Those deeds proved fatal to him. The English and Dutch became jealous of this new power that seemed bent on taking over the entire island, and allied themselves with the sultan of Borneo to defeat the audacious warrior.

Gold first and weapons later succeeded in ripping the new kingdom apart. Traitors raised the various tribes in rebellion and hired assassins killed Sandokan's mother, brothers, and sisters. Powerful bands invaded Sandokan's kingdom in various locations and bribed the leaders and their troops, while looting, massacring, and committing unheard-of atrocities.

Sandokan struggled with desperate fury, defeating some and crushing others, but all was in vain. Treason caught up with him inside his own palace, and his relatives were felled by the weapons of the assassins that the white people had hired. In a night of fire and slaughter, he was barely able to save himself and a small company of daring followers.)

Literary and extraliterary reasons converge to allow this successful identification process. John Cawelti points out that, because of its escapist thrust, formulaic literature creates a unique psychological bond between audience and protagonist: 'Its purpose is ... to take me out of myself by confirming an idealized self-image' (18). The art of formulaic character creation, in other words, demands the establishment of a bond between the reader and a superior figure who inhabits a 'removed, imaginary world' (17). Because of his superhuman attributes, a character like Sandokan exists in a realm beyond conventional taboos. Within the limits of the written page and unlike in the 'real' world, where rules and restrictions are to be respected, in Salgari's fictional realm the hero can be non-white and fall in love with and marry the fair-skinned and blue-eyed Anglo-Italian Marianna, while enjoying the exclusive bond of homosocial affection with his Portuguese companion. 'Formulas,' writes Cawelti, 'transcend the boundaries and frustration that the reader ordinarily experiences ... [They] embody moral fantasies of a world more exciting, more fulfilling, or more benevolent than the one we inhabit' (38).

This psychological explanation also has ideological ramifications. Undoubtedly, readers sympathize with Sandokan's plea because Salgari depicts his opponent James Brooke as so unequivocally evil that no emotional alliance with him is conceivable. As he compels his readers to despise Brooke, Salgari by extension encourages them to scorn the mercilessly exploitative and violent imperialism that Salgari associates with Great Britain. This does not necessarily mean that Salgari expresses consistent and unequivocal anti-imperialist convictions in his novels. Under its black-and-white moral veneer, Salgari's jungle cycle offers a complex, shifting, and often sketchy rendition of colonial politics. Comparable to the colonial uncertainties that characterized the colonial exhibits at Italian expositions, the jungle cycle's colonial stance remains unresolved. The only undisputable trait is its anti-British emphasis, which underscores the need that Italy felt to break free from the cultural weight of the greatest imperial power in Europe. This need was precisely one of the factors that opened the debate to the possibility of a *different* kind of colonialism, a colonialism Italian-style that, as late as 1911, was still to be invented and ideologically sorted out.

If the basic human contrasts at play in Salgari's novels simplify the identification process between reader and protagonist (we obviously side with the handsome hero and despise the loathsome villain), the association between white bourgeois audience and exotic hero is successful because Sandokan's exoticism is, after all, just skin-deep. While Salgari often reminds his Western readers of Sandokan's racial and religious otherness, he also provides us with elements of deep familiarity. Thus, it is by familiar Christological references that Sandokan and his twelve faithful warriors present themselves as the sacrificial lambs in a world given over to greed, aggression, and murder: 'Non restavano in piedi che dodici uomini, dodici tigri però guidate da un capo il cui valore era incredibile ... Allora i tredici pirati, pazzi di furore, asssetati di vendetta, si slanciarono come un sol uomo all'arrembaggio' (Only twelve men were left alive, but they were twelve tigers, and led by a man whose valour was unbelievable ... The thirteen pirates, crazy with fury and thirsty for vengeance, leaped all together and boarded the enemy ship) (*Le tigri di Mompracem* 34).

Salgari both writes and erases Sandokan's difference as he has him carry out the same formulaic plot functions that mark the heroes of conventional Western adventure tales.[10] More specifically, by giving Sandokan more-than-human features in his hopeless battle against his imperial foe, Salgari typecasts him as an 'avenger hero,' one in a long tradition of popular champions who fearlessly battle against the agents of injustice and untiringly rally support for society's victims: women, the poor, the weak, and the oppressed. After Sandokan loses his kingdom by betrayal,

errò parecchi anni sulle coste settentrionali del Borneo, ora inseguito come belva feroce, ora senza viveri, in preda a miserie inenarrabili, sperando di riacquistare il perduto trono e di vendicare l'assassinata famiglia, fino a che una notte, ormai disperato di tutto, e di tutti, s'imbarcò su di un *praho* giurando guerra atroce a tutta la razza bianca.

... [Sandokan] era forte, era prode, era valente e assetato di vendetta ... Diventò il terrore dei mari, diventò la tigre della Malesia.

... [Sandokan è] un vendicatore che piange sovente sua madre, i suoi fratelli e le sue sorelle cadute sotto il ferro degli assassini, un vedicatore che mai commise azioni infami, che rispettò in ogni tempo i deboli, che risparmiò le donne e i fanciulli, che saccheggiò i nemici suoi non per sete di ricchezza, ma per levare un giorno un esercito di prodi e riacquistare il perduto regno. (*Le tigri di Mompracem* 153) (he roamed for several years along Borneo's northern coast, at times hunted like a wild beast, other times with no food, and subjected to inexpressible woes. Sandokan went on hoping to regain his lost throne and to avenge his murdered family, until one night, despairing of everything and everyone, he boarded a *praho*, swearing to engage in a terrible war against the entire white race.

... Sandokan was strong and daring, valiant and thirsting for vengeance ... He became the terror of the seas, he became the Malayan Tiger.

... [Sandokan] is an avenger who often weeps for his mother, brothers, and sisters who fell under the murderers' iron; an avenger who never committed infamous deeds, who always respected the weak, spared women and children, and did not raid his enemies out of greed for riches but to build a gallant army and conquer his lost kingdom.)

Salgari follows the narrative conventions of a specific sub-genre of the adventure novel, that of the avenger story. Avenger stories typically feature a young man of extraordinary promise and ambition who is wronged, betrayed, jailed, or exiled by the evil intrigues of one or more villains, and barely escapes death. Spurred by an initial act of betrayal, the story concentrates on the hero's return, often under a false identity or in disguise, and narrates his protracted and rightful vengeance (Green 123–4; Cawelti 39–40). Like Rudolf von Gerolstein in Eugene Sue's *Les Mystères de Paris* (1842), Edmond Dantès in Dumas's *Le comte de Monte-Cristo* (1844), Captain Nemo in Jules Verne's *Vingt mille lieues sous les mers* (1870), and Frank von Holfenstein in Karl May's *Der Verlorene Sohn* (1886), Sandokan is one of the many incarnations of the Robin Hood archetype, the hero who inspires unflinching loyalty and demands unconditional emotional support in his fight to protect the defenceless and the virtuous against the wicked and the powerful.[11]

Removed from reality, avenger heroes belong to the world of romance, their actions devoid of historical probability or even biological normality (Sandokan, a godlike figure, routinely dodges bullets and avoids death while everybody around him meets a gruesome end). However, one must not assume that, as romances, these tales carry no ideological weight or historical significance, and that all contemporary relevance becomes lost in the midst of immemorial archetypes. Their links with contemporary politics are symbolic rather than literal. For example, if gothic avenger stories, with their mad monks and wicked barons, marked the Enlightenment middle class's criticism of the corrupt feudal order, their nineteenth-century French descendants lived under the spell of Napoleon. From his quick rise to power, exile at Elba, escape, return to France, and engagement in the Hundred Days campaign, Napoleon became the real-life model for many popular avenger stories, the most famous of which is Dumas's *Le comte de Monte-Cristo*. As is well known, in *Le comte de Monte-Cristo*, Edmond Dantès's fate is associated with Napoleon, as he is betrayed and imprisoned for life at the beginning of the story with the accusation of being a Bonapartist agent plotting to help Napoleon escape from Elba in 1814. Dantès's enemies are therefore Napoleon's enemies, and they become the symbols of the immorality, greed, and hypocrisy of which the France of the Restoration was generally accused (Green 130). As he swims to freedom and proceeds to carry out his vengeance by enlisting his enemies' children against them, Monte-Cristo paints his personal war with the colours of a broader cause. He comes to stand for the rebellion of principled youth against middle-aged compromise, reviving the ideals of the French Revolution in order to shame the realities of the Restoration.[12]

Dumas's novels greatly influenced Salgari's imaginative world, and Salgari followed Dumas's blueprint in building his romance upon historical foundations. Undoubtedly, Dumas's idealized and romanticized portrait of Napoleon could hardly be a viable model in Italy, especially after the experience of Campoformio. Yet, it would be a mistake to follow the majority of Salgari critics in claiming that Sandokan was born *ex nihilo* from Salgari's extravagant imagination. It would be equally difficult to argue that Salgari was eccentrically sustaining values that were completely foreign to the West, given the enormous international success of his novels. Sandokan's alter ego did not begin his odyssey in the remote South China Sea or the rugged island of Corsica, but in the port town of Nizza. This hero was Giuseppe Garibaldi.

A Life Exposed: The Man, the Myth, and the Nation

It is easy to forget, today, that Garibaldi died only a year and a half before Salgari invented Sandokan. The years that followed Garibaldi's death in 1882 featured numerous official celebrations and popular events commemorating *L'Eroe dei Due Mondi* (The Hero of Two Worlds). The protagonist of numberless memoirs, biographies, historical accounts, and fictional adaptations, Garibaldi became the moral backbone of De Amicis's best-selling tearjerker *Cuore*, and chroniclers such as Giulio Cesare Abba, Giuseppe Bandi, and Giuseppe Guerzoni recorded memorable episodes from his military and public career. Early biographers such as Jessie White Mario, Maria Speranza von Schwartz, and George Trevelyan circulated the *Generale*'s life story in Italy and abroad; and Giosuè Carducci, Giovanni Marradi, Cesare Pascarella, Giovanni Pascoli, Aleardo Aleardi, and Gabriele D'Annunzio gave poetic form to Garibaldi's feats. Giovanni Fattori, Domenico Induno, Federico Faruffini and other painters produced official portraits and celebratory canvasses while the illustrations, vignettes, and caricatures included in popular magazines such *L'illustrazione italiana* and *L'illustrazione popolare* made Garibaldi's face well known in every household. Taking the cue from Turin's Museo del Risorgimento nazionale, museums collected and displayed memorabilia that bore witness to his deeds. Staple features at most national and international expositions, the Padiglioni del Risorgimento greatly contributed to the popularization of the Garibaldi saga, especially in its most iconoclastic and anecdotical features. From narratives to paintings, from chocolate wrappers to collector's cards, the red-shirted, poncho-enwrapped *condottiero* permeated all facets and all levels of post-unitary Italian culture.

When Salgari was completing *Le tigri di Mompracem*, Garibaldi had already been turned into a national myth, his life interpreted so as to form the central chapter in Italy's foundational epic. Garibaldi's material existence, in other words, had already been reconfigured into verbal and iconic representations. Textual and visual narratives, in turn, are interesting not because they provide a consensus about who the *true* Garibaldi was and what he *really* did, but because they volunteer important information about the way in which a specific society organizes its historical understanding. It is on the conceptual level of this understanding that the apparently unlikely characters of Garibaldi and Sandokan overcome the historical versus fictional divide and tread common ground by performing the same cultural functions and achieving analogous ideological ends.

Garibaldi's massive presence in Italian culture during the mid- and late-nineteenth century may suffice to justify the claim that Garibaldi influenced Salgari's depiction of Sandokan.[13] However, without discounting these broad cultural connections, a specific text seals the bond between the historical and the fictional hero. This text is *Les Mémoires de Garibaldi* (*The Memoirs of Garibaldi*) as assembled, edited, and expertly filled in by that master of real-life and fictional adventure, Alexandre Dumas. Hypotext for the Sandokan cycle, *The Memoirs of Garibaldi* mixed strong truth-claims with equally obvious fictional details, creating a protagonist who claims referential accuracy while sharing many traits with the heroes of the formulaic narratives, historical romances, and adventure tales that Dumas had so prolifically written.

The author of *Le Comte de Monte-Cristo* and *Les trois mousquetaires* was Garibaldi's friend, chronicler, and fellow soldier. Sharing Garibaldi's republican ideals and determined to 'mingle [his] recital with action' (Dumas, *On Board* 117), Dumas joined the Generale's volunteers in his famed expedition of *I Mille* to Sicily, which he narrated in a series of war letters published in the Parisian *La Presse* and, later, in the volume *Les Garibaldiens: Révolution de Sicile et de Naples* (1861). Bourgeois readers in Paris revelled in the colourful narrative of Dumas's adventures 'with a filibuster' in the exotic south of Europe, and Dumas immediately rewarded his readers' favourable reception with *Les mémoires de Garibaldi*, which *Le Siècle* published serially (*On Board* ix). Issued in book form in 1860, the *Memoirs* became an instant best-seller. Translations into Italian proliferated quickly, and numerous Italian magazines rushed to offer, almost simultaneously, the 'only authorized version' of Dumas's original. Because of their timeliness on the eve of Italy's unification and the consummate readability that Dumas imparted to them, The *Memoirs* had an extraordinary impact on the construction of the Garibaldian myth. However, with the wane of Romanticism and the rise of positivism and realism, *The Memoirs of Garibaldi* began to suffer from their connection with the father of the French *feuilleton* at least as much as they had initially profited from it. Suspiciously regarded as unreliable and heavily fictionalized, the narrative of 'the marvelous events of [Garibaldi's] adventurous career' (Dumas, *Memoirs* 30) became part of a once-young country's picturesque lore. Moreover, after Garibaldi published his own autobiography, the *Memoirs* lost much of their genre's appeal, namely, the first-hand exposition of self-experience, and were quickly forgotten.[14]

The *Memoirs* present an excentric and composite (auto)biography, resulting from the recollections that Garibaldi dictated to Dumas during a stay on Lake Como and from the holograph journals and notes that Garibaldi had entrusted to Dumas. However, Dumas was no mere scribe. Besides editing Garibaldi's own narratives, he also included sections providing background and contextual information that he deemed lacking in Garibaldi's originals. Remarking that Garibaldi was too self-effacing and modest in his own autobiographical efforts, Dumas used accounts that were provided to him by other witnesses to Garibaldi's deeds, such as his comrades Augusto Vecchi, Agostino Bertani, Gaetano Sacchi, and Giacomo Medici (*On Board* 115).

Garibaldi may have been an unpretentious and gruff writer, but his fellowship with Dumas and his familiarity with Dumas's novels demonstrate that he quickly mastered the rules of the adventure tale and learned how to emplot his battlefield heroism to fit the construction of a literary hero. The *Memoirs*, therefore, proved to be doubly useful to Salgari. First, they provided a literary model that, while professing autobiographical truth, exploited a storyteller's devices, fictional topoi, and all the clichés of the adventure novel with consummate skill. Second, unlike later biographies that focused on Garibaldi's Italian feats, the *Memoirs* gave ample space to Garibaldi's youth in Latin America. During Salgari's lifetime, official Italian culture successfully strove to smooth away the Latin American Garibaldi, concentrating instead on the mature Generale whose life was tailored to fit the Italian national epic. This Garibaldi was the courageous yet obsequious military leader whose laconic 'ubbidisco' (I obey) when ordered to stop his victorious advance toward Trent in 1866 spoke for discipline, restraint, and ultimate subservience to royal authority. In sum, this Garibaldi was the suitable model for a new monarchy striving to renounce all revolutionary excesses by emphasizing interclass accord, international diplomacy, dynastic legitimacy, and overall institutional stability.

Dumas's young and brash Garibaldi is a completely different type. Eliminating the randomness and unpredictability of a lived life, Dumas extrapolates from Garibaldi's childhood the events that foreshadow the man he will turn out to be. Thus prefigured, life is turned into a narrative plot, and the allegedly autobiographical record shares all the formal and thematic features of the adventure tale. From the start, young Garibaldi is a free and unconventional spirit, a born rebel with a double cause: a natural passion to protect 'everything that was little, weak and suffering' (*Memoirs* 33), and – quite precociously – a political agenda regarding 'a mother-country to avenge and to set free' (*Memoirs* 35). Garibaldi inherits from his father, a ship's captain, a vocation for sailing the seas, and Dumas singles out a youthful escapade on the Mediterranean to demonstrate that Garibaldi has an 'inclination for a life of adventure' (*Memoirs* 34). The *Memoirs* engage readers with narratives of Garibaldi's early 'voyages to the Levant,' featuring the young sailor from Nice getting his sea legs while witnessing frightful storms and shipwrecks and undergoing capture and despoliation by Greek pirates.

After being sentenced to death for taking part in the patriotic insurrection of 1833–4, Dumas's Garibaldi dons the garb of the avenger hero: pursued, disguised, and under a false identity, he engages in a daring escape from the Sardinian authorities and plans his revenge against those who have wronged him while leading a toilsome existence of 'exile, struggle and persecution' (*Memoirs* 44). Like Sandokan and Monte-Cristo, Garibaldi exists at the margins of 'civilized' society and outside the law: he briefly serves on a Turkish brig and on a war frigate in the service of the Bey of Tunis, and subsequently moves to Rio de Janeiro, where he joins the Mazzinian expatriates and sympathizes with the cause of the newly founded republic of Rio Grande do Sul, which is fighting for independence from the Brazilian empire. It is at this point that Garibaldi's avenging mission acquires a broader scope. Proclaiming himself a champion of the oppressed and the defender of all peoples fighting for liberty, Garibaldi, now thirty, offers his seafaring skills to the Rio Grande's secessionist leadership, who furnishes him with letters of marque to cruise against Brazil and, specifically, to ambush and capture military and commercial ships belonging to the Brazilian government. In a chapter aptly entitled 'A Corsair,' Garibaldi/Dumas writes: 'We fitted out for war the *Mazzini*, a vessel of about thirty tons only, and in this we started coasting. We put to sea with about sixteen companions in adventure. We were sailing under a Republican flag, and were consequently "corsairs." With sixteen men aboard a barque, we were declaring war against an empire' (*Memoirs* 51). Just like Sandokan's *praho*, Garibaldi's barque hosts a motley and cosmopolitan crew of men chosen for their formidable physical prowess, tested loyalty, and boundless courage:

> I had ... a new recruit, a colossal Frenchman, a Breton by birth, whom we used to call 'Gros-Jean,' and another man named François, a true filibuster, and a worthy member of the roving brotherhood ...
>
> The life we led was an active one and full of danger, because of the numerical superiority of our enemy; but, at the same time, it was attractive, picturesque and quite agreeable to my disposition ... The horde which accompanied me, a real cosmopolitan lot, was composed of men of all nations and of all colours. (*Memoirs* 71–2)

By re-baptizing the Mazzini *Farrapilla*, from the Brazilian expression *Farrapos* (ragamuffins), the name that the Brazilian empire had contemptuously given to the inhabitants of the rebel republics of Latin America, Garibaldi overwrites the cause of political independence with the romanticized theme of the revenge of the dispossessed against the all-powerful. By recasting Garibaldi as a kind of seafaring Robin Hood, Dumas simplifies a very fluid and complex political reality involving multiple nations, contrasting ideologies, and conflicting local interests, and presents it under simple dichotomies of tested popular appeal:

> On one side, there was ... strength, wealth and power fighting on behalf of despotism. On the other side, a poor little republic – a dismantled city, an empty treasury, a people without resources and unable to pay their defenders but fighting for their liberties.
>
> Garibaldi did not hesitate a moment. He went straight to the aid of the people and of liberty. (*Memoirs* 164)

It is not surprising that Salgari similarly watered down the historical intricacies of European expansion and competition in the South China Sea, and built his jungle cycle on equally simplistic moral dichotomies. What is interesting is that, in spite of England's powerful political and cultural sway over its European neighbours and in spite of Italy's own budding colonial efforts, Italian readers would still succumb to the spell of the romanticized legacy of the Risorgimento to the point of unanimously choosing the adventure of national freedom and national legitimacy (Sandokan) over that of imperial conquest and colonial expansion (James Brooke).

Garibaldi's and Sandokan's moral economies subsist because, consistent with the spirit of the avenger tale, the two heroes succeed in justifying their rebellion and outlawry by denouncing the hypocrisy and injustice of the dominant laws, and by demonstrating that they are the bearers of a purer and nobler ethos. In his corsair actions, Garibaldi never engages in indiscriminate plunder and violence and is keen on pointing out that despoiling the Imperial ships of their charge should not be regarded as a mere action of piracy, but as serving a higher political goal, that of filling the Republican cause's coffers while intercepting intelligence communications and disrupting the provision of the Imperial troops. Similarly, Sandokan never plunders for the sake of plundering but in order to put an end to his people's subjugation to an invading empire. Violence, in other words, is not an end in itself, but it is justified in the name of a higher justice, a better good, or a restoration of peace. These noble corsairs are quick to reward brave enemies and unfailingly respect women and civilian passengers. Garibaldi's first engagement as a corsair is narrated to expound precisely this moral code:

Whilst I, like some sea-bird, was perched aloft in my observatory, I caught
sight of a schooner sailing under the Brazilian flag ... We ... directed our
course straight upon the schooner ... On hailing her, we made ourselves
known, and called upon her to surrender ... We then boarded her and took
possession.

I next saw a poor devil of a passenger, a Portuguese, coming towards me
with a casket in his hand. He opened it. It was full of diamonds, which he
offered me as a ransom for his life. I closed the box again and handed it
back to him, assuring him that his life was in no danger and that, consequently, he might keep his diamonds for an occasion when they might be
more useful. (*Memoirs* 51)

Salgari's narrative parallels Dumas's: Sandokan's first attack against a
Chinese ship in *Le tigri di Mompracem* serves to establish the moral coordinates of Sandokan's pirate enterprise as he rewards the bravery of the
few survivors by sparing their lives and liberally compensating them for
the loss of their ship (20–1).[15]

Similarly, an almost mortal wound at the inception or at a climactic
point in the hero's adventures conventionally serves the function of
heightening pathos, underscoring the hero's exceptional courage and
resilience and his ability to overcome impossible odds. One could think,
for example, of Ivanhoe being badly wounded at the tournament at
Ashby-de-la-Zouche, Robin Hood receiving a blow to his side in a duel
with Sir Guy of Gisborne, and D'Artagnan's unfortunate skirmish at the
Jolly Miller's tavern in Meung.[16] Garibaldi's first fight against the Imperialists, at the Barranca of San Gregorio (*Memoirs* 60), reaches its climax
when Garibaldi receives a ball between the ear and the carotid artery
and is left senseless on his ship's deck among the wounded and the
dead. In his first major engagement with a British cruiser, Sandokan is
shot in the chest after boarding the enemy ship. Having jumped over-
board to avoid capture, he barely escapes death by drowning. These
brushes with death underscore the enormity of the challenges, losses,
and human expenditure that adventure heroes must accept. Rather
than inspiring self-analysis and spiritual brooding, these dramatic events
are used to point out the worthiness of the hero's cause and the
strength of his unwavering convictions.

Just as their moral landscapes are similar, the settings of Garibaldi's
and Salgari's narratives show comparable features. The analogies
between these distant locales – Garibaldi's Atlantic Ocean with its
islands, the Paranà and La Plata Rivers cutting through the virgin tropical forest, and the lagoon of Los Patos, in the Rio Grande region, on

Garibaldi Boards and Captures the Ship 'Luisa.' Gustavo Sacerdote, *La vita di Giuseppe Garibaldi, secondo i risultati delle più recenti indagini storiche con numerosi documenti inediti.* By permission, Civica Raccolta delle Stampe 'Achille Bertarelli,' Milan, Italy.

one hand; Sandokan's South China Sea with the Malayan islands, and the Indian Sundarbans, with their maze of marshes and rivers flowing into the Ganges and forming its enormous delta, on the other – are possible because they arise from similar descriptive and exotic conventions. More importantly, these distant settings resemble one another because they serve the same narrative function. Following the dictates of the adventure tale, Garibaldi's and Sandokan's wild and sublime environs are both a formidable challenge and a trusted accomplice to them and their daring companions. As we have seen in Salgari's comparison between Sandokan and the stormy ocean, nature becomes the stage on which these heroes' simple ideals are unequivocally and unambiguously acted out – the backdrop that intensifies by force of analogy their charismatic and titanic personalities.

Like Sandokan, Garibaldi suffers the consequences of shipwrecks, loses friends in battle and by drowning, undergoes capture, imprisonment, and torture, and leads his men in battles that are conventionally marked by extraordinary numerical imbalance.[17] One is naturally re-

'Garibaldi is Wounded during an Enemy Boarding.' Illustration by Edoardo Matania for *Garibaldi e i suoi tempi* by Jessie White Mario.

minded of Robin Hood, a land corsair who engages in tireless guerrilla warfare in Sherwood Forest, and who must deal with the sheriff of Nottingham, whose soldiers are far more numerous and better equipped than his own. Similarly, D'Artagnan and the three Musketeers' motto, 'All for one – one for all!' would appear ludicrous, given the overpowering forces the Musketeers take on, were they not always successful. Dumas and Garibaldi make the most of this formula, and treat their readers with a breathtaking account of such disproportionate engagements. Off the Brazilian coast, Garibaldi's two small vessels with a 'horde of seventy men' (*Memoirs* 72) take on the Imperialists armed with thirty warships and a steam ship. Later, Garibaldi's 'three armed vessels' resolutely open a 'very unequal contest' against a war fleet that appears to be 'incomparably stronger' than his own (*Memoirs* 91). In 1842, at the command of a small flotilla flying the flag of the Oriental Republic, the name that the republic of Montevideo (today's Uruguay) had given itself, Garibaldi wages a war against forces four times stronger than his own (*Memoirs* 165). Similarly, land engagements present the same disproportion, as Garibaldi's most devastating battle on the banks of the Uruguay River sees his 190 'giants' face 1,500 imperial troops (*Memoirs* 185). Perhaps the most famous of Garibaldi's battles occurs at Caballu-Cuatia on the Paranà River, where his three ships engage Argentina's seven vessels under the command of the fabled Admiral Brown, until, at the end of the third day of battle, Garibaldi orders his few surviving men to set his ships on fire rather than surrender them to the enemy.

Sandokan, too, consistently engages enemy forces that are 'three or four times more numerous' than his own (*Le tigri* 26). The decision of Yanez's first mate to set the *Marianna*'s powder magazine on fire to avoid relinquishing his ship to the hordes of attacking Dayaks in *Il re del mare* (The King of the Sea) echoes Garibaldi's analogous unconventional choice. Garibaldi's narrative of the Imperialist fleet ambushing him while he was seeking shelter in the port of Imbituba is echoed by Salgari's description of Sandokan's battle against a British cruiser. Garibaldi/Dumas writes:

> Just off the Isle of Santa Catharina ... we fell in with a Brazilian *patacho* ... We discovered the Brazilian vessel right on our prow. There were no means of avoiding her, so we bore down on her and opened the attack resolutely. We started firing and the enemy replied; but the combat was indecisive on account of the heavy seas.
>
> ... We entered [the port of] Imbituba ... [and] had to prepare for resistance.
>
> ... Day had scarcely broken on the morrow when we became aware of three vessels bearing down on us ... The enemy, favoured in his manoeuvre

by the freshening breeze, continued to sail on, tacking about for short distances and bombarding us furiously ... In the meantime, we, on our side, fought with the most obstinate resolution ... By reason of our numerical weakness, the losses on our side were much heavier than those of the Imperialists. Our deck was already covered with dead and wounded; but although the flank of our vessel was riddled with shots, although our masting had been heavily damaged, we were resolved not to yield, but to die, to the very last man, rather than surrender. (*Memoirs* 90–1)

In *Le tigri di Mompracem,* Sandokan suffers analogous initial losses and escapes into a natural harbour formed by the mouth of a river, only to find himself trapped by the British cruiser. Like Garibaldi, he is forced to engage in a desperate battle, marked by a predictable outcome:

I tre legni, decisi a soccombere, ma non a retrocedere, non si scorgevano quasi più, avvolti come erano da immense nuvole di fumo ... ma ruggivano con egual furore e i lampi si succedevano ai lampi e le detonazioni alle detonazioni.

Il vascello aveva il vantaggio della sua mole e delle sue artiglierie, ma i due *prahos,* che la valorosa Tigre conduceva all'abbordaggio non cedevano. Rasi come pontoni, forati in cento luoghi, sdruciti, irriconoscibili, già coll'acqua nella stiva, già pieni di morti e di feriti, continuavano a tirare innanzi malgrado il continuo tempestare di palle.

Il delirio si era impadronito di quegli uomini e tutti altro non chiedevano, che di salire sul ponte di quel formidabile vascello e se non di vincere, almeno di morire sul campo del nemico. (*Le tigri di Mompracem* 28)

(The three boats, resigned to succumb but not withdraw, could barely be seen, enwrapped as they were by immense clouds of smoke ... yet they roared on with undiminished fury, lightning following lightning and thunder following thunder.

The vessel had the advantage of its size and its artillery, but the two *prahos* that the valiant Tiger led did not give up. Flattened like pontoons, with a hundred holes, torn apart and unrecognizable, with the water already swamping the hull, already full of dead and wounded, they kept on, in spite of the unceasing hail of cannon fire.

Delirium had taken over the men, and they asked nothing else than to storm the deck of that formidable vessel and, if not win, die on the enemy field.)

Garibaldi is Shipwrecked. Illustration by Edoardo Matania for *Garibaldi e i suoi tempi* by Jessie White Mario.

Garibaldi's three-day resistance on the fortress of Los Ratos against Admiral Brown's squadron recalls Sandokan's defence of Mompracem in *Le tigri di Mompracem,* as well as Yanez's resistance inside Tremal-Naik's fortified farm in *Il re del mare.* In turn, these episodes repeat the broader adventure topos of the defence of a fortified city or island, the most famous example of which may be the defence of La Rochelle in *The Three Musketeers.*

Predictably, given the patent numerical disparity, the adventure hero suffers excruciating losses, yet his defeats merely prefigure brilliant victories to come. In Dumas's *Memoirs,* Latin America functions as the training camp where the young *condottiero* can gain experience and prepare for the *real* war that he will fight in Italy. Dumas is keen to point out that Garibaldi's legend grows larger despite, or perhaps because of, his Latin American setbacks, and the *Memoirs* display Dumas's melodramatic ability to intensify the glory of the Italian outcome with the pathos of Garibaldi's initial Latin American adventures.

In their fight against the British Empire, Sandokan's *tigrotti* are indeed the daring children of Garibaldi's own 'tigri' (*Mémoirs* 196). Not only does Salgari recycle the defining topoi of the adventure tale that, in turn, Dumas had so craftily exploited in his *Memoirs of Garibaldi* but Salgari reveals his imaginative indebtedness to Dumas by repeating specific narrative details and analogous incidents, going so far as to mimic some of the *Memoirs*' stylistic and lexical peculiarities.[18] In spite of these massive analogies, the two narratives also reveal some fundamental differences. Salgari's tone is more subdued and elegiac – if Garibaldi's world basks in a tropical dawn, that of Sandokan is fading into the sunset. Perhaps this difference is most evident in Garibaldi's/Dumas's and Salgari's respective representation of women. Undoubtedly, Anita Garibaldi and Marianna mirror each other, as they both inspire love at first sight and thus underscore the hero's passionate and wilful nature. Both die of sudden and incurable illnesses (malaria and cholera) while in flight from enemy forces, and both are pregnant when death strikes. However, Anita is a woman-warrior, an Amazon who rides a horse and uses a gun 'like a man' and eagerly follows Garibaldi in his dangerous missions and wandering existence. By sharing all of the male hero's superhuman traits, Anita is a rightful participant in Garibaldi's divinely sanctioned epic adventure: 'She was in a little boat with two rowers, and these poor devils bent down as low as possible to keep out of the way of balls and bullets. But she, standing in the poop, amid the hail of grapeshot – erect, calm, and proud – seemed like a statue of Pallas; and God, who stretched out His protecting arm over me, brought her, too, beneath its shadow' (*Memoirs* 97).

Marianna, on the other hand, is a pliable and languid beauty of fifteen who predictably succumbs to the hero's uninhibited ardour. If Dumas and Garibaldi masculinize Anita to make her a worthy member of Garibaldi's adventuring forces, Salgari gives Marianna an emasculating power: as docile as she is charming, Marianna represents all the trappings of feminine passivity. A modern Circe who destroys adventure, heroism, and action, Marianna represents the seduction of everyday affections and the comforts of the bourgeois home in a world without history, a paradise island of feminine tranquillity: 'Sì, se tu lo vorrai ti porterò in una lontana isola coperta di fiori e di boschi, dove tu non udrai più parlare della tua Labuan, né io della mia Mompracem, in un'isola incantata del grande Oceano, dove potremo vivere felici' (Yes, and if you want it, I shall bring you to a far-away island covered with flowers and forests, where you will never hear of your Labuan nor I of my Mompracem, an enchanted island in the immense Ocean, where we will be able to live happily) (*Le tigri di Mompracem* 59). While Anita underscores that Garibaldi is predestined to become Italy's national hero in tones that popularize Mazzini's messianic utopianism, Marianna becomes the vehicle of Sandokan's negative predestination. Sandokan is a star-crossed leader whose actions and choices appear guided toward a tragic downfall by unseen and sinister powers. A puppet of fate, Sandokan is trapped between two equally undesirable outcomes: defeat and death in manly efforts, or peace and oblivion in feminine exile:

– Fatalità! ...
– Quante volte ho tentato di spezzare la catena! Quante volte quando mi assaliva il pensiero di dover un giorno, per sposare quella donna, abbandonare il mio mare, por fine alle mie vendette, abbandonare la mia isola, perdere il mio nome di cui andavo un dì tanto altero, perdere i miei tigrotti; ho cercato di fuggire, di porre fra me e quegli occhi affascinanti una barriera insormontabile! Eppure ho dovuto cedere, Yanez. Mi sono trovato fra due abissi: qui Mompracem coi suoi pirati, fra il balenar dei suoi cento cannoni e i suoi vittoriosi *prahos*; là quell'adorabile creatura dai biondi capelli e gli occhi azzurri. Mi sono librato a lungo esitando e sono precipitato verso quella fanciulla dalla quale, lo sento, nessuna forza umana saprà strapparmi. Ah! Sento che la Tigre cesserà di esistere! (*Le tigri di Mompracem* 78–9)

(Fatality! ...
How many times have I attempted to break the chain! How many times have I tried to escape, and create an impassable barrier between those enthralling eyes and me! I did so every time the thought of having to leave my ocean and put an end to my avenging feats assailed me; every time I felt that in order to marry that woman, one day I would have to abandon my island and renounce the name of which I was once so proud, and my tiger cubs. Yet, I had to give up, Yanez! I found myself caught between two chasms: on one side Mompracem, with its pirates, the thundering of its hundreds of cannons and its victorious *prahos*; and on the other side that adorable creature with blonde hair and blue eyes. I hovered, hesitating, for a long time, and then hurled myself headlong towards that girl from whom no human force can ever tear me away. Ah! I feel that the Tiger is about to end his existence!)

Salgari understood that his metropolitan readers would favour a character such as the Anglo-Italian Marianna over the exotic Anita. While Marianna satisfied the bourgeois and domestic ideals of modern Italy with her alluring and passive femininity, the androgynous Anita belonged to the Risorgimento, a time of struggle, adventure, and freedom on which contemporary Italy looked with both desire and anxiety. By representing the nemesis of the Risorgimento Zeitgeist, Marianna heralds the conclusion of the Age of Heroes. If Salgari eliminates the threat of the feminine with Marianna's timely death, his very act of writing delays Sandokan's demise. Like Scheherazade's untiring narratives, Salgari's sequels of episodes in the two jungle cycles serve to exorcize temporarily an apocalypse that is always just around the corner, and that is as inevitable as it is compulsively postponed. The end of writing corresponds to the demise of adventure, the exile of heroes, and the triumph of the banalities and contingencies of history over the self-enclosed and brilliant geometries of myth.

Salgari's imaginative creation of Sandokan's world follows the convention that defines the exotic as all that corresponds to laws, feelings, mores, and values that are different from and often antagonistic to all that governs the reader's everyday existence. In spite of all his strange and seductive otherness, however, Sandokan's roots are in what I would call, somewhat oxymoronically, an autochthonous exoticism, namely, an exoticism based on temporal rather than geographical distance. As my comparison with Garibaldi proves, Sandokan repeats the core values of a heroic and bygone time: the Italian Risorgimento. In this context, the Malayan archipelago, with all its divided and enslaved tribes, becomes a somewhat mechanical *analogon* of pre-unification Italy, and Sandokan's battles against the imperial usurper are readable as the exotic counterpart of the nineteenth-century wars of independence in Europe, fuelled by similar principles of national unity and political freedom.

As they return to the forefront in the unfamiliar world of Sandokan's Malayan archipelago, these ideals appear both significant and remote. If Sandokan's passions are Garibaldi's own, by being cloaked in Sandokan's exotic garb these passions appear estranged from the reader's present. In his careless and free expenditure – be it of love, riches, or violence – Sandokan represents opposition to the bourgeois culture of acquisition, preservation, and self-control. His generous and impulsive actions, heroic excesses, and unconventional yet uncompromising ethic make of Sandokan the very opposite of the political expediency and bureaucratic hurdles that according to many marked the post-unification era in Italy and that had been summed up in Depretis's politics of *trasformismo*.

While expressing nostalgia for the values of a heroic and idealized national past, Salgari's jungle cycle also reveals the conceptual dissonances implicit in the effort to revive these values while adapting them to suit a country aiming to disseminate an image of monarchic legitimacy and social stability within its borders and imperial expansion and conquest beyond them. Sandokan's project of monarchic restoration founded on family privilege, tribal prestige, and unquestioned authority has none of the democratic thrust of Garibaldi's own ideals. Garibaldi's romanticized descriptions of his sense of deep, horizontal comradeship with all the members of his crew, and his notion of a community of equals based on a fraternal sharing of values, is totally absent from Sandokan's world. Salgari limits Garibaldi's notion of universal brotherhood to the self-reflective and mutually interdependent relationship between two exceptional individuals, Sandokan and Yanez.[19] The rest of Sandokan's 'tigrotti' are amorphous and interchangeable and serve to fulfil the function of the hero-worshiping masses, whose cult of a charismatic leader makes their absolute loyalty appear illogical and their self-sacrifice eerily unmotivated.

Mompracem's imaginative topography, with Sandokan's hut perched atop a mountain and protected by the huts of the various tribal chiefs below, portrays a feudal, atavistic, and brutally hierarchical world. Reminiscent of Manzoni's description of the Innominato's castle, this vertical organization is based on the fearsome authority of a demagogical leader whose unquestioning followers are as eager to die for him as they are to disperse when he fantasizes about a domestic existence with his beloved Marianna. Sandokan's aggressive and conquering hubris contrasts with the self-consciously unselfish connotations of Garibaldi's republican and cosmopolitan ideals as narrated in his *Memoirs*. If Garibaldi's notion of a hero was 'a man who ... adopts some other country as his own and makes offer of his sword and his blood to every people struggling against tyranny' (*Memoirs* 39), Sandokan's heroism acquires a more sinister hue. Sandokan fights the British to restore his own crown and privilege over the territories that he had progressively conquered from rival monarchs by subjugating and slaughtering other tribal and ethnic groups, groups that presumably valued their independence as much as Sandokan valued his own. Quite paradoxically, if seen in this light, Sandokan and James Brooke look more alike than different, and Sandokan ends up embodying some of the expansionistic ideals against which he was battling so fervently and heroically.

Pursuing Salgari's comparison between Europe and the South China

Sea region would be methodologically preposterous from the perspective of historical analysis. However, from a symbolic point of view, it is revealing. This comparison displays the epistemic inconsistencies and ideological ambiguities of a young country attempting to reshape its national self-image in order to mesh its founding ideals with new imperial intimations. These inconsistencies, so clearly embodied in Sandokan, demonstrate that a nation's process of identity-formation is a dynamic, relational affair that must negotiate the merger of collective memories with current investments, and socio-ideological continuities with cultural changes and epistemic disruptions. It also shows how the very concept of Nation proved to be far more elusive and hybrid than the beautifully lyrical 'una d'arme, di lingua, d'altare, / di memorie, di sangue e di cor' (one in arms, language, and altar / one in memories, blood, and heart) (19) of Manzonian coinage. Seduced by the songs of empire and the promises of technology, in the first decade of the twentieth century Italy flexed its industrial muscles and nurtured its budding colonial ambitions, while continuing to be cast in a peripheral and subordinate role on the West's imperial stage. In spite of the rhetoric of its international expositions, Italy was perceived – and kept perceiving itself – as a bit player in the imperial 'great game.' While wholeheartedly sharing what Raymond Williams calls the 'structures of feeling' that founded and supported the practice of Empire, Italy also had other, often repressed, stories to tell. The territorial and cultural heterogeneity of what was popularly defined as the 'garden' of Europe or the 'door' to Africa shows how these 'structures of feeling' were criss-crossed with contradictory experiences, interspersed with hybrid domains, and shot through with alternative narratives that destabilized the hegemonic and centralizing cultural and political ambitions that Italy aggressively pursued at that time.

The Fall of a Crystal Palace: *Le meraviglie del Duemila*

If Salgari's jungle cycle differs from conventional exposition narratives in its nostalgic tone and in its selecting a defeated outsider rather than an imperial conqueror as its protagonist, *Le meraviglie del Duemila*, one of Salgari's least-known novels, is, at first glance, a typical exposition narrative. Contrary to the past-oriented inspiration of the jungle cycle, *Le meraviglie del Duemila* invents the future. Set in the early 1900s in New York City, the heart of modernity, technology, and progress, *Le meraviglie* does not attempt to defer the spectre of death but tells the story of a resurrection. The protagonist, James Brandok, is an American bachelor who, unlike his resourceful and pragmatic compatriots, lives in a half-wakeful state, unable to participate in the vigorous optimism of his age. His youth and immense wealth cannot overcome the depression that haunts him, leading him to contemplate suicide. Toby Holker, a physician and long-time friend, arouses him from his melancholy state when he confronts him with an amazing proposition: that of arresting their aging processes by placing both their bodies in a hibernation-like state for one hundred years in order to reawaken in the year 2003. Holker has discovered the extraordinary properties of a mysterious Egyptian plant, 'the flower of resurrection,' which allows the temporary suspension of life. James eagerly agrees, and the two friends retreat into a solitary crystal-domed sepulchre after leaving written instructions for their descendants on how to bring them back to life in the next century.

Salgari's idea, a combination of Washington Irving's *Rip Van Winkle* (1819) and the fairy tale *Sleeping Beauty*, was not particularly original. It reflected the age's popular fascination with the mass-packaged Egypt of many World's Fairs, which reduced the mysteries of the Pharaonic past to the wonders of the pyramids with their ancient inhabitants. It also recycled popular literary materials, and critics have duly recognized Salgari's indebtedness to numerous sources: Albert Robida's *Vingtième siècle* (1883), Edward Bellamy's *Looking Backward 2000–1887* (1887), H.G. Wells's *When the Sleeper Wakes* (1899), and Jules Verne's *In the Year 2889*.[20] Though turn-of-the-century Italian science fiction never achieved the value and international circulation of its French, British, and American counterparts (the Italian word for science fiction, 'fantascienza,' was not even coined until 1952), Italian readers were not unfamiliar with the genre, as demonstrated by the popularity of novels such as Agostino della Sala-Spada's *Nel 2073: Sogno d'uno stravagante* (1875), Paolo Mantegazza's *L'anno tremila: Sogno* (1897), and Luigi Barucchi's *Un'escursione nel 3004: Racconto fantastico*.

These narratives reveal their age's fascination with the spectacular technologies and exotic wonders displayed at World's Fairs. The tourists who boarded the fanciful railway for the Tour du monde in 1900 Paris or participated in the Viaggio all'estremo Nord in 1906 Milan were the same who read Verne's *Le tour du monde in 80 jours* and Salgari's *Al Polo Nord* and *Una sfida al Polo*. The enormous telescope that allows people to see the moon in amazing detail in *Le meraviglie del Duemila* is modelled on the faux telescope, sixty metres long, which showed lunar landscapes at the Palais des illusions in 1900 Paris. Salgari's suicide, on the eve of the grand opening of Turin 1911, prevented the realization of a quintessential 'Exposition event': the transformation of *Le meraviglie del Duemila* into a 'Ballo Excelsior futurista' modelled upon Manzotti's famous ballet.

Mirroring the technological fervour of the early twentieth century, *Le meraviglie* has unanimously been regarded as 'un libro ... [che] autorizzava a credere nella possibilità, in un futuro ormai imminente, di realizzare ... [il] sogno ... d'un mondo migliore, l'avvento d'una giustizia sociale che le conoscenze tecniche d'allora, in piena espansione, autorizzavano a ritenere non illusione chimerica' (a book ... [that] allowed people to believe in the possibility in a by-now imminent future, of realizing ... [the] dream ... of a better world, the achievement of social justice that the ever-growing technical expertise of that age promised would be real and not a mere illusion') (Viglongo, 'L'editore ai lettori: *Le meraviglie*' xi). Undoubtedly, Brandok's and Holker's successful resurrections in the year 2003 initiates a journey among technological wonders. 'Meraviglia' and its adjectival and adverbial cognates are the most recurring terms in the novel, together with 'extraordinary,' 'fantastic,' and 'miraculous.' Holker and Brandok discover with amazement that the people of the twenty-first century commute in marvellous flying machines, get current news from apparatuses that anticipate television sets, and receive their precooked meals directly at home via electrically powered conduits. The whole world is illuminated cheaply and efficiently with radium, and colossal hydroelectric generating stations harness the power of Niagara Falls and the Gulf Stream. In a utopia where 'la scienza ha vinto' (science won) (*Le meraviglie* 41), wars have been abolished, the world can be toured in one week, and one can befriend a Martian and buy sodas from vending machines.

Readers of nineteenth- and early-twentieth-century science fiction often engage in comparing once-futuristic utopias with actual reality. As I write these pages, the year 2003 is already history, New York's skyscrapers have reached far more vertiginous heights than the twenty-three floors that Salgari envisioned in his novel, and their vulnerability has proven that we are still far from the end of armed conflicts. Of course, the value of *Le meraviglie del Duemila* must not be measured against the accuracy of Salgari's prophetic visions. The novel's worth lies rather in Salgari's skilful adaptation of the romantic concept of the sublime to a world ruled by technology. *Le meraviglie del Duemila* stages the conflict between two forms of the sublime: the natural and the technological. This conflict lends a tragic quality to a novel that critics have too hurriedly labelled a futuristic utopia.

There are numerous definitions of the natural sublime, and while the concept has undergone significant transformations from Longinus to Burke, scholars generally agree that to be sublime objects must affect the mind 'with a sense of overwhelming grandeur or irresistible power; calculated to inspire awe, deep reverence, or lofty emotion by reason of [their] beauty, vastness, or grandeur' (*Oxford English Dictionary*). For my analysis of Salgari's use of the term, the most useful definition is perhaps Immanuel Kant's. In his *Critique of Judgment*, Kant speaks of two kinds of sublime experience: First, the mathematical sublime defines a feeling of extreme magnitude and absolute vastness, such as that experienced when viewing a forest or a polar expanse from a mountaintop. Second, the dynamic sublime entails the contemplation of scenes that arouse terror by displaying the overwhelming, often destructive power of nature in motion:

> Bold, overhanging, and, as it were, threatening rocks, thunderclouds piled up the vault of heaven, borne along with flashes and peals, volcanoes in all their violence of destruction, hurricanes leaving desolation in their track, the boundless ocean rising with rebellious force, the high waterfall of some mighty river, and the like, make our power of resistance of trifling moment in comparison with their might. But, provided our own position is secure, their aspect is all the more attractive for its fearfulness; and we readily call these objects sublime, because they raise the forces of the soul above the height of vulgar commonplace, and discover within us a power of resistance of quite another kind, which gives us courage to be able to measure ourselves against the seeing omnipotence of nature. (110–11)

According to Kant, a sublime spectacle may initially inspire the feeling that humanity is utterly powerless and insignificant before nature's astonishing might. However, Kant emphasizes that contemplating the sublime makes us understand that nature can only challenge our physical being, yet ultimately leads us to feel superior to nature by virtue of our superior reason: 'Sublimity, therefore, does not reside in any of the things of nature, but only in our own mind, in so far as we may become conscious of our superiority over nature within, and thus also over nature without us' (114).

In the age of technology, Kant's rational control over nature cemented itself in the great works of manufacturing and engineering with which 'man' was able to harness the sublime power of nature. As World's Fairs optimistically repeated, in the modern utopia of progress the natural sublime had no other option but to either collaborate or be crushed by a sublime engendered by sheer human skills. This was what scholars such as Perry Miller and Leo Marx aptly defined the 'technological sublime' of the machines that marked human triumph over space and time.[21] Railroads opened up forests, bridges spanned rivers and lakes, tunnels disembowelled mountains, and channels tore land open for communication and commerce. The locomotive, the steamboat, the telegraph, and, later, all the many applications of electricity symbolized the age's conquest of matter and, in a momentous reversal of roles, nature became the silent observer of, and submissive witness to, man's magnificent achievements. In Ralph Waldo Emerson's early enthusiastic words, 'Nature is thoroughly mediate. It is made to serve ... It offers all its kingdoms to man as the raw material which he may mould into what is useful ... The world becomes, at last, only a realized will, – the double of the man' (28). Lords of technological creation, men had built their own mechanical Eden, soon to be brightened with the shimmering lights of an eternal electrical dawn.

By setting his novel in the United States, Salgari mirrored the fascination this country held upon the European imagination. If, in Europe, there was deep ambivalence toward technology and the process of industrialization met with numerous detractors, since the Jacksonian era the United States had maintained a more optimistic belief in the possibility of reconciling the natural with the technological sublime. While Salgari was writing *Le meraviglie del Duemila*, innumerable tourists were flocking to Niagara Falls to see how Westinghouse had harnessed the Niagara River's raging waters to the largest hydroelectric power station in the world. The electric transformation of the falls had also been the major theme of the 1901 Pan-American Exposition in Buffalo, which displayed a 400-foot electric tower, covered with 40,000 small bulbs, with a 60-foot model of Niagara Falls flowing from its side (Nye 149). In 1907, the year of publication of *Le meraviglie del Duemila*, General Electric had caused a widely publicized sensation when it had heightened the natural sublime of Niagara Falls by illuminating it at night using powerful searchlights. Niagara Falls and its hydroelectric plants became the emblem of how the United States had been able to subsume new technologies within the framework of the natural sublime to increase human happiness by achieving widespread prosperity and progress.

Salgari captures this fascination by having the 'resurrected' Holker and Brandon take one of their first trips to Niagara Falls, where they admire 'i colossali impianti elettrici che forniscono la forza a quasi tutti gli stabilimenti della federazione' (the colossal electric plants that furnish power to almost all the Federation's factories) (46). Even more amazingly, the scientists of the year 2003 have channelled the energy of the Gulf Stream by building 'delle enormi isole galleggianti' (enormous floating islands) that capture and exploit the ocean's currents at almost no expense (117). Holker's and Brandon's subsequent journeys across the globe reveal the spectacular technological developments of the year 2003. Futuristic vessels that can travel equally well on land and underground, as well as in water and air, transport them to the North Pole, which is now reachable via a marvellous tunnel that cuts below the polar ice cap. Conversations with fellow travellers reveal that modern technologies have freed people from need and given them time for extended leisure. Natural resources are being exploited fully and, when depleted, replaced with affordable man-made substitutes. Crime is virtually non-existent.

This perfect utopia has a sinister side. Crime is absent from this world because all thieves, murderers, outlaws, as well as anarchists and dissidents of all kinds, are imprisoned in airtight submarine cities and polar colonies. Away from the 'civilized' world, these communities are self-governed, their borders overseen by international patrols of 'vigilanti' (controllers). In the event of a rebellion, these patrols are charged with the mass execution of all dissenters with blasts of 'torrenti di acqua elettrizzata al massimo grado' (streams of water electrified to the utmost degree) (42), which sink the ill-fated city into the ocean. Merciless means, Brandon and Holker sheepishly comment, but necessary perhaps to 'mantenere in equilibrio il nostro pianeta' (keep our planet in balance) (100).

If, initially, Salgari appeared to echo many of his contemporaries' enthusiasm for the wonders of American technology, his fanciful exploration of a world obsessed with notions of balance and order evoke Henry Adams's more pessimistic views on progress. As is well known, Adams developed the theories of physicist William Gibbs to extend the notion of entropy from the realm of physics to that of historical processes. A corollary to the second law of thermodynamics, entropy defines the tendency of all systems to gradually degenerate into chaos, as energy disperses more and more randomly. All complex systems progress toward an increasing lack of differentiation: order slowly falls victim to disorder, and disorder ends up in stasis. According to Adams, over time entropy increases: 'the world is running down' (Slade 77).

Salgari's brave new world has apparently waged a successful offensive against entropy. Like two of Thomas Pynchon's characters in his short story 'Entropy,' in *Le meraviglie del Duemila* people live in airtight apartments neatly stacked one upon the other. When they travel, they do so in hermetically sealed compartments, protected from random encounters, meteorological turmoil, and other chance events. They have perfected orderly lives in a politically, socially, and ecologically stable environment. This is a world based on order, rational control, and efficiency, a world that resembles anthropologist Burton Benedict's description of World's Fairs: 'Everything is man-made and nature is excluded or allowed in only under the most rigorously controlled conditions ... man is totally in control and synthetic nature is preferred to the real thing' (5). Significantly, Brandok and Holker gain access to this world only after inventing their own counter-entropic utopia: a hermetically sealed enclave, detached from the rest of the world and covered with a crystal dome that maintains it at the constant temperature of −20° Celsius in which they 'sleep' for one hundred years (14).

It soon appears evident to our time travellers that in spite of all its 'animazione straordinaria [e] febbrile' (extraordinary [and] feverish animation) (61), this overorganized world is exceedingly homogeneous and static. Innumerable botanical and animal species have become extinct and, besides having lost racial and ethnic differentiation, people are all of one 'mind,' dissent and opposition having been either crushed or purged from the system. There are no accidents, no surprises, no singularities, and no eccentricities in this world. If healthy systems are composed of many different elements that interact in various relationships among one another, as entropy increases, these elements lose their differentiation: homogeneity ushers in stasis. Paradoxically, in Salgari's New York of 2003 the war against entropy has resulted in increased entropy. A hyper-rational city, Salgari's New York has built all kinds of rational systems to control and regulate all that was unpredictable, charismatic, and vital. As a consequence, the entire metropolitan system has moved toward inflexibility, repressive stability, or, in Max Weber's terms, 'routinization.' Spontaneity and originality have no place in this systematized and perfectly arranged utopia.

However, as society has become more rational and more complexly subdivided, the individual appears unable to grasp the totality of the system, or to comprehend and explain its functioning. Even from above, there is no unifying perspective from which the whole can be viewed and understood. In a curious reversal from World's Fairs' 'bird's-eye views,' in *Le meraviglie* New York City when viewed from above appears as a formless amalgam of oversized buildings, shapeless and ubiquitous assemblages with no beginning and no end. Size, detail, and number overwhelm the viewer, who loses the sense of a unifying plan or human purpose in this futuristic metropolis. The vast humanity that dwells in these places has no discernible language, but utters unintelligible and mechanical noise:

> Vie immense apparivano sotto agli aeronauti, se così si potevano chiamare, fiancheggiate da palazzi mostruosi di venti, venticinque e perfino di trenta piani, che dovevano contenere migliaia di famiglie ciascuno, la popolazione di un villaggio. Mille fragori salivano fino agli orecchi dei due risuscitati, prodotti chissà da quali macchine gigantesche: fischi, colpi formidabili, detonazioni, scoppi. (*Le meraviglie* 51)

> (Huge avenues appeared below the aeronauts, if we can describe them as such. These avenues were lined with monstrous buildings of twenty, twenty-five, and even thirty floors. Each building was likely to contain thousands of families, the population of a village. A thousand noises produced by who-knows-what gigantic machines reached the ears of the two resurrected men: whistling noises, formidable bangs, blasts and explosions.)

If Salgari's New York of the year 2003 appears to be undergoing what Fausto Maijstral, the protagonist of Pynchon's *V*, would call a 'slow apocalypse' – a process through which Western civilization slowly succumbs to entropy, finally becoming 'subject to the laws of physics' (316, 321) – once they leave New York, Salgari's protagonists experience what we may term a 'fast apocalypse.' Here, repressed conflicts suddenly erupt, and the system is blown apart with unprecedented violence, bringing utter disintegration and chaos. Brandok and Holker's journey to Europe sets the scene for this apocalyptic scenario, as they become forced participants in a crescendo of dramatic events. Everything begins with a show of the natural sublime:

> La bufera ... aumentava di miglio in miglio ... Lo spettacolo che offriva l'oceano da quell'altezza era spaventevole e nello stesso tempo ammirabile. Montagne d'acqua, nere come fossero d'inchiostro e colle creste invece candidissime e quasi fosforescenti, si rovesciavano in tutte le direzioni, accavallandosi e rimbalzando a grande altezza. (*Le meraviglie* 112)

> (The storm ... increased mile after mile ... The spectacle that the ocean offered from that elevation was terrifying and marvellous at the same time.

Mountains of water, waves as black as ink with candid and quasi-phosphorescent crests, broke in all directions, crashing down and rearing up again to a great height.)

Predictably, the natural sublime is the backdrop against which the men of 2003 can display the potential of the extraordinary vessel in which they are travelling, a miracle of human ingenuity and a symbol of the achievements of human reason. To evade the fury of the elements in the air, the flying vessel can land on water and operate as a boat. In order to better withstand the raging waves, the crew drops anchor by the submarine city of Escarios, home to reformed anarchists and other 'undesirable' people. Surprisingly, our protagonists discover that the inhabitants of Escarios have initiated a bloody revolt after bingeing on a supply of stolen alcohol:

Gli abitanti della città sottomarina ... erano divenuti tutti pazzi. Urlavano, saltavano, si picchiavano, si gettavano a terra rotolandosi fra un frastuono orrendo, prodotto da sbarre di ferro che picchiavano furiosamente le pareti metalliche che li difendevano dall'invasione delle acque dell'oceano ...

Un uragano spaventevole imperversava sull'oceano Atlantico. Ondate alte come montagne si rovesciavano, con spaventevoli muggiti, contro le balaustrate di ferro ... e raffiche tremende passavano sopra la città sottomarina. (*Le meraviglie* 129)

(The inhabitants of the submarine city ... had all gone mad. They yelled, jumped, beat each other up, and threw themselves rolling onto the ground, among the horrendous din of the iron bars with which they hit the metal walls that protected them from the assault of the ocean ...

A horrendous storm raged in the Atlantic Ocean. Waves as high as mountains crashed, with a terrifying roar, against the iron railings ... and terrible gusts of wind blew over the submarine city.)

With the storm above and the inmates' revolt below, our protagonists become the protectors of human reason in a world fallen prey to folly, the keepers of normality in the surrounding chaos. They assume the duty of staving off disorder and maintaining unity. The adventures that follow rise to a crescendo of intensity, as Brandon and Holker witness the revolt and its tragic aftermath, and continue their voyage on the floating wreckage of the submarine city. First lost at sea, then trapped amid the seaweed in the Sargasso Sea, the castaways sight land only to be forced to endure the experience 'sublime ed insieme spaventevole' (sublime and at the same time terrifying) (158) of a volcanic eruption and a stampede of wild animals. Of course, in all these adventures, human resourcefulness and genius counter the unpredictability and fury of nature, until a passing flying machine rescues our heroes just in the nick of time. However, this victory is only apparent. The epic battle between the natural and the technological sublime demands its scapegoats. Reversing Kant's argument, Salgari's sublime spares the men's bodies but claims their minds. Unable to withstand the tension, Brandok and Holker succumb to madness, their disordered minds slowly lapsing into a catatonic inertia. Entropy has won.

Like Jules Verne in his *Voyages extraordinaires*, Salgari uses science and its miracles as the narrative motor of *Le meraviglie del Duemila*. Resembling that of the early Verne, Salgari's utopian project displays 'man's' ability to dominate nature by his sheer will, ingenuity, and scientific knowledge. However, like the later Verne, Salgari also presents a world at the end of time's arc, a world that, more in line with the laws of thermodynamics than with the dreams of myth, undergoes an entropic 'apocalypse' with nothing to herald a new beginning. In *Le meraviglie del Duemila*, the 'flower of resurrection' ultimately betrays its promise. With a tragic twist, reminiscent of the Hawthorne of 'Rappacini's Daughter,' Salgari contradicts the technological optimism of the World's Fairs' age and sombrely concludes that the cult of science heralds no rebirth.

4 Guido Gozzano's Imperial Ambiguities

Reclaiming the Context: On Gozzano *gazzettiere* and the Archaeology of *Verso la cuna del mondo*

In 1917, the prestigious Milanese publishers Fratelli Treves issued Guido Gozzano's *Verso la cuna del mondo: Lettere dall'India* (Toward the Cradle of the World: Letters from India), a collection of fourteen travel sketches describing some of the cities and customs of India. Since Gozzano had died prematurely in 1916, the publishers had charged Giuseppe Antonio Borgese with assembling, editing, and prefacing the volume. By 1916, Borgese was already one of the most influential arbiters of Italian literary taste, and his critical authority, combined with the Treves's reputation and Gozzano's own standing in the contemporary poetic arena, converged to give *Verso la cuna del mondo* the status of a 'classic,' in the sense of T.S. Eliot's definition, which identified a work endowed with formal precision and ideological consistency and conveying a sense of 'comprehensiveness' and 'universality' (10–11).[1] In his preface to the volume, Borgese emphasized these ideas of compositional unity when he argued that he had organized 'molti suoni fievoli ... in una triste armonia ... [e] molte macchie di colore ... [in un] quadro' (many soft sounds ... into a sad harmony and [...] many spots of colour ... [into a] painting) (63).

Critics approached the Treves volume already expecting to discover 'un libro d'arte' (an art book) (Calcaterra, 'Le opere' xvii), that is, a self-enclosed text, characterized by thematic coherence and formal unity, rather than a sequence of loosely connected travel narratives. Despite the fact that the chapters comprising *Verso la cuna del mondo* had appeared as separate pieces in several magazines and in the daily paper

La Stampa between 1914 and 1916, *Verso la cuna del mondo*, these critics argued, revealed a teleological thrust that went beyond the simple gathering together of its parts and endowed them with a deeper logic. Given that the volume's chapters did not follow the chronology of the original publications, much exegetical energy went into assessing whether Gozzano himself had drafted the volume's sequence before his death, or whether it was Borgese who arranged the *disjecta membra* into the itinerary displayed in *Verso la cuna del mondo.*[2]

Notwithstanding the familiar claims regarding the (in this case all too real) 'death of the author,' Carlo Calcaterra's authoritative conclusion that Gozzano had indeed devised the collection's structure drew renewed interest in its organic design and overarching meaning.[3] Furthermore, the discovery that the narrative's itinerary did not correspond to Gozzano's actual journey to India but was, for the most part, a literary invention led interpreters to isolate *Verso la cuna del mondo* in a supra-historical and symbolic realm.[4] Gozzano's literary excursion starting in Bombay (Mumbai), the 'door to India,' through Goa, Kandy, Madura (Madurai), Madras (Chennai), Haiderabat (Hyderabad), Delhi, Agra, Giaipur (Jaipur), Cawnpore (Kanpur), and ending in Benares (Varanasi), the 'cradle of the world,' became a spiritual journey, in the best tradition of allegorical and existential quests.[5] Some interpreters read this itinerary as a deeply personal pilgrimage toward physical and spiritual healing. Since Gozzano was suffering from late-stage tuberculosis, they considered the Indian journey as triggering Gozzano's much debated deathbed conversion (Calcaterra, 'Le opere' xxxi; Mor 9). Upon returning from India, these interpreters contended, the former *sofista subalpino* abandoned his proverbial scepticism to embrace a spirituality liberally mixing traditional Catholicism with popular elements of a Westernized and simplified Hinduism (Calcaterra, 'Le opere' xxviii–xxxi; Guglielminetti 42).[6] The unoriginal theme of the modern pilgrim seeking enlightenment in the East easily lent itself to universalizing readings as well. Especially in consideration of the ongoing world war, some scholars viewed Gozzano's failed quest for healing as a sign of the ills of the whole of the West and an allegory of an entire civilization's state of malaise (Guglielminetti 42–3).

Undoubtedly, the quest for humankind's origins, one of philosophy's traditional subjects, had gained new momentum since the age of social and scientific Darwinism. The recovery of our primordial beginnings was the necessary starting point for anybody seeking to draw the trajectory of humanity's evolution in order to restore a consolingly meaningful present, in either a scientific or a religious perspective. Perhaps more than any highbrow theorization, Gozzano's and Borgese's quests for the cradle of the world echoed many popularized renditions of their age's systematizing and totalizing tendencies. The World's Fairs' displays courageously titled 'A History of the World' or 'A Brief History of Humanity,' for example, visibly illustrated these universalizing goals and made them accessible to a wide public.

For those critics who did not accept the complexities or the clichés of the allegorical journey, Gozzano's Indian writings were evidence of the decadent writer's evasion from the here and now of contemporary life (De Rienzo, 'Introduzione' 9). In this light, Gozzano's *Verso la cuna del mondo* complied with Victor Segalen's definition of the exotic text as one that stages the artist's 'fuite éperdue du présent mesquin' (mad escape from the dull present) (19) and his or her retreat into a distant world of aesthetic delight. Segalen's 'beau spectacle' (beautiful spectacle) (19) mirrors Gozzano's aesthetic approach to exotic objects: 'io vivo della loro bellezza, la gusto, la faccio mia, cerco di gettarne una scintilla nelle mie lettere' (I live in their beauty, I enjoy and appropriate it, and attempt to throw a spark of this beauty into my letters) ('A Candida Bolognino' 169). While underscoring the escapist implications of his Indian narratives, Gozzano's critics also conceded that these texts engaged the exotic only superficially, as a detour in an intellectual journey that, ultimately, remained self-centred, isolated, and utterly devoted to the poet's own interior landscapes.

Whether deeply spiritual or impressionistically descriptive, *Verso la cuna del mondo* was generally interpreted as a text wilfully severed from the realities of contemporary life. 'I letterati tradizionali,' wrote Antonio Piromalli, describing Gozzano and his generation, 'non partecipano all'attività pratica, i problemi interiori dell'uomo e la vita individuale dello spirito sono i motivi dell'arte ... L'artista, velleitario, si contrappone alla società ... e si isola dalla realtà in un egoismo individualistico e nell'irresponsabilità della vita dello spirito' (Traditional men of letters do not participate in practical activities. Man's interior problems and his personal spiritual life are the themes of their art ... The fanciful artist opposes himself to society ... and isolates himself from reality into an individualistic egotism and in the irresponsibility of his spiritual life) (3–4). Borgese made a similar point in his own reading of Gozzano's travels to India:

In India [Gozzano] cercava soprattutto se stesso, il se stesso fisico e morale: un po' di buona salute, un po' di quiete e d'oblio promessigli dalla dottrina vagamente intravveduta del nirvana, e forse un ampliamento del suo dolce orizzonte canavesano ...

I suoi tentativi d'interessarsi alle cose esterne, quali sono realmente, non mancano: ma scissi, deboli, abbandonati ben presto ... Non ignora Kipling, eppure non lo ricorda mai, perfino temendo la vicinanza di quell'imperiale britannico appetito di esistere ... Ammira gl'inglesi conquistatori e organizzatori, senza che questa ammirazione oltrepassi l'accento giornalistico e tocchi la soglia della storia. (64)

(In India [Gozzano] mainly sought his own Self, his physical and moral Self: a bit better health, a bit of tranquillity and the oblivion that the vaguely perceived doctrine of Nirvana promised him. Perhaps he was also striving to enlarge the sweet horizon of his own Canavese region ...

Gozzano made a few attempts to interest himself in external things, as they really are, but they are fragmented and weak attempts, and soon abandoned ... He is not unaware of Kipling, yet he never remembers him, being afraid of even getting near that British imperial appetite for existence ... He admires the conquering and organizing Britons, without letting his admiration go beyond a journalistic tone and enter the realm of history.)

Later and more substantial readings revealed that Gozzano's letters were a crafted mosaic, made of pieces borrowed from numerous texts, including Pierre Loti's *L'Inde (sans les Anglais)*, Angelo De Gubernatis's *Peregrinazioni indiane*, Ernst Haeckel's *Lettere di un viaggiatore nell'India*, Italo Pizzi's *L'Islamismo*, Paolo Mantegazza's *India*, Théôphile Gautier's *Caprices et zigzags*, André Chevrillon's *Dans l'Inde*, and Fedinand De Lanoye's *L'Inde contemporaine*. An erudite exercise in intertexuality, *Verso la cuna* inspired equally erudite *Quellenforschungen*, and while unearthing the text's many literary sources, interpreters consistently swerved away from all referential and contextual analyses.[7]

All these readings shed much light on Borgese's edition of *Verso la cuna del mondo*. The numerous publications that, over the years, reproposed or slightly altered Borgese's systematizing editorial feat demonstrate the enduring success of his collection.[8] However, approaching Gozzano's Indian letters only through Borgese's edition raises two significant problems. First, it forces us to overlook the letters on Indian topics that Borgese, with a critical auto-da-fé, deemed extraneous to his edition's narrative structure.[9] Second, it neglects the archaeology of Borgese's successful volume. Gozzano's Indian sketches were part of the surprisingly prolific narrative output of Gozzano the *gazzettiere*, as Gior-

gio De Rienzo, quoting Gozzano himself, humorously defined the celebrated poet's other professional life, the one guided by the spectre of
currency rather than the muse of art (*Guido Gozzano* 133–9). Reaching a
broader and more heterogeneous readership than that which Borgese
envisioned for *Verso la cuna del mondo*, Gozzano's Indian letters were
originally published in Turin's leading daily *La Stampa*, and in three
periodicals: *La Donna, Bianco rosso e verde*, and *La Lettura*, between 1914
and 1916. They were part of a steady journalistic production that
included novellas and short stories, but also occasional pieces such
as sketches on historical places and characters, and brief pieces of
reportage on contemporary events, including a few devoted to the 1911
International Exposition in Turin.

Taken as a whole, Gozzano's journalistic output reveals a writer who,
far from being isolated in the empyrean spheres of poetic activity, was
attuned to contemporary cultural preferences and readily available to
gratify them. By anticipating and reflecting public opinion, Gozzano
acted as an eloquent mouthpiece for the northern Italian bourgeoisie's
evolving ideology in the crucial years that led to the First World War.
Besides displaying his well-known tendency toward ironic role-playing
and literary posturing and his willingness to comply with the various
magazines' individual philosophies, Gozzano's mutable opinions also
reflected the broader changes and the uncertainties of contemporary
politics. If, for example, as early as 1914, Gozzano condemned the
impending world war in pieces such as 'Guerra di spetri' (A War Among
Spectres) and 'La belva bionda' (The Fair-Haired Beast), once the traditionally neutral *La Stampa* swerved to promote Antonio Salandra's
pro-war national politics, Gozzano concocted a number of patriotic narratives such as 'La scelta migliore' (The Better Choice), 'Gli occhi
dell'anima' (Eyes of the Soul), and 'Un addio' (A Farewell).

Examining some of the most significant among Gozzano's Indian letters together with some of his articles on the 'Fabulous Exposition' of
1911 reveals that Gozzano was a subtle interpreter of the enthusiasms
and the contradictions of his age's exposition mentality, and a sophisticated, if often ambiguous, reader of a society in rapid evolution.[10] Repa-
triated to their original publication sites and stripped of the ideological
and formal consistency with which Borgese festooned them, Gozzano's
narratives reflect the complexities of their age's cultural politics. If,
rather than attempting to minimize these pieces' fragmentary, redundant, and frequently contradictory features, we emphasize instead their
discontinuities and inconsistencies, we discover that they reveal symp-

toms of an ideology in a state of transition, in a world undergoing quick and dramatic changes.

Gozzano's articles exemplify a type of journalistic reporting that was innovative in its forms and culturally specific in its content. Attentive to the needs of the expanding marketplace, this journalism was reflective as well as constructive of the ideological preferences and aesthetic taste of the new bourgeoisie, and responded to the technological innovations that both characterized and influenced the style of modern illustrated magazines. Giuseppe Prezzolini identified these innovative features in his discussion of *La Lettura*:

> [le] riviste tipo magazine inglese, come 'La lettura' ... hanno forte diffusione e forti entrate di pubblicità ... Tutto in esse deve avere il sussidio dell'illustrazione. Sono le riviste tipiche per ferrovia, che si comprano per passare il tempo in un tragitto noioso. Ma anch'esse desiderano buone firme e, pur dovendo tener conto del loro pubblico, apron le porte a buona letteratura quando c'è. (66)

> ([the] magazines inspired by the British model such as 'La lettura' ... have widespread sales and bring in much advertising money ... Everything in them must be backed up by illustrations. They are the typical magazines for a train trip, which people buy to pass the time during a boring commute. But they also want big-name writers, and though they have to consider their readership, they do publish good literature when it is available.)

As Prezzolini explains, the press played a leading role in the process of cultural democratization that accompanied the socio-economic changes of early-twentieth-century Italy. Modelling themselves upon British magazines, several Italian periodicals catered to the new middle-class urban public while striving to maintain their traditional readership from the cultivated elites. Since they operated between high and mass culture, these magazines' efforts to expand their readership brought a series of significant changes. *La Lettura*, for example, pioneered attempts to alter its formats so as to fit the 'misura dei ritagli di tempo che, nel corso del mese, il lettore medio può dedicare alla lettura' (measure of the scraps of time that, in the course of a month, the average reader can devote to reading) (Camerlo 14).[11] If narratives became generally shorter, in the best cases their style abandoned conventional academic abstractions and became more incisive, pithy, and overall more accessible. During his tenure as the editor of *La Lettura*, the writer Giuseppe Giacosa repeatedly stated that he would evaluate all contributions to his magazine based on their readability and ability to satisfy the needs of an increasingly busy, inquisitive, and hurried readership (1–5). Typical articles evolved from an average of eight to ten pages with a few small illustrations to an average of four or five pages, a third of which were taken up by photographs and illustrations (Camerlo 17).

Together with the format, topics changed, too: In the notes that he jotted down for later inclusion in *Movimenti spirituali e correnti letterarie* (Spiritual Movements and Literary Currents), Renato Serra commented that modern readers no longer wanted the critical article. They favoured instead the illustrated piece, featuring 'aneddoti; immagini rapide; tutto quello che interessa, ferma gli occhi' (anecdotes, rapid images, all that is interesting, and strikes the eye) (172). These new magazines' emphasis on the variety and multiplicity of their topics influenced the spread of mixed narratives, that is, of a writing style that Giovanni Ragone identified as the practice of the 'manipolazione degli ambiti,' or the amalgamation of different stylistic and generic backgrounds (704). These mixed narratives included, for example, Federico De Roberto's and Adolfo Albertazzi's fictionalized renditions of historical events and the romanticized biographies of famous women with which Alfredo Panzini achieved success later in the 1930s, and that Gozzano anticipated in pieces such as 'La Garibaldina.' Perhaps the most successful examples of mixed narratives were those devoted to travel. Perfected by writers such as Edmondo de Amicis, Luigi Barzini, Vico Mantegazza, Luciano Magrini in *La Lettura*, Grazia Deledda in *La Donna*, and of course Gozzano himself, these travel narratives found room for excursions into innumerable other disciplines such as geography, history, politics, literature, art, archaeology, and anthropology. These narratives popularized the figure of the *giornalista-letterato*, the arbiter and interpreter of cultural mores, equally at home searching libraries and archives and exploring exotic locales. Trained to mediate specialized knowledge by making it accessible and palatable, the *giornalista-letterato* catered to audiences eager to expand their cultural horizons in pleasant and effortless ways.

With their broad circulation, magazines devoted to national and international expositions exemplified and popularized this new style of writing. In spite of a certain amount of repetitiousness from one exposition to the next, these magazines featured an impressive variety of articles, combining anonymous and mostly descriptive pieces with renowned writers' more substantial contributions. *Torino e l'esposizione italiana del 1884: Cronaca illustrata della esposizione nazionale industriale ed artistica del 1884,* or *L'esposizione di Torino 1911: Giornale ufficiale illustrato dell'esposizione internazionale delle industrie del lavoro,* just to cite two examples, hosted pieces signed by De Amicis, Giuseppe Faldella, Camillo Boito, Salvatore Farina, Enrico Thovez, and Gozzano. Just as other periodicals favoured mixed narratives, the exposition magazines' pieces, featuring the conventional 'stroll' along the fairgrounds or through specific exposition sectors, often combined multiple topics. Sociological and ethnographic notes were liberally mixed with popularized technical reports and with historical and geographical overviews containing summarized and simplified scientific expositions. Pieces on contemporary politics shared space with brief biographies of patrons, inventors, or historical characters. Consequently, these magazines' contributors included professional reporters as well as novelists, poets, economists, scientists, anthropologists, politicians, and public servants. Comparable to the eclectic architectural forms that World's Fairs' designers favoured, these magazines reflected the age's exposition mentality and diffused the writing style that marked 'exposition texts' in general.

In an age when photographs were meant to directly capture the real, their increased use in magazines underscored the positivistic myth of journalistic objectivity, and they functioned as visual confirmation of the written word. The photographic reports that Luigi Barzini sent to *La Lettura* and *La Domenica del corriere* from the Russo-Japanese front in 1905 marked an epochal shift into the way journalism was practised, and brought the immediacy of the unfolding war to all bourgeois living rooms. Illustrated magazines thus exploited modern photographic technologies and utilized the illustrative power of the printed image for aims of realistic documentation and factual persuasion. *Bianco rosso e verde,* for example, an openly committed periodical that started publication on 1 July 1915 to celebrate Italy's belated entrance in the arena of the First World War, introduced itself as an 'Illustrazione quindicinale' (bimonthly illustrated magazine), drawing attention to its visual component. 'Di parole il nostro periodico sarà scarso' (Our periodical will cut down on words) ('Presentazione' 1) stated its first director, playwright Giannino Antona-Traversi, thus emulating the ideal of the 'lettura breve, rapida' (quick and rapid reading) ('Il nostro programma' iv) that was typical of the new illustrated magazines.[12] *Bianco rosso e verde's* collaborators (including Gozzano, Salvatore di Giacomo, Rosso di San Secondo, Guido Mazzoni, Amalia Guglielminetti, Anton Giulio Bragaglia, Marino Moretti, Ada Negri, and Alfredo Panzini) bought into the magazine's dual inspiration.[13] Narratives addressing the ongoing war were featured along with other pieces exploiting exotic themes and combining the magazine's colonial thrust with its escapist fantasies.[14] Thus, while upholding the positivistic myth of narrative objectivity and journalistic accuracy, *Bianco rosso e verde* reflected the tension, common to the age's popular press, between the promise of realism and the utilization of forms of disengaged divertissement and spectacular invention. This new type of consumeristic journalism, perhaps best represented by the monthly *La Donna,* both reflected and constructed the refined ambitions and expansive dreams of the newly prosperous Italian bourgeoisie.[15]

The 'Compendium of the World': Gozzano's India as World's Fair Exhibit

Gozzano captured some of these ambitions and dreams when he portrayed India as a visual cornucopia, a spectacle of profuse referentiality, and a land that obediently offers itself to Western inventorying eyes. Whether he is describing the multicoloured crowds and bazaars of Hyderabad, the dazzling gems adorning the body of a dancing girl, or the aimless flow of life in Jaipur, the itemized catalogue remains his prime hermeneutical device, the encyclopedic account his stylistic blueprint. In 'Le grotte della Trimurti' (The Caves of *Trimurti*), for example, the typical coup d'oeil over the fairgrounds translates itself in the description of a breathtaking view, as seen from the dynamic and progressive vantage point of a moving boat. Gozzano marvels at the 'policromia gaudiosa' (cheerful polychromy) (4) and 'bellezza varia' (varied beauty) (4) of the grand harbour of Bombay, with the Island of Elephanta in the background:

> Dobbiamo attraversare il porto della grande metropoli asiatica; la lancia passa come un moscerino ronzante tra i fianchi delle navi: navi di tutta la terra: inglesi, francesi, olandesi, giapponesi, australiane, americane; di tutti i tempi: colossali alcune, nuove, intatte, saggio imponente dell'ultima civiltà; altre di forma arcaica, di età non definibile, zattere immense con una sola grande vela, che osano attraversare l'Oceano Indiano dall'Africa all'India, affidandosi per lunga esperienza a quel dato soffio di monsone in quel dato giorno stabilito: velieri decrepiti che fingono di ignorare ancora l'istmo di Suez, poichè la tassa di transito che si paga a porto Said varia dalle trenta alle cento e più mila lire, e ripetono il loro viaggio secolare circumnavigando l'Africa, l'Arabia, la Persia; velieri panciuti, d'una tinta uni-

forme di vecchio legno fradicio, dalle vele gialle a sbrindelli e a rattoppi, così decrepiti che fanno pensare alle galee portoghesi che ripararono per la prima volta in Buona-Bahia (Bombay), ai negrieri, ai pirati che furono per tanti secoli i signori indisturbati di questi mari e di queste terre. ('Le grotte' 4)

(We must cross the harbour of the great Asian metropolis; the launch flies by like a buzzing gnat among the ships' sides: ships from all over the world: English, French, Dutch, Japanese, Australian, American; ships of all eras, some huge, new and intact, imposing examples of the latest civilization, others archaic in shape, and of indefinable age. They are immense rafts with a single great sail that dare to cross the Indian Ocean from Africa to India, trusting through long experience to that specific monsoon breeze on that specific established day; decrepit sailing ships that pretend to ignore the Suez Canal, because the transit fee that is charged in Port Said varies from thirty to over a hundred thousand liras, and they repeat their age-old journey, circumnavigating Africa, Arabia, and Persia. They are round-bellied, with the uniform hue of rotten wood and with yellow tattered and patched sails. They are so decrepit that they remind one of the Portuguese galleys that took refuge for the first time in Buona-Bahia (Bombay), and of the slave merchants and pirates who were the undisputed lords of these seas and lands for so many centuries.)

Bombay harbour offers a compendium of the world; it is a storehouse packed full with heterogeneous and amazing merchandise craftily scattered all over the place, yet ultimately ready to be brought together and displayed for the viewer's inspection. Liberally mixing geographical spaces and historical times, the harbour is indeed a permanent Universal Exposition, a simultaneous world where the similar and the discordant, the near and the distant, the present and the past, the huge and the diminutive, converge and coexist all at once. One is reminded here of the 'multicoloured and polyphonic tides' that Filippo Tommaso Marinetti celebrated in his Futurist Manifesto. In Gozzano's own words:

Ecco l'Esplanade, dove l'ansare delle automobili, lo scalpitìo degli equipaggi, si fonde col vociare di una folla composta di dieci razze diverse e il suono di venti bande militari. È la passeggiata, il Bois de Boulogne di Bombay; interessante, misto, illogico, come un quadro futurista: tutti i veicoli: carrozzelle indigene, tirate da zebu gibbosi, dalle corna dorate, elefanti gualdrappati fino a terra di velluti ricchissimi, dai quali non emergono che i quattro zoccoli enormi, le zanne tronche, la proboscide, gli orecchi agitati di continuo come due ventagli; carrozze di cavalli candidi precedute da araldi ansanti e vocianti: e dentro è adagiata la moglie, la figlia di un funzionario inglese, e la biondezza della signora, stilizzata secondo l'ultimo figurino europeo, fa uno strano contrasto con la magnificenza esotica e arcaica dell'equipaggio, con i turbanti e i velluti dei cocchieri, con la nudità bronzata degli araldi. ('Le Torri' 14)

(Here is the Esplanade, where the panting of the automobiles and the clatter of the crews blend with the shouting of a crowd composed of ten different races and the sound of twenty military bands. This is the promenade, the Bois de Boulogne of Bombay: interesting, varied, and as illogical as a Futurist painting. All the vehicles – hackney cabs drawn by humped zebus with gilded horns, elephants caparisoned to the ground with sumptuous velvets, under which all that can be seen are four enormous feet, the mutilated tusks, the trunk, the ears constantly in motion like two fans; carriages drawn by snow-white horses, preceded by panting, shouting heralds: inside recline the wife and daughter of a high English official, and the lady's blonde hair (styled in the latest European way) creates a strange contrast to the exotic and archaic magnificence of the retinue, the turbans and velvets of the coachmen, and the heralds' bronzed nudity).

As this example makes clear, Gozzano does not subscribe to a simple aggregative listing technique, and his exotic inventories do not furnish mere sequences of unrelated objects. While aiming at thoroughness, Gozzano's catalogues highlight striking contrasts and unexpected juxtapositions. Haunted like his contemporaries by the fear of Western standardization with its grey triumph of universal sameness, Gozzano revels in his personal poetics of 'le cose stridule' (strident things) ('Un vergiliato' 185), which recalls the 'picturesque contrasts' that contemporary critics such as Ernesto Ferrettini saw as characteristic of all World's Fairs' aesthetics ('Un'ora' 247). Gozzano thus invites his readers to experience the 'shock' caused by the bizarre contact between the known and the unfamiliar, the archaic and the modern, and the here and the elsewhere: 'Barbarie pittoresca e civiltà vittoriosa, tutte le razze e tutti gli idiomi, tutte le linee e tutte le tinte si contendono, stridono in questo convegno del Mondo, che offre tante cose rare all'amatore dell'anacronismo e del paradosso' (Picturesque barbarism and victorious civilization, all the races and all the languages, all the lines and all the colours compete and clash with each other in this Congress of the World, which offers so many rare things to the lover of anachronism and paradox) ('Le grotte' 4).[16]

Unlike other practitioners of the exotic, Gozzano does not seek to capture an otherness uncorrupted by Western contact, still existing in the remote and primeval East, and does not feel bound to safeguard the 'exotic' against the rush of an entropic modernity. Certainly, Gozzano plays – half nostalgically and half humorously – with these literary clichés, but he is no mourner for the ruined tropics. For him, India's colonial exoticism ultimately rests upon the coupling of distant, often contradictory, terms. It results from the pairing, yet never merging, of those highly crafted representations of the East and the West that the river Po had also conveniently separated at the 1911 International Exposition in Turin. Gozzano lingers on the description of an Indian chauffeur, whose forehead sports both a bright red plastic visor and a tattoo with the trident of Vishnu ('Le Torri' 13), and comments on the 'vertiginous speed' of modern automobiles swirling around an ageless fakir lost in motionless meditation on the steps of the Victoria Memorial ('Le Torri' 13). Indian railways exude 'un fascino esotico indefinibile' (indefinable exotic charm) ('Da Ceylon' 42) with the swish of their *pankas* alternating with the hum of electric fans, and his sense of the picturesque finds inspiration in the light carriages made of lacquered bamboo placed on modern bicycle wheels ('L'impero' 73). Equally exotic is the sound of gongs and flutes, playing counterpoint to the bell chimes of the Catholic missions, the acoustical parallel to the necklaces mingling Hindu idols and the phallic lingams with images of Christian saints and crosses ('Da Ceylon' 45). In 'Glorie italiane all'estero: gli orrori del Paradiso' (Italian Glories Abroad: The Horrors of Heaven), Gozzano exemplifies the practice of the contrastive catalogue thus:

Abbiamo intorno la folla più varia: Cingalesi dal passo lento, dal profilo perfetto, nobili nella loro nudità bronzata come principi di leggende, tamili foschi ... donne native dal naso, dagli orecchi, dai piedi ingioiellati d'ori gialli e massicci, sacerdoti buddisti dal manto giallo e dalla testa rasa. In quest' ambiente indigeno si sovrappone, senza confondersi, l'elemento europeo: signori e signore in veste di tela o di seta candida, col cappello caratteristico del tropico. (138)

(The most varied crowd surrounds us: slow-paced Sri Lankans with their perfect profiles, noble in their bronzed nudity, like fairy-tale princes, dark Tamils ... native women, their noses, ears, and feet bejewelled with solid yellow gold, Buddhist monks in their yellow mantles and shaven heads. The

European element – ladies and gentlemen dressed in white cotton or silk,
wearing the typical tropical hats – superimposes itself without merging into
the native environment.)

The 'shock' deriving from Gozzano's poetics of 'le cose stridule'
could be related to the Russian formalists' *ostranenie*, literally, the aesthetic practice of 'making strange' through which the artwork upsets
routine modes of perception and inspires a new, non-jaded vision of
reality. By defamiliarizing and creatively deforming the normal and the
usual, the poet stimulates perceptive mechanisms worn out by everyday
habit: 'le cose vicine, anche bellissime, non si vedono più' (we can no
longer see the things that are near to us, even if they are splendid),
states Gozzano ('Le grotte' 3). Unforeseen juxtapositions engender a
sense of perceptual alertness and, by awakening the viewer's critical
attention, inspire a deepened awareness not only of what is different but
also of all that is familiar. In his draft of an *Essai sur l'exotisme*, Segalen
defined the exotic experience precisely as an experience of shock: 'la
réaction vive et curieuse au choc d'une individualité forte contre une
objectivité dont elle perçoit et déguste la distance' (the lively and curious reaction to the shock caused by a strong subjectivity in the act of
enjoying the distance of a perceived object) (25). For Segalen, this
experience of shock is always reciprocal and transformative. Reciprocity,
of course, does not mean that the power of one culture to affect another
is equal. As is often the case when Western and extra-European civilizations meet (one can think of the Maori in *Les Immemoriaux*), the encounter is tragically destructive only for the latter.

In contrast to what happened in Segalen's case, in Gozzano this encounter is rarely transformative. With a few exceptions that I shall discuss in
detail later, his cultural values and ideological presuppositions remain
unaltered. Therefore, like those displayed at World's Fairs, Gozzano's global inventories function as optical devices that intensify the viewer's sense
of visual responsiveness, while remaining framed within conventional
interpretative mechanisms. By thus depriving it of all subversive edge,
Gozzano confines his poetics of the 'shock' to the practice of superficial
chromatic contrasts in a series of two-toned vignettes with which he ultimately waters down the complexities of all cultural encounters:

Avanziamo lungo un piroscafo inglese giunto da poco ... Lungo una sca-
letta troppo fragile scendono i viaggiatori ... Una signora biondissima si
rifiuta al passo ... un gigante di bronzo l'afferra senz'altro, la solleva in alto,

la passa a un altro gigante ignudo, che la depone delicatamente ... nella
barca tra i suoi bagagli ... Quella biondezza e quelle braccia candide avvinte
disperatamente alle spalle barbare mi hanno fatto pensare una romana
della decadenza, una *flava coma* contesa da due schiavi nubiani un poco
irriverenti. ('Le grotte' 5)

(We sail past a newly arrived British steamer ... The passengers climb down
the all-too-precarious gangway ... A platinum-blonde lady refuses to step
down ... and a bronze giant unhesitatingly grabs her, lifts her into the air,
and hands her to another likewise naked giant who delicately deposits her
... in the boat among her luggage ... The blonde woman, with her white
arms clinging desperately to the barbarian's shoulders, made me think of a
Roman woman of the end of the Empire, a *flava coma* fought over by two
slightly irreverent Nubian slaves.)

The 'shocking' encounter between the vulnerable white beauty and the
swarthy 'giant' implies the possible violation of an unwritten rule or of a
set of social premises. At first glance, India appears as the theatre that
unhesitatingly stages the prologue to an act that may well mock Western
biases, the prejudice against 'miscegenation' in the first place. However,
Gozzano frames this vignette within a narrative that reiterates rather
than challenges the norm. That of the 'black giant,' it turns out, is a
tightly framed shot, and there is no sequel to the specific event of this
vignette, as Gozzano immediately cuts back to another panoramic view
of the Bombay harbour, showing 'un brulichio di forme nere; tutti *indu*
di bassa casta, che vanno, vengono in file ordinate e opposte come le
formiche, o si passano dall'uno all'altro, in catena, le gerle di carbone,
le balle di cotone' (a swarm of black shapes; all low-caste Hindus who
come and go, filing past one another in opposite directions like ordered
lines of ants, or form a chain handing one another baskets of coal and
bales of cotton) ('Le grotte' 5). De-anthropomorphized and reduced to
the size of insects, the chain gang of pariahs working for Western trade
confirms the power of European rule. Even slavery, Gozzano concludes,
is a small price to pay if one considers that Christianity has liberated
these people from the caste system and introduced them to the idea of
'una possibile salvezza, la speranza di poter pretendere dalla morte ciò
che non ha dato la vita' (potential salvation, the hope to be able to
demand from death that which life has denied them) ('Le grotte' 6).

Gozzano's conclusive statement, a sort of voice-over to the panoramic
shot of Bombay's harbour, literally wills emancipation and transgression

out of *this* world. Framed within this larger picture, the 'strident' element of Gozzano's vignette becomes what Umberto Eco would define as an *'authorized* transgression,' a brief parenthesis that emphasizes by way of contrast the surrounding celebration of conventional social models and cultural expectations ('The Frames' 6). However brief, Gozzano's parenthesis is not entirely inconsequential. Although it offers a mere hint of transgression within a normative script – nothing more that a ripple in the otherwise smooth narrative of Western conquest – Gozzano's vignette also discloses the West's deep-seated cultural fears. By describing a virile India acting upon a feminized and threatened England, Gozzano overturns the clichéd allegory of a feminized land awaiting and welcoming the advances of a male-gendered West, and thus unveils Europe's unacknowledged colonial anxieties.

With vignettes like this one, Gozzano aimed at satisfying editorial requests to provide pleasurable entertainment to a hurried and curious readership. In their quick succession, Gozzano's vignettes also recall the expositions' dioramas and panoramas, with their ambition to set up the wondrous world of modernity as a sequence of pictures that everybody could see. In his Indian narratives, Gozzano repeatedly stated that his India was to be experienced as a painting or a scene. In this case from 'Da Ceylon a Madura,' one could speak of a *maréorama*:

> Dal Picco d'Adamo alle foreste del litorale tutto è avvolto in pochi secondi da una cortina di nubi tondeggianti, cupe e concrete come se scolpite nel marmo livido, mentre il cielo intorno e sul nostro capo resta azzurro e tranquillo; nella cornice fosca, simile all'ovale di nubi artificiose di certi Inferni e di certi Diluvii, guizzano, s'intrecciano lampi azzurri e violetti, e lo scenario interno s'accende di un riverbero sanguigno, profilando in nero i palmizi scapigliati; un'acquata torrenziale ... riga il centro del quadro di striature oblique di cristallo. (40)

> (In a few seconds, from Adam's Peak to the coastal forests, everything is engulfed in a curtain of billowing clouds, dark and solid as if carved from bluish marble, while the sky around and above us remains blue and peaceful. In the dark frame, resembling the oval of artificial clouds in certain pictures of Hell and Floods, blue and violet thunderbolts criss-cross and flash. The inner scenery sparkles with bloody red flashes, outlining the dishevelled palm trees in black. A torrential rain ... streaks the centre of the picture with oblique glass-like stripes.)

It is not surprising that Gozzano inverts the relationship between art and life, invention and reality. One is bound to think, of course, about one of the clichés of the Decadents' poetics, as popularized by Oscar Wilde's famous aphorism: 'Life imitates Art far more than Art imitates Life' (*Epigraphs* 82).[17] Gozzano is also displaying his age's exhibition mentality as the 'logic of techniques, dictionaries, frames, tableaux, descriptive systems, or rhetorical processes in general' that structure and interpret the real for us (Hamon 79). Modern exotic travellers and fairgoers give themselves over to the exercise of the gaze and look at a world made of carefully framed reproductions. As we have discussed earlier, from towers or portholes, telescopes, balconies, windows, and camera lenses, this ubiquitous machinery of representation directs and monitors the viewer's gaze. The world, even the exotic world, offers itself up not as undefined reality, but as a further model of the real, a disciplined spectacle, a pre-represented plot, a diorama of juxtaposed images, a visual arrangement. 'Io mi compiaccio,' Gozzano writes as he arrives in Agra, 'di osservare nella realtà misera e cenciosa, ma pittoresca, le figure e le cose troppo lette nei libri' (I find delight in observing, within this destitute and tattered, but picturesque, reality the figures and the things that I too often read about in books) ('Fachiri e ciurmadori' 91).

Given these premises, how can fairgoers and exotic travellers experience a sense of wonder (Gozzano's 'shock') in responding to a reality that is already a twice-told tale and, in its prefigured forms, has no more real novelty to offer? In 'Il dono della meraviglia' (The Gift of Wonder), Gozzano describes the 'folla varia e cosmopolita' (varied and cosmopolitan crowd) that visits the 1911 Turin exposition 'con lo scopo precipuo di *meravigliarsi*' (with the specific aim to experience *wonder*) ('Il dono' 195). In the modern world, Gozzano argues, wonder is rarely the result of an encounter with the absolutely new. Only children 'sanno godere con meraviglia delle cose nuove' (know how to enjoy new things with a sense of wonder) ('Il dono' 195). For everybody else, 'le cose non esistono ... se la cultura non le ha prima rivelate' (things do not exist ... unless culture has revealed them first) ('Il dono' 195). For Gozzano, modernity's sense of wonder, then, does not result, as an *exote* such as Segalen would have claimed, from the shocking and unmediated encounter with difference, but depends instead upon pre-established cultural preferences: 'non ci meravigliamo che delle nostre predilezioni ... Io conosco più di un uomo e più d'una donna intelligente che va all'Esposizione col solo desiderio dell'acquario, del Padiglione della moda, della Kermesse, dei vaporini sul Po ... La diversità ... che di tutto fa meravigliare è un dono assai raro' (We only feel a sense of wonder about the things that we already like best. I know more than one intelligent man or woman who goes to the exposition with the sole desire to see the Aquarium, the Couture Pavilion, the Kermesse, or the boats on the river Po ... The sense of diversity ... which allows one to feel wonder for everything, is a very rare gift) ('Il dono' 196).

The 'new,' Gozzano concludes, enjoys a paradoxical status in the modernist sensibility because it can be known and felt with wonder only if it is not *really* new, but comes framed within familiar structures. Novelty is an experience in the second degree, resulting from the stirring up of acquired notions, mnemonic traces, and stored images, which cannot lay claim to, but at best only evoke, a sense of novelty. While Gozzano would have agreed with Flaubert, who stated that the attentive European '*re*discovers [in the East] much more than he discovers' (*Flaubert in Egypt* 81), he often wavers between the pleasure of rediscovery and the sense of loss implicit in this cultural hypertrophy. In 'Il dono della meraviglia,' he mockingly describes the fairgoers as people 'incapaci di vedere, di sentire, se il *Baedeker* non vede e non sente per loro' (unable to see and unable to feel, unless their *Baedeker* sees and feels for them) ('Il dono' 196). At the same time, Gozzano does not place himself above his times. A belated traveller in an aging world, throughout his writings Gozzano self-consciously highlights the filters through which he experiences the world. His trip to India, in particular, is a pilgrimage among the many cultural memories that have already composed this world as a text or a picture for him.

Of Mazes and Masks: India as Counter-Exposition

If this were all of India, then the difference between East and West would be more a matter of surface than substance. In its engulfing power, the exposition mentality that we have drawn so far would order both East and West as pictures and displays, successfully submitting them to the laws of point of view and perspective, and organizing them into the World's Fairs' typical 'gran quadro sinottico' (great synoptic picture) (Gozzano, 'La città' 208). Gozzano, however, proceeds a step further and raises the logical question: What happens when the East, as the negation of the order and logic of the West, does not accept being framed within a 'picture' and thus either 'fails' to produce meaning or appears to defy the West's appropriative epistemology? Gozzano's evaluation of Indian art and architecture illustrates this hermeneutical quandary and provides an interesting, if somewhat predictable, answer to this question. If, in the West, classical beauty depends on principles of harmony and proportion and conveys a sense of wholeness and organic unity, India features an upside-down world built on the perverse negation of these valued notions. The description of Gozzano's trip to Elephanta Island in 'Le grotte della Trimurti' is a case in point: 'Le colonne si moltiplicano all'infinito, pendono spezzate dalla volta tenebrosa o s'innalzano monche come stalattiti. Il tempio è lavorato con un'arte pazientissima nei particolari ... ma noncurante delle proporzioni e dell'armonia dell'insieme' (The columns multiply into infinity, hanging suspended from the gloomy vault or rising mutilated like stalactites. The temple was built with an artistry that was painstakingly attentive to detail ... though careless about the proportions and harmony of the whole) (7–8). Approaching it with the criteria of classical aesthetics, Gozzano cannot but consider the Indian temple as a challenge to Western artistic sensibilities. The monstrous combinations of feminine and masculine attributes and of human and animal traits in the temple's bas-reliefs defy the principle of non-contradiction and the aesthetics that idealizes the human form. It is with calculated effectiveness that Gozzano juxtaposes the 'teogonia barbara e selvaggia' (barbarous and savage theogony) ('Le grotte' 9) depicted in the temple with the 'topografia mirabilmente equilibrata' (wonderfully balanced topography) of British Bombay ('Le grotte' 10).

By posing as the advocate of a strong rationalism, based on binary logic and hierarchical opposition, Gozzano does not tolerate what he perceives to be the disharmony and confusion of Indian aesthetics. In spite of Borgese's claims attesting to the journeyman's spiritual progression, the pilgrimage toward Madura – il cuore di Brama (the heart of Brahma, the fifth sketch in Borgese's edition) ('Da Ceylon' 43) – does not bring any change in the tenacious traveller. With their exaggeration of the colossal and the diminutive, the hybrid monstrosity of their images, and the incompleteness and proliferation of their forms, Madura's cyclopean temples defy aesthetic and logical conventions and give no hermeneutical crutches to the baffled European visitor. This is a reality of chaos that refuses to compose itself into a picture: 'la grande pagoda a Siva e a Minakshi "la dea dagli occhi di pesce" è per sè sola una città e un labirinto' (the great temple of Shiva and Meenakkshi, 'the fish-eyed goddess,' is a city in and of itself and a labyrinth) ('Da Ceylon'

45). In the bellies of these enormous mazes, shapes double in perceptive nightmares that erase all differences between the sacred and the
profane. Space seems to progressively dilate and Gozzano continually
alters his point of view without being able to identify the frontal perspective from which to organize, once and for all, the proliferation of
images.

Intended as loci for the display and the worship of the sacred according to the Hindu faith, for the Western traveller the temples of Madura
constitute instead a counter-exposition: they do not offer a vantage
point from which to enjoy an empowering coup d'oeil on a space ready
to disclose its topographical logic. There is no panoramic or panoptic
site here, from which the whole can be embraced in a comprehensive
manner, thus affording the exposure of meaning and inspiring a grand
totalizing synthesis. A product and a victim of the exposition mentality
that sees the world as a picture set up in front of a subject, here Gozzano
is hopelessly looking for something that would form a structure or a system, a framed totality. As Timothy Mitchell argues, the problem for the
writer or the photographer visiting the East 'was not only to make an
accurate picture of the East, but to set up the East as a picture. One can
copy or represent only what appears already to exist representationally –
as a picture. The problem, in other words, was to create a distance
between oneself and the world, and thus to constitute it as something
picture-like – as an object on exhibit. This required what was called a
point of view' (229). In Madura, Gozzano finds out, there is no such
place set apart, outside of the labyrinth, or above it. Instead of the exhibition of a cohesive organizing principle, Madura reveals a heterogeneous and flat textuality, an infinite display of disconnections, and an
undecipherable iconography than cannot be submitted to written semiotic mediation. Gozzano confirms this impression throughout his pilgrimage in Hindu India, and the Lambadahadam temples appear to
him as 'un ammasso babelico che supera, confonde ogni legge di gra-
vità, ogni concetto architettonico della proporzione e della linea' (a
Babel-like jumble that overcomes and confounds all laws of gravity, all
architectonic concept of lines and proportions) ('Un voto alla dea
Tharata-Ku-Wha' 129).

If, as Hamon remarks, literary architecture realizes itself in the form
of descriptions, and if these descriptions can occur through the main
rhetorical figures of metaphor, metonymy, and synecdoche, then Gozzano's narrative witnesses the frustrated attempt to *expose* Madura via
these rhetorical strategies. Hamon explains:

Exposition – both as a privileged ... moment and as a descriptive figure in literary texts – is able to submit itself to one of these [rhetorical figures] ... which are also the foundation for three conceptions of the world ... three sorts of realism ... We have, first of all, a hermeneutic realism, this is a 'vertical' realism, based on decipherments ... It is a realism essentially concerned with bringing to light, dismantling, revealing, and flushing out the real from behind its facades, its masks, or its outward appearances. Secondly, there is a 'horizontal' realism that clears the grounds, maps out exhaustive neighborhood routes, furls and unfurls encyclopedic juxtapositions, and furnishes methodical tables and classifications. Thirdly, there is a realism that apprehends the real as an intersection of norms, as a system which is itself the effect of a larger hierarchical system of values, scales, and constraints. (28–9)

Madura makes no sense metaphorically, or 'vertically,' as no deeper or inclusive reality emerges from the maddening display of the 'useless' details that accumulate chaotically upon its baffling surfaces. Madura is not, therefore, a '*hermeneutical* object' (Hamon 26), as its facades do not shelter any concealed meaning. In the rare cases in which Madura delivers some kind of hermeneutical clue, it is so debased and profane in the eyes of the Western viewer that it cannot possibly invest the transcendent, and rather than awe it inspires laughter: 'Passo dalla luce abbagliante nella penombra religiosa, m'addosso alla parete di granito, per orizzontarmi, e sento che il granito palpita e cede; è uno degli elefanti sacri, un colosso decrepito che sembra scolpito nella pietra stessa del tempio' (I walk from the blinding light into the religious dusk, and lean against the granite wall in order to get my bearings. I feel the granite pulse and give way. It is one of the holy elephants, a decrepit colossus, which seems carved out of the temple's stone itself) ('Da Ceylon' 46).

Madura makes no sense 'horizontally' or metonymically either. The temples do not define clear spatial contiguities; there are no partitions and thresholds joining and separating distinctive spaces. Madura is not a '*differential, discriminating* object that analyzes space through interfaces and proximities' (Hamon 27). 'La città profana continua nella città sacra' (The secular city continues inside the holy city) ('Da Ceylon' 46) writes Gozzano, bewildered by the optical illusions that the play of lights and shadows creates, and by the hybrid shapes merging in strange forests of columns 'di carne, di pietra, di metallo' (made of flesh, stone and metal) ('Da Ceylon' 47).

Consequently, nor does Madura make sense synecdochically, as a '*hier-*

archical object,' a system that defines interlocking components and architectural hierarchies (Hamon 28). Madura distorts all familiar value systems, all scales and relative spatial rankings, its spaces failing to construct an intelligible system of differences. Inside and outside, container and contained, sacred and profane, centre and periphery, parts and whole, lose their oppositional and therefore signifying codes. Unlike any Western church, Madura is not a space 'of interlocking volumes or proportional scenography' (Hamon 142), and does not provide the extended metaphor of transcendence that produces intelligibility and meaning. Gozzano's narrative can be interpreted as the negative side of Erwin Panofsky's famous essay on the Gothic cathedral, with its systematic exposition of 'the structural homology between scholastic rhetoric and the organization of medieval architecture' (Hamon 31), that is, its interpretation of the sacred space as metaphor or incarnation of a Scripture and a Word.

Unable to devise configurative patterns that can resolve spatial ambiguities, Gozzano cannot translate the temple into an expository narrative or a 'discreet, articulated, hierarchical, semiotic whole' (Hamon 32). Lacking metaphorical, metonymical, and synecdochical values and being deprived of the inaugural vantage point that enables full understanding of its inner meaning, Madura – the Indian 'sacred' – is limited to mere surfaces. However, these surfaces do not remain utterly undefined and unintelligible. Rather than conceding that different conceptual schemes and a different set of tools for gathering and deciphering information may be necessary to *understand* Madura, or accepting the sense of dispossession of a subject whose rational procedures cannot resolve the intricate hermeneutics of a space that breaks away from Western cognitive appropriation, Gozzano sticks to familiar evaluative strategies. Although Madura is, simply, not arranged as an exhibition, Gozzano nevertheless resorts to the typical cognitive tactics of the modern interpreter, and naturalizes the surfaces of Madura into objects of mimicry. In their unnatural, hybrid, freakish, extravagant, and ridiculous forms, and in their defiance of all laws of statics, symmetry, and proportion, they are seen as replicating European grotesques.

Emphasizing deformed bodies and bodily functions, the grotesque was at the opposite of sacred art that idealized the human form (Kayser 23). The upside-down world of Madura, the sacred city of Brahmanism, where 'strane divinità [sono] ... chiuse in gabbie dalle sbarre robuste' (strange gods [are] ... caged up behind strong bars) ('Da Ceylon' 47) and animals are free to roam the temple, fits right into the grotesque mould.[18] By activating the code of the grotesque Gozzano engages in a familiar discourse, that of contrastive comparison: Madura's grotesques forms the dark, sinister, and distorted side of a brighter and rationally ordered world. Furthermore, by arguing that Madura is grotesque, Gozzano is essentially stating that there is no place for the sublime in Madura, that is, for the only aesthetic discourse that Western thought deems worthy of defining the sacred.[19] Only the sublime in fact is able to convey that all-embracing, absolute necessity of a structure that exposes the logic of all its parts as they effortlessly unite in a harmonious, breathtaking whole. By contrast, the 'ridiculously distorted and monstrously horrible ingredients of the grotesque point to an inhuman, nocturnal, and abysmal reality' (Kayser 58). Therefore, Gozzano can conveniently conclude that the Indian sacred is incomprehensible for the simple reason that it is not sacred at all: it is a disproportionate and repulsive world of forgeries, travesties, and surfaces – a devilish denial of beautiful nature.

Just as he attempts to disclose and evaluate the meaning of Indian architectural forms for his Western readers, Gozzano proposes himself as the privileged interpreter of another quintessentially exotic and opaque surface, the body of a dancing girl (a bayadère) in 'La danza d'una Devadasis' ('The Dance of a Devadasi'). Reversing his typical claim of the hermeneutic precedence of art over reality, Gozzano claims that in order to *understand* the bayadère, one has to rid oneself of Western prejudice based on the images popularized in 'i libri d'avventura, le oleografie, i melodrammi, l'operetta' (adventure books, oleographs, operas, and operettas) ('La danza' 50) and observe her *directly*. What he sees, though, is a crafted and structured fiction, not unlike the exotic dances performed at many World's Fairs' Oriental villages.[20] Mise en abîme of diverse symbolic systems, the bayadère's dancing body displays itself as the esoteric commentary, the semiotic mediation, of an exceptionally closed text:

> Una Devadasis (ancella della Dea) cioè una bajadera di casta bramina, vanta, anzitutto, una nobiltà millenaria, poichè non può essere che figlia di una bajadera ... È facile comprendere come, anche per solo istinto ereditario, s'affini in una Devadasis l'arte del gesto, del passo, dell'atteggiamento, l'arte della voce e della maschera, l'attitudine letterata a penetrare, commentare insuperabilmente i capolavori della poesia indiana ...
>
> La danza è già cominciata quando prendiamo posto ... ho la fortuna d'aver dinanzi, a pochi passi, la danzatrice famosa ... Una snellezza alla

Rubinstein, non so se illegiadrita o ingoffata da un costume singolarissimo, formato di sete, di velluti, di tulli sovrapposti, che lasciano ignude le spalle e le braccia; ma dalle spalle alla gola, dalle spalle alle mani è uno scintillìo d'oro e di gemme, oro e gemme autentici, poichè così è prescritto dalla regola monastica, tutto un tesoro che tremola e corrusca sulla fine epidermide bruna: oro giallo del Coromandel, perle di Manaar, rubini, smeraldi, zaffiri di Ceylon; e dalle stoffe, dall'oro, dalle gemme emergono ignudi soltanto la maschera del volto, le mani, i piedi perfetti. ('La danza' 50, 54–5)

(A Devadasi (handmaiden of the Goddess), that is, a bayadère of the Brahamin caste, boasts, first of all, a nobility that goes back for thousand of years, since she can only be the daughter of a bayadère ... It is easy to understand how, just by mere ancestral instinct, a devadasi can refine the art of gesture, gait, carriage, the voice and the mask, the literary attitude to penetrate and masterfully interpret the masterpieces of Indian poetry ...

The dance has already started when we take our seats ... I am fortunate to have the famous dancer in front of me, just a few steps away ... She is as slim as Ida Rubinstein, though I do not know whether her figure is embellished or encumbered by a very unusual costume made of silk, velvet, and layers of superimposed tulle that leaves her shoulders and arms bare. Yet, from her shoulders to her throat, gold and gems sparkle, real gold, real gems, as the monastic rule prescribes. An entire treasure sparkles and glitters on her delicate brown skin – yellow gold from the Coromandel, Manaar pearls, rubies, emeralds and sapphires from Ceylon; and all that emerges out of the fabrics, the gold and the gems is the naked mask of her face, her hands, and her perfect feet.)

Just like the facades of the temples at Elephanta Island and Madura, the bayadère has an ostensive (or theatrically 'ostentatious') function. On stage for the pleasure and edification of her selected public, she performs an *exposition*. Like a parchment, a vellum, or a sheet of paper, her body is an inscribed surface, the site of a complex discourse made of multiple signifying agents: her mask-like expressions, her precious ornaments, the overlapping layers of her sacred garments, and the scripted movements of her dance.

In spite of his journey to authenticity, however, the Western pilgrim remains several times separated from meaning: The obscure metalanguage of dance and staged performance glosses a sacred text that has been made available to Gozzano via a flawed translation of a printed summary in Hindi, itself a copy of the inaccessible original. Thus, just like the famous temples, the bayadère's 'script' remains incomprehensible to the Western viewer. If all these surfaces (the bayadère's mask-like face and her layered clothing, or the temples' intricate bas-reliefs) appear to gloss a deeper text, to put it on *show*, to *expose* it, the excitingly esoteric and rich semantic core of that text is ultimately ungraspable. Epistemological conquest is thus denied to the eager Western voyeur:

La Devadasis non danza, s'avanza e retrocede con un ritmo prestabilito, seguendo la musica e le strofe ... Nessuno canta, ma tutti, musici e spettatori, sillabano a mezza voce i versi del poema sacro che la bajadera ripete per conto suo, come per rammentarsi o per intesa. Ma più nulla si sente, più nulla si vede che la maschera ovale, il sorriso triangolare, gli occhi già troppo lunghi, prolungati dal bistro fin sotto la benda dei capelli compatti, lucenti come se scolpiti in un ebano raro: una maschera che sembra staccarsi dalla persona, far parte a sè come un'evocazione spiritica. ('La danza' 55)

(The Devadasi does not dance. She moves forward and backward to a pre-established rhythm, following the music and the strophes ... Nobody sings, but all, musicians and spectators, chant sotto voce the lines of the sacred poem that the bayadère repeats to herself, as if to remember them or by common agreement. But I no longer hear and see anything besides the oval mask, the triangular smile, the already over-elongated eyes that the make-up extends even further, all the way to the veil of her compact hair, shining as if sculpted out of rare ebony – a mask that seems to detach itself from the body and exist on its own, like an evoked spirit.)

Arguably, the act of relating the bayadère's dance or describing the Indian temples is, in itself, a form of rewriting: a glossing over of the original narrative, a way to reactivate a body of knowledge. However, unlike the Romantic traveller to the Orient whose self-assured gaze penetrated the exotic mysteries of both bodies and temples – I think of Flaubert's *Salammbô* and the learned sensuality of Kuchuk Hanem – Gozzano simply fails to perform.[21] Bayadère and temples alike do not lay themselves open to activities aimed at the begetting of meaning, and to satisfying the urge to read, interpret, paraphrase, understand, and know. In her resistance to interpretation, the bayadère is a deeply disconcerting reminder of Gozzano's *own* lack of self-possession, of the limitations of his *own* heuristic skills. Therefore, with a predictable reaction, Gozzano responds to this hermeneutical resistance by first forcing a debased meaning upon the elusive body: 'Spettrali veramente sembrano le mani ... di questa Devadasis [che] all'estremità delle braccia immobili, s'agitano con un movimento vertiginoso di rotazione e di distorsione che sembra sconvolgere ogni legge anatomica' (The Devadasi's ... hands are truly ghost-like. At the ends of her immobile arms, these hands flutter with a dizzying rotating and twisting motion that seems to defy all laws of anatomy) ('La danza' 55). Gozzano sees a grotesque body on stage, a body distorted in unnatural poses, a twisting body that exposes an equally twisted text. Secondly, Gozzano denies the bayadère meaning altogether: in spite of all her accoutrements, the bayadère signifies nothing as *hermeneutical object*. There is absolutely nothing underneath the mask, nothing beyond the spectacle of this alienated body, this theatrical machine given over to something other than herself, ready to be used and reused with the predictable repetition of ritual.

While Gozzano initially implies that the bayadère's meaning is socially constructed (she may mean nothing, or appear grotesque, to the party of Western visitors, but is otherwise meaningful to her Indian audience), he later extends the meaninglessness to a wider, more absolute realm. According to Gozzano, once her scripted performance is over, the bayadère remains an empty shell for everybody, Indian and Western visitors alike: 'Le siamo intorno rispettosamente, per osservarla, ma sul suo volto è la completa assenza spirituale; è cessata la musica e la fiamma e si ha veramente l'impressione di accostarsi ad una lampada spenta, ad uno stromento che ha finito di vibrare' (We respectfully gather around her, to observe her, but her face reveals a complete spiritual emptiness; the music has ceased, and so has the flame within her, and one really has the impression of approaching a lamp that has been turned off, an instrument that has ceased to vibrate) ('La danza' 57).

Devoid of any inner independent life, the mediator of Indian spirituality has, paradoxically, no soul. Like the religion she embodies, or the ruined temples that dot the Indian landscape, Gozzano implies, 'la viva scultura del tempio' (the temple's living sculpture) is a fiction and a forgery, an idol rather than an icon. Behind all this mystified disapproval, Gozzano hides a telling act of displacement. He exorcizes the great spectre haunting the modern consciousness of the West, with its fear of alienation and loss of authenticity, by displacing both alienation and inauthenticity from the mind of the Western male observer to his quintessential Other: the body of an Asian woman. Significantly, it is at the end of the bayadère's baffling performance that Gozzano expresses his disappointment regarding his trip to India. His statement challenges the very title of Borgese's collection:

> L'occidentale, che ritorna in India, non riconosce più la sua cuna.
>
> So bene, questi Indu sono ariani del nostro ceppo, fratelli nostri, ma fratelli che rifiutano di tenderci la mano. Siamo troppo diversi. Ci dividono troppi millennii. Da troppo tempo ci siamo detti addio. ('La danza' 58)

> (The Westerner who returns to India does not recognize his cradle any longer.
>
> I am well aware that these Hindus are Aryans like us, our brothers, but brothers who refuse to hold out their hand to us. We are too different. Too many millennia separate us. We said farewell to one another too long ago.)

Casting himself as the forlorn traveller in a world brimming with false images and empty surfaces rather than disclosing humanity's original essence, Gozzano is, indeed, the anti-pilgrim. Knowledge, for him, does not result from contact with new ideas or revision of old beliefs, but only from recognition and confirmation of conventional and familiar views. Take, for example, the 'vision' that Gozzano experiences upon finally leaving the interior of the Madura temple:

> Si esce all'aperto ... E alla luce del tramonto, appare la grande piscina del tempio, un rettangolo di cento metri di lunghezza, chiuso ai quattro lati da scalee di marmo, circondato da colonne leggiadre, evocanti la grazia d'un peristilio pompeiano. Dopo l'ombra tetra e le fiaccole gialle e gli idoli spaventosi, l'anima si ristora in riva a quest'acqua cristallina, liscia come uno specchio, dove il cielo riflette con un nitore preciso le nubi sanguigne, alternate all'azzurro cupo, e le prime stelle della notte che giunge. ('Da Ceylon' (47–8)

> (We walk outside ... and, in the light of sunset, we see the great temple pool, a hundred metres long, rectangular, enclosed on all four sides by marble staircases surrounded by graceful columns, evoking the grace of a Pompeian peristyle. After the gloomy darkness and the yellow torches and the fearsome idols, the soul refreshes itself on the shore of this crystal-clear water, smooth as a mirror, in which the sky reflects its blood-red clouds and dark blueness and the first stars of the coming night with terse clarity.)

In the familiar features of classical structures and in the reassuring proportions provided by a space arranged according to symmetrical lines and enclosed by ninety-degree angles, the traveller is, once again, able to 'orient' and project himself into the outside world. This world reflects back a sense of identity based upon notions of balance, order, and measure. Architecture, here, reflects nature's sublime geometry, and its design is pleasurably intelligible because it reproduces known representational schemes, thus giving the traveller the consoling impression of being able to master the real.

A similarly empowering vision had captured Gozzano upon exiting from the darkness of the temples at Elephanta Island, when he rendered the visual shock caused by the tropical glare with the universalizing finality of this impersonal two-valued statement: 'Si passa dall'ombra alla luce, dalla barbarie alla civiltà, dal passato decrepito al presente vittorioso ... Dall'alto di quest'isola d'Elefanta – tomba del passato – si contempla l'isola di Bombay – cuna dell'avvenire – e nessun contrasto è più profondo e più significativo' (We move from shade to light, from barbarism to civilization and from decrepit past to victorious present ... From atop Elephanta Island – tomb of the past – one contemplates the island of Bombay – cradle of the future – and no contrast is deeper and more significant) ('Le grotte' 10–11). The sweeping view from atop the temple's mountain underscores the subject's panoptic power. A heap of crumbling and worthless ruins deprived of all aesthetic and spiritual value, the temple of Elephanta is exploitable only for its utilitarian use: a vantage point from which the Western traveller enjoys the dominating vistas of the ordered and sublime glories of Western imperial conquest.

Beyond the Exotic Surface: Gozzano's *Letters* as Hermeneutical Objects

Similarly clichéd renditions of Western superiority pervade the surface of Gozzano's Indian sketches, which are brimming with invidious praise for 'questi Inglesi, così forti e così ricchi, padroni di mezza terra' (these British people, so powerful and so rich, rulers of half of the earth) ('Le Torri' 14). At times, however, unforeseen messages circulate at the deeper levels of Gozzano's prose and a more original, ideologically troubled voice emerges. In 'Le Torri del silenzio' (The Towers of Silence), for example, Gozzano recounts a trip to Malabar Hill, in Bombay, following the invitation of a group of British acquaintances. The reason for the trip is twofold: it is an occasion to observe, albeit surreptitiously and from a distance, the Parsees' funeral rites, and a chance to participate in the picnic that a Lady Harvet is hosting in the lovely gardens of the Towers of Silence. 'La Torre del Silenzio: anzi, le Torri, poiché sono cinque le *Dakmas*' (The Tower of Silence: actually, the Towers, for there are five *Dakmas*) (12), Gozzano explains with the skilled precision of a Cook's tour guide, are the places where the Parsees deliver the corpses of their loved ones to the vultures. As is imaginable, in its cultural remoteness, the topic of the Parsee funeral ceremony was particularly apt to excite the curiosity and provoke the scandalized reaction of Gozzano's bourgeois readership:

> Ed ecco fra il candore dell'edifizio e l'azzurro del cielo un'enorme forma nera e sinistra: il primo avvoltoio; poi un secondo, un terzo; poi sei, sette coronano la torre ... Questi grifoni funerari superano veramente l'orrore di ogni aspettativa; si direbbe che la Natura li abbia foggiati secondo il loro tetro destino; hanno ali immense, possenti al volo, fatte per gli abissi del cielo, ma che nel riposo lasciano pendere lungo il corpo, trascinano nella polvere con una sconcia stanchezza, artigli formidabili, ma senza la linea nobile dell'aquila, artigli fatti per affondare nella carne putrida, non per lottare con la preda viva. E alla base del petto, sopra una collarina di piume fitte, si innesta un altro animale, un tronco di serpente ignudo, gialliccio, grinzoso, dalla testa calva, con un becco oscuro ed occhi dallo sguardo insostenibile, dove s'alterna la ferocia ingorda alla viltà e alla maliconia ...
>
> Lungo la strada, a mezza costa della collina, biancheggia ... il corteo funerario. È tutto candido; strana usanza opposta alla nostra, che ammanta di veli bianchi il dolore dell'ultimo addio. ('Le Torri' 16)

(Suddenly, a large shape, black and sinister, appears between the gleaming whiteness of the building and blue of the sky – the first vulture, then a second, a third, then six, seven crown the Tower ... The griffins of death truly exceed the horror of every expectation; one would say that nature has designed them according to their gloomy destiny. They have immense wings, powerful for flight, made for the abysses of the sky; yet in repose they let them hang next to their bodies, trailing them with a sense of obscene exhaustion in the dust; formidable claws, but without the noble profile of the eagle's, claws made for sinking into putrid flesh, not for struggling with live prey. At the base of their breasts, above a thickly plumed neck, another animal is grafted: the trunk of a naked serpent, yellowish, wrinkled, with a bald head, a dark beak, and eyes whose gaze, which alternates between insatiable ferocity and melancholy cowardice, is unbearable ...

Along the road, halfway up the hill, the funeral procession shines white

... Everything is immaculate whiteness; a strange custom the very opposite
of ours, a custom that shrouds the sorrow of final farewell in white.)

Gozzano's narrative proceeds through a series of vivid visual contrasts.
The juxtaposition between Christian and Parsee funeral rites, for example, rests upon the overarching chromatic contrast of blacks and whites,
and the same chromaticism marks the opposition between the snow-
white towers and their dark-winged inhabitants. Within this contrastive
visual framework, Gozzano inscribes other types of dualisms or oppositions. Half sky-dwelling and half earthbound, capable of soaring upwards
yet weighed downwards due to their ill-matched anatomy, the snake-birds
appear to be the result of a botched metamorphosis. In more symbolic
terms, they can be viewed as embodying a flawed resurrection, one per-
verted by the damning semiosis of the biblical serpent. This symbolism
acquires more sinister tones when Gozzano endows the vultures with
anthropomorphized attitudes (themselves contrastive, ferocity and cowardice), thus creating an unsettling parallel between the fiendish birds
and the human realm. In another juxtaposition, Gozzano intersperses
the portrayal of the Parsees' funeral cortege – each member symbolically
united with another in silent grief by holding the opposite ends of a
twisted handkerchief – to the description of the picnicking party. This
party does not share quiet pain but garrulous pleasure, and combines the
enjoyment of a colourful meal with the thrilling voyeuristic experience of
the exotic forbidden 'spectacle': 'Lady Harvet dispone ... la tavolozza ga-
stronomica dell'invidiabile appetito inglese ... latte, miele, thè, marmel-
late indigene ed europee, canditi, sott'aceto, salati, e frutti tropicali'
(Lady Harvet arranges the culinary wonders ... in which the enviable
English appetite delights ... milk, honey, tea, local and European jams,
pickles, relishes, candied and tropical fruit) ('Le Torri' 15–16).
  'Le Torri del silenzio' stands out among Gozzano's Indian sketches
because, rather than limiting himself to his customary visual contrasts,
here Gozzano creates a sense of cognitive shock by unveiling deeper
similarities among distant and contrastive situations. As in a well-built
baroque metaphor, binary oppositions curtail their absolute distance
and a single commonality shines forth. Readers experience a sense of
surprise as they progressively realize that the narrative's descriptive and
linear logic is traversed by the implicit simile between British appetite
(the 'invidiabile appetito degli Inglesi') and the vultures' hunger (their
'ferocia ingorda'), between Lady Harvet's juicy jams and the birds'
human repast. As a result, Gozzano the traveller cannot imagine the

macabre feast from the safe distance of the uninvolved European audience, and his initial eagerness to scoop out an exotic fruit suddenly turns into disgusted refusal.

If the medical doctor who dispassionately presents the details of a corpse's disposal while consuming his lunch represents the Western detached audience in the act of examining an alien cultural phenomenon, Gozzano's hostess, Lady Harvet, fills the immeasurable distance between the two worlds, and unsuspectingly brings the appalling candour of exotic death within the European compound. 'Una signora attempata e bellissima, tutta bianca, vestito, volto, cappello, capelli, con non altro di colorito che gli occhi azzurri' (A gorgeous, elderly lady whose sky-blue eyes provide the only chromatic contrast with the whiteness of her dress, face, hat, and hair) ('Le Torri' 13), Lady Harvet shares in the chromaticism of the funeral scene and thus appears now as a harbinger of doom, a female destroyer, a mask of death. The provider of heavenly culinary temptations in the Edenic setting of the Towers of Silence's garden, the elderly Lady Harvet becomes a figure of rapacious exploitation, a living corpse that scavenges on the remains of an ancient culture, the synecdoche of an entire nation's colonial yearning for political incorporation and economic consumption. 'The Towers of Silence' resonates with a surprisingly virulent, if oblique, anti-imperial criticism, and Gozzano's shocking imagery challenges the overall conservative practice of the '*authorized* transgression.' Reaching deeper than the initial contrastive chromaticism would have implied, Gozzano's surprising analogies unsettle conventional views of the relationship between Britain and India. As he moves beyond binary logic, Gozzano provides a startling counter-narrative to his own apologia of British imperialism.

Historiography as Assemblage: Intertexual Montages in 'L'Olocausto di Cawnepore' and 'Goa: "La Dourada"'

Contrary to Borgese's reconciling and totalizing project, Gozzano's Indian sketches reveal a contradictory subject whose relationship to India is complex indeed. In the course of his journey, Gozzano experiments with numerous identities, sometimes displaying an unassailable self whose beliefs are inflexibly predefined, other times revealing a more puzzling subjectivity, one that readjusts and realigns its ideological stances, sometimes going as far as reversing them. These shifts do not mark a progressive journey in the construction (or dissolution) of selfhood as presented by classic epistolary novels such as Ugo Foscolo's

Ultime lettere di Jacopo Ortis. Seen together, Gozzano's letters from India constitute a non-linear juxtaposition of ideological and autobiographical experiments that never settle on a resolutory and univocal position.

Two of Gozzano's Indian narratives, 'L'Olocausto di Cawnepore' and 'Goa: "La Dourada"' may be examined together in order to discuss Gozzano's contrastive and ultimately unresolved ideologies. Unlike other extemporaneous Indian sketches, Gozzano carefully researched and meticulously wrote 'L'Olocausto' and 'Goa.' To borrow Gerard Genette's useful textual taxonomy, we can say that Gozzano's two narratives systematically expose their 'transtextuality,' or their 'textual transcendence,' that is, they self-consciously highlight the fact that they echo, reproduce, recontextualize, distort, or parody an interlocking network of other texts (1).[22] In 'L'Olocausto' and 'Goa,' Gozzano sees India as an inscribed page waiting to be rewritten: a palimpsest, accessible to those who are able to read through its scripted layers and extrapolate new meanings from the subtle variations on the already said. If Salgari surreptitiously removed fragments from someone else's script and blended them with his own authorial discourse, Gozzano flaunted his citational acts, drawing the reader's attention to the 'quotation marks' interspersed in his narrative. These quotations marks have a Janus-like duplicity, as they perform tasks of both intertexual and extratextual validation. Comparable to World's Fairs' pavilions, with their eclectic reuse of polyvalent and simultaneous architectural discourses, Gozzano's citational narratives purport to reproduce faithfully the extratextual world while claiming at the same time that this world exists inside a well-stocked library. Gozzano does not use his melange of authoritative citations in a dialectical way but, rather, in a self-validating one. Multiple voices thus join him in supporting what he presents as a generalized truth rather than as a subjective and self-consciously Eurocentric rendition of the historical and cultural past.

However, while 'L'Olocausto' reassembles a collective 'colonial library' in order to provide an idealized view of Imperial Britain and sustain Western colonial paradigms in general, 'Goa' casts a long shadow on the history of imperial politics, and dismantles the very imperial palace that 'L'Olocausto' had so painstakingly erected. Gozzano's textual architecture thus exposes a problematic and ultimately contradictory philosophy, as 'L'Olocausto' and 'Goa' first assemble and then take apart one of the founding concepts of British imperial politics in India, which Francis G. Hutchins aptly defined that of the 'illusion of permanence.' In celebrating imperial permanence and then ironically exposing the ephemerality of this very permanence, Gozzano does not embrace an anticolonial stance, but reveals a mixed attitude, combining imperial activism with nihilistic resignation. Modernity, Gozzano concludes, can both admiringly cling to and ironically break apart the heroic imperial history of a world that is inexorably moving toward its sunset.

'L'Olocausto di Cawnepore' is inspired by an episode of what was famously discussed, at the time, as the 'Great Indian Mutiny' of 1857. From May to September of that year, almost all of northern India was swept by a series of uprisings initiated by the Indian sepoy soldiers in the Bengal army, often with the support of the local population, against British rule.[23] Gozzano's piece describes some of the events that took place in the station of Cawnpore (Kanpur) between 4 June and 15 July 1857 pitting the rebel sepoys against the British officers and civilians who were stationed or resided there.[24] Besieged in a poorly fortified entrenchment, the British suffered heavy losses and eventually surrendered to the sepoy leader and newly appointed *peshwa*, Nana Sahib, who promised the British safe conduct down the Ganges to Allahabad. In what contemporary historians interpreted as Nana's betrayal, the rebels opened fire upon the British as soon as they embarked on the boats at the Sati-Chaura Ghat, on 27 June. After the massacre, about two hundred surviving women and children were imprisoned in a small house called the Bibighar and killed en masse just before the arrival of Generals Havelock's and Neill's victorious troops on 17 July. The British regime of retaliatory terror and indiscriminate executions instituted in Cawnpore soon after the Bibighar massacre put a brutal end to the sepoy rebellion.

In 'L'Olocausto' Gozzano characterized his interpretative engagement with 'that red page of Anglo-Indian history' in these words: 'Non invento: tolgo dalla raccolta del *Times* di quell'anno – sfogliata nella decrepita biblioteca del Queen's Hotel – tolgo fedelmente dalla nuda esposizione dei fatti quanto ne emana di tragica poesia' (I don't invent: I extract from the collection of the *Times* of that year – which I leaf through in the dilapidated library of the Queen's Hotel – I extract what tragic poetry emanates from the exposition of the naked facts) ('L'Olocausto' 104). The first statement contains a promise of factual accuracy: 'I don't invent.' By alluding to the insurrection's date and by mentioning his own alleged visit to the library of the Queen's Hotel in Cawnpore, Gozzano creates a convincing 'reality effect.'[25] He establishes his narrative around powerful temporal and spatial markers both on the level of the *discours* (that belonging to the narrating voice who visited the Queen's Hotel's library) and on the level of the *récit* (that of the narrated events, which indeed occurred in the summer of 1857). While these markers guarantee the narrative's concrete extratextual foundation, they also trigger a feeling of exotic distance, in both space and time. Clearly, the average Italian reader in 1915 did not possess specialized knowledge about events that had occurred in a remote location over half a century before. Therefore, while eliciting the readers' curiosity, these markers also made them aware of the different level of historical expertise separating them from the narrative's author. In turn, the author recruits numerous other 'trusted' interpreters to back up his own reading of the events of Cawnpore. The Cawnpore chronicle is thus an exceptionally closed text whose apparent multivoicedness, to borrow Mikhail Bakhtin's famous definition, turns out to be a crafted recycling of numerous 'authorized' sources. Unlike the mystified tourist visiting Elephanta Island, Madura, or Calem, the Gozzano of Cawnpore plays the role of the self-assured mediator, the authoritative decoder, the antiquarian-writer-traveller who performs, to borrow Hamon's pithy expression, 'a discourse about touring [and a] ... tour through discourse' (53).

This tour appropriately begins in the library of the Queen's Hotel, and 'L'Olocausto' leaves no doubt that the queen to whom Gozzano is referring is Victoria. Therefore, the original event, the Cawnpore insurrection, has only a deceptive referential foundation, elicited by the reality markers that Gozzano exploits. These referential markers guide us into an institutional space built upon the exotic land, where, according to the age's taxonomic zeal, all that was strange and distant has already been neatly indexed, catalogued, and displayed. Knowledge is ultimately fixed and stored away in discursive form. A foreign colonial power, aptly represented by Queen Victoria, encodes and controls this uniform script and ties it up with its own nationalist politics and restrictive and self-serving interpretations of the past.

As he conjures up the illusion of a close encounter between the object and its verbal representation, Gozzano is also fully aware that this object exists as a cultural construct – a body of writing. Yet Gozzano is keen on providing us with all that is necessary to 'authenticate the "real"' (Barthes, 'The Reality' 15), and he establishes the truth of his narrative by firmly grounding it in a prime textual authority, a renowned newspaper such as the *Times*. Publishing eyewitness reports, circulating cables received from the 'disturbed provinces,' and collecting moving abstracts of letters and current intelligence from correspondents, the 1857 *Times* was indeed the first source of information on the progress of the insurrection. The conviction that a written document, especially one that has eyewitness authority, can provide an objective and truthful presentation of events belongs to that referential illusion which founds the aesthetics of realism. Besides the obvious allusion to Giovanni Verga, Gozzano's 'nuda esposizione dei fatti' (exposition of the naked facts) mimics the referential ostension that, as we have seen, marked the exposition mentality and made the World's Fairs reflective microcosms for the entire world.[26]

The fundamental difference between the *Times* reports and Gozzano's own narrative resides in their respective formal structures. While the accounts of the *Times* form a loose and fragmented chronicle that maintains all the openness, immediacy, and contradictions of history in the making, the narrative that Gozzano constructs from his temporal vantage point appears as an extraordinarily closed text. From a formal point of view, then, Gozzano's assertion of extracting the tragic poetry from the historical chronicle corresponds to Aristotle's famous definition of tragic and epic plots as dealing with 'a single action that is whole and complete and has beginning, middles, and end.'[27]

Significantly, for Gozzano, the poet's task is to 'extract' (tolgo) a form that is already embedded within the events themselves, and to emphasize the emotional valences that belong to these events rather than to the poet's sensibility in interpreting them. In Gozzano's eyes, therefore, a narrative does not impose formal structures upon the outside world in order to make events meaningfully intelligible, but, rather, reproduces the inner order of history itself. Ultimately, in Gozzano, the function of the poet is to make readers come to terms with data that are only apparently 'strange, not to say exotic, simply by virtue of their distance from us in time and their origination in a way of life different from our own' (White 49). The poet does so by shaping these data according to familiar formal structures that Western thought had long since come to consider universal: 'for poetry is a more philosophical and serious business than history: for poetry speaks more of universals, history of particulars' (Aristotle 33).[28] The mimetic fallacy embedded in Gozzano's formal argument becomes clear if we compare his words with an 1865 interpretation of the 'mutiny' issued by G.D. Oswell:

> The story of the Indian Mutiny will ever exercise a fascination over the minds and imagination of men. It has, indeed, a world-wide interest. Drama must always appeal to the human race. And in this particular story

the world has seen depicted not one only, but a whole series of immortal dramas. What a theme for the great World-Dramatists and for the great World-Poets is here! Not one single element that goes to make up a World-Drama or a great World-Epic is wanting. Scene succeeds scene with dramatic swiftness: figures heroic who would not have done despite to an Homeric stage: figures tragic and pathetic such as only the genius of a Shakespeare could adequately present: figures half-divine and wholly dæmonic such as only a Milton could have called up from the vast deep of his almost inspired imagination: all these move across the stage. It would be a theme, moreover, for a modern Indian Epic: but who could be found capable of undertaking such tremendous a task? (xxiii–xxiv)

Like Ferdinand De Lanoye, who, in *L'Inde contemporaine* (1858), familiarized his European readers with 'le théatre et les acteurs du dernier acte du grand drame de l'insurrection' (the theatre and the actors of the last act of the great drama of the insurrection) (526), Oswell views past actuality as an 'untold story' that is simply there, waiting to be unearthed and exposed. The formal closure of the insurrection's narratives is not intended to provide an order that the interpreter constructs retrospectively. This order is instead meant to mirror the innermost form of the real, which, ironically, bears a striking resemblance to the classic narrative principles of exposition, intrigue, and outcome. The writer and consumer of these narratives is the detached and cultivated bourgeois – the World's Fairs' flâneur – who has mastered the exotic world and its intrinsic violence by reducing it to the familiar forms of a spectacle, so that 'the original strangeness, exoticism of the events is dispelled [as] they take on a familiar aspect, not in their details, but in their function as elements of a familiar kind of configuration' (White 49). Emplotting the Indian Mutiny as a set of dramatic episodes within a larger and ultimately triumphal epic is thus explained by the assumption that this was the form intrinsic to the events themselves, rather than the form through which the 'illusion of permanence' expressed itself, that is, the way in which European interpreters sought to justify, celebrate, and most of all maintain Britain's presence in India.[29]

Although Gozzano concentrates on just one episode of the 1857 insurrection, the reflectionist approach that founds these grand imperial epics of the British in India, and presents them as exact copies of what actually happened, underscores his narrative as well. Nowhere is this translation from the referential to the symbolic orders so apparently unobstructed than in the citation that opens Gozzano's narrative: 'Remember Cawn-epore!' A nameless highlander, Gozzano explains, inscribed these words with the tip of his sword, on a stone covered with the victims' dried blood. The fusion of biological and discursive realities is complete here. That nameless bard and earliest historian issues a written directive for Western collective memory, whose task becomes that of preserving this 'truthful' merging of the empirical into the symbolic through the acts of reading, remembering, and eventually rewriting.[30] The material form of the citation functions as a monument, whose object is to memorialize a fixed, unchangeable memory, literally carved with blood in stone:

Remember Cawnepore! Non so staccare gli occhi dalla targa di cristallo che ha conservato, dopo cinquant'anni, le due parole disegnate da un *highlander* innominato sul cubo di granito. Il soldato era certo tra quelli che ebbero il còmpito tremendo ... di entrare nella casa della strage, di restaurare le pareti crollanti, di raccogliere i resti, di detergere il sangue 'che saliva fino alle caviglie.' Sopra un macigno sconnesso, dove il sangue aggrumato – sangue di bimbi biondi, di donne bionde! – offriva una pagina rossa, il soldato aveva disegnato, con la punta della spada, a grandi lettere accurate, le parole tragiche.

Remember Cawnepore! Nessuno ha dimenticato, ma certo l'umile soldato non immaginava che il cubo fosse più tardi rimosso e la sua iscrizione, tutelata dal cristallo, figurasse oggi nelle cripte del Fatal Well: il pozzo fatale. Il sangue ha preso col tempo una tinta di fuliggine, dove le due parole spiccano più chiare. ('L'Olocausto' 103–4)

(*Remember Cawnpore!* I cannot take my eyes off the glass plate that for fifty years has protected the two words that a nameless highlander carved on the granite stone. The soldier was certainly among those who had the terrible task ... of going into the house of the massacre, to restore the crumbling walls, gather the remains, clean the 'ankle-deep blood.' On a disconnected stone, where the clotted blood – blood of fair women and fair children – created a red page, the soldier had drawn, with the tip of his sword, in big and accurate letters, the tragic words.

Remember Cawnpore! Nobody forgot, but certainly the humble soldier did not imagine that the stone would be later removed, and his inscription, protected by the glass, would be displayed today in the chambers beneath the Fatal Well. With the passing of time, the blood has acquired the colour of soot, where the two words stand out in a lighter hue.)

Instead of bleaching them into oblivion, time brightens the words of the dead: writing thus overturns the ravages of time and becomes memory's ally in preserving an icon – a 'true' image – of what is no more.

In its citational form, Gozzano's quotation also evokes a literary corpus that appropriated and repeated this memorializing mandate in order to validate its own rendition of the Cawnpore events. Aristide Calani, for example, in his aptly titled *Scene dell'insurrezione indiana* (Scenes from the Indian Insurrection, 1858), imagines the British women, imprisoned in the Bibighar and about to be murdered, 'che intingono le loro dita nel sangue e scrivono queste parole: Vendicateci! Ricordatevi di noi!' (dip their fingers in their blood and write these words: Avenge us! Remember us!) (886). Similarly, Gozzano's direct reference to the blood 'che saliva fino alle caviglie' (that was ankle-deep) recalls words printed in the *Bombay Times* on 10 August 1857: 'there were two inches of blood upon the pavement' ('The Disturbed'), which, in turn, are echoed by Charles North's 'the clotted gore lay ancle [*sic*] deep on the polluted floor' (76), and W.J. Sheperd's 'One small room was a pool of blood about two inches deep' (136). Similarly, George Trevelyan described the Bibighar's inner apartment as being 'ankle-deep in blood' (335), and T. Rice Holmes reiterated that 'clotted blood lay ankle-deep upon the floor' (290). The citational quality of Gozzano's introduction alludes to a textual ensemble, and to a process of textual layering in which verbal signs never engage their referents directly, but only after circulating through numerous other verbal spaces. Referents, therefore, are paradoxically both evoked and superseded by successive strata of written words. In one pithy paragraph, Gozzano adheres to a realist creed, acting as the antiquarian who 'deciphers stones and their inscriptions, collects relics and fragments,' repeats history's 'true echoes,' and captures the 'voices of the dead' (Hamon 149). He also admits that his facts will never be naked, because these facts are given to us cloaked and embroidered with all the intricate patterns of previous interpreters' inscriptions. In Gozzano's poetics, therefore, the poet's job consists of the act of 'truthfully' reworking other writers' scripts.[31]

Employing the notion of script in both a specific and general manner, in order to contextualize Gozzano's narrative in light of the 'idea of India' that was circulating in Italy and Europe around the beginning of the First World War, one should not limit oneself to identifying the most literal and immediate borrowings. One should also consider more indirect sources, the kind of miscellaneous materials that form the common memorial patrimony of a specific cultural ensemble, shaping its com-

pounded imagination. This patrimony can be called a group's 'collective learning,' which defines a small group (the bourgeois Turinese
intellectual circles to which Gozzano belonged, for example) but also,
in its broader traits, a much larger constituency (such as the Italian middle classes in general). Although a single influential and widely known
text can shape the collective imagination in a given field of knowledge
over an extensive period of time, a group's collective learning is generally made up of an assorted cultural corpus – one that, as shown in the
case of World's Fairs, is not necessarily limited to writing. A set of shared
ideological and ethical traits characterizes this corpus and disseminates
a specific world view, at a given moment in time. A certain group, more
or less consciously, shares a sense 'of the forms that significant human
situations must take by virtue of [its] participation on the specific processes of sense-making that identify [this group] as a member of one
cultural endowment rather than another' (White 49).

The cultural corpus on the Cawnpore events available in Europe
between 1858 and 1915 appears unerringly homogeneous in its assemblage of the same data and events, and in its use of the same formal
structures.[32] The *Times* reports provided the rough canvas upon which
stories were redrawn, following a predetermined sketch. Like Gozzano's, these narratives were generally organized around a chronological scheme based on two scenes of increasing horror and violence: the
killing of the British prisoners at the Sati-Chaura Ghat after Nana's
alleged betrayal of his promise of safe passage, and the massacre of the
surviving British women and children at the Bibighar.[33] With its crescendo in pathos, clear-cut moral dichotomies, and antagonistic protagonists (the 'Devil,' Nana Sahib, versus the 'Saint,' Colonel Wheeler), the
Cawnpore story elicited a visceral and unambiguous public response,
which every new text, with its dogged repetition of the same facts,
seemed devoted to inspire anew. By 1915, average European readers,
while remaining ignorant about specific details of the insurrection,
shared a set of preconceptions about how the mutiny had to be emplotted according to imperatives that were extrahistorical, aesthetic, and
ideological in nature, but that were considered, in a kind of collective
conceptual fallacy, as purely mimetic and referentially accurate. As in
classic epics, the claim to 'truth' advanced by innumerable stories dealing with the insurrection rested on the mere fact that they had become
familiar, part of a generally accepted tradition of materials selected and
shaped by the Western imagination.[34] In this context of sheer interpretative redundancy, the meaning and ideological specificity of 'L'Olo-

causto di Cawnepore' cannot be found within its stated conformity to the unvarnished reality. On the contrary, it will emerge from its reworking of previous representations, in the extent, that is, to which Gozzano adhered to or departed from the stock representations of the Indian 'mutiny' that were circulated in Europe between 1857 and 1915.

Writing from the vantage point of 1915, Gozzano follows his age's taste for sweeping overviews, and offers a list of the insurrection's reasons that reconciles and sums up previous interpretations:

> Compie ora il secolo dal giorno dell'occupazione sacrilega (1757–1857) predicano i Bramini; la profezia dei 100 anni sara coronata dallo sfratto degl'infedeli e da un'India degli indiani. I reggimenti di *sepoys* si sollevano ad uno ad uno, per cause minime: la proibizione di portare i grandi cerchi d'oro agli orecchi o di ridurre le lunghe barbe uncinate, un nuovo tipo di carabina che comporta cartucce da rompersi coi denti: e le cartucce sono unte di grasso di bue o di maiale: il bue, animale sacro per gli Indù, il maiale, animale immondo per i mussulmani; cause occasionali: le cause concrete sono ben altre. Gl'inglesi annettono uno stato dopo l'altro alla Compagnia. Lord Dalhousie ha tolto di colpo l'immenso Stato di Ouda, rifiutando al Marhaja spodestato la pensione e gli onori. Quasi tutti i sovrani indigeni delle province del Nord sono in vedetta, sicuri del popolo, forti di ricchezze immense e di una speranza quasi certa: l'aiuto della Russia ferita dalla campagna di Crimea, la Russia in vedetta all'Himalaja. ('L'Olocausto' 104–5)

(The Brahmins announce that it is now the one-hundredth anniversary of the sacrilegious occupation (1757–1857). The prophecy of the one hundred years will realize itself in the chasing away of the infidels and an India for the Indians. The sepoy troops rise up one by one, for minimal causes: the prohibition of wearing their big round golden earrings and the order to cut down their long forked beards, the use of a new kind of rifle the cartridges of which must be broken open with one's teeth: and the cartridges are smeared with cow's and pig's fat. The cow is an animal sacred to the Hindus, and the pig is an unholy animal for the Muslims. These are occasional reasons; the true causes are quite different. The British are annexing one state after another to the company. Lord Dalhousie has suddenly taken away the enormous state of Oudh and has refused the deposed Marahaja a pension and honours. Almost all the indigenous rulers of the northern provinces are on the lookout, sure about their people, strengthened by enormous wealth and an almost certain hope: help from Russia hurt by the Crimean campaign, Russia on the lookout in the Himalayas.)

By separating the 'occasional' reasons related to the sepoys' religious beliefs from the 'concrete' political causes that triggered the uprising, Gozzano appears to shape his historical overview according to strong evaluative codes that sift deep historical causality from mere surface pre-textuality. In spite of this statement, however, Gozzano ends up amplifying what contemporary historians such as Charles Ball labelled 'the religious prejudices of the high-caste sepoys ... and the visible mysteries of their idolatrous faith' (1: 35), that is, the 'occasional causes' that he had only apparently dismissed. Gozzano achieves this through an act of historical compression that collapses multiple historical time frames into a single discourse. European interpreters often argued that the expectations related to the hundredth anniversary of the battle of Plassey and the infamous cartridge incident that Gozzano describes were among the main causes of the 1857 insurrection.[35] However, unlike Gozzano, none of these interpreters listed the prohibition against the sepoys wearing gold earrings and long beards as triggering the revolt of 1857. Instead, they mentioned this prohibition only when discussing the introduction of European headgear as parts of the new regulations in the Madras army, which they believed had triggered the Vellore mutiny of 1806 (Corte 186). By compressing history, Gozzano remarkably expands the range of the 'unfounded and unreasonable' (Ball 1:49) motives that contemporary interpreters attributed to the sepoys 'primitive' religious habits, rather than to a mature sense of political independence. A verbal counterpart to the eclectic exposition buildings, compressing architectural chronologies into one space, or to equally fanciful displays telescoping multiple historical periods into one evocative show, Gozzano's narrative uses a technique of historical 'montage' that carries heavy ideological biases.

Moreover, in spite of his initial analytical posture, Gozzano's political overview lists the reasons for the insurrection one after another rather than critically. One of the most controversial issues among both contemporary and later historians was whether the 1857 uprising resulted from a large and premeditated conspiracy against the British government, or rather was the somewhat random and violent result of various and unorganized local grievances that were either limited to the sepoys or extended to wider segments of the population.[36] Several early historians subscribed to the conspiracy theory, and argued that Persia and Russia had fuelled the insurrection as part of a campaign to drive the English out of India.[37] By undervaluing foreign influences, or by connecting them to Indian plots, other scholars followed an indigenous trail leading to Nana Sahib as one of the uprising's chief conspirators. Early interpreters such as John Kaye, W.H. Russell, and Holmes saw Nana engaged 'in widespread intrigues before the outbreak of the Mutiny' (Majumdar 340).[38] Giovanni Flechia, in *Storia delle Indie Orientali* (A History of the Eastern Indies), a volume published in Turin in 1862, which Gozzano is likely to have consulted, discusses 'un'estesa congiura contro la continuazione del dominio inglese [in India]' (an extensive plot against the continuation of British domination [in India]) (1229). Even though Western historians hinted at these leaders' attempts to restore the ancient Indian dynasties to rule the country, they refused to characterize the insurrection in terms of a people's struggle for independence.[39] Rather, they saw the insurrection as the result of these leaders' 'misplaced' grudges and ambitions, particularly those of Nana Sahib for being deprived of his adoptive father's pension and title, following Lord Dalhousie's implementation of the doctrine of lapse.[40]

It has often been argued that our explanations of historical processes are determined more by 'what we leave out of our representations than by what we put in' (White 44). Although Gozzano borrowed extensively from historical and fictional accounts of the sepoys' 'mutiny' such as Calani's *Scene dell'insurrezione indiana* and Jules Verne's *La maison à vapeur* (*The Steam House*, 1860), he eliminated their interpretation of Nana as the mastermind of a vast insurrectionary movement. Calani's text, in particular, contains an astonishing letter attributed to a non-Western interpreter, a 'Bramino Ram-Mohun,' who characterizes the revolt as a nationalistic and patriotic endeavour, in tones reminiscent of those used for the Italian Risorgimento. Talking about the insurgents' hope for the 'sublime trionfo dell'armi nazionali contro l'oppressione straniera' (the sublime triumph of the national army against foreign oppression) (719), Ram-Mohun examines the siege of Cawnpore as a reaction to intolerable British abuses, refers to a newly established Indian national army, and defines Nana Sahib as one of the main leaders of a great national movement (722–43). Similarly, in *The Steam House*[41] Verne wrote: 'At the beginning of the year 1857, while the contingent of the British army was reduced owing to exterior complications, Nana Sahib, otherwise called Dandou Pant, who had been residing near Cawnpore, had gone to Delhi, and twice to Lucknow, no doubt with the object of provoking the rising, prepared so long ago, for, in fact, very shortly after the departure of the Nana, the insurrection was declared' (136).[42]

While interpreting the uprising as a popular and collective national independence movement (renaming the 'Great Mutiny' as the 'First

Indian War of Independence') is, generally, a theory supported by only more recent historians, it is interesting that Gozzano, who borrowed extensively from both Verne and Calani, chose to omit all references to Nana's conspiratorial efforts.[43] Although Gozzano appears to aim at historical thoroughness and objectivity in discussing the uprising's causes, through meaningful omissions he frames the cause of national independence in such a way that severs it from his own narrative of the facts of Cawnpore.[44] By weakening the insurrection's political foundations and depriving Nana and his sepoys of all ideological maturity, Gozzano devalues his own hypothesis of the existence of an independence movement: 'un' India degli Indiani' (an India for the Indians).[45] Gozzano's list of probable causes for the insurrection remains isolated from the account of its effects, which appear therefore as a gratuitous crescendo of random acts of violence. In spite of his best efforts at rational political analysis and social investigation, Gozzano implicitly claims, the 'mutiny' remains an incomprehensible event, to be relegated to the realm of destructive natural occurrences such as earthquakes, hurricanes, and volcanic eruptions.[46] This is the exotic as untamed, inexplicable, and unpredictable violence: the sudden explosion that temporarily wreaks havoc upon the ordered trajectory of progress, the absurd fury that lies outside the cause-and-effect logic of rational historical becoming: 'la razza bionda sa quale sangue scorra nelle vene di questi indiani dal sorriso abbagliante di fanciulla timida, dallo sguardo mansueto sotto le ciglia tenebrose; e ricordano, come si ricorda nella calma dei secoli, il furore sotterraneo della terra malfida' (the fair race knows what kind of blood runs in the veins of these Indians, with their brilliant smiles of shy maidens, their mild glances under dark eyelashes. The fair race remembers, as one remembers through the centuries' stillness, the subterranean fury of an unreliable land) ('L'Olocausto' 103).

The theme of treacherous violence, attributed to a land and a people still in the process of being brought into the light of Western civilization, had become a staple in most representations, whether historical or fictional, of the sepoys' insurrection. Significantly, in 1883, French playwright Jean Richepin staged *Nana Saheb*, an apparently conventional drama of politics and love transposed into the exotic setting of Nana Sahib's palace in Bithoor, Hindustan, during the crucial years of 1857–8.[47] Richepin was not interested in factual accuracy, and the historical events themselves remain marginal parts of the plot. However, the commonly held European views of these events permeate the entire play, shaping its ideological and moral messages. The core of the play is not the tragic love story between the beautiful Djamma (a role designed for the celebrated Sarah Bernhardt) and Nana Sahib, or the outcome of the bloody battles between the sepoys and the British troops. *Nana Saheb* is simply a lengthy variation on the themes of deception and betrayal. While the plot uses many ingredients of classical tragedy and exploits the familiar buzzwords of French classic plays – *le sang* and *la gloire* – it soon becomes apparent that, under the Indian sky, blood and glory are reduced to matters of brutal murder and selfish rapacity, as they have lost their traditional mate, *l'honneur*. Untrustworthy and deceitful, Nana's actions are prompted by jealousy and hatred, and Richepin denies him the ending appropriate to tragic heroes, that of catharsis and death, dooming him to live on as a victim of his own deceitful ways, banished from the lavish existence he once held in the palace of Bithoor.[48]

Wholeheartedly buying into the cliché of Indian 'malignant treachery ... and pitiless ferocity' (Ball 1: 330), Gozzano also fondly exploited the echoes of innumerable narratives that had brought to Europe a romanticized rendition of the elegantly structured British social life in India on the eve of the great insurrection. These included the immensely popular Oriental dioramas, which delighted thousands of Worlds' Fairs visitors with fanciful pictorial representations of the social life of the English in Britain (Altick 481).[49] The average European was thus 'familiar with the pattern of anglo-indian life ... the churches, the theatre, the assembly room, the race courses – occasional whist-parties or balls, western delicacies' (Gupta 46). In this perspective, the recurrent references to Nana Sahib's seldom missing 'an occasion for giving a ball or a banquet in European style to the society of the Cawnpore station,'[50] while historically inaccurate, were exploited to titillate Western curiosity about the 'excesses' of Asian splendour.[51] They were also the excuse to portray Indian attempts to compete with Western refinement as pathetically inept, and emulation was invariably reduced to grotesque mimicry.[52] These references were also meant to intensify the moral reprobation against Nana's betrayal during the siege and its aftermath:

[Nana] était de toutes les parties de chasse, de toutes les fêtes, de tous les bals; et sa fortune, fort belle pour un simple particulier, lui permettait de rendre aux Européens les politesses qu'il en recevait. Ce fut lui, dit-on, qui donna le dernier grand bal de la dernière saison; et presque toutes celles qui devaient être ses victimes dansèrent sous ses yeux, quelques-unes dans l'étreinte voluptueuse de celui qui devait être leur bourreau. Sensuel au suprême degré, la beauté des dames anglaises lui avait toujours inspiré une ardente convoitise. L'insurrection qui semblait devoir renverser la puissance anglaise dans l'Inde allait peut-être lui faire réaliser les deux rêves passionnés de sa vie, savoir: la restauration à son profit du trône des Peschwa, et un sérail peuplé de belles Anglaises. (De Warren 2: 224).[53]

([Nana] participated in all the hunting expeditions, all the parties and all the balls; and his fortune, which was awesome for a simple private individual, allowed him to repay the Europeans for all the kindness he received from them. It is said that it was he who gave the last great ball of the last season; and almost all of those who would become his victims danced under his eyes, some of them in the voluptuous embrace of him who would become their murderer. Sensual to the utmost degree, Nana had always felt an ardent greed for the beauty of the British ladies. The insurrection that appeared to overturn British power in India would have perhaps realized his life's two passionate dreams, that is: the restoration, to his own advantage, of the Peschwas' throne, and a harem peopled by beautiful British women.)

The moral censure against Nana's treachery is one of the commonplaces in all of the 'mutiny's' narratives, as witnessed by Edouard De Warren's previous description, or the hackneyed romance by M. Harding Kelly, *Dick's Love, or the Shadow of Cawnpore* (1914), a narrative hodgepodge featuring endless variations on the stock themes of native disloyalty and British valour: 'Through that week picnics, dances, private theatricals kept the English residents fully amused, and Nana Sahib, who was present at one of these evening gaieties, watched the happy, careless dancers with his false smile of pretended goodwill and friendship, while in his heart he was planning their destruction' (162).[54] Circulated in Europe in conjunction with the reports of the uprising, these narratives capitalized on the stark contrast between the sepoys' savage brutality and the exquisite grace of British costumes – de facto levelling the historical complexities of the insurrection to the timeless struggle between enlightened civilization and monstrous barbarity.

Numerous chronicles and fictional narratives describe lavish receptions organized in various British stations during the months that preceded the insurrection. Charles Ball, for example, observes that in May an unusually large number of European families 'had been attracted to Cawnpore ... in consequence of a series of balls and entertainments given by the officers of the garrison' (306). There is no precedent, however, describing an official ball in Cawnpore honouring Queen Victoria's birthday on the eve of the insurrection. Gozzano imagines that the ball was staged to convey the sense of British confidence and power in spite of the reports of widespread dissent within the ranks of the native soldiery:

> Giunge a Cawnepore la notizia che a Mirat – a dieci miglia dalla città – *i sepoys* hanno ucciso gli ufficiali inglesi, e il colonnello Stanes apre le sue sale ad una festa da ballo, quella sera stessa, per consiglio del generale Hugh Wheeler, e tutta la Colonia è invitata in gran gala diplomatica: la guarnigione europea, tutti i gentiluomini, tutte le signore. Nulla si deve temere, nulla si teme a Cawnepore: la popolazione sappia ben questo. A Wood-House l'orchestra alterna i valzer al *God Save the Queen*. Si festeggia il genetliaco di Sua Maestà la Regina Vittoria. ('L'Olocausto' 105)

> (The news reaches Cawnpore that in Mirat – ten miles away from Cawnpore – the sepoys have killed the British officers, and Colonel Stanes opens his doors to a ball, that very evening, following General Hugh Wheeler's advice. The entire colony is invited in full diplomatic attire: the European garrison, and all the gentlemen and the ladies. Nothing must be feared, nothing is feared at Cawnpore: the population must know this. At Woodhouse the orchestra alternates the waltzes with 'God Save the Queen.' Her majesty Queen Victoria's birthday is being celebrated.)

This smug and self-assured picture that Gozzano offers of the British rule in India contradicts other reports. Even an official British chronicle such as Kaye's monumental *History of the Indian Mutiny of 1857–58* describes in vivid detail the anxiety and confusion reigning in Cawnpore during the months preceding the insurrection, and comments on the widespread rumours about the decline of British power in both India and Europe.[55] Echoing concerns emerging from the *Bombay Times*, Trevelyan writes that there was 'much talk among those who did not love us concerning the decadence of England and the youthful vigour of the Russian power,' and describes the 'cheery vaticinations relating to the approaching downfall of the British rule' (55).[56] Trevelyan himself mentions Queen Victoria's birthday, but only to state that it was passed in silence: 'On the return of the Queen's birthday the usual compliment was omitted, lest the natives should interpret the firing of the salute as a signal for revolt. Even military loyalty dared not do honour to our sovereign in a garrison that was still nominally her own ... The Englishmen at Cawnpore, ignorant of what each day may bring forth, certain only that the catastrophe was not remote, sat, pistol in hand, and expected the inevitable' (78–9).[57]

Most British chroniclers consistently describe the anxiety caused by the perceived weaknesses of British rule on the eve of the 'mutiny.' However, an interestingly discordant note comes from Clemente Corte's *Le conquiste e la dominazione degli Inglesi nelle Indie*. Published in Turin in 1886, this text contains the description of a sumptuous ball that Robert Montgomery offered on 12 May 1857, just two days after the Meerut insurrection. Montgomery's ball, Corte writes, was intended to send a clear message regarding the power and ease of the British administration and military officials:

quella festa ... ricorda in qualche modo per le importanti conseguenze del fatto da cui fu susseguito il ballo dato dalla Duchessa di Richmond a Bruxelles prima della battaglia di Waterloo, poiché al disarmo dei Sipoys a Lahore è specialmente dovuto se Delhi ha potuto essere liberato e la ribellione contenuta. (183)

(Because of the important consequences of the event that followed it ... that ball in some ways recalls the ball that the Duchess of Richmond gave in Brussels before the battle of Waterloo. In fact, it was especially because of the disarmament of the sepoys in Lahore that Delhi was liberated and the rebellion contained.)

In a similar vein, discussing Lord Canning's role in quelling the revolt, Corte writes:

Con una calma che non si smentì mai il Governatore Generale mentre per una parte radunava alacremente i mezzi occorrenti per domare la rivolta, dall'altra parte mostrava col suo contegno la sua piena fiducia nell'esito definitivo della lotta.

Egli sentiva quanto importasse di evitare ogni atto che potesse lasciar credere agli indigeni che gli Inglesi dubitassero della vittoria e diffidassero della efficacia delle loro forze. In onta alle più sinistre previsioni egli volle che ... la festa della nascita della Regina (25 maggio), fosse celebrata colla solita pompa, con un ballo ufficiale e con salve di gioia dalle truppe del presidio. (193)

(With unfailing calm, the Governor General actively gathered the means necessary to quell the revolt while continuing to show in his demeanour that he had full confidence in the final outcome of the struggle.

He sensed that it was very important to avoid every action that might let the natives believe that the British had doubts regarding their victory and did not trust the effectiveness of their strength. In spite of all the most sinister forecasts he decided that ... the Queen's birthday (25 May) should be celebrated with the customary pomp, with an official ball and with a joyful salute from the guns of the garrison's troops).

Completely reversing Trevelyan's account, Corte's narrative appears to be, like Gozzano's, a creative manipulation of other tales of parties and dances given, on several occasions, at various British stations. As a whole, Corte's book glorifies European colonial imperialism in general, and the British conquest and rule in India in particular, all of it seen as central to a God-sanctioned plan: 'sotto la misteriosa ma saggia e benefica azione della Provvidenza ... fu stabilito l'Impero Inglese in India con tutti i beneficii che l'accompagnarono e primo quello di avere aperto la via alla estensione della supremazia degli Europei su tutta l'Asia.' (The British empire in India was established ... under Providence's mysterious yet wise and beneficent action, with all the advantages that accompanied it, first and foremost that of paving the way for the expansion of European supremacy all over Asia) (137, n 1).

Compared with other evaluations of the British Empire in India, including those written by British authors, Corte's text strikes the shrillest pro-British note in its enthusiastic defence of even the most criticized imperial policies, such as Lord Dalhousie's aggressive politics of direct annexation of lands belonging to the East India Company's princely 'allies,' and his strict implementation of the doctrine of lapse. Corte's 'concetto imperiale e civilizzatore' (imperial and civilizing principle) (150) justifies military aggression with a moral agenda, a notion which Gozzano fully embraces in his Indian writings. Citing the Count of Montalembert, Alexis de Toqueville, and Carlo Cattaneo, Corte interprets the 'mutiny' as Gozzano does, as 'une lutte engagée entre la barbarie et la civilization' (a struggle taking place between barbarism and civilization) (170), an epic and holy war whose ending is already predetermined, given the military power and spiritual worth of Western civilization. Resulting in the moral and material development of all Indian people, Corte declares British rule in India as a model for all European powers to emulate.

Gozzano accepted Corte's unique interpretation of the undaunted strength of the British rulers at the time of the insurrection. With an astonishing geographical adjustment, one that reminds us of the architectural transpositions in the expositions' 'dream worlds,' Gozzano rebuilt in Cawnpore the prime symbol of British military power in India: Calcutta's Fort William. Readers of the insurrection chronicles are familiar with the accusations levelled against Hugh Wheeler for having chosen an unsatisfactory site for the Europeans' entrenchment. Having opted for two large barracks 'not more ill-chosen than ill-fortified and not more ill-watered than ill-provisioned' (Chandra 1: 342), Wheeler had failed to prepare his troops to withstand a lengthy siege, thus sealing the Europeans' fate.[58] Describing Wheeler's entrenchment, William Howard Russell wrote: 'The difficulty, in my mind, was to believe that it could ever have been defended at all ... It [was] the most wretched defensive position that could be imagined' (1: 179). Censoring these facts, Gozzano places the Cawnpore garrison 'tra le mura tozze del forte inglese' (within the thick walls of the British Fort) ('L'Olocausto' 106). He proceeds to narrate the British downfall as caused by reasons other than lack of military valour: the arrival of the monsoon, rampant disease, lack of food and ammunition, the presence of women and children in the entrenchment, and, of course, Nana's betrayal.

As the emblem of British military occupation, Fort William also yielded another emotional clue for Western collective memory, for it 'had ignited generations of British schoolboys with passionate indignation and outrage against the "uncivilized natives" of India' (Wolpert 179) as the infamous site of the Black Hole of Calcutta tragedy of 1756. Just as happened during the Cawnpore massacre, on that occasion, too, Indian treachery and cruelty were cited as the causes of the horrendous fate suffered by the many British soldiers who suffocated in the fort's dungeon after it was captured by Nawab Siraj-ud-daula. Just like after the Cawnpore massacre, British retaliation came 'swift and harsh, putting the torch of martyrdom to the tinder of greed and personal ambition' (Wolpert 180), thus underscoring, in spite of occasional setbacks such as this one, the wonderful destiny of the British in India.

Besides these geographical changes, Gozzano took other significant liberties with Corte's narrative. Although Queen Victoria's thirty-eighth birthday occurred on 24 May and the insurrection started at Cawnpore on 4 June, Gozzano placed both insurrection and birthday on 14 May 1857.[59] While the discrepancy between 14 and 24 May may be ascribed to a mere typographical error, the coexistence of the two events is suspiciously meaningful. By transposing the festivities right at the garrison, and by falsifying the chronological record so that the ball celebrating the queen coincides with the sepoy insurrection, Gozzano placed Victoria, victory's namesake, in the middle of the strife, thus anticipating the rebels' defeat:

> L'Inghilterra provvede, combatte l'insurrezione con tutte le qualità sue migliori ... La città è in festa, nella bellissima notte tropicale. Le bionde *ladies* possono sfoggiare le loro spalle e i loro gioielli, gli ufficiali alternare le divise vermiglie alle immense crinoline di seta, nelle graziose volute delle contraddanze dei lancieri. Li protegge il Marhaja generoso, li tutela dall'alto, in effige, la graziosa sovrana ventenne, biondo-cerula sotto la corona dove scintilla la gemma unica al mondo. ('L'Olocausto' 105)

> (England takes care of everything and battles the insurrection with all its finest qualities ... The city is celebrating, in the gorgeous tropical night. The blonde ladies can display their shoulders and their jewellery, and the officers mingle their crimson uniforms with the ladies' immense silk crinolines, in the graceful turns of the 'Lancers.' The generous Maharaja looks after them and, from above, the portrait of a pretty twenty-year-old queen, blonde and blue-eyed under the crown sparkling with the most unique gem in the world, protects them.)

At the time of the insurrection, Victoria was thirty-eight years old, and contemporary portraits depict her as a dark-haired woman. Turned into a fair and blue-eyed Madonna in his iconic revision in Catholic terms, Gozzano's young queen epitomizes the virginal and vigilant Britain that will guard her subjects against the 'devil incarnate' Nana Sahib.

Gozzano's nurturing and protective Victoria corresponds to an image of the queen that the British government aggressively disseminated in India only after the bloody aftermath of the insurrection. Responding to the polemics caused by the excesses of British retaliatory violence in quelling the rebellion, and as a result of what was perceived as a weakness in the East India Company's administration, the British Parliament decided 'that the relations between India and the Sovereign should be drawn closer and this could best be brought about by a transfer of the Government of India from the East India Company to the Crown' (Oswell 1: 40).[60] With the Royal Proclamation of 2 August 1858, Victoria took the sceptre of India. On 1 November 1858, royal rule was dressed in motherly garb as the proclamation, translated 'into all the languages and many of the dialects of India' (Kaye 5: 277), was aimed at conveying 'feelings of generosity, benevolence and religious toleration' (Kaye 5: 273) and at emphasizing the 'prosperity following in the train of civiliza- tion' brought by a 'female sovereign ... to more than a hundred millions of Eastern people' (Kaye 5: 273). The early chroniclers of the rebellion thus created a gap between the British administration in India before and after the uprising: 'The people [of India] generally welcomed [the proclamation] as the document which closed up the wounds of the mutiny, which declared, in effect, that bygones were to be bygones, and that thenceforward there should be one Queen and one people' (Kaye 5: 277). The 'Illustrious Lady' thus replaced the 'Venerable Company,' which became the scapegoat held responsible for having allowed, if not caused, 'the conflict which had deluged the country with blood' (Kaye 5: 278). Pointing to 'an era full of hope alike for the loyal and the mis- guided, for the prince and the peasant, for the owner and the cultivator, for every class and for every creed' (Kaye 5: 278), Victoria brought the epic narrative of British imperialism to its celebratory triumph.

By claiming unbiased fidelity to referential truth while engaging in overt formal recycling, Gozzano engaged in a symbolic practice that World's Fairs repeatedly employed when putting together their ephem- eral shows. A chapter in the great imperial epics of British India, Goz- zano's 'L'Olocausto' was meant to retell the 'true' story of Cawnpore by repeating, and thus confirming, the conventional European interpreta- tions of this phase of the sepoys' insurrection. However, the adjustments and omissions that mark Gozzano's narrative also transform the histori- cal record in a significant manner. Gozzano evaded addressing the prob- lems faced and adjustments made by British imperialism in India by placing a majestic Victoria at the heart of the sepoys' revolt in Cawn- pore. As he forced his Cawnpore narrative to incorporate different phases in the chronology of the British imperialist adventure, Gozzano succeeded in making his narrative the quintessential case study of all the best, and all the worst, that the relationship between East and West had to offer. Gozzano's 'L'Olocausto' confirms the binary and oppositional hermeneutics that expressed itself visually in many World's Fairs' lay- outs, with their displays of Western industrial might on one side and their colonial exhibits on the other. Gozzano magnified the vices that Western interpreters attributed to the Indian character (idolatry, duplic- ity, violence, and ideological immaturity), and exalted the virtues of British rule in India, embodied by an idealized Victoria as the emblem of a benevolent, yet powerful, leadership. Just as expositions constituted idealized and condensed renditions of all the most significant products that participating nations had to display, as a whole, Gozzano's strategy of historical compression conferred an emblematic value upon the Cawnpore events. 'L'Olocausto' became the exemplary *fabula* concentrating, in one point, the whole trajectory of the 1857 insurrection.

'L'Olocausto di Cawnepore' reveals the admiration of large sectors of the Italian middle classes for the British imperial model. It also demonstrates how Italian interpreters such as Corte and Gozzano emphasized the ideology of permanence that founded that very model. 'L'Olocausto' reflects Italy's colonial aspirations on the eve of the Great War, and its desire to acquire international recognition as one of the great European imperial powers. It also demonstrates how Italy's colonialism was, to borrow Giovanni Bosco Naitza's interpretation, 'un fenomeno ... di mimesi, di imitazione e di emulazione volto soprattutto ad appagare ambizioni di prestigio in campo internazionale rispondendo nel contempo a certe tendenze militaristiche ed autoritarie presenti in campo nazionale' (a phenomenon ... of mimesis, imitation, and emulation designed to satisfy Italy's ambition of gaining international prestige and, at the same time, responding to certain militaristic and authoritarian tendencies that characterized the nation as a whole) (3). Supported by the military, the monarchy, and the northern bourgeoisie in general, Italy advocated the beginning of another triumphal age of expansion abroad, an age that would avenge the infamous colonial defeats of Dogali and Adowa. In spite of Gozzano's universalistic pretensions of abiding to absolute historical truth, the ideological slant of 'L'Olocausto di Cawnepore' emerges clearly from Gozzano's engagement with other 'Mutiny' narratives. 'L'Olocausto' shows that Gozzano's effort to merge the realist's cult for absolute referential accuracy with the formalist's engagement with a world of textual inscriptions fulfils a deeply political agenda. By setting the seal of authenticity upon Western readings of the sepoys' insurrection, as revised according to the interpretative strategies used above, Gozzano's narrative demonstrated how his exotic lore was deeply entangled with contemporary politics.

Like 'L'Olocausto,' 'Goa: "La Dourada"' displays its citational riches; however, unlike the Indian Mutiny narrative, it submits some of the cited or evoked texts to the transformative powers of parody. Parody, in Gozzano, implies a commentary on the art form that is being parodied: a kind of 'criticism in action' (what Gerard Genette would call a 'metatext') that spans beyond literature to include architecture and painting. With an astonishing reversal from 'L'Olocausto,' Gozzano's engagement with the epic genre (in this case Luis de Camoëns's *The*

Lusiads), reveals how modern readers can imaginatively relish, yet must analytically question, the original scope of the epic, that of singing the heroic beginnings and imperial destinies of 'chosen' nations and their heroes. Gozzano's own counter-epic, which describes his wanderings in the old Portuguese colonial city of Goa, exploits parody to both evoke and dismantle the epic paradigm on thematic as well as formal levels. However, if Gozzano resists the optimistic and future-oriented push of the epic, he is unable to embrace the pluralistic and anti-authoritarian implications of his own parodic shift: while bluntly reversing them, Gozzano remains nostalgically attached to the epic's teleological thrust, as well as to the concepts of purity, originality, and absolute distance that the epic genre traditionally supported. To overcome his predicament, Gozzano gives up epic altogether, and chooses the elegy for the defeated, rather than the victors' epic song, as the only apt tune for modernity. No longer tempted by the disruptive powers of parody, Gozzano ends up admitting that it is through mere repetition and borrowed words that he can vicariously recover the sense of distance, the aura, of a city which remembers, with sadness and nostalgia, the great and the powerful of a glorious age that has long disappeared.

Exposing what Philippe Lejeune would term the 'palimpsestuous' nature of writing, Gozzano opens his piece on Goa by explicitly tracing some important textual coordinates:

> Andare a Goa, perchè? I perchè sono molti, tutti indefinibili, quasi inconfessabili; parlano soltanto alla mia intima nostalgia di sognatore vagabondo. Perchè Goa non è ricordata da Cook, nè da Loti, perchè nessuna società di navigazione vi fa scalo, perchè mi spinge verso di lei un sonetto di De Heredia, indimenticabile. ('Goa' 19)

> (Go to Goa? Why? There are many reasons, all indefinable, indeed almost impossible to admit; they simply speak to my deepest longings as a wandering dreamer. Because neither Cook nor Loti mentions Goa; because Goa is a port of call for no shipping company; because an unforgettable sonnet by Heredia urges me to go there.)

Gozzano's narrative journey starts out by refuting his two most obvious narrative models. The first is the model provided by the famous Cook's tourist guidebooks, which supply Gozzano with all the practical and extratextual references to places, itineraries, and locations: a gold mine of concrete data on which to construct his often forged real-life itineraries. The second model, which stands in opposition to the first, is that repository of exotic descriptions and stylistic refinements which constitutes the most massive intertextual presence in all of Gozzano's Indian narratives, Pierre Loti's *L'Inde (sans les Anglais)*. Gozzano's journey to Goa, then, appears to find its inspiration in personal, nostalgic reminiscences:

> pochi nomi turbavano la mia fantasia adolescente quanto il nome di Goa: Goa la Dourada.
>
> Oh! Visitata cento volte con la matita, durante le interminabili lezioni di matematica, con l'atlante aperto tra il banco e le ginocchia ... Il viaggio sull'atlante mi pare la realtà viva, e pallida fantasia mi sembra questo cielo e questo mare: cielo e mare di stagno fuso, limitato da una fascia di biacca verde: la costa del Malabar ...
>
> Termina oggi il viaggio intrapreso a matita sull'atlante di vent'anni or sono, termina a bordo di questa tejera sobbalzante, una caravella panciuta, lunga trenta metri, alla quale è stata senza dubbio aggiunta la prima caldaia a vapore che sia stata inventata. Ma tutto questo è indicibilmente poetico e mi compensa della vuota eleganza dei grandi vapori moderni dalle cabine e dalle sale presuntuose di specchi e di stucchi Impero e Luigi XV, dall'odore di volgarissimo *hôtel*, dove è assente ogni poesia marinaresca, ogni senso della *cosa nuova* e dell'*avventura*. Qui tutto è poetico, e la mia nostalgia può sognare d'essere ai tempi di Vasco De Gama, di navigare alle *Terrae Ignotae*, alle *Insulae non repertae*. (19–20)

(... few names captured my adolescent imagination as powerfully as Goa: Goa the Golden.

I visited it with my pencil a hundred times during never-ending math lessons, with my atlas open between desk and knees ... To me the voyage over the pages of the atlas seems to be living reality, and this sea and sky, pale imaginings – sea and sky of molten tin, bordered by the Malabar coast, a strip of green ...

Today my voyage traced on an atlas twenty years ago is coming to an end, coming to an end upon this heaving teapot, a caravel with a rounded hull, thirty meters in length, in which has been installed what is doubtless the first steam engine ever invented. Yet this is all unutterably poetic, and more than compensates for the specious elegance of the great modern steamships with their cabins and presumptuous staterooms filled with mirrors à la Louis XV and à la Bonaparte, which smell like ordinary hotels, without the slightest trace of seafaring poetry, a sense of novelty and of adventure. Here everything is poetic. I can imagine myself living during the age of Vasco da Gama, sailing to *Terrae Ignotae* and *Insulae non repertae.*)

An apt vessel for Gozzano's poetic journey, the antiquated ship inspires his escape into that remote past in which sailing toward the unknown was geographically, intellectually, and aesthetically still a possibility.[61] Although modernity is succumbing to the sterile comforts of mass tourism, with its commodified goods and vicarious forms of travel, Gozzano's voyage into Vasco da Gama's past allows him to recover – with his typical emphasis on the ambiguity of his second-hand claim to originality – the wonder of 'il senso della *cosa nuova*,' the 'aura' that, according to Walter Benjamin, modernity has lost.[62] Gozzano's wavering between imaginative seductions (following a regressive trajectory, toward the personal past of the daydreaming schoolboy) and the appeal of the reality principle (the ship's progressive motion toward Goa) is only apparent. For the lover of poetic revisions and imagined worlds, Goa is already fixed in its colonial cliché, that of the 'Golden Goa,' the Rome of the East, the paradise-city 'rich on trade and loot' (Scammel 243) constructed by so many narratives from 1510, the date of Alfonso de Albuquerque's conquest, onwards (Pearson 14–39). If, for Gozzano, the world is accessible only through the mediation of reproduced forms, borrowed words, and pre-established points of view, then the pressing problem for him is to identify, by means of concrete experiments, what hermeneutical system, and what literary discourse among those inherited from a century-long tradition, is most suitable for re-presenting the long-gone 'wonder' of Goa for us, today.

Gozzano's reference to *Terrae Ignotae* and *Insulae non repertae* semantically doubles the concept of absolute novelty while formally estranging it in the distance evoked by the Latin quotation. Mediated, perhaps, by the epic pages of Virgil's *Aeneid*, (the 'ignotae ... terrae' of canto V, 793–5), Gozzano's first encounter with Goa occurs through one of the *Aeneid*'s hypertexts:

[Leggo] *Os Lusiadas*, le *Lusiadi* ... [in] un'edizione arcaica sucidissima, con in calce la *real alvairà*: la licenza dei superiori. Non conosco il portoghese e non mi giova ad avvicinarmi il poco spagnuolo che so, ma i versi sono così armoniosi, così perfette le rime che alla fine d'ogni strofe capisco esattamente ciò che il poeta ha voluto dire ... Il libro è ... l'opera nazionale portoghese, quanto sopravvive, ohimé, di tutta la grandezza coloniale dei giorni splendidi. Non per nulla, e non indegnamente, Camoens fu detto il Tasso del Portogallo. ('Goa' 21–2)

([I read] *Os Lusíadas*, The Lusiads ... [in] an incredibly soiled old edition with the *real alvaira*, the censors' licence, at the bottom of the title page. I do not know Portuguese and the little Spanish I know is of no use, yet the verses are so harmonious and the rhymes so perfect that at the end of each strophe I feel I understand exactly what the poet has meant ... *Os Lusíadas* is ... the Portuguese national literary work – alas, all that survives of the colonial greatness of those splendid days. With good reason, and not undeservedly, Camoëns was called the Portuguese Tasso.)

The epic code opens the doors of Goa, and this code is so comprehensive and familiar, in its fixed form, that the linguistic barrier does not prevent Gozzano from fully comprehending it. The poem is universally enjoyable and understandable because of its classical sense of poetic harmony. As Magris eloquently pointed out in his reading of Salgari, the epic celebrates the magnificent acts of foundation made by a nation's patriarchs and heroes. The origin of contemporary reality, the epic world is, in its arcane perfection, utterly detached from the present. The epic bard shares with his audience a sense of reverence toward a grand and inaccessible reality:

The epic world is an utterly finished thing, not only as an authentic event of the distant past but also on its own terms and by its own standards; it is impossible to change, to re-think, to re-evaluate anything in it. It is completed, conclusive, and immutable, as a fact, an idea and a value. This defines absolute epic distance. One can only accept the epic world with reverence; it is impossible to really touch it, for it is beyond the realm of human activity, the realm in which everything humans touch is altered and re-thought. This distance exists not only in the epic material, that is, in the events and the heroes described, but also in the point of view and evaluation one assumes toward them; point of view and evaluation are fused with the subject into one inseparable whole ... The epic world is constructed in the zone of an absolute distanced image, beyond the sphere of possible contact with the developing, incomplete and therefore re-thinking and re-evaluating present. (Bakhtin 17)

As in hagiographic and memorialistic writing, the epic representation follows the rules of idealization. Only what is worthy of being transmitted to posterity is remembered, after being elevated into the realm of *sublimitas*. As Bakhtin points out, the absolute past is an evaluative category, and epic concepts such as 'founder,' 'beginning,' 'first' are valorized temporal concepts, because it is in this past that the source of everything good for all later time is to be found. By definition, the epic discourse cannot be re-examined or re-evaluated: bordering on the sacred, it allows only one interpretation, that which is offered by tradition, and only one attitude, that of a respectful and admiring reverence. The source of all values, and the guarantor of the laws of contemporary reality, the epic past becomes an absolute category. Events and heroes belonging to it are fixed *sub specie aeternitatis*. Distanced from the present, and liberated from any risk of contact or revision, they are static and complete.

In 'Goa: "La Dourada,"' Gozzano evokes the epic discourse in a context that deliberately puts these presuppositions into a state of crisis. The sublimity of the skies does not attract Gozzano as much as the depths of the *Pedrillo*'s hold, with its jumble of miscellaneous wares:

Oggi sono sceso nella stiva. Quanta merce disparata abbiamo con noi! Pianoforti, macchine da scrivere, biciclette, balle di cotone a fiorami vivacissimi per le belle dei coloni, tre casse enormi, dove viaggia, divisa in tre parti, una statua gigantesca di San Francesco Saverio ... e un'infinità di sacchi pieni di cocci: cocci di stoviglie raccattati in tutti gli spazzaturai occidentali, frantumi a colori vivi. ('Goa' 21)

(Today I went into the hold. What a jumble of wares we are carrying! Pianos, typewriters, bicycles, bales of cotton cloth with vivid floral patterns for colonial belles, three enormous crates containing a huge statue of Saint Francis Xavier broken down into three parts ... and an endless number of sacks filled with bits of broken pottery, vividly coloured fragments collected from garbage dumps all over the West.)

An act of homage to one of the most common stylistic devices of the epic, the catalogue, Gozzano's list, with its obvious pluralizing and multiplying effects, hardly follows the contextual hierarchies of relevance that we saw operating in World's Fairs' displays that both celebrated and imposed order upon the fullness of the world. Without any totalizing framework, in Gozzano a sense of incongruity prevails, as does fragmentation, confusion, and waste. The sacred (the saint's statue) is, and remains, juxtaposed with the profane in a context (the *Pedrillo*'s hold) that is bound to debase the sacred rather than elevate the profane. The gigantic statue of Saint Francis Xavier chopped into three pieces expresses visually the divorce of the parts from the whole. The divided statue represents the modern fragmentation of that epic hero who used to be, as Bakhtin aptly put it, 'all of one piece' (35). Embodying the unity of universal and individual spheres, the epic hero gave form to the epic world, and the epic world recognized itself in its hero: 'And I'm resolved my inmost being / shall share in what's the lot of all mankind,' in the eloquent words of Goethe's Faust (2: 46–7). Here Gozzano pinpoints the crisis of the exposition mentality we have drawn so far: The West is beginning to question its own giants, casting doubt on the usefulness of its unifying and totalizing view of reality. The West that Gozzano depicts is a place of scattered and disjointed traditions, a place that can only ship its material surplus abroad, and export its own spiritual debris.

The hero of Camoëns's *Lusiads*, Vasco da Gama, undergoes a similar fate. After all, it is 'in the kitchen, between a cask of bananas and a tin of preserves' that Gozzano finds the soiled copy of the *Lusiads*:

Tutti gli elementi delle grandi epopee sono ricordati intorno alla figura dell'eroe: Vasco De Gama, e intorno alla sua gesta: la scoperta delle Indie Orientali. Eppure non so leggerlo senza un sorriso d'irriverenza. La figura dell'Ulisside portoghese è così grottesca, camuffata secondo l'ossessione classicheggiante del tempo: sembra di vedere gli stivali, il robone logoro d'un pirata medioevale spuntare sotto la corazza, il casco clipeato delle reminiscenze omeriche e virgiliane ...

Ed ecco Didone, camuffata da Ines de Castro ... e il Ciclope, parodiato dal gigante Adamastorre. ('Goa' 22)

(All the elements of the great epic are recalled and centred on the figure of the hero, Vasco da Gama, and his feat: the discovery of the East Indies. Still, I am unable to read it without an irreverent smile. The figure of this Portuguese Ulysses is so grotesque, disguised according to the classicizing mania of the times: one can almost see the boots, the patched outfit of a medieval pirate showing underneath his armour and the decorated helmet that recalls Homer and Virgil ...

Now we see Dido disguised as Inês da Castro ... and the Cyclops, parodied by giant Adamastorre.)

Measured against its Homeric and Virgilian hypotexts, Camoëns's poem proves unsuccessful as a serious epic. As we have seen, the *Lusiads*' style lives up to its noble models; and its formulaic diction, with its 'roving stereotypes, hemistichs, hexameters, groups of verses which the bard shamelessly reuses' (Genette 15), allows for universal comprehension. However, according to Gozzano, Camoëns involuntarily acts as a parodist, because his epic contents stray from the norm of epic *sublimitas.* Dido ends up looking too much like Dona Inês de Castro, Adamastor is a dismal copy of Polyphemus, and Vasco da Gama is an early version of Blackbeard attempting to impersonate Ulysses. Reduced to an empty shell, only a mask and a disguise, the seafaring hero crumbles into a series of details that cannot be organically combined into a whole, an incongruous jumble of disparate elements (boots, a pirate's patched outfit, a suit of armour, a classical helmet) that expose all their conventionality. Camoëns's characters, in other words, do not measure up to their superhuman predecessors. The 'total individuals' of the past are 'contemporized,' fragmented, and 'brought low' (Bakhtin 21). Here, the temporal coexistence of multiple scripts does not display the imaginative and creative freedom of the expositions' dream worlds, but causes instead a sense of incredulity and laughter.

The *Lusiads*' caricatural and parodic elements that Gozzano emphasizes are not inherent in the poem itself (Camoëns did not mean to make us laugh). They stem instead from a discrepancy between authorial intentions and readers' responses. Gozzano is not discussing, here, the failure of the epic as a genre. He leaves the Homeric and Virgilian originals untouched, and acknowledges the initial success of what he calls '[uno dei] capolavori più completi che il Rinascimento abbia dato alla letteratura europea' ([one of the] most perfect masterpieces of the European Renaissance) ('Goa' 22). But he is also keen on recording the changed reception of *The Lusiads.* If Camoëns intended to seriously imitate two epic models, the *Odyssey* and the *Aeneid*, today's disenchanted readers cannot but view this imitation through a distorting lens, creating unanticipated and meaningful reversals. Modern times impose a change in the readership's attitude, and the downgrading standards applied to the grand epics of the past cause a debasing of the sacred (Dido as Inês de Castro) rather than a sacralizing of the profane (Inês de Castro as Dido). No longer seen in its unreachable totality and self-enclosed unity, Camoëns's epic poem appears as an absurd collection of different world systems. Intermixing classic and Christian myths, the *Lusiads* produces an assortment of sacred and profane elements, again according to a principle of involuntary caricature: 'Tutto l'Olimpo Pagano e Cristiano presiede alla gesta. La Vergine Maria da una parte – una Vergine troppo paganeggiante – e Venere dall'altra – una Venere che sa di sacrestia e di Santa Inquisizione – si contendono a volta a volta l'eroe navigatore' (The entire pagan and Christian Olympus presides over the feat. The Virgin Mary on one side – an excessively paganized Virgin – and Venus on the other – a Venus who smacks of the sacristy and the Holy Inquisition – contend from time to time for the navigator-hero) ('Goa' 22).

Gozzano's metatextual strategy – his commentary on *The Lusiads* – draws attention to the contextual factors responsible for a significant textual transformation: the original generic contract is breached, and Camoëns's epic is refunctionalized to be read in a parodic mode. Gozzano thus highlights the contractual nature of the relationship between reader and text. Pertaining to 'a conscious and organized pragmatics' (Genette 9), this relationship is not stable and fixed once and for all, but is bound to evolve in space and time. In the *Lusiads'* case, the discrepancies between original authorial intentions and modern readers' interpretations shatter the exegetic totality that epic discourse requires. Gozzano's reader, in other words, accomplishes a typical modernist gesture, rejecting tradition's sway over the reception of all epic discourses: 'Epic discourse is a discourse handed down by tradition. By its very nature the epic world of the absolute past is inaccessible to personal experience and does not permit an individual, personal point of view ... Evaluated in the same way by all and demanding a pious attitude toward itself [epic discourse requires] ... a commonly held evaluation and point of view which excludes any possibility of another approach' (Bakhtin 16).

By transforming the sublime into the grotesque, Gozzano's readers abolish epic distance and leave the epic subject bare under the power of tight scrutiny and close examination. What was heavenly becomes a caricature. Parody and caricature, however, cannot belong to a world of saints and heroes and cannot narrate the feats of the cross and the sword. Gozzano's impertinent smirk overturns the respectful devotion that the epic absolute demands. This is the first signal of that desecrating process which forces the great and the powerful of the past to be demoted from their dignified status and take a great fall into a present that is vulnerable to humour and irony. Even Saint Francis Xavier (and all that he ideologically represents) cannot be put together again. Gozzano's close-ups on single details imply the perceptive familiarity that empowers humour and parody: 'Laughter has the remarkable power of making an object come up close, of drawing it into a zone of crude contact where one can finger it familiarly on all sides, turn it upside down, inside out, peer at it from above and below, break open its external shell, look into its center, doubt it, take it apart, dismember it, lay it bare and expose it, examine it freely and experiment with it' (Bakhtin 23). Nothing is left intact in the epic image of the absolute past: 'the entire world and everything sacred in it is offered to us without any distancing at all' (Bakhtin 26).

Gozzano's demythologizing of the epic code in the *Lusiads* and his opening it up to the relativity of the present has none of the liberating, pluralistic, and antitotalitarian features that Bakhtin attributes to this process. Gozzano remains the bearer of those values of purity, harmony, and cohesive unity, which become real judgments of value when he transposes them upon the extraliterary reality, as in this description of the Goanese *mestiços* he sees in the Old City:

[Questa] folla numerosa [è] così diversa dalla corretta eleganza degli Inglesi e dalla grazia dignitosa degli Indu, folla di meticci portoghesi che si riprodussero come la gramigna sotto questo cielo ... e che si chiamano pomposamente *Toupas* [*sic*], cioè europei 'che portano il cappello,' ma che d'europeo non hanno più nulla, con quelle spalle gracili, le gambe smilze, il volto olivagno, angoloso, dagli occhi vivi, ma scimmieschi sotto la fronte depressa; e hanno atteggiamenti grotteschi di cavalleria, sono lisciati, impomatati, portano in giro sigari enormi e compagne languide. ('Goa' 29–30)

([This] large crowd [is] so different from the correct elegance of the English and the dignified grace of the Hindus, a crowd of Portuguese mestizos who in this climate reproduced themselves like weeds ... and who pompously call themselves *Toupas* – that is, Europeans 'who wear hats.' Yet there is no longer anything European about them, with their delicate shoulders, their slight legs, their angular, olive-hued faces with vivid simian eyes under their low foreheads. They have a grotesque chivalric bearing, are well groomed and pomaded, carry around huge cigars, and have languid lovers)

Gozzano borrows this peculiar piece of information from Édouard De Warren, a French officer in the British army in India and author of two volumes on British India, originally published in Paris in 1844:

[H]éritant des vices plus souvent que des qualités des deux races dont ils sont le produit, les half-castes ont en général toute la lubricité de l'Indien et toute l'ivrognerie de l'Anglais, et cette combinaison en amène un grand nombre à un fin prématurée et sans reproduction. S'il y a progéniture, elle se confond le plus souvent avec les Topassies ou Topas, pour se perdre à la longue parmi les indigènes. On appelle Topas ou Topassies des indigènes qui portent chapeaux, mais qui n'ont rien de commun avec les Européens qu'une partie de l'habillement et le plus souvent la religion catholique. Il descendent généralement des ancien métis français, portugais et hollandais.(2: 121–2)[63]

(Having inherited the vices more often than the virtues of the races that have produced them, the half-castes are, generally, as lustful as the Indian and as intemperate as the English, and this combination leads a great many of them to an early and childless demise. If they do have children, they most often resemble the *Topassies* or *Topas*, and ultimately disappear among the indigenous people. We call *Topas* or *Topassies* the indigenous people who wear a hat, but who do not have anything in common with the Europeans, except for this article of clothing and, more often, the Catholic religion. They generally descend from the ancient French, Portuguese, and Dutch mestizos.)

Inspired by De Warren's description of Indo-Portuguese dressing habits, Gozzano turns De Warren's racist statements into a caricatural vignette, the primary function of which is, of course, derision. Degraded to laughable acts and exterior poses, this debased Goanese chivalry has no connection to its noble European origins other than that of parodic distortion, mimicry, or masquerade.[64] Gozzano confronts the surfacing of the material and corporeal, which Bakhtin relates to the vitality of popular culture, with all the duplicitous distance of vulgarization and irony. He examines sexuality from a position of contemptuous intellectual superiority, and then demeans it with the trite humour of an obvious double entendre (enormous cigars). Behind the scornful smile and the clichéd image, begging the readers' complicity, there remains a fundamental aversion, a visceral fear, of all that is felt as hybrid, as *métissage*. Instead of yielding a sense of lost authenticity, Gozzano's India reveals the absence of an untainted, original essence. 'Pure products,' to cite William Carlos Williams's famous dictum, have been replaced by promiscuous and ambiguous imitations of questionable origins.[65]

The issue of race relations in Portuguese India has been a matter of wide controversy, with praise or censure bestowed upon the practices of intermarriage and interbreeding, and much discussion about the nature and effects of acculturation and assimilation, and about the extent of the intermingling between the 'cultures and societies of the Portuguese and the local people with whom they interacted' (Pearson 104). Positions on this issue vary greatly, according, of course, to the ideological and cultural make-up of those who held them.[66] Overall, Gozzano's stance parallels earlier or contemporary British racial attitudes. In 1847, the British explorer and Orientalist Richard Burton wrote:

> The reader may remember that it was Albuquerque who advocated marriages between the European settlers and the natives of India. However reasonable it might have been to expect the amalgamation of the races in the persons of their descendants, experience and stern facts condemn the measure as a most delusive and treacherous political day dream ... As soon as intermarriage with the older settlers takes place the descendants become Mestici – in plain English, mongrels. ... It would be, we believe, difficult to find in Asia an uglier or more degraded looking race than that which we are now describing. The forehead is low and flat, the eyes small ... Their figures are short and small ... The mongrel men dress like Europeans, but the quantity of clothing diminishes with the wearer's rank. Some of the lower orders, especially in the country, affect a full-dress costume, consisting *in toto*, of a cloth jacket and black silk knee breeches. (87–8, 97)

In a typically Victorian tone, W.W. Hunter claimed, in 1899, that 'the Goanese became a byword as the type of an orientalised community, idle, haughty, and corrupt' (157). Interbreeding, in particular, was seen as one of the main causes of Portuguese decline in India. John Fryer, an English visitor to Goa in 1909, draws a picture that chillingly contradicts any idea of racial tolerance as well as the myth of the progressive and peaceful assimilation of two races within one Luso-tropical civilization based on miscegenation and Catholicism: '[In Goa] the Mass of the People are Canorein, through Portuguezed in Speech and Manners; paying great Observance to a White Man, whom when they meet they must give him the Way with a Cringe and Civil salute, for fear of a *Stochado* [rapier's blow]' (27). As in Gozzano's, in all of these descriptions the racist disdain for hybrids manifests itself through caricature: the mestizos' physique is caricatured by emphasizing lack of (classic) proportions. The behaviour and dress code is deemed to demonstrate exaggerated and distorted movements, as in Gozzano's description of the Goanese boy who shows 'una mimica eccessiva che rivela il rampollo di razza bastarda' (excessive mimicry revealing that he is the offspring of a bastard race) ('Goa' 27). The 'strange melange of European and Asiatic peculiarities' (Burton 100) is seen as a monstrosity indeed. All mestizos can do, Gozzano implies, is to 'ape,' 'stand-in for,' or reduce to a 'pastiche' original Western talents.[67]

If Gozzano's metatextual analysis decrees the impossibility of the epic in the modern world, his parodic revisions, with their mixture of high and low registers, their tendency toward caricature, and their contamination of the serious with the profane, have no egalitarian inspiration. They reveal the fear of promiscuity and erasing of social distinctions; the alarm that something may, someday, challenge the West's unitary identity and its distancing, dichotomy-based sense of authenticity. Parody, in Gozzano, rests on ambiguous epistemological grounds, as it stylistically and structurally exploits those very forms that it ideologically condemns. As one of the classic genres, Gozzano implies, the epic establishes a norm designating a typology and an interdiction, and parody is guilty of defying precisely this norm. As Jacques Derrida argues, tongue in cheek, whenever the notion of genre is at stake, whether it is a matter of *physis* or *techné*, one must not risk 'impurity, anomaly, or monstrosity,' lest it cause the demise of the genre itself: 'If a genre is what it is, or if it is supposed to be what it is destined to be by virtue of its *telos*, then "genres are not to be mixed"; one should not mix genres, one owes it to oneself not to get mixed up in mixing genres. Or, more rigorously, genres should not intermix. And if it should happen that they do intermix, by accident or through transgression, by mistake or through a lapse, then this should confirm, since, after all, we are speaking of "mixing," the essential purity of their identity' (204).

Gozzano comments on the same impossibility for the epic at the intertextual level. By degrading the epic code, Gozzano exploits, and sadly subverts, one of its fundamental themes, that of the quest. To the colossal pursuits of epic heroes (*sapientia mundi* and immortality, *salus et amor, virtute e canoscenza*), Gozzano opposes his own degraded and modest quest. Leaving his friends in Bombay, he travels alone, in an absurd and inexplicable search for 'il fratello sconosciuto di un amico dimenticato' (the unknown brother of a forgotten friend) ('Goa' 29), a Franciscan missionary by the name of Vico Verani. Gozzano's *descensus ad inferos* does not appear to have clear ethical or epistemological motives and must, rather, be related to the vague and irrational nostalgia for an unknown person whose last name contains the root of the word truth (*verità*): '[n]on ho altra mèta, altra indicazione in questa solitudine di

piante e di ruine che il nome di un italiano non conosciuto mai: e lo ri-
peto a tutti i rari passanti' (I have no goal, I have nothing to guide me in
this solitude of plants and ruins other than the name of an Italian I
never knew. I repeat it to every one of the few passersby) ('Goa' 27). A
pathetic pilgrim, Gozzano follows an equally unepic guide, whom he
presents according to the racist caricatural model discussed before:
'[era] un monello goanese che si [interessava] a quella ricerca con
grandi esclamazioni grottesche, e agitar d'occhi e di braccia' ('[he was]
a Goan urchin who showed his interest in my quest with loud grotesque
exclamations, rolling his eyes and waving his arms') ('Goa' 27). Gozzano's wanderings in the nightmarish city reveal that all that appears
familiar is only a hollow surface, pervaded by a sinister sadness:

La nostra malinconia ritrova ... a Goa lo spettro di cose nostre: conventi,
palazzi, chiese del Cinquecento e del Seicento: una vasta città che ricorda a
volte una via di Roma barocca o una piazza dell'Umbria ... La città è vastissima, ma sono pochi gli edifici completi. Avanzo a caso, senza una mèta ...
Un edificio m'attira, un palazzo del Seicento, imponente, dalle grate panciute, dai balconi a volute aggraziate, recanti al centro, in corsivo, un
monogramma o uno stemma padronale; e lo stemma è riprodotto in pietra
sul vasto androne d'ingresso. Il cortile è circondato da un doppio loggiato
barocco, a colonne spirali; ma il loggiato è crollato per una buona metà e
s'apre sopra la campagna selvaggia. Seguo il portico a caso, entro nella
vasta dimora. Ohimè! Vedo il soffitto; e, attraverso il soffitto, larghe chiazze
azzurre: il cielo del tropico. Dei tre ripiani, delle fughe interminabili di sale
e corridoi, non resta più traccia, tutto è crollato, e il palazzo non è che una
scatola, una topaja deserta, che serve di màgazzino per le noci di cocco. In
terra, fino a vari metri d'altezza, sono accumulati i grossi frutti chiomati
che fanno pensare a piramidi di teste tronche. ('Goa' 25–6)

(Still we find ... in Goa the spectre of our own civilization: convents, palaces, and sixteenth- and seventeenth-century churches, a vast city that at
times reminds me of a street in baroque Rome or a square in Umbria ...
The city is endless, but few of the buildings are still whole. I walk haphaz-
ardly, without a destination ... One building attracts me, an imposing seventeenth-century palace with curved window gratings, balconies with graceful
spirals, bearing in their centres, in italics, a monogram or proprietor's coat
of arms; and the coat of arms is also reproduced in stone in the vast
entrance hall. The inner court is surrounded by a baroque open double
gallery with spiral columns, but at least half of the gallery has collapsed and

opens upon the wild countryside. I wander along the arcade, enter the vast dwelling. Alas, I gaze up at the ceiling, and through the ceiling I see broad patches of blue: the tropical sky. There is no trace of the three landings, of the interminable suites of rooms and corridors. Everything has tumbled down, and the palace is nothing more than a box, a deserted rat's nest used as a storehouse for coconuts. On the ground, up to a height of several metres, are piled the large, hairy fruit, which make me think of pyramids of severed heads.)

By 1915, the legendary palaces that the Portuguese had built during the height of Goa's splendour in the mid-seventeenth to mid-eighteenth centuries had long disappeared due to the slow decline of the empire and the harshness of the tropical weather. However, Gozzano captures here an interesting architectural hybrid – an example of a colonial Portuguese/Italianate building – that bears notable symbolic rather than referential implications. The exterior stairway protected by a colonnaded porch, leading to the first floor and opening onto a walled courtyard like the one that Gozzano describes, was the defining element of early colonial buildings. Characterized by rigour and austerity, these imposing and martial-looking palaces, originally conceived by military engineers, were meant to convey the sense of Portuguese strength and permanence to the peoples recently conquered: 'In colonial Portuguese architecture, [the colonnaded porch] was used primarily as a means for illustrating the policy of global power and social dominance developed by the Portuguese. The viceroy placed his guards, outfitted in blue livery and halberds along the stairs. The nobility, and even the archbishop, imitated the viceroy's practices to the finest detail, with the number of their servants and the luxury of their presentation' (Carita 17).[68]

When a more elaborate practice of formal display replaced the earlier policy of military force at the end of the sixteenth century, buildings began to display an Italian Mannerist influence, which lasted throughout the eighteenth and nineteenth centuries (Carita 19). Built for leisure and ostentation, these palaces were not designed by military architects but reflected the economic power of the Church and the Society of Jesus. Architectonic features that the Jesuit Fathers imported from Italy included a variety of ornamental elements decorating the buildings' facades, such as elaborate moulding and fluting, capitals, balcony windows, and family insignia, recalling Gozzano's description of the 'volute aggraziate' and 'grate panciute,' with their noble family crests inscribed in cursive script. Gozzano's eclectic palace, reminiscent of the fanciful architectural melanges of World's Fairs' pavilions, exposes the powerful alliance between military and religious powers that marked Portuguese dominance in Goa. Now a hollow box and vacant habitat, the palace also bears witness to these powers' dismal decay. Like any fragmented and polyvalent object, the ruin demands semantic interpretation, as it points in two opposite directions: it both indicates a former totality and exposes this totality's absence, thus defining the present as an emptiness full of half-erased traces. Ultimately, however, for Gozzano the ruined palace involves the *decomposition* of the real rather than allowing the archaeological reconstruction of a former totality.

Goa's gutted palace transformed into a desolate mausoleum of truncated head-like coconuts provides a chilling contrast to the deceptive sense of permanence offered by another art form, that of celebratory portraiture:

[immagino] una tela di Velasquez o di Van Dyck [raffigurante] uno di quei *conquistador* mezzo mercanti, pirata, guerriero, esploratore che s'avanzano in tutta la pompa delle sete, delle piume, dei velluti, recando la consorte per mano, una pingue signora a riccioli simmetrici, sorridente nonostante il ferreo busto a imbuto, la gorgiera crudele; e la prole segue in bell'ordine, già tutta imbustata e corazzata come i genitori, e un servo negro reca una scimmia sulla spalla e un pappagallo nell'una mano, sollevando con l'altra una cortina di velluto, e tra le due colonne appaiono le galee potentissime, d'innanzi al porto di una città favolosa: Goa. ('Goa' 26)

([I imagine] a portrait by Velázquez or Van Dyck [representing] one of the conquistadors, half-trader, half-pirate, warrior and explorer, who advances in all the pomp of silks, plumes, and velvets, holding his consort by the hand, a plump lady with symmetrical curls, smiling in spite of her iron corset and cruel gorget; and the offspring follows in perfect order, already all corseted and armoured like their parents; and a negro slave carries a monkey on his shoulder and a parrot in one hand, and with the other holds up a velvet curtain; and between the two columns the mighty fleet lies at anchor before the fabulous city: Goa).

Gozzano's *ekphrasis*, more than describing a specific artwork, identifies here the conventions of a style, that of seventeenth-century celebratory painting. Either devoted to the commemoration of military victories or the celebration of aristocratic and royal families, these paintings presented thematic and formal elements akin to Gozzano's description. Naturally, given their function and the circumstances under which they were commissioned, these paintings were all intended to glorify their sitters, and often allegorized the events they depicted. In particular, the celebratory paintings of aristocratic families demonstrated the close connections between art and the illustration of socio-economic power. However close, these connections had to be mediated, and financial worth was often converted, and idealized, into the representation of military distinction for the male sitters, and opulent, regal elegance for the women. Discussing Rubens's oeuvre, Giorgio Doria humorously recalls the vogue of portraying 'meticolosi contabili su cavalli rampanti, mogli di oculati prestatori di denaro [vestite come] principesse' (meticulous accountants riding rampant horses, wives of shrewd moneylenders [dressed like] princesses) (24).[69]

In Van Dyck's Genoese works, the wealth of powerful aristocratic families such as the Dorias, Spinolas, and Lomellinis, which was amassed through trade and banking, was translated into the elegance of military postures, precious fabrics, and sumptuous decors, and communicated in the sheer dimensions of the paintings, in which the sitters were often painted from below to increase the sense of their power and size. The royal portraits were, understandably, even more ambitious. Rubens's and Velázquez's portraits of the Spanish royal family underscore the conventional tendency to 'regard the king as a quasi-divine person, as a "deity" or "demi-god on earth"' (López-Rey 57). A telling example, which Gozzano may have seen at the Uffizi Gallery in Florence, is the allegorical equestrian portrait of Phillip IV of Spain, where Velázquez and his workshop painted allegorical figures descending from the skies and presenting the majestic king mounted on horseback with a cross, a laurel twig, and a globe. From below, a richly clad and solemn-looking black youth offers Phillip a helmet.

Painting black characters, usually servants, and usually extravagantly dressed to emphasize the wealth of the sitter's family, was also a pictorial convention of the time, as attested, for example, by Van Dyck's portrait of Elena Grimaldi Cattaneo. By placing the diminutive black servant between two slender white columns and Elena's imposing figure, Van Dyck emphasizes, by contrast, Elena's height and the classic splendour of her surroundings.

In his description of the imagined painting by Van Dyck or Velázquez, Gozzano overturns these painterly idealizations through parodic redundancy and debasement. The representation of the black servant offering the viewer a first glance of the Portuguese conquest of Goa, while holding a parrot as well as a monkey, accentuates the colonialists' notion of the natives' grateful submissiveness, their turning them into apes or parrots of their conquerors. This image is just as self-consciously redundant a representation of exotic clichés as the portrayal of the little children as miniature copies of their self-satisfied parents is of the advance of Western conquest. In what has become a familiar act in 'Goa: "La Dourada,"' Gozzano peers at the conquistador, brings him down, and looks closely at him, thus revealing his composite nature. With a brilliantly ironic chiasmus ('uno di quei conquistador mezzo mercanti, pirata, guerriero, esploratore'), Gozzano tightly interweaves commerce with economic exploitation, and political aggression with exploration. As with Camoëns's epic celebration, Gozzano's analysis of the imagined painting rests upon an interpretative change that activates a parodic register absent from the original intention. Modernity, Gozzano implies, is bound to favour close scrutiny rather than idealized distance, in all realms of human experience: 'Ancora una volta tocco l'ultimo limite della delusione, sconto la curiosità morbosa di voler vedere troppo vicina la realtà delle pietre morte, di voler constatare che le cose magnificate dalla storia, dall'arte, cantate dai poeti, non sono più, non saranno mai più, sono come se non siano state mai!' (Once again I am deeply disappointed and pay the price of my morbid curiosity to see the reality of the dead stones too close up, wanting to verify that the things glorified by art and history, sung by the poets, no longer exist, will never again exist, are as if they had never existed) ('Goa' 26–7). Against the intentions of celebratory art to bestow permanence and timeliness, Gozzano's futile yet stubborn quest in the baroque inferno of Goa yields only one revelation: the *sic transit* which art itself cannot overcome.

For Gozzano, depleting the present of heroic possibilities means also negating the temporal model upon which the epic plot is traditionally organized. Once in the cradle of the world, Gozzano fails to decipher the code revealing the origins of all that is to come. In a world where the first word is absent or incomprehensible, history cannot follow a progressive order. The only word that permeates this repetitive history states the disquieting, because rationally undecipherable, presence of an absence: 'nessuno conosce Vico Verani ... La solitudine mi par più completa ... ora che so di aver seguita la traccia d'un morto nella città morta' (nobody knows Vico Verani ... The solitude seems more complete ... now that I know that I have been following the traces of a dead man in a dead city) ('Goa' 27).

If the epic 'was the form through which classical antiquity, Christianity and the feudal world had represented the basis of civilizations, their

Diego Velázquez. Equestrian portrait of Phillip IV of Spain. By permission, Uffizi Gallery, Florence, Italy.

Anthony Van Dyck. Portrait of Elena Grimaldi Cattaneo. Widener Collection. By permission, National Gallery of Art, Washington, DC.

overall meaning, their destiny' (Moretti 36), and if *The Lusiads* sang in
epic form 'the Portuguese achievement [as] ... part of a great providential design to win the world for the true faith' (Atkinson 25), Gozzano's
modernist rewritings interpret the history 'bestowed' upon the world
outside of Europe in a much more problematic way. While with 'L'Olocausto' Gozzano sang the permanence of 'monuments' and the ultimate epic triumph of Western progress, with 'Goa' he told instead a
story of ruins.[70] To complicate matters even further, Gozzano's story of
ruins is steeped in ambiguity: oscillating between the destructive powers
of irony and nostalgia's conservative drives, Gozzano nurses a sense of
emotional loss for what he himself helped analytically to destroy. It is
precisely this sense of loss that Gozzano chooses to emphasize by concluding his journey to Goa with a sonnet by José-Maria de Heredia:

Morne Ville, jadis reine des Océans!
   Aujourd'hui le requin poursuit en paix les scombres
   Et le nuage errant allonge seul des ombres
   Sur la rade où roulaient les galions géants.
Depuis Drake et l'assaut des Anglais mécréants,
   Tes murs désemparés croulent en noirs décombres
   Et, comme un glorieux collier de perles sombres,
Des boulets de Pointis montrent les trous béants.
Entre le ciel qui brûle et la mer qui moutonne,
   Au somnolent soleil d'un midi monotone,
   Tu songes, ô Guerrière, aux vieux Conquistadors;
Et dans l'énervement des nuits chaudes et calmes,
Berçant ta gloire éteinte, ô Cité, tu t'endors
   Sous les palmiers, au long frémissement des palmes. (143)

(Sad city, of old time the Ocean's queen!
   To-day the shark in peace pursues his prey,
   And in thy road where giant galleons lay
   Shadows of drifting clouds alone are seen.
Since Drake's assault, his miscreants' rapine,
   Thy walls have crumbled in a black decay
   And seem, where Pointis rent them, to display
A zone of glorious pearls of somber sheen.
Between a burning sky and fleecy sea,
   While the sun sleeps through noon's monotony,

Thy dream is of the old Conquistadores;
In enervating nights of tropic calm,
Beneath the unending shudder of the palm
Thou slumberest, cradled in thy vanished glories.) (O'Hara 125)

However extensive, Gozzano's citation is incomplete. By removing the poem's epigraph (*Cartagena de Indias* 1532 – 1583 –1697), Gozzano transforms Cartagena, the city that Heredia's ancestor, Don Pedro de Heredia, founded in 1532 in what is now Colombia, into Portuguese Goa. Gozzano thus eliminates Goa's unheroic and prolonged decline by inventing a dramatic defeat at the hands of Sir Francis Drake's army. If, in the preceding examples, Gozzano had subverted the epic model by way of parody, here he bluntly relativizes it. As he emphasizes the sudden replacement of one colonial power (Portuguese) with another (British), Gozzano also implies that the end of one epic tale entails the beginning of another, with new protagonists acting out a similar script.

In 'Goa: "La Dourada,"' Gozzano overcomes his impasse between wanting to dismantle the epic model and nostalgically longing for that very model by delegating the representation of that longing to another voice. Through the filter of Heredia's poetic persona (the implicit 'Je' of the sonnet), Gozzano undertakes a drastic change in textual perspective. The elegy for the defeated replaces the winner's epic, and the gaze of a sympathetic observer substitutes for the parodist's close scrutiny. The resulting vision, broad enough to span the ages, effectively and calmly paraphrases the Darwinian law of the survival of the fittest. The broad panorama of the historical past shows a sequence of rulers, replacing one another in bloody competition. The present displays a Goa divorced from the progressive historical models imposed by the West. Yet, no independent historical scheme takes the place of Western rule. Having reverted to the rhythms of nature, Goa is now a ghostly home to the 'peoples without history,' as Hegel would have called them. There is no postcolonial projection in Gozzano, and the mournful city's sole identity is cast in the dream-like and passive remembrance of the heroic times when Goa, the *Guerrière*, had been invested with the individuality of its *Conquistadors*.

By quoting Heredia's sonnet verbatim, Gozzano delegates the representation of Goa to a different poetic persona: a 'Je' who omnisciently addresses a silent 'tu,' the city itself. Having renounced the creation of new meanings through the parodic transformation of the voices of the past, Gozzano completes his troubled journey to discover 'il senso della *cosa nuova*' by entrusting the construction of the elsewhere to the elegiac and conservative notes of the already said. If Heredia's Goa has no voice of her own, neither has Gozzano's. Gozzano's choice of direct quotation over individual creation involves renouncing the invention of possible futures – new worlds with new words – that may challenge Western visions of history and of modernity. By choosing to share Heredia's gaze of nostalgia and mourning, Gozzano implicitly confesses that, ideologically as well as aesthetically, utopianism is not within his reach here.

Meddling with the Sex of Angels: Gozzano's Readings of Albrecht Dürer's *Melancholia I*

If in 'Goa: 'La "Dourada"' Gozzano renounces his own voice in order to melancholically repeat Heredia's poetic script, in 'Un vergiliato sotto la neve' (A Guided Tour Under the Snow) he emphasizes his inventive and personal engagement in re-presenting the outside world. Like 'Goa,' 'Un vergiliato' is the story of a first encounter, this time not with an exotic city but with a marvellous one, the city of the 1911 International Exposition in Turin. Meticulously staged, as is typical of Gozzano, this first encounter takes place some time before the official spring opening of the exposition, on a snowy February day: 'Vorrò vedere l'Esposizione oggi, per la prima volta, in questo turbinio di candore abbagliante ... La neve copre la città di un'immensa pagina bianca sulla quale è facile disegnare le più strane fantasie' (I will want to see the exposition today, for the first time, in this whirlwind of dazzling whiteness ... The snow covers the city with an immense white sheet on which it is easy to draw the strangest fantasies) ('Un vergiliato' 175–6). Just like his India, Gozzano's city is a palimpsest: an inscribed surface that the snow has smoothed over like wax, which offers the perfect canvas for a further rewrite. On this frigid winter day, the inscribed surface is still just a draft: the exposition buildings are unfinished and, for the most part, empty. Encumbered 'dalle travi, dalle corde, dalle stuoie' (by the planks, the ropes, and the mats) ('Un vergiliato' 178), these buildings do not yet conceal their prefabricated structures and ephemeral construction materials. Even in their makeshift state, they already convey a message of industrial might, and inspire predictable feelings of 'meraviglia [e] ... ossequio per le grandi opere umane, [e per] lo sforzo dell'umanità concorde' (wonder [and] ... regard for the great human works, [and for] the efforts of a concordant humanity) ('Un vergiliato' 180).

If this is the official message that the exposition plans to disseminate, Gozzano pays only lip service to it, and ends up being a resistant and discordant reader. As is common in his writing, in 'Un vergiliato' Gozzano's interpretation is mediated. This time, his filter is Jeannette, a childhood friend whom he meets on the way to the fairgrounds, and whom he sees as a symbol of 'quanto c'è di più presente, di più febbraio 1911' (what there is of most modern, most February 1911) ('Un vergiliato' 176). An apt guide into the world of modernity, Jeannette represents the emancipated woman who has achieved financial independence, professional success, and sexual freedom. In her ability to reinvent herself from 'Giovannina ... piccola popolana' (Giovannina from the lower classes) to Jeannette 'direttrice di una ditta primaria' (director of a leading firm) ('Un vergiliato' 176), an importer and promoter of French fashion in Italy, Jeanette has realized the Italian provinces' material dreams. From her journeys to Paris, Vienna, and Berlin she has acquired a sense of worldly *savoir faire* and fashionable style. Through her lovers, she has claimed access to superfluous and pricey luxury items. Thanks to her own shrewdness and industry, she has achieved a measure of economic well-being rarely available to women of her own socio-cultural background. Jeannette embodies the spirit of the World's Fairs. Just as the expositions' ephemeral edifices display a false 'vetustà fatta di graticci, di stuoie, di cemento abilmente invecchiato' (antiquity made of trellises, matting, and craftily aged cement) ('Un vergiliato' 181), so Jeannette has perfected the art of the makeover: 'Non si è fatta bella. "Si è fatta," semplicemente. La scaltrezza del buon gusto ha dato al suo corpo magrissimo la linea parigina. Dalle parigine ha imparato a dipingersi gli occhi e le labbra' (She has not turned into a beauty. She has simply 'made herself up.' The guiles of good taste have given a Parisian look to her very slender body. She has learned how to paint her eyes and lips from the women of Paris) ('Un vergiliato' 177).

Even though, as a 'popolana ... travestita da gran signora' (low-class woman ... dressed up as a lady) ('Un vergiliato' 177), Jeannette mirrors the expositions' ambiguity between appearance and reality, neither she nor the world she represents constitutes a hermeneutical challenge for Gozzano. Unlike the baffled traveller in India, this pilgrim knows how to strip the real of its artificial garments, and, from the outset, what he sees turns conventional exposition pictures upside down:

Entriamo da un ingresso secondario che pure ha tutta l'imponenza di un ingresso trionfale: dal grande piazzale del monumento al Principe

Amedeo, dove il gruppo del Calandra emerge nero, bizzarramente oppresso da cumuli candidi. E intorno ricorre un semicerchio d'intercolunni, coi capitelli, le urne, le ghirlande ... Apro una porticina laterale ... Un uomo lascia la caldaia dove rimestava la pece bollente, si fa innanzi trasecolato, poi sospettoso ed ostile. ('Un vergiliato' 178)

(We enter from a secondary entrance, which nevertheless has all the imposing looks of a triumphal entrance, in the great square with the monument to Prince Amedeo. The sculptured group by Calandra stands out in black against bizarre and oppressive mounds of snow. Around it, there is a semicircle of intercolumns, capitals, urns, and wreaths ... I open a little side door ... A man leaves a cauldron where he was stirring boiling tar, and comes toward us, first baffled and then suspicious and hostile.)

Typical exposition narratives describing a visitor entering the fairgrounds for the first time – usually through a 'triumphal gate' and at the exposition's grand opening – undergo a bizarre twist here. After lingering on the funereal monument to Prince Amedeo, Gozzano describes an infernal space, guarded by an aged, tar-stirring Cerberus, and scattered with funeral icons and intimations of death. A she-Virgil in net stockings and high heels, Jeannette leans on a more wisely dressed pilgrim relying on his tour book to lead them through the snow-covered fairgrounds. In light of this masquerade, Gozzano's title choice of 'vergiliato' (the rare koiné is quintessentially D'Annunzio) constitutes a parodic trick. If Dante's *Inferno* is a very serious business, Gozzano's modern hell exists as a debased analogy of its tragic model – not a *città dolente*, but a melancholy one:

[È] strano, indefinibile il senso che incute questa città vastissima, dall'architettura grandiosa, a cupole, a colonne, questa città eretta per adunare quanto c'è di più veemente, di operoso, di febbrile nel mondo, avvolta nel suo sudario candido e silenzioso ...

[Jeannette] non pensa certo di ricordarmi col suo atteggiamento un'altra donna: la Melanconia, di Alberto Durero.

C'è fra la piccola crestaia che m'accompagna e la donna del pittore di Norimberga un'analogia che mi fa sorridere e mi piace, come tutte le cose stridule.

La Melancolia, vestita di corazza, ha le ali simboliche, e le chiome sparse, coronate di lauro. Medita, perplessa, dinnanzi all'opera dell'uomo con la gota sorretta dal pugno; intorno sono gli strumenti della maggiori con-

quiste umane: gli ordigni delle arti e delle scienze, dalla clessidra alla bus-
sola, dalla bilancia alle seste; e alle spalle della donna pensosa si stende una
lontananza di acque e si vedono le città e i porti e i navigli, tutti i prodigi
che l'uomo ha ideati e compiuti col macigno, col legno, col metallo. E la
donna ripete: *Cui bono? Melancolia!* ('Un vergiliato' 184–5)

(The feeling that this enormous city provokes is strange and indefinable,
with its grandiose architecture, its domes, and columns. This city, built to
bring together whatever is most intense and active in the world, is now
enwrapped in a white and silent shroud ...
    [Jeannette] certainly does not realize that her attitude reminds me of
another woman: Melancholia by Albrecht Dürer.
    Between the little milliner who accompanies me and the woman of the
Nuremberg painter there is an analogy that makes me smile, and that
pleases me like all jarring things.
    Melancholia, dressed in a suit of armour, has symbolic wings and wears a
laurel crown on her flowing hair. With her cheek resting on her fist, she is
perplexedly meditating in front of the works of man. Around her are the
tools of the major achievements of humanity: the instruments of the arts
and the sciences, from the hourglass to the compass, and from the scales to
the sextant. Behind the pensive woman, there stretches an expanse of
water and one can see cities, harbours, and ships. All the prodigies that
man has invented and accomplished with stone, wood, and metal are here,
and the woman repeats: *Cui bono? Melancolia!*)

Studies devoted to Albrecht Dürer's *Melancholia I* (1514) such as Raymond Klibanski, Erwin Panofsky, and Fritz Saxl's *Saturn and Melancholia*,
closely analyse the symbolic and figural complexity of Dürer's image.
Melancholia I belongs to those works of art that do not merely represent
a 'first-order' world of visual objects, but engage a 'second-order' body
of elements, that is, conceptual notions and intellectual signs that evoke
a rich cultural history (Klibanski 321–2). Unsurprisingly, Gozzano's own
reading of Dürer's esoteric imagery finds its meaning against this cultural history. Following the great majority of iconographic interpretations, Gozzano genders Melancholia in the feminine. In his multivolume *The Anatomy of Melancholy*, Robert Burton similarly described
Melancholia as 'a sad woman leaning on her arm' (334). In a cultural
framework closer to Gozzano, Giosuè Carducci interpreted Dürer's figure as an 'angelo femina di forti e leggiadre forme, coronata dalla
fredda ninfea e dal funebre apio la bella testa onde fluisce la chioma in

Albrecht Dürer. Melancholia I (engraving, 1514). By permission, Metropolitan Museum of Art (Harris Brisbane Dick Fund).

trecce disciolte' (a female angel, strongly yet gracefully built, her beautiful head of flowing, unbraided hair crowned by the cold nimphaea and the funereal apius) (275).[71]

While following these readings, Gozzano goes a step further than his predecessors when he underscores his gendered reading of Dürer's figure with his signature *oppositional* technique: the womanly Melancholia sits idle and pensive, gazing, perplexed, upon the many achievements, the 'works' and 'prodigies' of a hyperactive and unreflective 'man.' The objects that Gozzano selects from the engraving's visual riches are those that define man's imperial and military hubris: sextants and compasses to conquer space, hourglasses and scales to impose the time and law of the West upon the lands beyond the waters.

Describing Melancholia's pensive idleness was not an original exegetical choice: as a passionate reader of Théophile Gautier's poetry, Gozzano may have recalled the moving lines of his 'Melancholia': 'Je ne sais rien qui soit plus admirable au monde, / Plus plein de rêverie et de douleur profonde, / Que ce grand ange assis, l'aile ployée au dos, / Dans l'immobilité du plus complet repos' (Nothing is more admirable in the world. / More full of reverie and deep suffering, / Than this great angel sitting with her wings folded on her back, / In the immobility of the most complete repose) (87). What is unique to Gozzano is that Melancholia wears man's imperial garb: Gozzano reads Dürer's flowing dress as a suit of armour and transforms Carducci's nimphaea and apius into a laurel crown. Given the wearer, the armour and the laurel speak of imperial glory as well as of this glory's melancholy ephemerality. The laurel, however, also implies the notion of poetic fame. As early as Aristotle and Marsilio Ficino, the feeling of melancholia was linked to the exercise of poetry and philosophy. Melancholia marked people who devoted themselves to contemplative knowledge, were prone to interior withdrawal, and felt compelled to investigate the supreme mysteries of the divine. Married to creative imagination and visionary trance, melancholia ushered in prophetic and oneiric revelations (Yates 56; Riva 139; Agamben 11–12).

Contrary to man, the shortsighted *artifex* of an imperial world, Gozzano's womanly Melancholia is the inspired diviner of the long timespan. Hers is a prophetic history that belittles man's transient triumphs by placing them in the context of a non-anthropocentric and cosmic timescale. Progressive time – the time of the Universal History of Western conquest – comes to terms here with a *longue durée*, a cosmic or natural time that overcomes humanity's relative cultural constructs and has no knowable chronology. In 'Un Natale a Ceylon' ('A Christmas in Ceylon'), a sketch devoted to his stay on Adam's Peak in today's Sri Lanka, Gozzano underscores this point by ironically dismantling the concept of progressive and redeeming becoming that the reference to the Christmas holiday implies. Ceylon exists in a 'una quinta stagione senza nome' (a fifth season without a name) ('Un Natale' 36), a season that never changes. A modern counter-Adam, cast in what the legend argues was the location of the Earthly Paradise, Gozzano does not experience the absence of transience as a blessed prelapsarian condition. On the contrary, Gozzano's 'cosmic' time is alienating because it mocks all anthropocentric constructs – the 'man-made' time of the hourglass – and by way of contrast reveals the ultimate fleetingness of all that human beings devised to create their 'illusions of permanence.'

Associated with Chronos Saturn, with autumn and winter, Melancholia reveals the distressing truth of the inexorable decay of all things and the vanity of all human glories. Her forward-looking gaze does not build consoling utopias but translates the passing of time in the dusky and elegiac tones reminiscent of Heredia's sonnet on Goa. Gozzano's wintry pilgrimage in the frozen landscape of Valentino Park becomes a journey amid estranged cultural memories. From Dante to Dürer, these memories wreck havoc upon the progressive and triumphal trajectory of the 'Fabulous Exposition.' A month before its official opening, Turin 1911 is already a frozen corpse 'avvolta nel sudario che distenderà sulle cose il cataclisma apocalittico, il gelo finale' (enwrapped in the shroud that the apocalyptic cataclysm and final chill will stretch upon all things) ('Un vergiliato' 185). A nihilistic dystopia that foreshadows the dissolution of progress, Gozzano's exposition narrative trip through the 'moritura città del Valentino' (the dying city of Valentino Park) ('I crisantemi' 205) traces an itinerary to the end of modernity. In this context, Gozzano's otherwise conventional praise 'del nostro passato glorioso, del florido presente, della nostra ascesa rapida e magnifica nel divenire civile' (of our glorious past, our flourishing present, and our rapid and magnificent ascent in civilization's progress) ('Il padiglione' 201) becomes just the swan song of a fleeting instant of human glory.

That Gozzano's exposition articles hit a strident note in contemporary World's Fairs cant is hardly surprising. One would expect a similarly nihilistic approach in a piece significantly entitled 'La città moritura' (The Dying City), devoted to the closing of the 1911 exposition. Instead, if compared to 'Un vergiliato,' this article contains an astonishingly different reading of Dürer's famous engraving:

Fare bisogna, non sognare soltanto; il sogno è il compenso concesso alle tregue. Su questo ponte fittizio, dove mesi or sono contemplavo l'esposizione nascente sotto una cortina di neve candida, contemplo oggi l'esposizione agonizzante sotto un sudario di foglie morte. Ed oggi, come allora, mi ritorna al pensiero, la Melanconia eternata da Alberto Durero ... ma la ripenso oggi con diverso cuore.

Ripenso il grande Angelo terrestre dalle ali d'aquila che simbolizza il genio dell'uomo, lo spirito seduto sulla macina con il cubito poggiato al ginocchio, con la gola sorretta dal pugno, tenendo nell'altra mano le seste del calcolo e il libro della scienza. Intorno sono sparsi gli stromenti delle opere umane; in una clessidra scolpita scorre la sabbia silenziosa del tempo; e si scorge in fondo la terra con i suoi continenti e i suoi mari, con le città e i porti; e quelle città e quei porti li ha costruiti l'uomo; egli ha tagliato la pietra, abbattutto il pino per le navi, temprato il ferro per la lotta.

Egli stesso ha imposto al tempo il congegno che lo misura. Assiso non per riposarsi, ma per meditare un altro lavoro, egli fissa la vita con occhi forti e sereni. ('La città' 209)

(One must act, not just dream. Dreaming is the prize awarded to truces. Today, on this artificial bridge, where months ago I contemplated the exposition that was coming to light under a layer of pure white snow, I can observe the exposition dying under a shroud of dead leaves. And today, just like back then, I am reminded of Melancholy that Albrecht Dürer made eternal ... but I think of it in a different spirit.

Again, I think about the great terrestrial Angel with eagle's wings symbolizing man's genius. I see the spirit of man sitting on a millstone, his elbow resting on his knee, his fist supporting his cheek, a sextant and the book of science in his other hand. Scattered around are the tools of man's works, and the silent sand of time flows in a sculpted hourglass. Far away, one sees the earth with its continents and oceans, cities and ports. Man built those cities and ports; he cut the stone, and felled pine trees to make ships, and tempered iron for the struggle.

Man himself has imposed upon time the device that measures it. Sitting down, not at rest but pondering his next feat, man looks upon life, his gaze strong and serene.)

It is certainly not far-fetched to assume that this interpretation suited Gozzano's publishers much better than the first one did, and one may even venture to suggest that publishers' demands may have prompted

Gozzano's about-face. However, as is typical of Gozzano, this revised *ekphrasis* offers at least two further interpretative levels, one intertextual and the other contextual.

From his first to his second rendition of Melancholia, Gozzano modernizes the stale figure of prosopopoeia by using intertextual clues to make it a multi-faced and elusive 'personified abstraction.' What has so far eluded critical attention is that Gozzano's second reading of Dürer's *Melancholia* closely follows Gabriele D'Annunzio's own *ekphrasis* at the conclusion of *Il fuoco*:

> Il grande Angelo terrestre dalle ali d'aquila, lo Spirito senza sonno, coronato di pazienza, stava seduto su la pietra nuda, con il cubito poggiato al ginocchio, con la gota sorretta dal pugno, tenendo su l'altra coscia un libro e le seste nell'altra mano. ... E intorno erano sparsi gli strumenti delle opere umane; e sul capo vigile, presso l'apice di un'ala, scorreva nella duplice ampolla la sabbia silenziosa del Tempo; e scorgevasi in fondo il Mare con i suoi golfi con i suoi porti con i suoi fari calmo e indomabile, su cui, tramontando il Sole nella gloria dell'arcobaleno, volava il vipistrello vespertino recando inscritta nelle sue membrane la parola rivelatrice. E quei porti e quei fari e quelle città, li aveva costrutti lo Spirito senza sonno, coronato di pazienza. Egli aveva tagliato la pietra per le torri, abbattuto il pino per i navigli, temprato il ferro per ogni lotta. Egli stesso aveva imposto al Tempo il congegno che lo misura. Assiso, non per riposarsi ma per meditare un altro lavoro, egli fissava la Vita con i suoi occhi forti ove splendeva l'anima libera. (511–12)

> (The great Angel of Earth with the eagle's wings, the sleepless spirit crowned with patience, sat on the bare stone with his elbow on his knee, his cheek supported on his hand, a book on his other knee, and a compass in his other hand ... All round him were scattered the instruments of the works of man, and on his watchful head, near the summit of a wing, the silent sands of time ran through the hourglass; and in the background there was the sea with its gulfs and its ports and its lighthouses, the calm, unconquerable sea over which, when the sun had set in its rainbow glory, the twilight bat would fly with the revealing word written on its membrane. And those ports and those lighthouses and those cities were the work of the sleepless spirit crowned with patience. He had broken the stone for the towers, cut down the pine tree for the ships, tempered the iron for every struggle. He himself had laid on Time the instrument that measures it. Seated not to rest, but to meditate on some new work to be accomplished,

he fixed on life the powerful eyes shining with the free light of the sun.)
(*The Flame* 396–7)

Gozzano's reading emulates D'Annunzio's in reversing conventional interpretations and gendering the Angel of Melancholy in the masculine.[72] This Angel's wings are no longer abstractly 'symbolic,' but allegorize a virile spirit: man's genius. Gozzano makes an easy transition from the great 'Angel' to 'Man' as the protagonist of this energy-filled scene, fully identifying one with the other. If traditional iconography read the Angel's folded wings as expressing the frustration of Melancholia's spiritual ennui – her saturnine tedium – for both D'Annunzio and Gozzano they come to represent 'la tensione e la veglia, ricerca di nuove immagini visibili solo agli occhi di chi è senza sonno' (the tension and the wakefulness, and the search for new images to be seen only by those who are sleepless) (Ritter Santini 271). The lack of sleep that D'Annunzio mentions is a well-known feature of epic heroes: leaders, generals, and kings are often portrayed as alert and sleepless on the eve of battle. With his imperial eagle's wings, the wakeful Man/Angel embodies the qualities of a heroic genealogy, a brood of pensive nation makers and conquerors.

Both D'Annunzio and Gozzano take further liberties with former interpretations of *Melancholia I* by depriving the 'strange medley of objects' (Yates 50) that Dürer etched near the angel of Melancholia of all their obscurely esoteric senses, and prosaically seeing them as 'stromenti delle opere umane.' Indicative of man's heroic achievements, these objects are valuable for their pragmatic function and not for their symbolic power. The ideology promoted here is a utilitarian one, and its philosophy one of conquest and material gain. There is obviously no space left for Melancholia's negative 'feminine' side in D'Annunzio and Gozzano, who see the great Angel as the 'sanguine' symbol of Man's will rather than a 'melancholy' woman absorbed in deep meditation. In D'Annunzio's context, Dürer's figure embodies the 'spirito italico,' creatively and actively building Italy's new utopias of glory (Riva 150–1).

In the complex symbolism of *Il fuoco*, the great Angel is also a metaphor for the artist as prophet and seer, the 'Vate' of D'Annunzio's own poetic and political ambitions. *Il fuoco*'s protagonist, Stelio Effrena, transmutes the melancholy and aptly named female protagonist, Foscarina, into a sublime opus, a work of art liberated from the tyranny of time. If the utilitarian tools of man's science imposed their own unit of measurement upon time, the mystical and sublime tools of artistic creation – Melancholia's *imaginatio* – overcome time altogether. D'Annunzio's aesthetic heroics take on a different nuance in the context of Gozzano's interpretation. First, Gozzano makes clear that his musing on the 'revised' Dürer occurs on a 'ponte fittizio' (artificial bridge) ('La città' 209), an almost catachrestic symbol for the fairgoer's transition from reality into the man-made dreamland of the exposition. Gozzano's fantasy of man's power, his reading of 'man's genius' playing God with space and time, occurs within this artificial scenery, the stage-like setting of Turin 1911:

> L'Esposizione fu per molti mesi 'il paese fuori del mondo'; ed è stato questo, forse, il suo fascino più grande e più sottile ... Tutti esulavano per qualche ora nella città fittizia ... la folla accorreva per rintemprare lo spirito in un ambiente nuovo, in un'atmosfera meno grigia di quella che circonda la nostra vita consueta.
>
> ... [L'esposizione] ci offriva il soggiorno inverosimile, senza miserie e senza necessità, realizzava il sogno del paese felice che tutti portiamo in noi con una nostalgia senza nome. ('La città' 207)

> (The exposition was, for many months, the 'land outside of this world'; and this was its greatest and subtlest charm ... Everybody escaped into the fictitious city, for a few hours ... The crowds ran to the Exposition to recharge their spirits in a new environment, in an atmosphere that was more colourful than that which normally surrounds our everyday life.
>
> ... [The exposition] offered us an incredible sojourn, without despair and necessity, and realized the dream of the happy land that we all carry within us with a nameless nostalgia.)

Borrowing a well-known image from Pirandello, one may argue that while building his stage, Gozzano makes us aware of the rent in this stage's paper sky. For Gozzano, though, this rent does not reveal the tragic emptiness behind. It rather shows a melancholy backstage encumbered with the West's obsolete illusions and discarded myths: 'Iddie, Eroi, Ninfe, Stagioni, Ore, Vittorie, tutte han perduto gli archi, le saette, le ghirlande, le cornucopie, le faci, gli emblemi della lotta, dell'abbondanza, della gioia' (goddesses, heroes, nymphs, seasons, hours, and victories: they all have lost their bows, arrows, garlands, cornucopias and torches, all the emblems of struggle, abundance and joy) ('La città' 208).

The Leopardian last illusion, art, undergoes a similar fate. In its desecrating irony, Gozzano's *plagiat* of D'Annunzio's celebration of the artist's creative might drastically revises art's power in the modern world. By borrowing D'Annunzio's words, Gozzano argues that the modern poet is a reader and reuser of tradition. If, in 'Goa: "La Dourada,"' Gozzano had renounced inventing the future *tout court*, here he relativizes this future. Seen together, Gozzano's two readings of Dürer's *Melancholia* cannot but argue that there are as many futures as there are new angels wishing to invent them, as many historical *emplotments* as there are historians imposing their ideologies upon the passing of time. If for D'Annunzio, the 'Immaginifico,' the role of the artist is to 'obscure' the truth to reach a higher truth, Gozzano can only attest to the relativity and changeability of truths, their ephemerality. 'Io sono camaleontico, chimerico, incoerente, inconsistente' (I am chameleonic, chimerical, incoherent, and inconsistent'), Andrea Sperelli, the artist-protagonist of D'Annunzio's *Il Piacere*, exclaims with pride (359). The same may be argued for Gozzano, but in the twilight of his writing, there is no place for pride. Modernity has the *facies nigra* of Dürer's *Melancholia*,[73] and Gozzano's wavering between the anticipation of more relative and plural futures and the nostalgia for the absolute certainties of the past ultimately reveals his suffered involvement in one of the *cruces* of modernity: the ethics of aesthetics.

Production for Profit and Creation for Pleasure: Beauty, Truth, and the Role of the Artist in the World of Universal Expositions

'"Beauty is truth, truth beauty,' – that is all / Ye know on earth, and all ye need to know"' argued with chiastic rigour one of the most famous ekphrastic poems of the Western canon. In a typically mediated and displaced manner, Gozzano's addressed the ethics of aesthetics in his own ekphrastic reading of one of the world's wonders, the Taj Mahal. Gozzano translates his sensory engagement with the Taj Mahal's architectural magnificence and chromatic splendour into the mystical language of revelations and miracles. This language, he claims, is the only appropriate rendition of the monument's self-reflexive formal perfection:

> Sullo scenario a due tinte: l'azzurro del cielo e il bronzo cupo dei cipressi, s'innalza la più immacolata e gigantesca mole sognata da questi sultani amici del candore ... L'azzurro del cielo, il candore delle nubi e dei marmi, il bronzo cupo dei cipressi, tutto è riflesso in un gran lago tranquillo che raddoppia il miracolo. ('Agra' 85–6)

(Against the background of two colours – the blue of the sky and the dark bronze of the cypresses – rises the most immaculate and gigantic structure ever dreamed by these white-loving sultans ... The azure of the sky, the whiteness of the clouds and of the marble, the dark bronze of the cypresses, everything is reflected in a large, serene lake that redoubles the miracle.)

Self-sufficient in its totalizing and refined beauty, the Taj Mahal imposes its own logic upon the surrounding space and thus reverses the reflectionist economy of realist aesthetics, forcing nature to imitate art's sophisticated forms. This is art as sheer spectacle, and cult-like ostension: a supreme exposition of the beautiful in an absolutized, aristocratic, and rarefied environment that would have thrilled Oscar Wilde, Walter Pater, J.K. Huysmans, Paul Verlaine, and Gabriele D'Annunzio. A similarly decadent fascination with a ritualized art that stuns the senses guides Gozzano's description of the Palace of the Great Moghuls:

Siamo giunti nel regno dei marmi immacolati, nella città superna dei tiranni. Un terrazzo immenso, la sala delle udienze, candido come tutti gli altri edifizi, con non altro che un trono di marmo nero, per il Gran Mogol; intorno ricorrono arcate che dànno l'illusione d'una grotta di latte congelato, a stalattiti geometriche, dove il candore è sottolineato da una linea d'onice nerissima. L'onice, l'oro, l'argento, la turchese, il porfido sono usati con scaltra leggerezza, in gracili motivi floreali o in linee che seguono il frastaglio complicato delle trine marmoree, all'infinito ... Tutto è di marmo immacolato, e l'eleganza si mostra soltanto nel traforo e nella cesellatura, portate all'ultimo limite di un'arte inimitabile. ('Agra' 83)

(We have arrived in the realm of the immaculate marbles, in the supreme city of tyrants. An immense terrace, the audience hall, as white as all the other buildings and containing nothing but the Great Moghul's black marble throne is surrounded by a series of arches that give the illusion of a cavern of frozen milk, of geometrical stalactites, where a line of jet-black onyx emphasizes the surrounding whiteness. Onyx, gold, silver, turquoise, and porphyry are used with deft lightness, in delicate floral motifs or lines that follow the complex ornamentation of the lacy marble into infinity ... Everything is of immaculate marble, and elegance displays itself only in the fretwork and engravings perfected to the ultimate limits of inimitable art).

Gozzano's description of the Great Moghuls' palace would have complied with Walter Pater's aesthetic tenets, as expressed in his seminal essay entitled 'Style.' Pater argued that 'true *composition*' (24) results from the artist's 'skilful economy of means' (17), and from a creative exercise 'sustained by yet restraining the productive ardour' (24). Only through the utmost formal restraint, meticulous precision, and fastidious refinement of creative skills can the artist ultimately exceed all mimetic boundaries. Similarly, Gozzano interprets the artistry in the Palace of the Great Moghuls as displaying a virtuosity of technical control and apparent formal simplicity as means to achieve the aesthetic sublime of 'inimitable art.'

In his *ekphrasis*, Gozzano mimics this controlled yet expansive style, and conflates descriptive accuracy with imaginative suggestions and evocative imagery. By describing the architectural features of the Moghuls' Palace as imitating the lightness of lace and evoking the diaphanous evanescence of frozen milk, Gozzano presents concrete referents while conjuring up the figurative elegance of purely discursive ornaments, and foregrounding his subjective aesthetic sensibility and metaphorical inventiveness. If we remember that classical rhetoric assigned to *description* the task of materializing beauty through language, then it should not surprise us that the mimetic function in Gozzano's *ekphrasis* both evokes and dissolves its material foundations. While purporting to objectively capture the real through the reality markers that pepper his narrative and thus sustain referential illusion, Gozzano relies on unusual imagery and definitions of incalculability (such as 'all'infinito' or 'all'ultimo limite') to create a self-reflexive phantasmagoria that exposes the artifice inherent in all representations, the Great Moghuls' as well as his own:

> [L]a vita dei Gran Mogol è tutta nello scenario che ho d'intorno. [Ammiro] la zenana, l'arem che occultava gelosamente i più bei fiori di carne, poi i terrazzi immensi delle udienze, le sale di giustizia dove il sultano e la corte, abbigliati di stoffe vivaci e di gioielli, formavano sul marmo candido un quadro che abbacinava il popolo genuflesso. ('Agra' 84)

> (The scenery that surrounds me represents the life of the Great Moghuls. [I admire] the zenana – the harem that jealously concealed the rarest flowers of the flesh – the immense audience halls, and the halls of justice where the sultan and his court, in colourful garments and jewels, formed a picture against the white marble that dazzled the kneeling people.)

With this verbal rendition of the Moghuls' visual displays, Gozzano participates in a world of crafted appearances, and creates a fiction in the second-degree. In fact, if Gozzano's *ekphrasis* points to its own self as rhetorical construct as well as to the external referential world, this world, we find out, exists as a fiction, an aesthetic product, a formal display. With the familiar strategy employed in his description of the bayadère's dance in 'La danza d'una Devadasis,' Gozzano grounds his narrative on the principles of realistic mimesis only to move the mimetic goal further and further away from us. He thus forces us to wander with him in a space of layered textuality, an artificial world of *objets d'art* that exist in a purely aestheticized and ceremonial sphere. What prevails here is what Benjamin would call an art that 'originated in the service of a ritual' ('The Work of Art' 223). The ritual, in the case of the Palace of the Great Moghuls as Gozzano interprets it, conflates the cult of politics with the fin de siècle theology of art based on the cult of beauty. The 'two different planes' on which works of art can be received and valued according to Benjamin, their 'cult value' and their 'exhibition value,' become one and the same in Agra. The objects of cult enhance their value via their exhibition and vice versa, their 'aura' increasing, rather than diminishing, through display. However, a problem arises in the conflation of cult and exposition values where these objects' *truth* is concerned. If with the bayadère's performance Gozzano eluded the problem because the dancer was, ultimately, neither *true* nor *beautiful* to him, in Agra the beautiful puzzlingly corresponds to all that is referentially ambiguous. To put it simply, this is a world where nothing is what it appears to be:

Si passa di sala in sala, e le sale sono senza porte, così che formano prospettive di sogno immacolato, allee di trine candide che si prolungano all'infinito. Stupisce la nitida freschezza di queste lastre sottili di marmo, traforate fino all'inverosimile; lastre che ricordano immensi ricami a giorno, tesi tra due colonne e non pareti concrete: la mano vi si appoggia con esitanza, meravigliandosi della rigidezza secolare. ('Agra' 84)

(One walks from hall to hall. The halls have no doors, so that they form vistas from immaculate dreams, corridors of white lace that extend into infinity. The limpid freshness of these thin marble slabs is astonishing. Fretted with unbelievable skill, these slabs do not remind one of stone partitions, but resemble huge openwork embroidery stretched between two pillars. One hesitates to touch them, and marvels at the centuries-old hardness.)

This is a world of dream-like appearances and trompe l'oeil realities, where stone is carved so as to imitate lightly embroidered textures, and ephemeral surfaces conceal a beauty made to withstand the assault of time. Agra thus constitutes the opposite of those buildings that, at World's Fairs, imitated the pricey strength of marble and stone while built with cheap materials destined for imminent demolition. However, in spite of the many obvious differences, Gozzano implies that ancient Indian autocracies and Western liberal democracies share some fundamental traits in their 'exposition mentalities.' Both cultures, in fact, display wonders that flourish on the ambiguities between appearance and reality: 'Avanziamo quasi increduli, temendo dell'incantesimo creato da un negromante, di uno scenario che debba dileguare come la Fata Morgana' (We walk forward, almost incredulous, fearing that this is a magician's spell that will soon vanish like a mirage) ('Agra' 86).

By mimicking the Decadents' style, Gozzano reconciles art with cult. Yet, he also deconstructs the original and absolute truth-value carried by the artwork in its ritual function. In the cradle of the world, Gozzano learns, time and again, that humanity exists in and through displays and representations, self-expositions that highlight the ambiguity and multiplicity of all creative and hermeneutical exercises. With a typical ironic twist, in the autocratic world of the Great Moghuls Gozzano drafts an epistemology founded on uncertainty and the plurality of meaning. In engaging aesthetics as a viable if complex hermeneutical tool, this epistemology values the role of the individual imagination in reaching a 'truth' that may be as multifaceted as there are interpreters investigating it.

If Agra, the city of the tyrants, teaches this anti-absolutistic epistemology to the modernist pilgrim, in the social utopia of Hyderabad Gozzano reaches a different kind of aesthetic wisdom. Hyderabad represents a joyful enclave, where people do not subject themselves to the demands of labour in order to satisfy their basic needs, but live instead in the idyllic enjoyment of superfluous commodities:

La vita quotidiana è fatta di necessità. Ora questa gente non fa nulla di necessario. Tutti i negozi, sotto le arcate, ostentano le più deliziose cose inutili: gioielli, sete, velluti, vasi d'argento e di bronzo, babbucce ricurve, scimitarre cesellate e gemmate, veli tinti pur ora e tesi ad asciugare al vento, leggeri come la nube che si sfalda, vivi di tutte le tinte più delicate; profumi, essenze contenute in alti vasi suggellati o in barattoli dalla forma singolare, segnati di lettere cabalistiche. E fiori, fiori in abbondanza, piramidi di magnolie, di ibischi, di rose decapitate che i mercanti vendono a peso, come i frutti, e che la folla infilza per via, improvvisando la ghirlanda quotidiana più necessaria del pane; strana folla che vive di colori, di profumi, di sogno, d'apparenza! ('I tesori di Golconda' 65)

(Everyday life is made of needs. Now, these people do nothing out of necessity. All the shops beneath the arcades display the most charmingly superfluous things: jewellery, silks, velvets, silver and bronze vases, curved slippers, engraved and gem-studded scimitars, newly dyed veils hung up to dry in the breeze, light as dissolving clouds, aglow with the most delicate hues; perfumes and essences contained in tall sealed vases or in unusually shaped jars, marked with mysterious writing. And flowers, flowers in abundance – pyramids of magnolias, hibiscus and decapitated roses, which the merchants sell by weight, like fruit; the crowd strings them together on the streets, improvising their daily garlands, which are more necessary to them than bread: a strange crowd that lives on colours, scents, dreams, and appearances.)

Blessed members of an archaic community that predates the individualistic alienation and aggressive market competition of the technological West, these spontaneous people engage in the production of useless objects of beauty, their collective goal not mere profit but the sense of aesthetic fulfilment that those objects generate. The transient loveliness of a wreath of flowers defines their non-empirical and hedonistic appreciation of all that is purely decorative, their full engagement with the fleeting present, and their unproductive enjoyment of ephemeral pleasures. Their joie de vivre remains tied to all that is gratuitous in life, and their existence is measured on the slow time of *otium* and leisure. Gozzano's wordplay with the vocabulary of worship (the daily wreath more necessary than bread) removes the very notion of necessity from the practical sphere, and places it into a ceremonial world of ritual. With a typically aestheticizing move, Gozzano depicts the inhabitants of Hyderabad as devoted to the cult of pleasure for pleasure's sake, forgetful of the future and blessedly engaged in a perfect present. One is reminded, here, of Nietzsche's praise of the non-productive use of time devoted to idle contemplation, which he claimed the modern West had lost by favouring instead the restless activity of its 'the cash-amassing bankers' in *Human, All Too Human* (132).

Of course, the alter ego of Hyderabad is embodied by the utilitarian, self-centred, and rational West, which busily builds taxonomies for cognitive display and material possession, and exists exclusively in the private, mechanical time of profit and acquisition. From the nineteenth century, Johan Huizinga argued in *Homo Ludens*, Western culture became increasingly marked by 'utilitarianism, prosaic efficiency, and the bourgeois ideal of social welfare ... Work and production became the ideal, and then the idol of the age. All Europe donned the boiler-suit' (191–2). This is the West that Oscar Wilde scornfully accused of having forgotten the laws of beauty and of being too intent on exploiting the utility value of cheaply made and mass-produced objects rather than 'enjoying cultivated leisure ... or making beautiful things, or reading beautiful things, or simply contemplating the world with admiration and delight' (*The Soul* 27). In a controversial article, Gozzano himself chastised the 'folla cosmopolita e amorfa' (cosmopolitan and amorphous crowd) ('Rosolie' 187) that flocked from one World's Fair to the next to celebrate the 'rifioritura del cattivo gusto' (blossoming of bad taste) ('Rosolie' 189). Here, Gozzano's signature catalogue of 'le cose stridule' (strident things) mocks the modern aesthetics of the ugly:

> Chincaglierie feroci, bronzi con la naiade che regge il giaggiolo della lampadina elettrica ... orologi in alabastro con la ninfa accosciata [*sic*], piedistalli a spirale rivestiti di raso chermisi a frange d'oro, negretti di velluto, ballerine igrometriche che annunciano il tempo col colore del gonnellino ... statuette d'illustri italiani, illustri italiani convertiti in bottiglie di vetro col tappo sulla testa: Garibaldi, Mazzini, Cavour, che per commemorare il 1861 si empiranno di vino, d'olio, d'aceto. E su tutte queste scelleratezze scolpite o dipinte la data memorabile 'Ricordi di Torino – Esposizione 1911.' E il forestiero trova perfettamente appagati i suoi gusti e compera e paga. ('Rosolie' 188)

> (Horrible trinkets, bronze sculptures with a Naiad holding an iris flower that contains an electric bulb ... alabaster clocks with a squatting nymph, spiral pedestals covered in red satin with golden fringes, little black boys made of velveteen, hygrometric ballerinas announcing the weather by the colour of their skirts ... statuettes of illustrious Italians, and illustrious Italians transformed into glass bottles with the cork on their heads: Garibaldi, Mazzini, and Cavour will be filled with wine, oil, and vinegar to commemorate the Unification of Italy. And, on all these sculpted and painted obscenities, the memorable date: 'Souvenir of Turin – Exposition 1911.' The visitor, who finds his taste perfectly satisfied, buys and pays.)

If, in Turin, the goldsmith to whom Gozzano confides his 'fisime estetiche' (aesthetic whims) scornfully replies that he is a merchant before being an artist ('Rosolie' 189), in Hyderabad, people pursue a more innocent moral economy that, neglectful of self-interest, appreciates all that is unproductive, unquantifiable, extravagant, and beautiful, such as perfumes, colours, appearances, and dreams.

In spite of these premises, however, Gozzano makes it clear that this counter-economy does not exist beyond and above the rules of the marketplace. In Hyderabad, just as in Turin, London, or Paris, the shops display ephemeral objects of luxury in order to arouse the desires of potential buyers who, implicitly, must possess the means to fulfil those desires. Gozzano catches the merchants in the act of weighing and thus pricing the natural beauty of flowers, which will then be woven into a superfluous and artistic ornament, the garland. However, in Hyderabad the process of commodification remains restricted and self-enclosed. Comparable to what, in other contexts, anthropologists such as Igor Kopytoff and Arjun Appadurai have termed 'terminal commodities' (23), the ephemeral garland is likely to make only *one* journey from production to consumption. In the *art pour l'art* enclave of Hyderabad, once the garland has completed its journey from seller to purchaser, it enters a process of transvaluation and thus becomes decommodified. In a new understanding of value, the garland's worth depends now on a complex interplay of aesthetic, emotional, spiritual, ritual, social, and symbolic investments.

Gozzano does not interpret this phenomenon as something that exists beyond or against the market economy of the West, but in fact depends upon it. In Gozzano's view, in other words, Hyderabad exists because of Britain's 'illimitata generosità' (unlimited generosity) ('I tesori' 65):

Il Nizzam, sovrano d'Haiderabat, sa che invece di armati, l'Inghilterra manda sacchi di grano e che la carestia – endemica ormai in questa zona sempre più riarsa – si farebbe sentire ogni anno senza l'illimitata generosità dei custodi accerchianti. E Haiderabat vive nella sua favola millenaria, intatta come dieci secoli or sono, bella di tutte le eleganze e le raffinatezze ereditate da Bagdad, da Persepoli, da Bisanzio. ('I tesori' 65)

(The Nizam, ruler of Hyderabad, knows that instead of armies, England sends sacks of grain, and that famine – by now endemic to this increasingly arid region – would come back every year but for the boundless generosity of the surrounding wardens. Hyderabad lives its millennial fairy tale, untouched after ten centuries, beautiful with all the charms and refinements that she inherited from Baghdad, Persepolis, and Byzantium.)

By sending grain to these otherwise starving populations, Britain frees them from the stark rule of need and allows them to revel in the consumption of their blithe fairy-tale gifts. Gratuitous pleasure, Gozzano implies, is pricey indeed, and he portrays Britain as a very improbable type of donor who bestows upon Hyderabad the unselfish gift of an existence in an aristocratic and refined realm of sheer beauty, luxury, and material surplus.

Gozzano is not merely juxtaposing an archaic society with its instinctual and generous flair for the beautiful against the rational and calculating West. Unlike many practitioners of popular exoticism, Gozzano does not see the people of Hyderabad as the inhabitants of a primeval paradise, still uncompromised by the touch of Western greed. In Gozzano's view, modern productivity and the practical mentality of the West have indeed created this paradise by exorcizing the spectres of hunger, disease, and mortality that plagued these populations, ultimately allowing them to worship freely at the altar of beauty. However, if the festive parasite, *homo aestheticus*, needs the calculating *homo oeconomicus* to exist, then *homo oeconomicus*'s material gifts to India cannot logically add up to selfless acts of *largitio* but, rather, gratify his acquisitive and domineering ideology. This ideology, though, receives an ironic rendition in one of the very few self-portraits that Gozzano offers of himself as the Western traveller in India: 'Rientro nell'albergo abbagliato dalla troppa luce e dai troppi colori, umiliato in questa folla elegante tra la quale la mia figura occidentale in casco e gambali deve passare come il fantasma d'un mendicante' (I return to my hotel, dazzled by too much light and too many colours, humbled by the elegant crowds, amid which, in my Western gaiters and helmet, I must look like the ghost of a beggar) ('I tesori' 65). In an interesting reversal, Gozzano's colonial and militaristic persona loses its hard materiality, and becomes both evanescent and pleading, an image of lonely and absurdly masqueraded need, in a lush picture of stunning collective and expansive beauty.

By collapsing the contrastive foundation of conventional binary opposites, Gozzano reveals how two dominant ideologies coexist, in close and uncomfortable quarters, in his thought. One is rational, pragmatic, and utilitarian, and the other is aestheticizing, ritualistic, and expansive. While it thrives in this non-normative, disinterested, and communal ethos, art for Gozzano is inevitably implicated in the laws of supply and demand of the marketplace. Gozzano's narratives on Agra and Hyderabad conceal his implicit meditation on the role of the artist and the value of aesthetics in modern liberal economies. The mirror image of

Hyderabad's idealized artistic community is the artist who, in the West, chooses the refinements of art over the crass rules of the marketplace. However, as Gozzano the *gazzettiere* found out, this choice is not really available in the modern world. The rules of the marketplace have penetrated and organized all the spaces of modernity, forcing the ideologies of the beautiful and the useful to live in far closer quarters than their dichotomous ideals would prefer.

Conclusion

Since the fabled Great Exhibition at the Crystal Palace in 1851, World's Fairs have constituted ordered display cases of goods as well as ideas. Like the merchandise exhibited for the public's desiring eyes, these ideas were arranged and packaged for quick assimilation and eager consumption. If the expositions' cornucopia of commodities stunned the fairgoer with a sense of abundance, extravagance, and novelty, the power of the World's Fairs' ideas derived from the fact that they were both few and redundant. From one fair to the next, recurring notions displayed themselves in novel garb: they were notions about national identity and exotic otherness, imperial competition and civilization's advance, social stability and capitalist growth, and technological progress and bourgeois affluence. Kaleidoscopic in their arrangement of elements, World's Fairs exploited recurring ordering and characterization principles that hierarchically ranked and objectified societies, confirmed the pre-eminence of host nations, and, as a whole, asserted the supremacy of white civilization.

On the all-inclusive stage of universal expositions, differing ideologies, multiple messages, and contrasting representational codes nonchalantly coexisted: nationalism married cosmopolitanism, the gospel of world peace included statements of martial might and colonial aggression, the display of regional and ethnic particularities cohabited with globalizing drives, and intimations of realistic accuracy flaunted spectacular artifices. Janus-like, the founding ideas of the World's Fairs were thus both normative and integrative, heralding the future while remaining tradition-bound – they were parochial as well as universal, unifying yet Manichean. This ideological omnivorousness made World's Fairs formidable consensus-creating machines, operating on efficient technologies of social stabilization and cultural homogenization.

If, in agreement with post-colonial scholarship, we can argue that nations themselves are narrations, then the expositions' master-narratives were indeed among the West's most effective modes of self-representation. Foundational and progress-bound, these narratives defined national identities in absolute and essentializing terms. They communicated by means of a lingua franca that was global, authoritative, and comprehensive, steeped in unflinching generalities and absolute certainties about the essence of peoples, races, genders, and cultures. While these narratives' cultural influence and global diffusion was both formidable and unprecedented, one should not forget that such grand epics of emancipation and enlightenment engendered subversive subtexts and meaningful counter-discourses. These counter-discourses spoke through disruptive silences, significant absences, and puzzling paradoxes. They exposed biases and prejudices, thus uncovering social disparities and racial conflicts. Beyond their harmonious surface, they revealed epistemological tensions, ideological contradictions, and conceptual dissonances.

Engaging in this kind of contrapuntal reading of the discourses of the World's Fairs allows us to cast a discriminating eye on the concept of the imperial paradigm, thus complicating its concurring and univocal connotations. Edward Said, among others, convincingly argued that, if metropolitan Europeans and Americans are today facing a plethora of voices asking for their narratives to be heard, these voices have been here for a long time. In Said's words, 'to ignore or otherwise discount the overlapping experiences of Westerners and Orientals, the interdependence of cultural terrains in which colonizers and colonized coexisted and battled each other through projections as well as rival geographies, narratives, and histories, is to miss what is essential about the world in the past century' (Culture xx). *World's Fairs Italian Style* argues that 'rival geographies, narratives, and histories' were disruptive, if often marginalized, parts of the imperial narrative itself and examines the currents of disturbance and dissonance that destabilized the imperial flow from *within*, thus weakening the binary epistemology that relentlessly pitted the civilized and advancing West against the non-Western world.

As Salgari's exposition novels point out, cultures inevitably absorb 'foreign' traits, negotiate alterities and differences, and give narrative form to overlapping and ambiguous conceptual domains and mixed ideological territories. In Gozzano, these territories are inhabited by troubling and troubled subjects, caught between pro-imperialist apologies and anti-imperial resistances – between commitment and nihilism, attempting (and often failing) to negotiate an array of conflicting interests, multiple ideological references, composite aesthetic positions. In this perspective, Italian exposition narratives are especially significant because of Italy's belated and marginal status within the imperial West, and because of its cultural fragmentation and hybrid history, which made Italy a site of both hegemony and subordination, both centre and periphery – an aspiring imperial power whose colonization started from the inside. The formation process of the Italian national (and, later, imperial) identity was dynamic and fraught with inner tensions. Neither settled nor self-evident, nation making in Italy negotiated local traditions, competing interests, and evolving sites of authority and subordination, resulting in a work in progress that was as ephemeral and as urgently pursued as the many fabulous exposition that dotted the Age of Nations and Empire.

Notes

Throughout the text I have provided translations for passages quoted in languages other than English. I used published translations when available and cited the sources accordingly. In other instances, the translations are mine. Titles of books, articles, and other publications are translated when they are written by or relevant to the main authors discussed in this study.

Introduction

1 The difference in designation between 'international exposition,' 'universal exposition,' and 'World's Fair' was often only a matter of semantics (complicated by translation from one language to another) rather than content. Following Brigitte Schroeder-Gudehus, I consider the denominations 'international exhibition' (or 'exposition') and 'World's Fair' as equivalent (9–10).

2 See, for example, the volumes by Aimone and Olmo; Allwood; Baculo, Gallo, and Mangone; Benedict; Findling; Greenhalgh; Mainardi; Plum; Rydell and Gwinn; Schroeder-Gudehus and Rasmussen.

3 On the relationship between expositions and free time, see Bassignana, *Le feste*, and Harris.

4 I follow the definitions listed in the *Random House Unabridged Dictionary*, 2nd ed. (1993).

5 For the next several years, Salgari worked for five publishers at once: Treves, Speirani, Paravia, Bemporad, and Donath.

6 On Salgari's publishing ordeals, see 'Il capitano e gli editori' in Gonzato (135–51).

7 Details on D'Azeglio's famous phrase in Banti 203–5.

8 For a detailed history of national and international expositions in Turin and

Milan, see especially Bassignana, *Le feste*, Aimone, 'Le esposizioni,' and Pichetto and Devalle.

9 The architectural exposition in 1902 Turin and the 1906 fair in Milan were designated as 'international expositions' but did not reach the scope of Turin 1911.

10 I am using the term 'rhizomatic' in Gilles Deleuze and Félix Guattari's definition, as the kind of thought that attempts to thwart unities and break up dichotomies. Proceeding non-linearly, rhizomatic thought pluralizes, disseminates, and emphasizes differences and multiplicities.

1. Prologues to World's Fairs

1 See, especially, Spadolini and Vernizzi.

2 As early as 1864, the Tipografia Nazionale R. Jona issued a volume significantly entitled *Avvenire di Torino e la sua trasformazione in città industriale e manifatturiera. Proposte e suggerimenti al Governo, al Parlamento e al Municipio.*

3 The proponents of this project, which was eventually rejected in favour of a more modest re-naming of a major thoroughfare as Via Garibaldi, envisioned the Via Sacra as dedicated 'agli uomini benemeriti della patria, con busti sopra piedistalli: comprendendovisi finora i Re Carlo Alberto, Vittorio Emanuele II, Umberto, il Duca di Genova, il generale Garibaldi, C. Cavour, C.L. Farini, D. Manin, C. Balbo, V. Gioberti, B. Ricasoli, A. Lamarmora, G. Mazzini, M. d'Azeglio, R. Settimo' (to the fatherland's meritorious men, with busts placed on pedestals: including so far Kings Carlo Alberto, Victor Emmanuel II, and Umberto, the Duke of Genoa, General Garibaldi, C. Cavour, C.L. Farini, D. Manin, C. Balbo, V. Gioberti, B. Ricasoli, A. Lamarmora, G. Mazzini, M. d'Azeglio, R. Settimo) (Tamburini 9).

4 Camillo Benso di Cavour and Giuseppe de Vincenzi, the official representatives of the Italian Kingdom at the Universal Exposition in London, instituted the Museo. For detailed information, see the study on the creation of the Museo industriale by Carlo Olmo and the volume by G. Codazza.

5 The exposition was held in 1858 rather than in 1856 in order to not follow too closely the 1855 Universal Exposition in Paris (Cerrato 54). Pier Luigi Bassignana identifies an earlier attempt in the short three-day exposition held on the occasion of Napoleon's visit to Turin in 1805 (*Le feste* 20). In spite of its limited success, this exposition is noteworthy because it demonstrates that the project of self-assertion and the patriotic celebration of Italian industry (in spite of foreign domination) was awkwardly combined with the desire for assimilation with the age's cultural mecca, Paris.

6 Sculptures, paintings, and other artefacts had formed more than 30 per cent of the products displayed in previous expositions (Bassignana, 'Preludio' 19).

7 Gabriele Capello, who built train carriages for the soon-to-be-booming railroad industry, and the Albani brothers, who introduced important innovations in the field of chemical production, won prestigious prizes in London (1851) and Paris (1855).

8 Several publications demonstrate the general interest in the world of scientific progress and industrial development that the expositions presented. Gustavo Strafforello's *Storia popolare del progresso materiale degli ultimi cento anni* (Popular History of the Material Progress of the Past Hundred Years) (1871) and Alessandro Anserini's *Compendio della storia delle arti industriali* (Compendium of the History of the Industrial Arts) (1875) were addressed to a popular readership. Raffaele Pareto and Giovanni Sacheri's monumental *Enciclopedia delle arti e industrie* (Encyclopedia of the Arts and Industries) (1878–98) was one of the first cumulative efforts in this field.

9 See also Amabile Terruggia's synthesizing definition: 'Non v'ha dubbio che per [esposizione] debba intendersi una rassegna la più fedele, sincera e completa possibile dei prodotti naturali od industriali delle regioni che vi prendono parte' (Undoubtedly, an [exposition] must consist of the most faithful, sincere, and complete review that is possible of all the natural or industrial products of the participating regions) (26).

10 On metropolitan parks in late-nineteenth-century Europe, see Fanelli.

11 Brad Epps underscores a set of different symbolic ramifications regarding location choices for the Barcelona World's Fairs in 1888 and 1929. Deciding to exploit sites that were 'redolent of repression' (the Citadel in 1888 and Montjuïc in 1929), Barcelona transformed these locales' iconography from repression to diversion, from pain to pleasure, from stagnation to productivity (167). A similar point could be made about the choice to use Turin's Piazza d'Armi for some of its early national exhibits. I contend, however, that the transformation from authoritarian order to spectacular diversion is only a matter of surface, the laws controlling diversion often being as strict as those controlling state-sponsored discipline.

12 The Crystal Palace's impact on popular imagination was such that in 1850 the city of Turin planned to build a winter garden enclosed in a glass structure reminiscent of the Crystal Palace. This structure was to be graced by native and exotic plants and flowers, and feature gleaming creeks and waterfalls, reading rooms and conversation nooks, and splendid salons for parties and receptions (Roccia 18). Although never completed, this project inspired

many, including a young engineer who, in 1876, designed an equally unrealized *Wintervergnügungsgarten*. This 'trasparente giardino' (transparent garden) would include elegant shops and cafés, thus creating a system of leisure as consumption similar to that studied by Walter Benjamin in the Parisian arcades.

13 Similar to a gigantic hothouse, Paxton's palace contained powerful metaphorical investments. It evoked the idea that all that was carefully assembled and displayed inside represented the budding spirit of progress. Its declaredly ephemeral destiny implied that progress was not to be bound within a fixed frame, destined as it was to continually move forward. However, by providing the ideal and controlled 'climate' for the show of British wealth on the eve of Victoria's proclamation as empress, the Crystal Palace also emphasized the idea of the stability of British supremacy, and suggested the idea of a power that was bound to last indefinitely.

14 The idyllic atmosphere is equally evoked by the names of the first *Società di canottaggio* (Rowing Societies): Eridano, Armida, Leda, Medora (Roccia 31).

15 Describing the 1893 World's Columbian Exposition, a reporter wrote: 'Night is the time of [the fair's] greatest splendor ... Thousands upon thousands of incandescent light bulbs trace in delicate threads of light the outlines of the façades ... Blinding searchlights seem to make iridescent living things of cold, dead statues. The lagoon becomes a sea of dancing lights, edged by a ribbon of dazzling brightness. It is a fairy-land, an enchanted place' (Wade 73).

16 Though limited to the American experience, David E. Nye's chapter titled 'The Electrical Sublime: The Double of Technology' in his *American Technologicl Sublime* furnishes interesting comments on how electricity 'dematerialized the built environment' of the World's Fairs, transforming their buildings into 'enchanting visions' and 'shimmering artificial patterns' (150) that emphasized 'release from toil' (192) and evoked 'something mysterious, hinting at romance' (Oppenheim 192).

17 If the Turin Exposition was the first to benefit from electric illumination, its escapist rhetoric was not new. The *Cronaca illustrata della esposizione nazionale-industriale ed artistica del 1881* in Milan praises Giuseppe Ottino who, 'colla fantasia di un orientale' (with an Oriental fantasy), created a magic spectacle of two hundred thousand gas lights. The enthusiastic reporter comments that Ottino transformed Milan into a garden of Armida, and a 'paradiso terrestre' (an earthly paradise). Describing what he calls an escape into *The Thousand and One Nights*, the reporter lingers on the reproduced facade of an Indian pagoda: 'La luce raggia da dodici colonne ardenti: sei d'una parte e sei dall'altra d'una porta che s'apre nel mezzo, e piove da nove trapezi

l'uno sovrapposto all'altro, i quali figurano appunto la cupola d'un tempio d'India' (The light radiates from twelve burning columns: six on one side and six on the other side of a door that opens in the middle. The light pours down from nine trapezia, one above the other, to create the dome of an Indian temple). This enchanting spectacle did not ignore the here and now of current politics, and the 'illuminazione *féerique*' (enchanted illumination) also featured an enormous white 'U' intertwined with a cerulean 'M,' from the initials of the king and queen of Italy, Umberto and Margherita (*Milano e l'esposizione italiana del 1881* 31).

18 Roberto Romano convincingly connects the exposition craze in the late nineteenth century with the proliferation of its highbrow counterpart, the scientific congress. Both aimed at presenting up-to-date and exhaustive surveys of human knowledge and production, and Romano calculates that eighty-two scholarly meetings occurred during the 1906 Exposition in Milan (217). *L'esposizione nazionale del 1898* devoted a detailed article on the various congresses that took place simultaneously with the exposition ('I congressi' 225–6). Cesare Lombroso's classificatory obsession in the field of criminal anthropology found its most appropriate venue in a series of congresses held during numerous expositions (in 1889 Paris, 1892 Brussels, 1896 Geneva, 1901 Amsterdam, 1906 Turin, and 1911 Cologne). The influence of the expositions upon scholarly meetings runs even deeper than Romano suggests. If before the advent of the fairs' phenomenon scholarly congresses were purely instructional, during the expositions' heyday, congresses began to exploit amusement features typical of the exhibitions. The twenty thousand visitors to the Third National Geographic Congress that was held in Venice in 1887, for example, could admire documents and memorabilia of travels and explorations, participate in lectures held by such personalities as Ferdinand de Lesseps, Richard Burton, Alexandre Alberto Serpa Pinto, and also enjoy the popular entertainment that fairs usually offered. In the words of one participant, during the congress Venice became, indeed, a 'city of marvels': 'Il Congresso è terminato, e mi è rimasto nell'anima come un sogno pieno di luce e di memorie. Principi, ministri, inaugurazioni, luminarie in piazza e alle isole, escursioni ... regate sfarzose, serenate romantiche, e i mille riflessi della laguna' (The Congress is over but it lingers in my soul as a dream full of light and memories. Princes, ministers, inaugurations, lights in the piazzas and the islands, excursions ... sumptuous regattas, romantic serenades, and the thousand reflections of the lagoon) (Bertacchi 301). The tremendous didactic and escapist power of fairs cannot therefore be limited to the world of popular culture alone, and their cross-cultural and interclass influence deserves careful scrutiny.

19 See Sinclair 84. The emphasis on either amusement or instruction was the variable element of this popular equation. The *New York Tribune* of 18 May 1876, for example, underscored the pedagogical value of the Chicago Columbian Exposition. The reviewer praised the fairgoers because they approached the fair 'not as show place but as a school.' 'In the groups surrounding an exhibit,' the reporter continued with a puritanical sense of duty, 'the faces of Americans, keen, alive, quick-eyed, are distinguishable from all others,' especially from the French, who notoriously approached expositions as if they were going 'to a grand fête' ('First Week' 4). Conversely, in Italy, Giovanni Saragat denounced the hypocrisy of current definitions of fairs as the ideal locations for factory workers to learn about industrial progress, and lamented the lack of well-informed guided visits to the Turin exposition of 1884 ('Tipi umani' 219). In spite of the establishment of workers' parties – often invested with the task of writing detailed reports – and the organized tours for various *Società operaie di mutuo soccorso*, the attendance of the working classes at the fairs remained low in Italy. Contemporary reporters often superciliously remarked that, instead of using these opportunities as a means of professional training, workers were only attracted by the fairs' amusement sectors.

20 On how expositions facilitated the creation of various workers' organizations, see Bassignana, *Le feste* 136.

21 In these years of unrest, Prime Minister Francesco Crispi was given exceptional powers to control the press, confine political suspects, and dissolve the Socialist party. For an extensive analysis of the proletarian struggles in fin-de-siècle Italy, see Merli. For a detailed account of the relationship between the developing workers' unions in Italy and the 1911 Universal Exposition, see Parisella.

22 Turin was thus mimicking Le Play's 'Histoire du Travail' (introduced in the 1867 Paris exposition), consisting of national shows depicting the various phases through which each nation had passed before reaching its present state of civilization. As Linda Aimone reminds us, the rhetoric of political, economic, and, as we shall see, military might ultimately found its most convincing representation in the 'misura dello sviluppo industriale concretamente realizzato' (amount of industrial development concretely realized) ('Nel segno' 156).

23 Interestingly, Louis Figuier described the Eiffel Tower as an 'observatory' and compared it to a 'captive balloon' with a 'splendid view.' If astronomers in an observatory could map out the skies, visitors to the tower could observe the city-as-chart, reducing it to a panoramic photographic plate: 'No noise rises to this height: the city, so feverish and active, seems like the resting

place of silence and immobility. It is a heap of stones, from which no noise emerges' (470–3).

24 The Stigler Tower contained an elevator that carried eight to ten people up to a viewing platform, approximately thirty-seven metres from the ground. The Stigler elevators were used in the most luxurious hotels in Europe and in a handful of aristocratic private homes. Besides experiencing the technological innovation of the hydraulic-powered system that operated the elevator and enjoying the unprecedented view over the fairgrounds, visitors could bask in the plush interiors of the elevator's cabin, thus participating in a world that was beyond their financial reach (Dionisio 41).

25 Another popular and much emulated vantage point to view the various exhibits was the 'Pont roulant,' a giant moving platform from which visitors at the 1878 and 1889 Paris Expositions could look down on the machinery in motion in the Galérie des machines (Allwood 79). For a detailed reading of the *Rapport sur l'Exposition universelle de 1855* see Abruzzese's *Arte e pubblico* 49–55.

26 These are the classical passions that the experience of the 'sublime' brings forth, as famously theorized by Edmund Burke: 'The passion caused by the great and sublime in nature, when those causes operate more powerfully, is Astonishment; and astonishment is the state of the soul, in which all its motions are suspended' (Burke 53).

27 See, for example, De Luca 194–206, and *L'esposizione internazionale di Milano* 5–11; *Torino e l'esposizione italiana del 1884* 22; Robustelli 2–3; and *L'esposizione nazionale del 1898* 84–5.

28 In the official publication of the 1911 exposition we can find a suggestive description of a diorama: 'Una scena di grandi dimensioni, dipinta in una guisa speciale su una tela senza estremità visibili, illuminata con un gioco speciale di luce, mentre lo spettatore rimane nell'oscurità; tutto il primo piano è in plastica, decorazioni, mobili, mannequins, riuscendosi così ad una perfetta fusione, ad una assoluta illusione del vero animato' (A scene of great dimensions, painted in a special way on a canvas without visible borders, illuminated by a special play of lights, while the audience remains in darkness. Everything in the foreground is made out of plastic: decorations, furniture, mannequins, thus obtaining a perfect fusion with, and a total illusion of, animated reality) (*L'esposizione di Torino 1911. Giornale ufficiale* 170). For a more detailed description of the mechanics of dioramas and panoramas, see 'Panoramas: Topics of the Times' in Altick 173–83.

29 'The world exhibitions ... open up a phantasmagoria that people enter to be amused ... The phantasmagoria of capitalist culture reaches its most brilliant display in the World Exhibition of 1867. The Empire is at the height

of its power. Paris reaffirms itself as the capital of luxury and fashion' ('Paris' 153).

30 See also Boito 321–3, 330–4, and 346–50.

31 The courtyard, for example, was that of the Castle of Fenis, the soldiers' quarters belonged to the Castle of Verrès, the dining room to that of Strambino, and the kitchen was exactly the same as the kitchen in the Castle of Issogne.

32 This dual engagement of the codes of realism and the spectacular emerges clearly in a volume with the impressive title of *The Magic City: A Massive Portfolio of Original Photographic Views of the Great World's Fair and Its Treasures of Art, Including a Vivid Representation of the Famous Midway Plaisance with Graphic Descriptions by America's Brilliant Historical and Descriptive Writer J. W. Buel.* Buel tailored the expression 'splendid realism' to describe the three hundred magnificent photographs reproducing the 'Magic City By-the-Lake' and claimed that photography was the most appropriate medium to faithfully capture and preserve the 'charm, the witchery, the magnificence of the Fair' (1). While the vivid referentiality of Buel's photos issued a claim of authenticity, their formalism emphasized the fair's spectacularity. The photos of individual buildings, for example, heightened their monumentality by favouring low-angle shots. Bird's-eye views and wide-angle shots enhanced the fairground's geographical extension and spatial grandeur. In the photos of human beings, particularly those that relate to the ethnic and colonial displays, Buel preferred highly stylized and staged poses.

33 As Chris Bongie shows in his perceptive study on the exotic in fin-de-siècle literature, Pasolini's position on this issue was quite subtle. On the one hand, Pasolini argued that the elsewhere did not exist any longer, or was about to disappear. Air travel had overcome all spatial boundaries and industrial power had reached a transnational dimension: 'l'entropia industriale comprende ormai, praticamente l'intera umanità. Non si può più andare "verso l'Orizzonte" ... Siamo tutti qui' (by now, the industrial entropy comprises practically the whole of humanity. We can't go 'toward the Horizon' any longer ... We are all here) (149). On the other hand, Pasolini claimed that this was true only 'in theory.' For the great majority of people, the elsewhere was still available as an imaginative possibility, as the romance of travel, adventure, and discovery. Intellectuals, though, possessed a different knowledge, and this knowledge inspired Pasolini's mournful question: 'Ma gli scrittori appartengono all'élite che va in aeroplano, o che almeno sa che tutto questo sta per finire: e come si fa a fingere di non sapere?' (But writers belong to the elite who travel by plane, or who at least know that all of this is about to end: and how can they pretend they do not know it?) (150).

34 This dream of geographical control and display was well represented by the gigantic terrestrial globe displayed at the Liberal Arts Palace at the 1889 Paris exposition. Visitors could reach the top of the globe by elevator and descend via an inclined walkway running around the globe.

35 John C. Eastman, a visitor to the 1893 World's Columbian Exposition in Chicago, described the fair as 'brilliant with the colors of all nations. It is a kaleidoscope of the world, that furnishes a passing panorama of life in every zone' (13).

36 Besides the appreciation for the variety of national types, Wilson's comments are significant for this study because they reveal that in spite of the events of the Risorgimento the notion of who exactly the 'Italians' were was still not inclusive of all parts of the peninsula. The 1904 Louisiana Purchase Exposition at Saint Louis brought this tendency of ethnic display to its spectacular climax on Pike Day, when a huge parade of five thousand people and two thousand animals marched to represent every part of the globe: 'Japanese men pulled their jinrikishas. Arabian horses were harnessed to the Persian kajagas and zebus to the chariots of India. Sledges with teams of Alaskan dogs had place in the procession. Ostriches and giraffes were attached to modern sulkies to illustrate their training. Zebras and the fat-tailed sheep of Africa supplied motive power of dog carts. Caparisoned elephants and dromedaries carried on their backs the colonies from Cairo and Turkey. Bronchos were as numerous as the Indians of the Wild West Congress ... There were groups of nautch and devil dancers, geisha girls, whirling dervishes, buck and wing dancers ... Industries were portrayed by the groups from Jerusalem, by the Swiss from the Tyrolean Alps, by the weavers of Ireland, the tea pickers of Ceylon, the candy makers of Persia, the carvers from Japan. Flower girls and singers from Paris, merchants from Stamboul, gypsies from Spain, plantation darkies from the South, fire fighters, deep sea divers, Chinese silk weavers, fire worshippers from Persia, basket makers of the Zunis and scores of other groups had places in this polyglot parade' (Francis 601).

37 Prominent political personality Tommaso Villa was a deputy in the Italian Parliament for forty-four consecutive years, and then became a senator. He served as the minister of internal affairs and the minister of justice in the second and third Cairoli governments. He was also a member of the Turin city council for forty-three years (see Levra).

38 For a list of the exhibited documents and objects, see Arrigoni 1–66. Descriptions of the Padiglione del Risorgimento Italiano are also found in *Torino e l'esposizione italiana del 1884* 19–20, 63–4, 179–80, 395–6, 363–7 and in Robustelli 10–14.

39 The first national exposition in Italy was held in Florence in 1861 right after

the country's unification. Quintino Sella, a politician and renowned engineer, planned the exposition with the aim of cementing the country's cohesion and providing a review of its economic situation. The Italian state almost entirely financed the exposition by shouldering the then-astronomical expense of more than 3.5 million liras (one thousand liras in 1861 were roughly equivalent to 1.3 million liras in the late twentieth century). Victor Emmanuel II's official participation in the opening ceremony, and the hymn that Giosuè Carducci wrote to celebrate the king on this occasion ('Alla croce di Savoia,' with music by Carlo Romani), served to consolidate the monarchic idea. Interestingly, contemporary newspapers highlighted the fair's patriotic component by giving ample space to the plight of the 'terre irredente' (unredeemed lands) and publishing a letter from the Friuli region to the exposition's organizing committee. In this letter, the representatives from Friuli protested the Austrian government's refusal to allow Friuli's participation in the exposition.

40 The dash toward the future and the desire for novelty generated works of daring experimentalism as well as inventions bordering on comic absurdity. The Sonzogno edition of the Philadelphia exhibition catalogue somewhat doubtfully described Lewis's flying machine as a 'battello aereo a pedali con il quale l'inventore si ripromette di poter correre per l'aria' (pedal-operated aerial boat with which the inventor plans to be able to dash through the air) (618). Besides Lewis's visionary attempt, the catalogue listed a *cinofero*, that is, a 'velocipede azionato da cani' (velocipede operated by dogs) and a *pettopiuma*, which was a machine designed to 'spiumare ogni specie di volatile' (pluck any kind of bird) (*L'esposizione universale di Filadelfia* 433, 535). The 1881 exposition in Milan featured the 'velocipede sospeso' (hanging velocipede, see page 30), a bizarre invention consisting of a wheel that turned into an iron ellipsis elevated from the ground. The wheel was turned by a handle connected to an oscillating bench where up to two people could comfortably sit. Among the future practical uses of this device its inventor mentioned the possibility of crossing valleys without having to go up and down the mountains (*Milano e l'esposizione italiana del 1881* 106).

41 See, for example, *Torino e l'esposizione italiana del 1884: Cronaca illustrata dell'esposizione nazionale industriale ed artistica del 1884* 2–6, 11–18; and 'Torino nelle pagine delle scrittore più popolare d'Italia' (*L'esposizione di Torino 1911: Giornale ufficiale illustrato* 65–6).

42 To borrow Barthes's comments on the Eiffel Tower as allowing for the creation of the conceptual category of 'concrete abstraction,' we can argue that the totalizing bird's-eye view from the Superga hill makes the whole of the

landscape below 'comprehensible' without depriving it of its 'material concreteness' ('La Tour Eiffel' 1387).

43 'Le strade essendo lunghissime, presentano successivamente varii aspetti;
andando avanti diritto per una strada sola, si attraversa una parte di Torino
commerciale, una piccola parte di Torino elegante, un quartiere povero, un
quartiere affollato, un quartiere deserto ... E non si trovan grandi contrasti'
(The boulevards are very long, and they display a succession of various features; going straight along a single boulevard, you cross a small section of
commercial Turin, and a part of elegant Turin, a poor neighbourhood, a
crowded neighbourhood, a deserted neighbourhood [...] And you don't find
great contrasts) (20).

44 In that massive attempt at classification of knowledge that marked post-
Enlightenment society, the University of Turin oversaw the establishment of
new disciplines, such as criminal anthropology and statistics, and contributed to the systematization of others, such as geography, physiology, pa-
thology, history, and mathematics. An international leader in the fields of
economics, political science, and jurisprudence, the University of Turin
especially underscored the practical and functional value of its academic disciplines, and by sponsoring collaborative projects with Turin's Regio museo
industriale, the university expressed the city's industrial and entrepreneurial
vocation. Publishing firms also contributed to the university's systematizing
programs. Turin-based publisher Hermann Loescher, for example, launched
prestigious academic journals such as the *Giornale storico della letteratura italiana*, the *Rivista storica italiana*, and the *Archivio glottologico italiano*, all geared
toward providing a scientific foundation to the historical, literary, and linguistic patrimony of the new Italian nation. Similarly, Giuseppe Pomba,
owner of the Unione Tipografico Editrice Torinese (UTET), published Niccolò Tommaseo's *Dizionario della lingua italiana* and the *Enciclopedia popolare*,
one of the most widely sold efforts at gathering, ordering, and classifying
data of general culture in the late nineteenth century. Pomba paired with
Michele Lessona, holder of the chair of zoology at the University of Turin, to
translate and divulge Charles Darwin's evolutionary theories. Together, these
initiatives bestowed scientific rigour to a certain idea of the Italian nation –
an idea that partly depended on Italy's hierarchic placement in the deterministic ladder of 'civilized' countries – and granted Turin the intellectual
ownership of this idea. They also diffused this idea well outside of Italy by
helping Turin to join the European avant-garde of modern scientific culture.

45 As Carol A. Breckenridge points out: 'The world of collecting was consider-
ably expanded in the post-enlightenment era. With the emergence of the
nineteenth-century nation-state and its imperializing and disciplinary

bureaucracies, new levels of precision and organization were reached. This new order called for such agencies as archives, libraries, surveys, revenue bureaucracies, folklore and ethnographic agencies, censuses and museums. Thus, the collection of objects needs to be understood within this larger context of surveillance, recording, and classifying' (195–6, n 1).

46 On different kinds of recontextualization of commodities, see Appadurai 15–16.

47 This dream of universal appeasement was one of the recurring themes in national and international expositions. The Esposizione Internazionale Operaia held during the Esposizioni Riunite in 1894 Milan, for example, aimed at displaying 'gli elementi del problema sociale che vuol essere risolto in pace col benefico concorso di tutti' (the elements of the social problem that we must resolve in peace and with the beneficial participation of all) (Pavoni 18).

48 In his reflections on photography in *Camera Lucida*, Barthes uses the Latin term *punctum* to define the detail or details that 'bring out' the concealed meaning, the kind of subtle 'beyond,' of a certain photographed image.

49 Expanding his perspective even further, De Amicis compares Turin with the young American cities, and provides an original view of a Turin without history 'venuta su da pochi anni, nel primo sboccio della sua verde adolescenza' (grown in just a few years, in the early blossoming of its green adolescence) (64).

50 The Olympic Games emphasized their historic mingling of athletics, politics, nationalism, and spectacle when, starting in 1900 Paris, they were held in connection with World's Fairs. They also quickly absorbed the commercial and commodifying tendencies of all World's Fairs. In 1900 Paris, for example, the fencing competition was held as a sort of sideshow in the exhibition's cutlery area. When hosting, in 1904, the Olympic Games as well as the Louisiana Purchase Exposition, the city of Saint Louis inaugurated the 'Anthropological Days,' in which races were reserved for black, pygmy, and Asian athletes. One of the great attractions of the 1911 exposition in Turin was the Stadium, a massive arena built to host all kinds of sporting events, obviously with an eye to holding future Olympic Games. The largest in Europe, the Stadium could hold up to forty thousand people and covered the entire area previously occupied by the Piazza d'Armi. In the mind of its designers, with its size and the sophisticated design of its multiple concentric tracks, the Stadium would place Turin at the forefront of modern athletics.

51 The ballet gained such tremendous acclaim that it was repeated over one hundred times that year alone in Milan (Pappacena, 'The Transcription' 249).

52 The Regio staged it again and with equal success for the Carnival-Lent season of 1883–4 (Pappacena, 'L'*Excelsior* di Luigi Manzotti' 9).

53 In Vienna, *Excelsior* remained in the Court and State Opera Company's repertoire continuously from 1881 to 1910, totalling a record of three hundred and twenty-nine performances. In 1883, *Excelsior* landed in the United States and was staged hundreds of times in Boston, San Francisco, and New York. The reproduction of *Excelsior* that choreographer Imre Kiralfy staged at Niblo's Garden in New York City was particularly spectacular and so well-received that it was performed one hundred times at that location. Similar enthusiastic responses came from Latin America, where theatres in Rio de Janeiro, Buenos Aires, and Montevideo strove hard to keep up with the demands of ever-increasing audiences. For a complete list of performances in the world, see Pappacena, '*L'Excelsior* di Luigi Manzotti' 19–21.

54 In 1885, Carlo D'Ormeville wrote that the ballet was a 'capolavoro, che resterà leggendario ... e non teme l'ala distruggitrice del tempo' (masterpiece, which will remain legendary ... and does not fear the brush of the destroying wing of time) (2). Similarly, in 1888, the theatre journal *L'Asmodeo* stated that *Excelsior* 'conserva quel prestigio di originalità e novità, che fanno di questa composizione del Manzotti un vero capolavoro' (keeps that prestige of originality and innovation that make this composition of Manzotti's a real masterpiece) ('Cronaca milanese' 2). In 1910, Gino Monaldi concluded that 'Universali furono la gloria e la fortuna di questo ballo' (the glory and fortunate reception of this ballet were universal) (221).

55 More than twenty years after *Excelsior*'s premiere in 1882, set designer Caramba (Luigi Sapelli) staged a new version of the ballet that would give it a novel 'historic-political vitality and pertinence.' In this 1908–9 version, electricity was the great protagonist, with its modern applications, including lighting, the telegraph, and the telephone. In the same spirit, in the midst of the First World War in 1916, furnished his own interpretation of 'progress and civilization' by capitalizing on the ballet's militaristic slant, and developing its plot from the early barbaric raids to the fire of the cathedral of Reims and the invasion of Belgium. In 1931, choreographer Giovanni Pratesi revisited *Excelsior* in a fascist key, celebrating in autarchic tones the Italian genius and the 'memorable Italian deeds.' In 1967, director Filippo Crivelli and choreographer Ugo Dell'Ara staged a postmodern and self-consciously ironical version of *Excelsior* for the thirtieth edition of the *Maggio Musicale Fiorentino*, with the celebrated dancers Carla Fracci and Paolo Bortoluzzi in the leading roles. Renewing *Excelsior*'s initial success, Crivelli and Dell'Ara's magnificent revival was such a hit that it was reproduced in many Italian theatres for the next thirty years. (Pappacena, 'The New *Excelsior*'

314–5). Due to its popularity, *Excelsior* quickly overcame its own formal boundaries and was adapted to other art forms, such as the whimsical version for the puppet theatre that the Compagnia Colla staged in 1895 in Milan, and the cinematic adaptation of *Excelsior* that pioneer film director Luca Comerio completed in 1913 and that unfortunately survives only in fragments today. As late as 1952, *Excelsior* reappeared in a scene of Alessandro Blasetti's *Altri tempi* (Other Times), a film documenting the transition from the nineteenth to the twentieth centuries. In 1965, Susanna Egri revisited the ballet in *Spettacolo a Milano* (A Spectacle in Milan), a film made for the Italian state television facility Studio 3. Soon after its balletic debut, *Excelsior* exported its optimistic themes to the popular world of variety shows and operettas, starring celebrated actors such as Carlo Dapporto, Totò, Wanda Osiris, and Anna Magnani (Data 40). For more specific information about the cinematic renditions of *Excelsior*, see Data, Calò ('Il film *Excelsior* di Luca Comerio'), and Musumeci.

56 The stock imagery derived from *Excelsior* literally became part of all Italian households, as scenes and performers were often reproduced in popular magazines such as *L'Illustrazione italiana*. Even the boxes of the Liebig brand of broth cubes, which were staple cooking ingredients in Italian kitchens at the time, contained small cards portraying Manzotti's celebrated ballerinas with their extravagant costumes and backdrop of spectacular settings.

57 The first of the great Alpine tunnels to be completed, the Mount Cenis rail tunnel was built under the Fréjus Pass by Italian and French crews from 1857 to 1871. A major example of the power of applied engineering, the tunnelling of Mount Cenis pioneered several new technologies, such as the use of dynamite in blasting rock and of sophisticated compressed-air machinery. In the dedication to his readers, Manzotti writes: 'Vidi il monumento innalzato a Torino in gloria del portentoso traforo del Cenisio ed immaginai la presente composizione coreografica. È la titanica lotta sostenuta dal *Progresso* contro il *Regresso* ... è la grandezza della *Civiltà* che vince, abbatte, distrugge, pel bene dei popoli, l'antico potere dell'*Oscurantismo* che li teneva nelle tenebre del servaggio e dell'ignominia. Partendo dall'epoca della Inquisizione di Spagna arrivo al traforo del Cenisio, mostrando le scoperte portentose, le opre gigantesche del nostro secolo' (I saw the monument erected in Turin to the glory of the mighty drilling of Mont Cenis Tunnel and conceived this choreographic composition. It is the titanic struggle sustained by *Progress* against *Regression* ... it is the greatness of *Civilization* that, for the benefit of all peoples, conquers, demolishes, and destroys the ancient power of *Obscurantism*, which held them in the darkness of bondage and ignominy. Beginning with the epoch of the Spanish Inquisition, I carry the story right

to the Mont Cenis Tunnel, and display the portentous discoveries, and the gigantic works of our century) (Manzotti 78).

58 The railroad, the locomotive, and the Alpine tunnels were the protagonists of numerous expositions in Italy. With over one million visitors, the Esposizione nazionale di Milano in 1881 celebrated the tunnelling of the Gotthard, 'strada maestra fra l'Italia e il mondo europeo' (main road between Italy and the European world) (*Documenti* 7). In 1906, the Simplon Pavilion was hailed as 'la rappresentazione trionfale dell'ultimo miracolo che ... il genio e il lavoro umani hanno saputo e voluto compiere' (the triumphal representation of the latest miracle that ... human genius and labour have been able and willing to achieve) (*Esposizione di Milano 1906* 49).

59 New employment possibilities, enhanced opportunities for travel and leisure, and the promise of overall higher standards of living were also parts of this bourgeois narrative. Other stories, such as the one told via the working model of the Suez Canal during the 1867 exposition in Paris (complete with ships passing through it), provided the same messages, and so successful were they that as late as 1915, the Panama-Pacific Exposition in San Francisco displayed a five-acre working model of the Panama Canal. Visitors could view it by riding aboard theatre chairs on a moving platform.

60 On Romualdo Marenco, see Ferrando. The term *ballo grande* was coined to define the spectacular character of Manzotti's productions, which, besides *Excelsior*, included two equally extravagant ballets, *Amor* (1886) and *Sport* (1896). Along with *Excelsior* forming a trilogy devoted to *ballo grande*, *Amor* and *Sport* developed the spectacular, celebratory, and propaganda-laden features introduced in *Excelsior*. *Amor* stages the progress of humankind from the original chaos to the final apotheosis of freedom and universal love. In a sequence of scenes, Manzotti stages the discovery of art, architecture, music, and sculpture in ancient Greece, and the Roman mastery of the arts of politics and empire. The scenes presenting the decadence and destruction of Rome are the pretext to stage the victory of Milan and the Lombard League over Barbarossa. Anticipating a theme dear to Fascist propaganda, *Sport* is a glorification of all kinds of sports and those who excel in them: horse racing, cycling, big-game hunting, and athletics.

61 This notation is contained in Giovanni Cammarano's choreographic score of the ballet. While a ballet's libretto is generally used by the public and simply tells the ballet's story, the choreographic score is a much more detailed text that includes specific descriptions and sketches of the dancers' movements and contains extensive stage directions (Pappacena, 'The Transcription' 253 and 'From Giovanni Cammarano' 299).

62 This kind of exotic dancing was not particularly original. Manzotti exploited

a successful trend in the world of popular ballet as well as World's Fairs' spectacles, which would soon involve the newborn cinema as well. In 1896, Auguste and Louis Lumière, for example, created *Danse Egyptienne*, *Danse Javanaise*, *Danse Mexicane*, and *Negres dansant dans la rue à Londres*. Méliès presented the fanciful *Danse au serail* (1897). Similarly, the catalogue ANICA (Associazione nazionale industrie cinematografiche audiovisive) of Italian silent film lists *La danza del ventre e del fuoco* (1909), *Danze internazionali* (1909), and *Danze russe* (1911).

63 While sporadic negative remarks did occur (Tchaikovsky, for example, was incensed by the ballet's inanity and described it as 'bête au délà de toute expression' (stupid beyond all words), respectable journals such as *La Gazzetta musicale di Milano*, *La Gazzetta dei teatri*, *L'Asmodeo*, *Il Teatro illustrato*, and *Les Annales du théâtre et de la musique* provided poignant and detailed reviews that portrayed Manzotti as an innovator of unique genius. Most of all, throngs of ballet lovers continued to crowd theatres in Italy and abroad, making Manzotti one of the wealthiest and most sought-after choreographers of his time.

64 That the two kinds of exhibitions, the World's Fairs and the Excelsior Ballet, emerged from a shared mentality became especially evident in Paris, where *Excelsior* was staged at the Eden theatre, designed more as an amusement house than a conventional theatre. The auditorium was decorated in 'the Egypto-Assyrio-Indian style' that fascinated the masses in search of escapist fantasies. The various cafés and bars in the theatre hallways represented different cultures – Spanish, Russian, Swiss – following a trend introduced at the Paris Universal Exposition of 1867.

65 As the creator of motion, heat, and power, electricity was endowed with organic, life-giving metaphors: 'The Palace of Electricity contains the living, active soul of the Exhibition, providing the whole of this colossal organism with movement and light ... Without electricity the Exhibition is merely an inert mass devoid of the slightest breath of life ... A single touch of the finger on a switch and the magic fluid pours forth; everything is immediately illuminated, everything moves' (Allwood 102).

66 Carolyn Marvin reminds us that in these years in large North American and European cities a new kind of show was born: the 'electric spectacles' that attracted large crowds with the projection of cones of light evoking real images or purely decorative shapes.

67 For a less literary jolt, visitors at the 1881 exposition in Milan, could touch 'una ragazza dalle braccia denudate, posta in una specie di fossa, [che] dispensa[va] scosse elettriche a chi le v[oleva] purché paga[sse] pochi centesimi' (a bare-armed girl placed in a sort of pit, [who would] dispense electric

shocks to whoever want[ed] them in exchange of a few cents) (*Milano e l'esposizione italiana del 1881* 199) .

68 Cantù was the Honorary President of the Fine Arts Exhibit at the 1881 National Exposition in Milan.

2. Turin 1911: The 'Fabulous Exposition'

1 While Turin's fair was mainly devoted to industrial production, Rome hosted the historical, artistic, and ethnographic exhibits, and Florence concentrated on the exhibits of floriculture and the 'Art of the Italian Portrait' exhibits.

2 I am quoting from the Executive Committee's Program, which stated: '[si vuole] riflesso nella grande Mostra il concetto logico ed organico col quale procede e si svolge la legge economica del lavoro e della produzione' ([we want] the Great Exposition to mirror the logical and organic idea with which the economic law of labour and production progresses and unfolds itself) (*Torino esposizione 1911* 18). These progressive destinies were still gospel to the Unione liberale monarchica, the association of high-middle-class and aristocratic entrepreneurs who provided ideas and funds for the fair.

3 Discussing the development of World's Fairs in general, Linda Aimone argues that early in the twentieth century, expositions became sophisticated propaganda machines aimed at impressing more than informing their ever-growing public ('Le esposizioni nello specchio' 22).

4 The 'serate elettriche' (electric soirées), in particular, with their displays of moving, coloured beams of light, cast a spell over the expositions' pavilions, enhancing the uncanny appearance of this 'grande città effimera' (great ephemeral city) (Sobrero 258).

5 To offer some comparisons: the Great Exhibition in 1851 attracted approximately six million people to London. The 1855 Universal Exhibition in Paris had over five million visitors, and the 1876 Exposition in Philadelphia registered over nine million. The Chicago Fair of 1893 set a record with approximately twenty-five million visitors. For more exhaustive data, see Baculo.

6 See, for example, the description of the project for the 1881 Exposition in Milan: 'Nel padiglione principale la facciata è nello stile rinascimentale ... per dare un'impronta di grandiosità ... Verso il bastione lo stile [è il] pompeiano ... Nella parte laterale ... una costruzione leggera, svelta, ricca, ci trasporta sulle rive del Canal Grande [...] riproducendo le linee e i trafori e le finestre dello stile orientale ... [Segue] un padiglione di legno, in istile russo per noi originale, che ci trasporterà col pensiero alle stazioni delle steppe ... Un tempietto pompeiano [sarà usato] per pasticceria, il padiglione

turco-moderno per caffé e ristorante, un portico in istile rinascimento per birreria ... Un padiglioncino in istile arabesco [sarà decorato di] fregi in marmi e pietre artificiali, perfette imitazioni in cemento di quelle naturali' (The main pavilion's façade is in the style of the Renaissance ... to give the imprint of grandeur ... Toward the fortress the style [is the] Pompeian ... On one side ... a lightly built, agile, but richly decorated building takes us to the shores of the Grand Canal ... by reproducing the lines, embroideries and windows of the oriental style ... A wooden pavilion [follows], in the Russian style that is for us original and that will carry our imagination to the stations of the steppes ... A small Pompeian temple [will be used] as confectionery, the modern Turkish pavilion as café and restaurant, a Renaissance style portico as beer house ... A small pavilion in the Arabian style [will be decorated with] friezes made of artificial marbles and stones, perfect plaster imitations of the natural ones) (*L'esposizione italiana del 1881 in Milano* 6).

7 These designs became the models for all the buildings commissioned by the fair's Italian underwriters (the designs for the national buildings such as the Pavilion of Siam or the Russian Pavilion were left to the individual nations).

8 Political power disclosed itself most visibly in the army, or better, in the spectacle of the army, as Lewis Mumford understood well in his seminal study devoted to the city in history, where he addressed the topic of the relationship between city planning and political power in the baroque period: 'In view of the importance of the army for the ruling classes, it is no wonder that military traffic was the determining factor in the new city plan ... The building forms a setting for the avenue, and the avenue is essentially a parade ground: a place where spectators may gather, on the sidewalks or in the windows, to review the evolutions and exercises and triumphal marches of the army – and be duly awed and intimidated. The buildings stand on each side, stiff and uniform, like soldiers at attention: the uniformed soldiers march down the avenue, erect, formalized, repetitive: a classic building in motion. The spectator remains fixed. Life marches before him, without his leave, without his assistance: he may use his eyes, but if he wishes to open his mouth or leave his place, he had better ask for permission first' (369–70).

9 Juvarra's fancifully mixed forms reflect a complex reality, and address the political quandary of a minuscule kingdom that, after Vittorio Amedeo's conquest of the royal title with the Treaty of Utrecht (1713), was determined to find spectacular military and diplomatic ways to preserve its own sovereignty, in spite of the contrasting interests of the age's political giants, France and Spain.

10 As at the theatre, the spectacles within the fairs' precincts were available to those who paid an admission ticket (a practice imposed for the first time at

the 1855 Universal Exposition in Paris). Incidentally, if at the theatre specific seating areas maintained social hierarchies and limited intermixing, fairs' special passes and differently priced tickets performed a similar controlling function. For example, the widespread practice of instituting Sunday as the day of free access counterbalanced the institution of the 'elegant day,' whose expensive admission tickets signalled that access and special events were reserved for the wealthier classes (Picone Petrusa 12). In spite of these limitations, the technologies of the spectacle that fairs perfected allowed fairgoers to enjoy, albeit vicariously and fictionally, many of the experiences (such as travel in exotic locales) that still were the preserve of the wealthier classes.

11 Bradd Epps reminds that *urbs* 'is ... a Latin word, as in *urbum*, related to "plow" or "hoe," the instrument that ... the Romans, with the aid of a sacred oxen, used to demarcate the terrain, or territory, of a human settlement.' Epps goes on to explain that the demarcated terrain is also a circumscribed space, a bounded domain like the walled enclosures of traditional cities (152).

12 The practice of the facsimile resulted in the creation of interesting buildings, often altered in their dimensions, obviously estranged from their original locations, and transformed in the construction materials employed. The 1893 Columbian Exposition in Chicago, for example, featured the facsimile of a medieval Norwegian church's crypt, the copy of a colonial residence in Virginia, and that of the Franciscan monastery of Santa María de la Rábida, in Palos, Spain, where Columbus found hospitality and assistance in 1485. With an even more bizarre touch, fairgoers in Chicago could admire the facsimile of an ancient Moorish minaret made entirely of Bohemian crystal and ingeniously illuminated to host the electricity exhibit. Celebrating the centennial of the French Revolution, the 1889 Exposition in Paris appropriately proposed a reconstruction of the Bastille, which even included, at designated times, the coup de théâtre of a prisoner's escape.

13 Paolo Boselli (Savona 1838 – Rome 1932) was the Secretary General of the Italian commission at the 1867 World's Fair in Paris and later served as President of the Regio museo industriale in Turin. In his long political career, he served under several successive governments as Minister of Public Education, Agriculture, Industry, Commerce, and Finance. A political conservative, in 1922 he supported the rise of the Fascist party.

14 The same point may be made about the Palermo Exposition of 1891. Its architect, Ernesto Basile, chose what he defined as the 'Sicilian' architectural style, a derivation of the Arab and Norman-Gothic styles. While purporting to express 'i caratteri naturali e storici' (the natural and historical characters) of the Sicilian people, this style failed to reach a broader national constituency (Nicoletti 75).

15 While tightly enmeshed in politics, in 1911 Rome the art exhibits were also regarded as the manifestations of an economy in full boom (albeit elsewhere). As early as 1861, Pietro Selvatico, the author of *Le condizioni dell'odierna pittura storica e sacra in Italia, rintracciate nella esposizione nazionale in Firenze nel 1861,* had not minced words about the subordination of art to the market economy: 'senza una certa misura di questo riprovato mercantilismo, è ben difficile far ricche le nazioni in modo da porle in grado di possedere il danaro d'avanzo per infondere prosperità alle arti del bello ... Tralascino dunque i retori di scalmanarsi tanto contro il secolo tuffato nei profitti pecuniari, perché se i popoli non guadagnano largamente colle industrie, colla agricoltura, col commercio finiremo come la repubblica di San Marino, a mandare cioé, all'Esposizione Nazionale, una casatella di formaggio, due bottiglie di svigorito vinello, ed un cattivo fucile (without a certain amount of this disparaged mercantilism, it is very difficult to enrich nations in a way as to put them in the position to own the extra money to make the fine arts prosper ... Rhetoricians should therefore refrain from agitating against our century, which has plunged into making economic profit, because if people don't earn a great deal with industry, agriculture, and commerce, we will end up like the Republic of San Marino, and send to the National Exposition a wheel of cheese, two bottles of weak wine, and a bad gun) (23).

16 Giovanni Bolzoni composed the musical score and E. Augusto Berta wrote the lyrics.

17 Combining the rhetoric of peace with the display of military might was a common trait of all World's Fairs. The Chicago World's Columbian Exposition, for example, placed a replica of the battleship *Illinois,* standing 'grim and stern, white as though pale through long and arduous struggle with a desperate foe' near the main pier where the steamers from downtown Chicago delivered the fair's visitors to the dreamland of peace and prosperity (Allwood 89).

18 On 7 October 1911 Giolitti gave a historic speech at the Teatro Regio in which he argued that the war against Turkey for the conquest of Libya was to be considered a new Crusade.

19 On the use of souvenirs as tools to create 'the illusion of the fairs' permanence' against their own ephemerality, see Zachman 206–7.

20 The expositions' visual displays performed the same function by presenting reproductions that claimed to be both realistic and evocative of a much broader geographic reality. The guidebook for the 1906 exposition in Milan, for example, matter-of-factly praised the Villaggio Africano Menges because it captured some of the variety of the African continent, with its 'ricco campionario vivente delle bestie di quei paesi, con annessa popolazione di indi-

geni non meno viventi' (rich living inventory of the animals of those countries, with alongside them the population of indigenous people, equally alive) (*Esposizione internazionale di Milano Aprile–Novembre 1906* 11). Similarly, the 'Via del Cairo' was supposed to be a 'vero lembo d'Egitto' (true corner of Egypt) as well as an authentic catalogue of 'diverse epoche, razze e civiltà' (different ages, races and civilizations) (*Esposizione internazionale di Milano Aprile–Novembre 1906* 30).

21 In June 1882, Italy declared its sovereignty over the Bay of Assab in the Red Sea.

22 Writing about the 1876 Centennial Exhibition in Philadelphia, a reporter from *The Nation* hoped that future expositions would pay better attention to the 'kaleidoscope' of the world, featuring 'American aborigines ... Australian blacks ... the last of the Tasmanians ... and from India and Egypt, types of their numerous populations.' Such a gallery, the reporter continued with taxonomic and cataloguing zeal, 'would furnish endless entertainment and much information concerning the races of mankind, besides throwing light upon the problem of their origin and order of differentiation (L.N., 'The International Exhibition' 238). At the 1893 Columbian Exposition in Chicago, the 'Midway Plaisance' (a boulevard linking Jackson and Washington Parks designed as 'the unofficial section of the fair [and] ... strictly commercial in its purposes') was described as 'a living ethnographic museum [where] all the exhibits except the natives are for sale' (Eastman 13). It featured Irish, Javanese, Lapland, American Indian, Eskimo, Chinese, Turkish, and Dahomey villages hosting three thousand people. The Midway also included a Chinese tea house, a 'little Algeria and Tunis,' a Japanese bazaar, a 'Street of Cairo,' a Persian concession, and an Indian bazaar (Tenkotte 22).

23 At the 1893 Columbian Exposition in Chicago, the belly dancing by Fahreda Mahzar, otherwise known as Little Egypt, was said to have been 'the only attraction to pull more money than the giant Ferris Wheel' (Kyriazi 75). The few notes of disapproval toward the Midway Plaisance came from people who did not object to the reification of human beings but who worried about the negative influence that 'immodest' dancing might have upon Western observers. Some fair officials defended these dances on account of their ethnic specificity. Others commended the whole Midway Plaisance on philanthrophic grounds, arguing that it was a commercial venture established as a source of income for poorer countries in order to allow them to finance their own exhibits at the fair.

24 For a detailed presentation of these displays, see Francis 522–34 and 564–72.

25 The climax of the classification and display obsession was reached with 'The

Creation' exhibit, a pageant of world's history ending with 'The Hereafter' complete with the River Styx (Allwood 114).

26 This was the age of the sideshow: Buffalo Bill's Wild West Show came to Italy in 1890 with its extravaganza of Indians, cowboys, athletes, rifle experts, and other attractions. See also Salgari's description of Buffalo Bill's Wild West show in Verona, Italy, in *Una tigre* 67.

27 For a similar argument, see Tenkotte 11–12.

28 Reviewing the 1884 exposition in Turin, Giovanni Robustelli praised the 'piccola ma pure eloquente Mostra Africana' (little but nevertheless eloquent African display), arguing that rather than 'far voto di castità coloniale' (make a vow of colonial chastity), Italy was ready to test its 'poderosa virilità' (powerful virility) by accomplishing the 'conquista [...] delle vergini sabbie del deserto africano' (conquest ... of the virgin sands of the African desert) (5).

29 Regarding the fairs' exploitation of a poetics of 'contrasts,' see also Alfredo Comandini's comments on the juxtaposition of antiquity and modernity at the 1911 Turin exposition (12).

30 'The Great organizing principle of the Victorian Fair,' writes James Gilbert, 'was the idea of universal culture, a complex notion defined, in part, by European (often with a French accent) opposition between civilization and savagery. This division was moral, physical, and visual. In several early expositions, planners designed a central area of the fair featuring industrial merchandise in displays embellished by gleaming symbols of Western culture and a periphery displaying the colonial dependencies of the host nation' (17). The Paris Exposition of 1889, for example, featured the impressive exhibition of the French École militaire starring its colonial troops, surrounded by the edifices of the French colonies and protectorates. Together, these displays expressed the idea of a centralized yet ever-expansive France.

31 This collaboration resulted in an interesting exhibit devoted to the history of Franco-Italian relationships, with which the Italian organizers stressed a sense of historical continuity between its own past and that of its powerful foreign ally. The exhibit was intended to 'donner par une présentation artistique et documentaire, parlant aux yeux aussi bien qu'à l'esprit, la sensation de cette indiscontinue fusion des deux peuples; rendre tangibles aux moins avertis les liens multiples qui, depuis tant de siècles unissent les deux nations; rappeler les éfforts dépensés, les affections communes, glorifier le sang répandu et les gloires partagés; montrer enfin les deux sœurs latines serrant la main au jour de triomphe' (give, through an artistic and documentary presentation that speaks to the eyes as well as to the spirit, the sensation of this constant fusion of the two peoples; to make the multiple links that for

so many centuries have united the two nations tangible to those who are less aware of them; to remember the efforts made and the affections shared; to glorify the spilled blood; to exalt the shared dangers and glories; in sum to show the two Latin sisters holding hands on the day of their triumph) (*Catalogue de l'exposition* 7).

32 See also Comandini's awed description of the 'dominante palazzo' (domineering palace) with which Great Britain aimed to 'fare pompa della sua imperiale potenza' (make proud display of its imperial power) (12); and Sobrero's statement that, of all national flags, the Union Jack was 'il più attivo richiamo di tutta l'Esposizione, per la vastità l'ordine la bellezza della mostra che annunciano' (the most active invitation of the entire exhibition, because of the size, order and beauty of the exposition they announce) (Sobrero 258).

33 This also explains why, given the explicit and massive influence of France and Great Britain, the Direzione Centrale degli Affari Coloniali somewhat surprisingly stated that it wanted to give 'alla sua esposizione un carattere strettamente e gelosamente italiano' (a strictly and jealously Italian character to its exposition) (*Le mostre coloniali* 6). While depending, culturally and economically, upon more powerful colonizing giants, Italy felt the urge to assert its own colonizing style and thus establish its right to be an equal player in the colonial game.

34 I am adapting a definition that Benedict Anderson devised to discuss how media created imagined communities underlying the nation state in his *Imagined Communities*.

35 On the spectacular and competing pageants of Empire that France and Britain held in numerous twentieth-century expositions, see Rydell *World of Fairs* 63–72. For a detailed analysis of the India exhibit at the Crystal Palace, see Breckenridge.

36 The Unione Tipografico Editrice Torinese translated Darwin's works between 1871 and 1877. Darwin's thought influenced the positivistic approaches to biology and anatomy that placed the University of Turin at the cutting edge of contemporary scientific research in the late nineteenth century.

37 In the pages of *Milano e l'esposizione italiana del 1881*, Gaetano Sangiorgio welcomed the display of 138 regional costumes, 'prima che l'azione livellatrice del secolo faccia sparire per sempre gli usi, i costumi, le tradizioni dei nostri popoli' (before our century's levelling action forever wipes out the uses, customs, and traditions of our peoples) (24–5, 194).

38 The fabled Mille Miglia originated in Turin in 1901.

39 World's Fairs inspired this view; as *Shepp's World's Fair Photographed* wrote of

the Chicago World's Columbian Exposition, 'Everywhere there is motion; electric Launches, Gondolas, the Intramural Railway, the Sliding Railway, the Ice Railway, and the Movable Sidewalk; land and water alike are alive with happy people' (Shepp and Shepp 322).

40 A universe packed full of curious and unusual objects, the bazaar created a carefully engineered illusion of the Orient with its clichéd mysteries and exotic dreams: 'Vi si trovano ... delle graziose pantofole dette dell'harem ... tappeti antichi e moderni ricamati a mano, arabescati, altri ricamati in argento ed oro su fondo di raso; coperte da letto ricchissime ... sgabelli turchi lavorati a mosaico ... armi antiche, turche e persiane, elmi, scudi, scimitarre, pugnali cesellati con grandissimo gusto d'arte ... Fra le cento e le mille curiosità delle nostre Esposizioni anche il bazar orientale è degno di essere visitato. Servirà ... a dare un'idea ... di un mondo misterioso, lontano, mistico, sensuale a cui tendono con intensità di desiderio tutti i sognatori e gli artisti delle nostre grandi città' (One will find ... graceful slippers called the harem's slippers ... hand-embroidered and arabesqued rugs, both antique and contemporary; other carpets embroidered in silver and gold on a satin base; sumptuous bedspreads ... Turkish stools in a mosaic pattern ... antique Turkish and Persian arms, helmets, shields, scimitars, and daggers, engraved with great artistic skill. [...] Among the hundreds and thousands of curiosities of our Expositions, the Oriental Bazaar is worth visiting, too. It will ... offer an idea of a mysterious, remote, mystical, and sensual world, toward which all the dreamers and artists of our metropolises aspire with intense desire) (Selvafolta 40).

41 Once again, this display was not unique to Milan. The 'Piker,' as the visitor of the 1904 Louisiana Purchase Exposition was called, could discover 'the North Pole in twenty minutes, a feat beyond Arctic explorers. The distinguishing feature of this show was an Atlantic liner two hundred feet long by fifty feet wide, with every appointment of the modern seagoing vessel. Gang planks connecting the vessel with the immense theatre lying next to the ship carried the passenger into the main illusion which consisted of a trip to the North Pole, the grinding of the vessel through ice fields and bergs, an electrical effect giving a startling illustration of the Northern aurora, and the final discovery of the Pole' (Francis 600).

42 This narrative was accompanied by a second volume entitled *Osservazioni scientifiche eseguite durante la spedizione polare di S.A.R. Luigi Amedeo di Savoia Duca degli Abruzzi* (Scientific Observations Executed During the Polar Expedition of H.R.M. Luigi Amedeo di Savoia, Duke of the Abruzzi).

43 During the scramble for Africa, the journalist-explorer Henry M. Stanley's expedition in search of David Livingstone remained, perhaps, the unsurpassed example of imperialistic reporting in the nineteenth century.

44 Amedeo's brother, the Count of Turin, attracted equal popular attention as he expanded the boundaries of the Savoy myth by participating in widely advertised tiger hunts in India and Thailand (then Siam), and by surveying the Italian colony of Eritrea in search of goldfields. Tommaso di Savoia, Duke of Genoa, travelled extensively in Ethiopia, and his letters were published in 1936 under the title *Precursori dell'impero africano*. With Admiral Umberto Cagni (1863–1932) – the 'pilota di eroi' whom Giovanni Pascoli praised in verse after his victorious landing in Bu Mellana, near Tripoli, in 1911 – Luigi Amedeo trekked to the North Pole from 21 February to 22 June 1899, leaving from Christiania (today's Olso) with the ship *Stella Polare*. Forced by frostbite to stop his march, the duke left the task of completing the adventure to his second in command, and Cagni hoisted the Italian flag at longitude 86° north after a long and exhausting march across the ice.

45 In a letter that publisher Antonio Donath sent to Salgari, this political aim is clear: 'Insomma lei mi avrà capito. Io terrei assaissimo che questo volume fosse una glorificazione del valore italiano e in ispecie del Duca, e che fosse un incitamento per la gioventù: istruttivo ed educativo' (In sum, you understand me. It is most important to me that this volume should be a glorification of Italian bravery and, specifically, the Duke's, and an encouragement to young people: that it should be instructive and educational) (cited in Pozzo, 'Io terrei' xliv).

46 Salgari emphasized the popular and accessible nature of his volume in a note addressed to his readers: 'La relazione ufficiale, che S.A.R. il Duca degli Abruzzi sta preparando, è destinata agli scienziati; il racconto che ho scritto per voi, invece, è tessuto su quanto sinora l'Augusto Principe ha comunicato alla stampa e al pubblico; ma vi ho intercalato quanto si conosce sulle regioni iperboree, cercando di rendere popolare, attraente ed istruttiva la storia dei viaggi polari, dall'ultimo dei quali la nostra cara Italia ha gloria ed onore' (The official report that His Royal Highness the Duke of the Abruzzi is writing is addressed to scientists; the narrative that I wrote for you, instead, is woven out of what the Prince has so far communicated to the press and the public; but I have inserted what is known about the Arctic regions, trying to infuse popularity, beauty, and instructiveness to the history of travels to the Pole, our beloved Italy having gained glory and honour from the latest one of these travels) (cited in Viglongo ix).

47 Unsurprisingly, narratives of real and imagined travels to the farthest edges of the world proliferated during the Imperial Age. Always attuned to popular trends, and often anticipating them, Salgari wrote several novels set in the North and South Poles. Widely successful, these novels were generally published in instalments in popular magazines such as *Il giornale dei fanciulli*, *Il*

giovedì, L'innocenza, Il novelliere illustrato, La biblioteca per l'infanzia e l'ado-lescenza and subsequently in single volumes, often in numerous successive editions. Among Salgari's polar narratives are *I pescatori di balene* (The Whale Hunters, 1894), *Le avventure del padre Crespel nel Labrador* (The Adventures of Father Crespel in Labrador, 1895), later included in the volume *Le grandi pesche nei mari australi* (The Great Fishing Adventures in the Antarctic Ocean, 1904), *Al Polo australe in velocipede* (To the South Pole by Velocipede 1895), and *Nel paese dei ghiacci* (In the Land of Ice, 1896). As international efforts to reach the northernmost point of the world intensified, so did Salgari's liter-ary output. *Al Polo Nord* appeared in 1898 and *Una sfida al Polo* in 1909, and they quickly reached the top of the best-seller lists. With their plethora of exotic-sounding terms such as *ice-fields* and *ice-bergs*, *streams* and *fjords* (the spelling is Salgari's), these novels dictated the contents of the average Italian reader's Arctic imagination. For specific comments about Salgari's 'polar lex-icon,' see De Anna.

48 Further details on this lawsuit are in Pozzo, 'Io terrei' xlvii–li.

49 Always careful to promote his adventures and aware of the advertising poten-tial of the newborn cinema, Luigi Amedeo climbed the Karakorum range in 1909 accompanied by Vittorio Sella, who realized the first cinematic report-age from the Asian mountains: *Sul tetto del mondo: Viaggio di S.A.R. il Duca degli Abruzzi al Karakoram* (On Top of the World: H.R.M. The Duke of the Abruzzi's Journey to the Karakorum.)

50 As Guy Debord points out in *La societé du spectacle*: 'Le caractère fondamen-talement tautologique du spectacle découle du simple fait que ses moyens sont en même temps son but. Il est le soleil qui ne se couche jamais sur l'empire de la passivité moderne' (The fundamentally tautological character of the spectacle flows from the simple fact that its means are simultaneously its ends. It is the sun that never sets over the empire of modern passivity) (13).

51 One should remember Nadar's famous photographs and the *The Douanier* Rousseau's paintings of hot air balloons.

52 At the Paris 1900 exposition, Raoul Grimoin-Sanson, an inventor of early motion picture equipment, devised 'a vast marquee containing white walls, a hundred metres in circumference, which would serve as an uninterrupted screen. In the centre was to be positioned the huge nacelle of a balloon equipped complete with anchor, ropes, ballast and ladders, and underneath this would be located ten projectors synchronized to a central motor. From the ceiling, curtain material would be draped to represent perfectly the cas-ing of the balloon. When the audience have assumed their places in the nacelle, the lights would be dimmed for the commencement of the journey

... leaving Paris, the balloon will travel around visiting Brussels, London, Barcelona and Tunis. The films projected on the walls depict scenes from these various cities, thereby creating the illusion of a tour of the capitals' (Allwood 103). Although the show was shut down for fear of fires, Grimoin-Sanson's idea explains well the thirst for vicarious travel. Elsewhere in the exhibition, visitors struggled with seasickness in the Maréorama's heaving viewing platform. Built like the deck of a steamship, this platform stood against a painted background that created the illusion of a voyage in a stormy Mediterranean Sea from Marseilles to Algiers.

3. Emilio Salgari: Writing Exposition Style

1 French magazines specializing in *feuilletons* had perfected the art of the promotional advertisement. For one of the novels of Ponson du Terrail's *Rocambole* series, for example, La Petite Presse printed posters that mimicked the style of these public announcements that typically bore the caption 'Passants Lisez et Prononcez.' People who stopped to read what they thought was the announcement of an important political event were instead treated to the entire first chapter of the new novel (Neuschäfer 216).
2 On the specific difficulties involved in compiling a correct bibliography of Salgari's works, see Pozzo, 'Bibliografia,' and Sarti.
3 *Il corsaro nero*, for example, sold more than one hundred thousand copies in record time (see Di Fazio Alberti 55).
4 For detailed analyses of literary genres as socio-cultural and historical phenomena, see Corti, Steinmetz, and Levin.
5 Salgari borrowed the names of these Indian ships from Ferrario's volumes, which included illustrative sketches of the various vessels.
6 I use the term 'racialism' to define the movement of ideas that originated in Europe between the mid-eighteenth and the mid-twentieth centuries. For a broader illustration of racialist principles, see Todorov.
7 The most obvious archetypes being the Philoctetes episode in *The Odyssey* and the story of Sinbad in *The Arabian Nights*.
8 Said expands his argument by stating that the entire genre of the novel accompanies and is a part of the conquests of Western society: 'the novel, as a cultural artifact of bourgeois society, and imperialism are unthinkable without each other. Of all the major literary forms, the novel is the most recent, its emergence the most datable, its occurrence the most Western, its normative pattern of social authority the most structured; imperialism and the novel fortified each other to such a degree that it is impossible ... to read one without in some way dealing with the other' (*Culture* 70–1).

9 The systems may vary: Defoe's Robinson Crusoe (with his many literary brothers in the *Robinsonaden* genre), for example, learns to master the island's hostile environment through physical work, technical and intellectual skill, persistence, temperance, and sheer practicality. Crusoe thus transforms his crude island into an earthly paradise (minus a woman) that celebrates freedom and manly independence, fortitude, and resourcefulness. Verne's *The Mysterious Island* (1874) emphasizes the same positivistic enthusiasm for man's technical and scientific achievements and values, in a nineteenth-century context: the new adventurer meets Nature face-to-face and acts on her, forcing her to yield her secrets and bend to his power.

10 I am using the term 'function' following Vladimir Propp's definition in his *Morphology of the Folktale*.

11 One should recall here that the Robin Hood that Percy translated from popular legends in 1765 not only inspired Walter Scott's *Ivanhoe* but was also rewritten in prose by Dumas in *Robin Hood le proscrit*. Perhaps the novel that most inspired Salgari was Verne's *Twenty Thousand Leagues under the Sea*, where the protagonist, Captain Nemo, engages in a relentless act of vengeance to satisfy the wrong that he and his people had originally suffered. Though Verne kept the secret of Nemo's origin in that book, in *The Mysterious Island* he reveals that Nemo was an Indian prince who had lost his kingdom to the British during the insurrection of 1857.

12 Green points out that Dantès's moral development from a proud and ambitious soul to an inflexible and indifferent individual because of his enemies' actions and his immense wealth and power was also intended to remind contemporary readers of Napoleon (130).

13 Giovanni Arpino and Roberto Antonetto mention that Garibaldi's 'legend' may have inspired Salgari, without, however, bringing this idea to full development (27).

14 Garibaldi started compiling *Le mie memorie* in 1849 and completed the definitive edition in 1872.

15 Similarly, in a chapter entitled 'The Affair of Salto San Antonio' Garibaldi lingers on the anecdote of an enemy soldier who broke through their lines on a galloping horse in an attempt to set the straw roofs of Garibaldi's encampment on fire. Garibaldi comments that this man, though unsuccessful, had nevertheless 'carried through a very brave enterprise' and therefore stops his men from shooting him by proclaiming: 'We should spare the brave: they belong to our race' (186).

16 If the natural world is the locus where these heroes must prove their value, the island is another of the adventure tale's *loci communes*. Mompracem, like Garibaldi's Caprera and Dantès's Monte-Cristo, is the hero's inner sanctum

and the objective correlative of his psychical and ethical make-up. Wild, rugged, solitary, inhospitable, and remote, the islands define the moral coordinates of the all-male world of Western adventure.

17 Garibaldi's guerrilla warfare on the lagoon of Los Patos, for example, consisted of ambushing the ships that happened to be separated from the rest of the Imperialist fleet, and resulted in random killing, despoiling, and fleeing under the cover of darkness. This warfare succeeded in harming communication, spreading confusion, and effectively blocking the Imperialist forces from attaining a swifter, if inevitable, victory.

18 The most common shared and recurring expression in these action-packed narratives is 'fu l'affare di un secondo' ('it was the matter of a second'), as in 'to spring from the bowsprit to the figure-head and thence on to the deck was the matter of a second or two' (*Memoirs* 192).

19 Yanez can be interpreted as an imaginative rendition of Garibaldi's friend, Nino Bixio, whom contemporary biographies portray as more cynical and astute than the General and who died in the Malay Archipelago.

20 This novel was first published in English in the American magazine *The Forum* and then translated into French with the title *La journée d'un journaliste americain en 2889.*

21 For extended bibliographical information on the use of the term 'technological sublime,' see Nye xv–xvi.

4. Guido Gozzano's Imperial Ambiguities

1 Founder of the literary journal *Hermes*, Borgese held a chair in German literature at the University of Turin (and, later, in Rome and Milan as well). By 1917, he had successfully combined his academic interests with a prolific career in journalism and essay writing. His widely read contributions on literature and current politics for *Il corriere della sera* made him one of the most influential cultural voices of the early twentieth century (see Luti 19–22).

2 The order and places of publication of the Indian narratives that were later collected in *Verso la cuna del mondo* (VCM) are as follows: 'Un Natale a Ceylon' *La Lettura* (January 1914); 'La Torre del silenzio' (in *VCM* 'Le Torri del silenzio') *La Stampa* (9 March 1914); 'L'isola d'Elefanta' (in *VCM* 'Le grotte della Trimurti') *La Stampa* (31 March 1914); 'La danza d'una Devadasis' *La Stampa* (15 April 1914); 'Golconda: la città morta' (in *VCM* 'I tesori di Golconda') *La Stampa* (12 June 1914); 'Il vivaio del Buon Dio' *La Stampa* (15 June 1914); 'Il fiume dei roghi' *La Stampa* (10 July 1914); 'L'India ribelle?' (in *VCM* 'Le caste infrangibili') *La Stampa* (20 April 1915); 'L'olocausto di Cawmpore' (in *VCM* 'L'Olocausto di Cawnepore' *La Donna* (20 April 1915);

'Goa: "La Dourada"' *Bianco rosso e verde* (15 November – 15 December 1915);
'Le città della favola: Agra' (in *VCM* divided into 'Agra: l'immacolata' and
'Fachiri e ciurmadori') *Bianco rosso e verde* (30 January 1916); 'L'impero del
Gran Mogol' *Bianco rosso e verde* (15 February – 15 March 1916); 'Giaipur: la
città rosea' (in *VCM* Giaipur: città della favola' *La Donna* (20 August 1916);
'Da Ceylan a Madura' (in *VCM* 'Da Ceylon a Madura') *La Donna* (20 September 1916).

3 According to Carlo Calcaterra, 'Il titolo *Verso la cuna del mondo*, fu designato
   dal Gozzano stesso al fratello Renato alcuni giorni prima della morte ... Il
   Gozzano in persona indicò anche l'ordinamento del libro dando istruzioni
   per la cura dell'edizione' (A few days before his death, Gozzano told his
   brother Renato that the volume should be titled *Verso la cuna del mondo* ...
   Gozzano himself also specified the ordering sequence of his narratives and
   gave editing instructions for the volume) ('Note' 1220–1). See also
   D'Aquino Creazzo, 'Introduzione' xxviii.
4 Gozzano left Genoa, Italy, on 16 February 1912. He arrived in Bombay on
   March 8, and from March 15 to April 10 he stayed in Sri Lanka, taking one
   trip to Benares (Varanasi), and returning to Bombay for his final departure
   on March 15. In mid-April he was back in Italy. See D'Aquino Creazzo,
   'Introduzione' vi; Grisay 427–30; De Rienzo, *Guido Gozzano* 157–60.
5 The spelling of Indian names and locations often varies from source to
   source. I used the authors' own spellings when citing directly, and adopted
   the most prevalent spelling in all other cases, giving the current versions in
   parenthesis.
6 For evidence of this spiritual evolution in Gozzano's own testimonies and
   letters, see De Rienzo, *Guido Gozzano* 131 and 215–16.
7 On the sources of *Verso la cuna del mondo* see Grisay, Sanguineti, Mondo, Mor,
   Porcelli, Casella, and D'Aquino Creazzo, 'Introduzione.'
8 In 1937, Treves published a new edition of *Verso la cuna del mondo* as the fourth
   volume of the *Opere di Guido Gozzano*. This 'definitive edition' followed the
   same narrative sequence as the original one: An introductory note to the
   reader endorsed Borgese's organizing principles and claimed that it had
   been Borgese, and not Gozzano, who had devised the collection's overall
   design ('Al lettore' ii). In 1948, Calcaterra and Alberto De Marchi included
   Verso la cuna del mondo in their edition of Gozzano's *Opere*, which followed the
   same narrative sequence of Treves's volumes, and contained Calcaterra's
   statement about Gozzano having decided the volume's sequence. De Marchi's 1961 edition of Gozzano's works reiterated that Gozzano had drafted
   the volume's 'disegno generale' (overall design), which it did not alter
   ('Note' 1411). Similarly, in his detailed introduction to the 1971 Marzorati

edition of *Verso la cuna del mondo*, Antonio Mor deferred to Gozzano's *auctoritas* and repeated the assertion that Gozzano had devised the volume's design before his death (22). No structural changes appeared in subsequent editions, including Marziano Guglielminetti's in 1974, Gianni Guadalupi's (also in 1974), Nico Orengo's in 1980, and Giusi Baldissone's in 1984. Giorgio De Rienzo was the first to reject Borgese's organizing principles in his 1983 edition of *Verso la cuna del mondo* for Mondadori. De Rienzo organized the various Indian letters according to the sequence of their original publication in *La Stampa* and the other periodicals, and claimed that 'c'è più di un sospetto per considerare … arbitraria la composizione postuma del libro di Gozzano. Manca qualsiasi attestazione espistolare su questa volontà d'autore e manca qualsiasi testimonianza d'archivio' (There is more than one reason to suspect that the posthumous composition of Gozzano's book is arbitrary. There are no letters and no archival testimony to corroborate this authorial design) ('Introduzione' 10). Shortly after, in 1984, Pietro Cudini edited for Garzanti *Un Natale a Ceylon e altri racconti indiani*. This volume's preface echoes De Rienzo's statement in arguing that 'sinora … non sono comparsi documenti che possano attestare una sicura paternità gozzaniana alla strutturazione complessiva dell'opera' (to this day … we have not discovered any documents that attribute the paternity of the overall structure of this work to Gozzano) (12). Cudini concludes that in the absence of such documents, the only viable edition is the one that reproduces the chronology of the original publications. Unfortunately, De Rienzo's and Cudini's editions are compromised by the fact that they were unable to find the original publication sites for some of the *Lettere*, which they were thus forced to include in separate appendices. Notwithstanding more recent editions (one in 1995 for Millelire Publications and one in 1998 for EDT), the most accurate and systematic edition of *Verso la cuna del mondo* remains Alida D'Aquino Creazzo's (Olschki, 1984), from which I cite. Besides providing a painstakingly accurate study of Gozzano's literary borrowings, D'Aquino Creazzo identifies Gozzano's important contributions to *Bianco rosso e verde*, which Cudini and De Rienzo overlooked. Though D'Aquino Creazzo breaks new ground in systematizing and correctly identifying the original publication sites for Gozzano's Indian narratives, she does not discuss the socio-historical implications of her discoveries and, somewhat surprisingly given her philological efforts, ends up reproducing Borgese's own narrative structure. D'Aquino Creazzo justifies her choice according to a familiar logic. She states that, though there is still no archival evidence that Gozzano arranged his pieces according to the sequence that Borgese proposed, this sequence is by no means 'arbitrary,' as De Rienzo claimed, but conveys a sense of organic wholeness ('Introduzione' xxviii).

9 These narratives are 'Un voto alla dea Tharata-Ku-Wha' (A Vow to the Goddess Tharata-Ku-Wa) (*La Stampa*, 30 January 1914), 'Sull'oceano di brace'
   (On the Burning Waves) (*La Stampa*, 16 February 1914), and 'Glorie italiane
   all'estero: gli orrori del Paradiso' (Italian Glories Abroad: The Horrors of
   Paradise) (*Bianco rosso e verde*, 15 January 1916). 'Un voto' and 'Sull'oceano'
   were later included in the collection *L'altare del passato*) (An Altar to the Past).

10 Gozzano wrote several short articles on Turin 1911. 'Torino suburbana: la
   gran cuoca,' 'Il padiglione della città di Torino,' and 'Superga' were originally published in *L'esposizione di Torino 1911: Giornale ufficiale illustrato
   dell'esposizione internazionale delle industrie del lavoro*. 'Un vergiliato sotto la
   neve' appeared in *La lettura* (April 1911). 'All'esposizione del lavoro:
   l'Acquarium' (The Acquarium at the Industry Pavilion) and 'La città moritura' (The Dying City) were published in *Il Momento* (respectively, 16 June
   and 9 November 1911). *Il Momento* also published 'Rosolie di stagione' (Sea-
   sonal Maladies) (4 May 1911) and 'Il dono della meraviglia' (29 June 1911).
   The *Bollettino ufficiale dell'Esposizione Internazionale di Torino* (1 November
   1911) hosted 'I crisantemi alla mostra dei fiori' (The Chrisanthemums at the
   Flower Exhibit)

11 As a free monthly publication affiliated with the most widely read, and therefore most profitable, Italian newspaper, *La Lettura* was a steady presence in
   middle-class Italian households between 1901 and 1945. *La Lettura* favoured
   humanistic subjects, with articles about literature and literary studies, the
   visual and performing arts, music, and history. In the sciences, *La Lettura*
   hosted pieces on anthropology, medicine, and psychology. The last pages
   included advertisements and serialized novels, the topics of which generally
   favoured sensation and adventure.

12 With the ongoing war as its main topic, Antona-Traversi promised factual
   accuracy and timely reporting with 'importanti e dirette corrispondenze
   tanto dal fronte italiano che dal fronte francese' (important and direct
   reports from the Italian as well as the French fronts) ('Il nostro programma'
   iv). The first issues contained extensive photographic reports from 'the theatre of the war,' with images of battlefields, trenches, alpine battalions, war-
   planes, marching troops, and gutted buildings. The narrative sections
   included short edifying pieces reporting, for example, symbolically charged
   events such as the crossing of the Isonzo River during the march toward Trieste and humanitarian endeavours such as those undertaken by the 'grande
   armata bianca' of the Red Cross's nurses. A section devoted to 'I cantori di
   guerra' published war poems such as 'Le cri' by Henry Bataille (*BRV* 3: 4),
   and the page entitled 'Frammenti di gloria' included short celebratory biographies devoted to war 'heroes.'

13 Besides the Indian narratives, Gozzano contributed his 'Dittico della pace e della guerra' (A Diptyc to Peace and War). Though enriching the variety of its inspiration, *Bianco rosso e verde* kept the ongoing war as its main topic. The sociologist Émile Durkheim, for example, provided a long serialized piece on the German mentality and the war, and Gerolamo Lazzeri wrote short stories on war themes and literary analyses on war literature.

14 See, for example, Cesarina Lupati's exotic short stories, such as *Canillita, novella d'oltremare.*

15 Launched in 1905, *La Donna* shared some important features with *La Lettura.* Among its contributors were Ada Negri, Matilde Serao, Vittoria Aganoor Pompilj, Grazia Deledda, Amelia Rosselli, Amalia Guglielminetti, Carlo Chiaves, Marino Moretti, and Borgese. *La Donna* enjoyed the advantages of affiliation with two major daily newspapers, Rome's *La Tribuna* and Turin's *La Stampa.* By the turn of the century, Luigi Frassati's *La Stampa* had become the leading advocate of liberal democracy in Italy, often in dialectic opposition with Luigi Albertini's more conservative *Corriere della sera.* While initially opposing Crispi's imperialistic program and his repressive and authoritarian leadership, by 1910 *La Stampa* was actively encouraging Italy's colonial involvement in North Africa. *La Stampa* enthusiastically encouraged Giolitti's Libyan enterprise 'non solo per motivi di orgoglio nazionale ma per onorare la "missione civilizzatrice e fecondatrice"' (not only for reasons of national pride but to honour the 'civilizing and fertilizing mission') of the Italian nation (Castronovo, *La Stampa* 204). *La Stampa* thus revealed that, on the eve of the First World War, Italy's imperialistic ambitions were no longer a prerogative of the conservative classes alone, but were part of the liberal elites' political agenda as well.

16 For an analysis of Gozzano's aesthetics of the 'strident things,' see Sanguineti 135–47.

17 See also 'Torino d'altri tempi' (Torino of Times Past): 'non l'arte imita la vita, ma la vita l'arte; le cose non esistono se prima non le rivelano gli artisti' (Art does not imitate life, but life imitates art. Things do not exist until an artist reveals them) (*Cara Torino* 146). See also, in *Verso la cuna del mondo,* 'Il fiume dei roghi' (The River of the Pyres): 'Devo liberarmi dal ricordo di troppe descrizioni – da quelle deliziosamente arcaiche di Marco Polo a quelle moderne e sentimentali di Pierre Loti – per entrare nella realtà, vedere la cosa troppo attesa con occhi miei. Ma ... se risalgo alle origini prime della mia memoria vedo la città sacra in un'incisione napoleonica ... Benares va vista dal Gange, come la ribalta dalla platea' (I have to free myself from the memories of too many descriptions – from the delightfully archaic ones by Marco Polo to Pierre Loti's modern and sentimental ones – in order to

experience reality and finally see the things I have longed for with my own eyes. But ... if I go back to the prime source of my memory I see the holy city in a Napoleonic woodcut in my playroom ... You have to see Varanasi from the Ganges, just like you see the forestage from the stalls) (111).

18 A similar concept in 'Un voto alla dea Tharata-Ku-Wha' (A Vow to the Goddess Thaata-Ku-Wha): 'ogni idolo è chiuso in una gabbia come un felino' (every idol is locked in a cage like a big cat) (130).

19 On the grotesque as contrastive device, see Kayser 58–9.

20 By the turn of the century, shows by troupes of bayadères, or nautch girls, had become World's Fair clichés, and several operas and ballets were written for and about them (Altick 251).

21 On the association between the Orient and sex, see Said, *Orientalism* 149–97.

22 Within the general heading of transtextuality, Genette identifies numerous categories, such as intertextuality (defined as the 'copresence between two texts or several texts,' which includes the literary practices of quoting, plagiarism, and allusion); paratextuality (or the relationship between texts and elements such as their titles and subtitle, prefaces, postfaces, blurbs and illustrations, covers etc.); metatextuality (or commentary, which defines the critical relationship of a text that speaks about another text); archtextuality (defining the general categories to which the text belongs, such as genre and type of discourse); and hypertextuality (the relationship uniting a text A, or hypotext, to a text B, or hypertext, such as the *Aeneid* to the *Divine Comedy*.

23 "The East India Company's army in India consisted of two sections, – one, in which both officers and rank and file were Englishmen, and the other, in which the commissioned officers were all British, but the rank and file, known as sepoys (anglicized from *Sipahi*) ... and junior officers, subordinate to the lowest class of English officers, were recruited from various parts of India' (Majumdar 29–30).

24 For a description of the station of Cawnpore, and the make-up of its troops, see Trevelyan 2–3 and 104–6. For more recent discussions, see Majumdar 85–8 and Gupta 47–8 and 73.

25 As is often the case with Gozzano, this reality effect is misleading. While the letter from Cawnpore published in *La Donna* is not dated, in the Borgese edition of *Verso la cuna del mondo* the same letter appears with the date of 16 February. While it is certain that Gozzano was not in Cawnpore on 16 February, it is doubtful that he was in Cawnpore at all (D'Aquino Creazzo 'Introduzione' vi; Grisay 427–30).

26 I am thinking, of course, about Verga's famous poetics of the 'fatto nudo e schietto' (naked and sincere fact) as expressed in 'L'amante di Gramigna' 1: 202.

27 In Aristotle's words: 'It is clear that epic plots should be made dramatic, as in tragedies, dealing with a single action which is whole and complete and has beginning, middles, and end, so that like a single complete creature it may produce the appropriate pleasure. It is also clear that the plot-structure should not resemble a history, in which of necessity a report is presented not of a single action but of a single period ... of which each event has only chance relationships to the others' (61).

28 See also Hegel's comments: 'To poetry alone is the liberty permitted to dispose without restriction of the material submitted in such a way that it becomes, even regarded on the side of external condition, conformable with ideal truth' (4: 41–2).

29 The conclusion of John Kaye's chronicle of the insurrection is a case in point: 'The History of the Indian Mutiny is, in fact, a record of the display of all the qualities for which Englishmen have been famous – of the qualities which have enabled the inhabitants of a small island in the Atlantic to accumulate the noblest and largest empire in the world, and which, so long as they remain unimpaired in their descendants, will enable them to maintain it' (5: 302).

30 Anonymity does not grant universality, of course. The bard was one of the Scottish soldiers who entered Cawnpore the day after the massacre and engaged in violent retaliations against the sepoys' own murderous acts. The locus of the utterance is therefore culturally and historically determined, and so are the memories that one is asked to select.

31 The elusiveness of this truth is evidenced by one of the first chroniclers of the mutiny, John Walter Sherer, who, reacting against the oft-cited words that Gozzano himself was to quote fifty years later, wrote: 'And I may say once for all that the accounts were exaggerated ... The whole of the pavement was thickly caked with blood. Surely this is enough, without saying "the clotted gore lay ankle deep," which, besides being most distressing, is absolutely incorrect' (1: 207–8). Gozzano's reworking of other writers' scripts is comparable to what Edward Said described as the citationary nature of Orientalism. The Orient that is thus assembled is obviously not a real place, but 'a set of references, a congeries of characteristics, that seem to have its origin in a quotation, or a fragment of a text, or a citation from someone's work on the Orient, or some bit of previous imagining, or an amalgam of all these' (*Orientalism* 176–7).

32 The bulk of the primary materials on the insurrection are, of course, British. There are almost no contemporary Indian reports, and the few existing ones come 'through a British filter: the depositions of native witnesses afraid that they may be hanged, the testimony of rebels at their trials, the journals

of Indians eager to demonstrate their loyalty to the ascending Raj' (Ward xviii).

33 While reports on Nana's actual involvement in the slaughter on the river vary, Gozzano and most European interpreters accepted the treachery theory, according to which Nana had sworn on his religion's sacred texts to allow safe passage to Allahabad to all surviving Europeans of the Cawnpore garrison, only to have them slaughtered shortly after they had embarked on the boats that were to take them to safety. On 20 July 1857 the *Bombay Times* reported: 'the force had accepted the proffer of safety made by the Nana Saheb [but] ... after getting them on boats, fire was opened on them from the bank, and all were destroyed' ('Melancholy Tragedy'). See also Kaye 1: 225; Forrest 1: 409 and 445–75; Trevelyan 227; Holmes 247; Thomson 166–7; Ball 1: 335–40; De Lanoye 538–9. For a fictional narrative exploiting the treachery theme, as well as the theme of British revenge, see the novel by J.E. Muddock. More doubtful opinions on Nana's role in the massacre are expressed by Sheperd 82, and Lang 412–13. For more recent interpretations see Majumdar 88; Sen 149–50, and especially Gupta 68–72 and 116–18. Interestingly, one of Gozzano's direct sources, Calani's *Scene dell'insurrezione indiana*, presents a wholly different picture, both of Nana and of the massacre at the river. Nana is a heroic and decisive leader, faithful to his promise of safe evacuation and dismissive of some of his most fanatical soldiers' desire to annihilate the British. Here the catastrophe is caused by a quid pro quo, as in Nana's absence the sepoys open fire when they believe that the British have betrayed their promise, having heard an explosion and musket fire coming from the entrenchment (272–748).

34 See, for example, the postscript to Ronald Bassett's *Blood of an Englishman: A Novel of the Siege of Cawnpore*. While conceding that much anti-Indian evidence was fabricated, Bassett concludes that 'the genuine circumstantial evidence is so sickeningly overwhelming that an objective picture of the circumstances can be recreated without difficulty' (346).

35 The battle of Plassey had started the East India Company's rule in India (23 June 1757). The *Times* gave ample space to the cartridge incident. As is well known, the introduction of the new Lee Enfield rifles in the sepoy army aroused the suspicion that the cartridges required by these rifles were greased with tallow made with cow and pig fat, thus becoming offensive to both the Hindu and the Muslim religious beliefs. According to reports in the *Times* the sepoys interpreted this fact as the government's ruse to start a wholesale conversion of the Indian people to Christianity.

36 The majority of European sources wholeheartedly dismissed the possibility that the insurrection was inspired by revolutionary or nationalistic feelings,

thus denying any political maturity to the Indian people. Early historians such as Charles Raikes agreed that the uprising was a mutiny of soldiers, 'not a mutiny growing out of a national discontent' (see Raikes 156).

37 Kaye 2: 25–31; Duff; De Lanoye 500–2.

38 In Kaye's interpretation: 'For months, for years indeed ... [Nana] had been quietly spreading [his] network of intrigue all over the country. From one Native Court to another Native Court, from one extremity to another of the great continent of India, the agents of the Náná Sáhib had passed with overtures and invitations, discreetly, perhaps mysteriously, worded, to Princes and Chiefs of different races and religions, but most hopefully of all to the Maráthás' (1:424); see also Holmes 92. For a more recent interpretation, see Thapliyal: 'The Nana's main object was to foment the revolt inside the country and to create circumstances favourable for help from outside the country. Internal disorder and external attack would help the Indians to mount their armed pressure upon the British and then to drive them away easily' (122–3). For a refutation of the pro-independence argument, see Gupta 63–4.

39 'Une insurrection digne de ce grand mot ... un drapeau national agitant une ombre électrique de l'Himalaya au cap Comorin [pour] une patrie indoue ... jamais' (An insurrection worthy of this great name ... a national flag waving and casting an electrical shadow from the Himalayas to the Comorin Cape for an Indian homeland ... never) (De Lanoye 495). De Warren was among the most eloquent deniers of a national movement: 'Pour qu'il y eût soulèvement général, il faudrait que les masses y fussent intéressées, qu'elles ne fussent divisées par aucun sentiment de haine, et c'est ce que les différences entre leurs croyances religieuses ne permettront jamais ... Il faudrait ... qu'il y eût une seule nation, une partie commune, des traditions, des idées, des intérêts communs' (For there to have been a general uprising the masses would have had to be involved, they would not have had to be divided by feelings of hatred, and their religious differences will never allow that ... There would have had to be ... a single nation, a shared contest, and common traditions and interests) (2: 170, 270). See also Corte, 170–3: Corte distinguished between the reasons of the Hindus (related to what they perceived as an offence against their religion) and those of the Muslims, who were instead moved by political reasons. Corte denies that the insurrection was a national movement, on the assumption that the leading classes did not participate in it: '[alla rivolta] non parteciparono generalmente che le infime e peggiori classi della società, e ... le pochissime persone appartenenti alle classi dirigenti che vi presero parte erano state spinte da risentimenti personali' (Generally, only the lowest and worst segments of society partici-

pated in the mutiny, and ... the few people from the ruling classes who took part in it were inspired by personal resentments) (172).

40   Although, according to Indian customs, royally adopted heirs had the same rights as first-born natural sons, in 1848 Dalhousie decided that, on the death of a prince without a natural son, no inheritance should benefit the adopted son, and the principality should be merged into the British Empire. Another kind of lapse applied to the pension awarded to local rulers as a compensation for land seized by the British. When the *peshwa* of Poona died without any natural heir, his adopted son, Nana Sahib, was denied his father's pension, an event that many contemporary historians believed to have led to the Cawnpore insurrection.

41   Part of the series of his *Voyages extraordinaires*, Verne built *La maison à vapeur* on the invention of an 'extraordinary vehicle' aptly called Behemoth, a cross between a sumptuous train and a rolling house, a steam house in fact, in the shape of a gigantic steel elephant pulling two enormous moving bungalows. This formidable travelling abode hosts an eccentric group of friends who journey together through 'the highways and byways' of northern India, each of them having a different goal in mind. Mr Banks, the engineer and inventor of the steam house, wishes to test his new prototype. Monsieur Maucler, the narrator, plans to 'visit [the] great cities [of India and] examine and study the principal monuments of antiquity' (125); Captain Hood, traveller and sportsman, is looking forward to 'bagging' his forty-first tiger; Colonel Munro, of the 93rd regiment of Highlanders, joins the party thinking about a different kind of hunt altogether. Eager to avenge the victims of the Cawnpore massacre, and especially his wife, Munro is on the trail of Nana Sahib, the tiger-man who has eluded his relentless quest for over ten years, and is as deadly, vicious, and stealthy as his animal counterpart. Verne's movable house throws its passengers headlong into breathtaking adventures and allows for the intersection of multiple narrative threads, including several descriptive pauses dealing with the geography and topography of northern India, a concise account of the sepoys' insurrection, and an imaginative narrative of its aftermath.

42   Ten years after the failed insurrection of 1857, Verne presents Nana as again engaged in plotting against the British and roaming through all Indian territories in order to collect 'men ripe for revolt': '[Nana] began the insurrection campaign. Now in the costume of a parsee, and now in that of a humble ryot ... he went long distances from the Pâl of Tandit, northward, to the other side of the Nerbudda, and even beyond the Vindhyas. If a spy had followed him in his wanderings he would, soon after the 12th of April, have found him at Indore. There, Nana Sahib, while preserving the strictest

incognito, put himself in communication with the extensive rural population employed in the culture of poppy fields. These were Rihillas, Mekranis, Valayalis, eager, courageous, and fanatical, chiefly sepoy deserters, concealed by the dress of native peasants ... When the hour came, a signal would be enough to excite them to throw themselves *en masse* on the invaders' (249). The European imagination was haunted by Nana's ability to elude pursuit, and he became the spectre haunting the rational edifice of European order in India. In his craft to disguise himself he came to represent all that could not be tamed and made to fit into the mould of the 'domesticated' and grateful native. The elusive Nana embodied the European fear of Asian otherness, the exotic in its most mendacious astuteness and uncanny violence.

43 V.D. Savarkar, for example, reinterprets Nana Sahib's actions in patriotic terms and argues that '[Nana] began to send missionaries all over India to initiate people into ... the glorious ideal of the United States of India and to induce them to join the Revolution' (77). Interpretations of the uprising as a popular political movement marked by patriotic fervour and nationalistic feelings can be found also in Sen 1–40; Chaudhuri 258–99; Misra 34–5, 177–8, 195–7; and Thapliyal 130–1. For a different point of view, see Majumdar 99–148. In his detailed account of the reasons for the insurrection, which include analyses of the various motives that provoked different classes and groups to take part in the insurrection, Majumdar claims that 'it is significant to note that there was no common end, common plan, or common organization. In most cases the outbreaks were purely local affairs' (102). Majumdar denies that Nana Sahib or other leaders 'had either the capacity or opportunity to organize a general conspiracy of an all-Indian character' (379).

44 Through peremptory statements like the one that opens the article, Gozzano denies, with a sort of *post factum* wisdom, the nationalistic hypothesis on a larger temporal scale: 'Per anglomania, per rivalità d'infinite caste, per interessi naturali e morali l'India non vuole e non può sollevarsi' (Because of its anglophilia, of the rivalries among its infinite castes, and of natural and moral interests, India cannot and does not want to rebel) ('L'Olocausto' 93).

45 In 'Le caste infrangibili' (The Unbreakable Castes), Gozzano is more explicit: 'Gl'indiani non formano un popolo e l'India non pensa e non può ribellarsi' (Indians do not form a single people and India cannot think about and is unable to rebel) (63).

46 This is a recurring metaphor in the accounts of the 'mutiny.' See Flechia's conclusion to the Cawnpore narrative: 'Si sarebbe potuto dire, per servirci di un esempio tolto dal mondo fisico, che i fuochi vulcanici avevano cessato, tranne che in un gran cratere imperversante tuttavia nell'Oude e in alcune

minori spaccature d'onde uscivano ancora sprazzi di fiamme; ma l'intera contrada palpitava e tremava ancora del terremoto, e la violenza della scossa sostenuta veniva attestata dalle rovine di cui era seminata' (One could say, to borrow an example from the physical world, that the volcanic fires had subsided, except in a great crater that was still raging in the state of Oudh, and in some minor cracks from which bursts of flames still emerged. However, the whole region still pulsed and shook from the earthquake. The violence of the shock was attested by the ruins that it scattered around) (1284). See also 'the smouldering fires of the volcano' in Ball 1:40 and 306.

47 Nana Sahib had inflamed the European imagination and become the protagonist of plays, novels, travel narratives, and memoirs. Sherer and Maude humorously comment that in English literature he was seen as one of the 'extraordinary monsters of ferocity and slaughter' while French authors portrayed him as 'a scented sybarite, who read Balzac, played Chopin on the piano; and lolling on a divan, fanned by exquisite odalisques from Cashmere, had a roasted English child brought in occasionally on a pike, for him to examine with his *pince nez*' (1: 214).

48 While the themes of dissimulation and deceit use the classic comedy motif of characters disguising themselves and passing for other people, the play does not close, comedy-style, with a recognition scene in which the two protagonists are finally reunited after much strife. If Nana initially feigns submission to the British by affecting English clothes and manners, he then betrays them by presenting himself as the incarnation of Shiva, the destroyer. At the end, in yet another masquerade, Nana dons a vagrant's garb in order to be able to see Djamma before her forced wedding to Nana's deceitful cousin, Tippoo-raj. On the verge of being recognized and killed, Nana manages to once again conceal his identity with Djamma's complicity, who lies to save his life. No longer a prince and deprived of kingdom, spouse, and genuine identity, Nana pays for his betrayal of the British not with loss of life, but with a different and more shameful kind of death. He becomes a pariah and is doomed to live on as an outcast, fixed in a borrowed self, shunned by the rest of society.

49 The 'Mutiny panoramas' were equally popular, their focal points being the slaughter of women and children and Cawnpore, and other graphic 'rebellion' scenes in Lucknow and Delhi (Altick 208, 177).

50 Trevelyan 59; Gupta 9. See also Martin 2: 249.

51 Reports of the 'sumptuous entertainments' that Nana and other native princes offered to their British conquerors captivated Western imagination. Trevelyan writes that 'The Maharaja of Bithoor exhibited a lively interest in the proceedings of our Government at home and abroad, in our history, our

arts, our religion, and our customs ... Nothing could exceed the cordiality which he constantly displayed in his intercourse with our countrymen' (62). Sheperd talks about the 'excellent entertainments [that Nana] gave to the officers and ladies of the station,' and comments that he 'was on friendly and intimate terms with many' (14–15). Nana's sumptuous balls for his soon-to-be European victims became a cliché in popular novels inspired by the Cawnpore events, like Graydon's, which starts with a chapter entitled 'The Nawab's Ball.' See also Pearce, Money, Henty, and Nisbet. On Nana's effective participation in European social life and his contacts with the English residents, see Gupta 7–9. For an overview of the fiction inspired by the 1857 mutiny, see Singh.

52 A report written by a 'gentleman of some literary reputation' was reproduced in several chronicles, including Trevelyan's: 'I sat down to a table twenty feet long (it had originally been the mess-table of a cavalry regiment) which was covered with a damask table-cloth of European manufacture, but instead of a dinner napkin there was a bed-room towel. The soup – for the steward had everything ready – was served up in a trifle-dish which had formed part of a dessert service belonging to the Ninth Lancers – at all events the arms of that regiment were upon it; but the plate into which I ladled it with a broken tea-cup was of the old willow pattern ... The pudding was brought in upon a soup-plate and the cheese was placed before me on a glass dish belonging to a dessert service' (57–8).

53 De Lanoye has an almost identical description: 'Nana-Saheb ... recherca la société des Européens et se fit facilement accepter par elle ... Le journaux de Bénarès et de Calcutta ont parlé longtemps du bal qu'il donna six semaines tout au plus avant l'insurrection, dont ... il était déjà un des plus actifs conspirateurs. A ce bal figurèrent la plupart des femmes et des jeunes filles qui devaient peu après être ses victimes; et pendant qu'elles suivaient, sous ses yeux ou dans ses bras, la mesure d'une valse allemande ... lui, marquait dans sa pensée, et celles qu'il livrerait aux fureurs du glaive, et celle qu'il réserverait pour ses plaisirs ... Chez cet être sensuel et dissolu, le désir de peupler son sérail de blondes et blanches beautés de l'occident ne fut peut-être pas un mobile de crimes moins puissant que la soif du pouvoir et de l'or' (Nana Sahib ... sought the company of the Europeans and they easily accepted him ... Papers in Benares and Calcutta spoke for a long time about the ball that he hosted at the most six weeks before the insurrection of which ... he was already one of the most active organizers. The majority of the ladies and young women who would shortly after be-come his victims participated in this ball. While they followed the rhythm of a German waltz ... under his gaze or in his arms, he identified in his mind those that he would leave to the

fury of the executioner and those that he would keep for his own pleasure ... In this dissolute and sensual being, the desire to people his harem of fair and white Western beauties was as powerful an instigation for his crimes as his thirst for power and gold) (534–5).

54 See also Trevelyan 62–3.

55 Kaye quotes from a letter by Fletcher Hayes describing the operations of transferring the European women, children, and non-combatants from their homes to the improvised entrenchments in Cawnpore: 'At six A.M. [on 22 May] I went out to have a look at the various places, and since I have been in India never witnessed so frightful a scene of confusion, fright, and bad arrangement as the European barracks presented ... I saw quite enough to convince me that if any insurrection took or takes place, we shall have no one to thank but ourselves, because we have now shown to the Natives how very easily we can become frightened, and when frightened utterly helpless' (2: 227). Discussing Nana Sahib's involvement in the insurrection, Kaye also writes that '[Nana] had been told ... that the power of the English in Europe was declining. He knew that we were weak in India – that vast breadths of country, over which Rebellion was running riot, lay stripped of European troops' (2: 235). See also Sheperd, 29 and 42.

56 The disastrous Crimean War (1854–6) was often cited as having contributed to the downfall of British prestige, thus fuelling the Sepoy revolt in 1857. See Russell 1: 168.

57 See also Forrest: 'On the 24th of May, the day on which the many millions beneath her gracious sway commemorated the birth of her Imperial Majesty, no salute was fired at Cawnpore lest the natives should interpret the roar of the guns as a signal for revolt' (1: 410).

58 See also Forrest 399–400.

59 Discussing the eve of the insurrection, Trevelyan refers to the celebration of a birthday, but he is talking about George III and the festivities that are traditionally held at Eton on the monarch's birthday on 4 June. Trevelyan's narrative emphasized the contrast between the peace at home and the looming tragedy in Cawnpore: 'The end was not remote ... On Thursday, the fourth of June: while far away on the banks of pleasant Thames, Eton was celebrating the birthday of her patron monarch, with recitations from Julius Caesar, and copious libations of unwonted champagne: At Cawnpore the men of the Second Cavalry were sharpening sabres, and distributing ammunition, and secreting their families and their property in the back-slums of the native city. In the mid-darkness of the succeeding night, when men were in their first sleep, three reports of a pistol, and a sudden and brilliant conflagration, showed that the hour had arrived' (87–8).

60 On the polemics and horror generated by the British mass executions, see
    Calani 905–6; De Warren 249–51, and especially Misra 294–9.

61 See Camoëns' proud opening of the *Lusiads*: 'This is the story of heroes who,
    leaving their native Portugal behind them, opened a way to Ceylon, and fur-
    ther, across seas no man had ever sailed before' (39).

62 'The concept of aura ... may usefully be illustrated with reference to the aura
    of natural [objects]. We define the aura ... as the unique phenomenon of a
    distance, however close it may be ... If, while resting on a summer afternoon,
    you follow with your eyes a mountain range on the horizon or a branch
    which casts its shadow over you, you experience the aura of those mountains,
    of that branch ... [T]he contemporary decay of the aura ... rests on two cir-
    cumstances ... namely the desire of contemporary masses to bring things
    "closer" spatially and humanly, which is just as ardent as their bent toward
    overcoming the uniqueness of every reality by accepting its reproduction'
    ('The Work' 222–3).

63 Édouard De Warren's book enjoyed a considerable fortune and was repub-
    lished with extensive additions soon after the Sepoy rebellion in 1858.

64 The reference to Indian's mimicry of British costumes is a recurring theme
    in Gozzano. See 'Le caste infrangibili' 59–60, 63, and 'Fachiri e ciurmadori'
    91.

65 See 'To Elsie.'

66 Pearson effectively compares the two renowned and widely differing inter-
    pretations by Brazilian sociologist Gilberto Freyre and British historian
    Charles R. Boxer. With other apologists of the Portuguese empire during the
    Salazar dictatorship, Freyre argued that centuries of interbreeding had cre-
    ated a remarkable racial harmony in India. He thus justified the retention of
    Portugal's colonies in the twentieth century. Conversely, C.R. Boxer provided
    a far less idyllic picture of early racial tensions between *reinoes* (Portuguese
    born in Portugal) and *indiáticos* or *castiços* (Portuguese born in India), *mes-
    tiços* or *descendentes* (people of Indo-Portuguese ancestry).

67 See also 'Le caste infrangibili' 60.

68 On the symbolism of space in the Portuguese palaces in India, see Kubler.

69 On Van Dyck's Genoese paintings, see also Barnes.

70 The theme of the ruin is a recurring one in Gozzano's Indian travels. In the
    dead city of Golconda, too, ruins bear testimony to the distant achievements
    of epic dreams as well as to the overall futility of those very achievements:
    'Golconda! Quella che fu per tanti secoli la meraviglia dell'Asia, la città dei
    diamanti favolosi e delle regine sanguinarie, Golconda favoleggiata nei
    romanzi d'amore e d'avventura dei secoli andati, Golconda la grande guerri-
    era e la grande voluttuosa ... [è] un fantasma' (Golconda! The city that for so

many centuries was the wonder of Asia, the city of fabulous diamonds and bloodthirsty queens, the setting for tales of love and adventure of centuries past, Golconda the great warrior and the great voluptuary ... [is] a ghost') ('I tesori' 67). This time not alone as he was in Goa, Gozzano visits Golconda with an authoritative guide, a professor from Munich, who introduces the dead city to him by way of his expository narrative of 'vicende epiche e ... monumenti famosi' (epic events and ... famous monuments) ('I tesori' 68). Uninterested, Gozzano's mind wavers between reminiscences of Dante's *Inferno* and references to eighteenth-century tales of adventure and *romans merveilleux*. Concluding that 'dinanzi alle ruine troppo riverite è consigliabile l'irriverenza' (before excessively revered ruins irreverence is advisable) ('I tesori' 70), with a predictable ironic move, Gozzano tears through the sublime fabric of the epic and chooses to know Golconda via a 'melodramma giocoso,' the popular 'La fille de Madame Angot' by Charles Lecocq.

71 Lea Ritter Santini points out that the majority of interpreters saw Dürer's *Melancholia* as an allegorical feminine figure (269). As late as 1979, Frances A. Yates describes the melancholic in the masculine: 'his typical physical pose, expressive of his sadness and depression, was to rest his head in his hands' (51), only to switch to the feminine when discussing Dürer's *Melancholia*: 'she supports her pensive head on her hand in the characteristic pose' (51). Klibansky, Panofsky, and Saxl also gender Melancholia in the feminine by connecting her to fifteenth-century French illustrations of *Dame Mérecolye* (304–5).

72 On the 'virility' of D'Annunzio's Angel, see Ritter Santini and Riva.

73 'The melancholic was dark in complexion, with black hair and a black face – the *facies nigra* or livid hue induced by the black bile of the melancholy complexion' (Yates 51).

Bibliography

Abruzzese, Alberto. *Arte e pubblico nell'età del capitalismo: Forme estetiche e società di massa.* Venice: Marsilio, 1982.

– 'Sapere la tecnica.' *Paesaggio metropolitano.* Ed. Giuseppe Bartolucci, Marcello Fabbri, Mario Pisani, and Giulio Spinucci. Milan: Feltrinelli, 1982. 93–110.

L'arrivo di Borghese a Torino.' *La Stampa,* 18 August 1907.

Agamben, Giorgio. *Stanzas: World and Phantasm in Western Culture.* Trans. Ronald L. Martinez. Minneapolis: U of Minnesota P, 1993.

Aimone, Linda. 'Le esposizioni nello specchio delle esposizioni.' *Le Esposizioni Universali, 1851–1900: Il progresso in scena.* Ed. Linda Aimone and Carlo Olmo. Turin: Allemandi, 1990. 13–49.

– 'Nel segno della continuità: le prime esposizioni nazionali a Torino (1884 e 1898).' *Tra scienza e tecnica: Le esposizioni torinesi nei documenti dell'archivio Amma: 1829–1898.* Ed. Pier Luigi Bassignana. Turin: Umberto Allemandi, 1992. 147–67.

Aimone, Linda, and Carlo Olmo. *Le Esposizioni Universali, 1851–1900: Il progresso in scena.* Turin: Allemandi, 1990.

'Al lettore.' *Verso la cuna del mondo: Lettere dall'India.* Vol. 4 of *Opere di Guido Gozzano.* Milan: Treves, 1937. ii–iii.

'Al villaggio e al castello medioevali.' *Torino e l'esposizione italiana del 1884: Cronaca illustrata della esposizione nazionale–industriale ed artistica del 1884.* Turin/Milan: Roux & Favale/Treves, 1884. 59–60.

Allwood, John. *The Great Exhibitions.* London: Studio Vista, 1977.

Altick, Richard D. *The Shows of London.* Cambridge, MA: Belknap, 1978.

Anderson, Benedict R. *Imagined Communities: Reflections on the Origin and Spread of Nationalism.* London: Verso, 1983.

Anserini, Alessandro. *Compendio della storia delle arti industriali: Dall'origine di ciascheduna agli ultimi progressi moderni.* Turin: UTET, 1875.

Antona-Traversi, Giannino. 'Il nostro programma.' *Bianco rosso e verde: Illustrazione quindicinale* 1.3 (15 August 1915): iv.

– 'Presentazione.' *Bianco rosso e verde: Illustrazione quindicinale* 1.1 (15 July 1915): 1.

Antonini, Maria Cristina. 'Le attrazioni alle riunite.' *Milano 1894: Le Esposizioni Riunite.* Milan: Silvana, 1994. 45–52.

Appadurai, Arjun. 'Commodities and the Politics of Value.' *The Social Life of Things: Commodities in Cultural Perspective.* Ed. Arjun Appadurai. Cambridge: Cambridge UP, 1986. 3–63.

Arcari, Paolo. 'Concludendo: 1898–1911–19 ...' *Le esposizioni del 1911 a Torino, Roma, Firenze: Rassegna illustrata delle mostre indette nelle tre capitali per solennizzare il cinquantenario del Regno d'Italia.* Ed. Guido Treves. Milan: Treves, 1911. 431–2.

Aristotle, *Poetics.* Trans. Gerald F. Else. Ann Arbor: U of Michigan P, 1970.

Arnaudon, Giacomo. *Sulle esposizioni industriali con alcune considerazioni intorno alle cause che possono influire sul progresso delle industrie.* Turin: Paravia, 1870.

Arrigoni, Luigi. *Documenti storici e autografi relativi alla storia del Risorgimento italiano posseduti ed illustrati in occasione della esposizione nazionale di Torino 1884.* Milan: Zanaboni e Gabuzzi, 1884.

Arpino, Giovanni, and Roberto Antonetto. *Emilio Salgari il padre degli eroi.* Milan: Mondadori, 1991.

Atkinson, William C. Introduction. *The Lusiads.* By Luis de Camoëns. Trans. William C. Atkinson. Harmondsworth, U.K.: Penguin, 1980. 7–36.

Audisio, Aldo, and Roberto Mantovani. 'La spedizione del secolo.' *La Stella Polare e il suo viaggio avventuroso.* Turin: Viglongo, 2001. xxv–xxxiv.

Avvenire di Torino e sua trasformazione in città industriale e manifatturiera: proposte e suggerimenti al governo, al parlamento e al municipio. Turin: Jona, 1864.

Baculo, Adriana, Stefano Gallo, and Mario Mangone. *Le grandi esposizioni nel mondo: 1851–1900.* Naples: Liguori, 1988.

Bakhtin, Mikhail M. *The Dialogic Imagination.* Ed. M. Holquist. Trans. C. Emerson and M. Holquist. Austin: U of Texas P, 1981.

Ball, Charles. *History of the Indian Mutiny.* 2 vols. London: London Printing and Publishing Co., 1858.

Banti, Alberto. *La nazione del Risorgimento. Parentela, santità e onore alle origini dell'Italia unita.* Turin: Einaudi, 2000.

Baricco, Pietro. *Torino descritta.* Turin: Paravia, 1869.

Barnes, Susan. J., Piero Boccardo, Clario Di Fabio, and Laura Tagliaferro, eds. *Van Dyck a Genova.* Milan: Electa, 1997.

Barthes, Roland. *Camera Lucida: Reflections on Photography.* Trans. Richard Howard. New York: Hill and Wang, 1981

- 'The Reality Effect.' *French Literary Theory Today.* Ed. Tzvetan Todorov. Cambridge: Cambridge UP, 1982. 11–17.
- 'La Tour Eiffel.' *Œuvres complètes.* Ed. Éric Marty. Vol. 1. Paris: Seuil, 1993. 1383–400.

Barzini, Luigi. *Da Pechino a Parigi in sessanta giorni: La metà del mondo vista da un'automobile.* Venice: Marsilio, 1985.

Bassett, Ronald. *Blood of an Englishman: A Novel of the Siege of Cawnpore.* London: Macmillan, 1975.

Bassignana, Pier Luigi. *Le feste popolari del capitalismo: Esposizioni d'industria e coscienza nazionale in Europa 1798–1911.* Turin: Allemandi 1997.
- 'Preludio alla Rivoluzione: Le esposizioni torinesi nel Piemonte preunitario.' *Tra scienza e tecnica: Le esposizioni torinesi nei documenti dell'archivio Amma: 1829– 1898.* Ed. Pier Luigi Bassignana. Turin: Allemandi, 1992. 13–36.
- ed. *Tra scienza e tecnica: Le esposizioni torinesi nei documenti dell'archivio Amma: 1829–1898.* Turin: Allemandi, 1992.

Basso, Alberto, ed. *Storia del teatro Regio di Torino.* Vol. 2: *Il teatro della città: Dal 1788 al 1936.* Turin: Cassa di Risparmio di Torino, 1976.

Beaumont, Cyril. *Complete History of Ballet: A Guide to the Principal Ballets of the Nineteenth and Twentieth Centuries.* New York: Garden City, 1941.

Benedict, Burton, ed. *The Anthropology of World's Fairs: San Francisco's Panama Pacific International Exposition of 1915.* Berkeley: Scholar P, 1983.

Benjamin, Walter. 'Paris, Capital of the Nineteenth Century.' *Reflections: Essays, Aphorisms, Autobiographical Writings.* Ed. Peter Demetz. Trans. Edmund Jeph-cott. New York: Schocken, 1978. 146–62.
- 'The Work of Art in the Age of Mechanical Reproduction.' *Illuminations.* Ed. Hannah Arendt. Trans. Harry Zohn. New York: Schocken, 1968. 217–52.

Bersezio, Vittorio. *Il regno di Vittorio Emanuele II: Trent'anni di vita italiana.* 8 vols. Turin: Roux e Favale, 1878–95.

Bertacchi, Cosimo. *Note geografiche: Saggi scientifici popolari sulle questioni più agi-tate in vari campi della geografia fisica, esploratrice, storica e descrittiva.* Turin: Isti-tuto Fornaris Marocco, 1887.

Bhabha, Homi K., ed. *Nation and Narration.* London: Routledge, 1990.
- 'The Other Question: Difference, Discrimination and the Discourse of Colo-nialism.' *Literature, Politics and Theory: Papers from the Essex Conference 1976–84.* Ed. Francis Barker, Peter Hulme, Margaret Iversen, and Diana Loxley. Lon-don: Methuen, 1986. 148–72.

Bianchi, Nicomede. *Storia della monarchia piemontese dal 1773 sino al 1861.* Turin: Bocca, 1877–85.

Boissay Charles. 'La galerie des machines.' *L'exposition universelle de 1867, illustrée:*

Publication internationale autorisée par la commission impériale. Ed. M. F. Ducuing.
Vol. 2. Paris: Commission Impériale, 1867. 322–23.

Boito, Camillo. 'Il castello medioevale all'esposizione.' *Torino e l'esposizione italiana del 1884: Cronaca illustrata della esposizione nazionale industriale ed artistica del 1884.* Turin/Milan: Roux & Favale/Treves, 1884. 321–3; 330–4; 346–50.

Bonaparte, Napoléon. *Rapport sur l'Exposition universelle de 1855 présenté à l'Empereur par S.A.I. le prince Napoléon.* Paris: Impr. Impériale, 1857.

Bongie. Chris. *Exotic Memories: Literature, Colonialism and the Fin de Siècle.* Stanford, CA: Stanford UP, 1991.

Borgese, Giuseppe Antonio. 'Premessa alla prima edizione.' *Verso la cuna del mondo: Lettere dall'India.* Vol. 4 of *Opere di Guido Gozzano.* Milan: Treves, 1937. 63–8.

Breckenridge, Carol A. 'The Aesthetics and Politics of Colonial Collecting: India at World's Fairs.' *Comparative Studies in Society and History* 31.2 (April 1989): 195–216.

Brennan, Timothy. 'The National Longing for Form.' *Nation and Narration.* Ed. Homi K. Bhabha. London: Routledge, 1990. 44–70.

Brown Goode, George. 'The Museum of the Future.' *Annual Report of the United States National Museum. Part II: Year Ending June 30, 1897.* Washington, DC: Government Printing Office, 1901. 243–62.

Buel, J.W. *The Magic City: A Massive Portfolio of Original Photographic Views of the Great World's Fair and Its Treasures of Art, Including a Vivid Representation of the Famous Midway Plaisance with Graphic Descriptions by America's Brilliant Historical and Descriptive Writer J. W. Buel.* St Louis, MO: Historical Pub. Co., 1894.

Burke, Edmund. *A Philosophical Enquiry into the Origins of Our Ideas of the Sublime and Beautiful.* Oxford: Oxford UP, 1990.

Burton, Richard. *Goa and the Blue Mountains, or Six Months of Sick Leave.* Berkeley: U of California P, 1991.

Burton, Robert. *The Anatomy of Melancholy.* Ed. F. Dell and P. Jordan–Smith. New York: Farrar & Rinehart, 1972.

Calani, Aristide. *Scene dell'insurrezione indiana.* Milan: Civelli, 1858.

Calcaterra. Carlo. 'Note di questa edizione.' *Opere di Guido Gozzano.* Ed. Carlo Calcaterra and Alberto De Marchi. Milan: Garzanti, 1948. 1193–231.

– 'Le opere e il poeta.' *Opere di Guido Gozzano.* Ed. Carlo Calcaterra and Alberto De Marchi. Milan: Garzanti, 1948. vii–xxxiv.

Calò, Maria Amata. 'L'*Excelsior* in pellicola: Dal cinema alla danza, dalla danza al cinema.' *Choregraphie* 3 (1995): 46–78.

– 'Il film *Excelsior* di Luca Comerio.' *Excelsior: Documenti e saggi/Documents and Essays.* Ed. Flavia Pappacena. Rome: Di Giacomo, 1998. 133–44.

Camerlo, Elisabetta. *La Lettura: 1901–1945. Storia ed indici.* Bologna: CLUE, 1992.

Camoëns, Luis de. *The Lusiads*. Trans. and intr. William C. Atkinson. Harmondsworth, UK: Penguin, 1980.

Cantù Cesare. *Storia universale*. Vol. 1. Turin: Pomba, 1838.

Carducci Giosuè. *Poesia e storia*. Bologna: Zanichelli, 1903.

Carita, Helder. *Palaces of Goa: Models and Types of Indo–Portuguese Civil Architecture*. London: Cartago, 1999.

Casella, Angela. 'Le isole non trovate.' *Studi novecenteschi* (July–Sept. 1976): 123–35.

Castronovo, Valerio. 'Da ex-capitale a città dell'industria.' *Torino nell'Italia Unita*. Vol. 5. *Storia illustrata di Torino*. Ed. Valerio Castronovo. Milan: Sellino, 1993. 1201–10.

– *La Stampa: 1867–1925: un'idea di democrazia liberale*. Milan: Franco Angeli, 1987.

– *Storia delle città italiane: Torino*. Rome-Bari: Laterza, 1987.

Catalogue de l'exposition rétrospective de la section française. Paris: Maquet, 1911.

Cawelti, John G. *Adventure, Mystery, and Romance: Formula Stories as Art and Popular Culture*. Chicago: U of Chicago P, 1976.

Cerrato, Bruno. 'Il ruolo della Camera di Commercio.' *Tra scienza e tecnica: Le esposizioni torinesi nei documenti dell'archivio Amma, 1829–1898*. Ed. Pier Luigi Bassignana. Turin: Allemandi, 1992. 37–63.

Chandra, Bholanatha. *The Travels of a Hindoo to Various Parts of Bengal and Upper India*. 2 vols. London: Trübner, 1869.

Chaudhuri, Sashi Bhusan. *Civil Rebellion in the Indian Mutinies, 1857–1859*. Calcutta: World Press, 1957.

Chevrillon, André. *Dans l'Inde*. Paris: Hachette, 1891.

Clifford, James. *The Predicament of Culture: Twentieth–Century Ethnography, Literature, and Art*. Cambridge, MA: Harvard UP, 1988.

Codazza, Giovanni. *Il Regio Museo Industriale di Torino. Suo ordinamento e descrizione delle collezioni*. Turin: Favale, 1871.

Comandini, Alfredo. 'Le origini dell'esposizione di Torino.' *Le esposizioni del 1911 a Roma, Torino, Firenze: Rassegna illustrata delle mostre indette nelle tre capitali per solennizzare il cinquantenario del Regno d'Italia*. Ed. Guido Treves. Milan: Treves, 1911. 10–13.

'Come nacque l'Esposizione.' *L'esposizione nazionale del 1898*. Turin: Roux e Frassati, 1898. 2–3.

'I congressi e l'esposizione.' *L'esposizione nazionale del 1898*. Turin: Roux e Frassati, 1898. 225–6.

'Corrispondenze.' *L'Asmodeo* 11 (11 November 1882): 8.

Corte, Clemente. *Le conquiste e la dominazione degli Inglesi nelle Indie*. Turin: Roux e Favale, 1886.

Corti, Maria. *An Introduction to Literary Semiotics*. Trans. Margherita Bogat and Allen Mandelbaum. Advances in Semiotics. Bloomington: Indiana UP, 1978.

Covino, Andrea. *Torino: Descrizione illustrata*. Turin: Le Beuf, 1873.

'Cronaca milanese.' *L'Asmodeo* 3–4 (11 January 1888): 2.

Cudini, Piero. 'Prefazione.' *Un Natale a Ceylon e altri racconti indiani*. Milan: Garzanti, 1984. 7–39.

D'Annunzio, Gabriele. *The Flame of Life*. New York: Boni and Liveright, 1900.

– *Il fuoco*. Rome: Istituto Poligrafico dello Stato, 1939.

– *Il piacere*. Milan: Mondadori, 1979.

D'Aquino Creazzo, Alida. 'Introduzione.' *Verso la cuna del mondo: Lettere dall'India*. By Guido Gozzano. Ed. Alida D'Aquino Creazzo. Florence: Olschki, 1984. i–xxxvi.

– 'La "letteratura dell'esotismo" e G. Gozzano; A proposito di un capitolo di *Verso la cuna del mondo.' Le ragioni critiche* 30 (1978): 333–55.

Data, Ernaldo. 'Gran rivista *Excelsior.' Excelsior: Azione coreografica, storica, allegorica e fantastica in sei parti e undici quadri*. By Luigi Manzotti. Turin: Edizioni del Teatro Regio, 2000. 39–46.

De Amicis, Edmondo. *Cuore*. Ed. Luciano Tamburini. Turin: Einaudi, 1972.

– *Torino 1880*. Turin: Lindau, 1991.

– 'Torino I: La città.' *Torino e l'esposizione italiana del 1884: Cronaca illustrata della esposizione nazionale–industriale ed artistica del 1884* Vol. 1. Turin/Milan: Roux & Favale/Treves, 1884. 2–6.

De Anna, Luigi. 'Gli articismi nelle opere di ambiente polare scritte da Emilio Salgari.' *Studi di lessicografia italiana* 12 (1994): 217–72.

Debord, Guy. *La societé du spectacle*. Paris: Editions Champ Libre, 1971.

De Cesare, Raffaele. 'Il Mezzogiorno all'Esposizione.' *Milano e l'Esposizione nazionale del 1881: Cronaca illustrata della esposizione nazionale–industriale ed artistica del 1881*. Milan: Treves, 1881. 258–9.

De Gubernatis, Angelo. *Peregrinazioni indiane*. Florence: Niccolai, 1886.

De Lanoye, Ferdinand. *L'Inde contemporaine*. Paris: Hachette, 1858.

Deleuze Gilles, and Félix Guattari. *A Thousand Plateaus: Capitalism and Schizophrenia*. Trans. Brian Massumi. Minneapolis: U of Minnesota P, 1987.

De Luca, Pasquale. *La primavera della patria: Il giubileo d'Italia e le esposizioni del 1911*. Buenos Aires: Corrientes, 1911.

De Marchi, Alberto. 'Note.' *Poesie e prose*. By Guido Gozzano. Ed. Alberto De Marchi. Milan: Garzanti, 1966. 1379–433.

De Rienzi, Louis-Grégoire Do</ény. *Océanie, ou cinquième partie du monde: Revue géographique et ethnographique de la Malaisie, de la Micronésie, de la Polynésie et de la Mélanésie*. Paris: Firmin Didot, 1836–8.

De Rienzo, Giorgio. *Guido Gozzano*. Milan: Rizzoli, 1983.

– 'Introduzione.' *Verso la cuna del mondo: Lettere dall'India*. By Guido Gozzano. Ed. Giorgio de Rienzo. Milan: Mondadori, 1983. 5–12.

Derrida, Jacques. 'La loi du genre / The Law of Genre.' *Glyph: Textual Studies* 7 (1980): 176–232.

De Warren, Edouard. *L'Inde anglaise avant et après l'insurrection de* 1857. Paris: Kailash Editions, 1994.

Di Fazio Alberti, Margherita. *Il titolo e la funzione paraletteraria*. Turin: ERI, 1984.

Diderot, Denis. *Encyclopédie, ou dictionnaire raisonné des sciences, des arts et des métiers. Extraits*. Ed. J. Charpentier and M. Charpentier. Paris: Bordas, 1967.

Dionisio, Agnese. 'La torre ascensore Stigler.' *Milano 1894: Le esposizioni riunite*. Ed. Rosanna Pavoni and Ornella Selvafolta. Milan: Silvana, 1994. 41–4.

'The Disturbed Provinces: Cawnpore.' *Bombay Times* 10 August 1857.

Documenti e immagini 100 anni dopo: Esposizione nazionale di Milano 1881. Comune di Milano: Ripartizione cultura e spettacolo, 1981.

Doria, Giorgio. 'Un pittore fiammingo nel "secolo dei genovesi."' *Rubens e Genova*. Genoa: La Stampa, 1977. 13–29.

D'Ormeville, Carlo. 'I teatri di Milano.' *Gazzetta dei teatri* 1 (1 January 1885): 2.

Duff, Alexander. *The Indian Rebellion: Its Causes and Results in a Series of Letters*. New York: Carter, 1858.

Dumas, Alexandre. *Le comte de Monte–Cristo*. Paris: Gallimard, 1981.

– *Les Garibaldiens: Révolution de Sicile et de Naples*. Paris: Calmann-Lévy, 1900.

– *The Memoirs of Garibaldi*. Trans. R.S. Garnett. New York: Appleton, 1931.

– *On Board the Emma: Adventures with Garibaldi's 'Thousand' in Sicily*. Trans. and Intr. R. S. Garnett. London: Ernest Benn, 1929.

– *Robin Hood le proscrit*. Paris: Calmann-Lévy, 1984.

– *Les trois mousquetaires*. Paris: Calmann-Lévy, 1884.

Eastman, John C. 'Eccentric features of the World's Fair.' *The Chautauquan* 17 (April 1893): 12–14.

Eco, Umberto. 'The Frames of Comic "Freedom."' *Carnival!* Ed. Thomas A. Sebeok. Berlin: Mouton, 1996. 1–9.

– 'Le lacrime del Corsaro Nero.' *Il superuomo di massa*. Milan: Cooperativa Scrittori, 1976. 13–24.

– 'A Theory of Expositions.' *Travels in Hyper Reality: Essays*. Trans. William Weaver. New York: Harcourt Brace, 1986. 291–307.

Eliot, T.S. *What Is a Classic?* London: Faber & Faber, 1944.

Emerson, Ralph Waldo. 'Nature.' *Essays and Lectures*. New York: The Library of America, 1983. 7–49.

Epps, Brad. 'Modern Spaces: Building Barcelona.' *Hispanic Issues 24*. Ed. Joan Ramon Resina. New York: Routledge, 2001. 148–97.

L'esposizione del 1884 in Torino. Illustrata. Milan: Sonzogno, 1884.

Esposizione di Milano 1906: Guida ufficiale. Milan: Max Frank, 1906.

L'esposizione di Torino 1911: Giornale ufficiale illustrato dell'esposizione internazionale delle industrie del lavoro. 2 vols. Turin: Momo, 1910–11.

Esposizione internazionale di Milano Aprile – Novembre 1906: Guida e pianta. Milan: Società Editrice Foto–Eliografica, 1906.

'L'esposizione internazionale di Torino.' *L'architettura italiana* 6 (May 1911): 1.

Esposizione italiana 1898: Arte sacra, missioni cattoliche, centenari religiosi. Turin: Roux e Frassati, 1898.

L'esposizione italiana del 1881 in Milano. Illustrata. Milan: Sonzogno, 1881.

L'esposizione nazionale del 1898. Turin: Roux e Frassati, 1898.

L'esposizione universale di Filadelfia del 1876: Illustrata. Milan: Sonzogno, 1877.

'L'*Excelsior* e la stampa francese.' *La Gazzetta dei teatri* 3 (18 Jan. 1883): 7–8.

L'exposition universelle de 1867 illustrée: Publication internationale autorisée par la commission impériale. 2 vols. Paris: Imprimerie Générale de Ch. Lahure, 1867.

Le esposizioni del 1911 a Roma, Torino, Firenze: Rassegna illustrata delle mostre indette nelle tre capitali per solennizzare il cinquantenario del Regno d'Italia. Ed. Guido Treves. Milan: Treves, 1911.

Le esposizioni riunite di Milano 1894. Unica pubblicazione illustrata autorizzata dal Comitato. Milan: Sonzogno. 1895.

Fanelli, Giovanni. *Fin-de-siècle: La vita urbana in Europa.* Florence: Cantini, 1991.

Ferrando, Enrico M. 'Incerte fortune di un genio minore.' *Excelsior: Azione coreografica, storica, allegorica e fantastica in sei parti e undici quadri.* By Luigi Manzotti. Turin: Edizioni del Teatro Regio, 2000. 47–57.

Ferrario, Giulio. *Il costume antico e moderno.* Florence: Batelli, 1823–6.

Ferrettini, Ernesto. 'Un'ora di vita d'Oriente all'esposizione: La grande *Kermesse.*' *L'esposizione di Torino 1911. Giornale ufficiale illustrato dell'esposizione internazionale delle industrie del lavoro.* Vol. 1. Turin: Momo, 1910–11. 246–51.

Feuerbach, Ludwig. *The Essence of Christianity.* 2nd ed. Boston: Houghton, Mifflin, 1881.

Figuier, Louis. *Année scientifique et industrielle de 1889.* Sarreguemines, France: Pierron, 1997.

Findling, John, ed. *Historical Dictionary of World's Fairs and Expositions, 1851–1988.* New York: Greenwood, 1990.

Finot, Louis, ed. *Le livre du centenaire de la Société Asiatique (1822–1922).* Paris: Geuthner, 1922.

'The First Week of the Exhibition.' *New York Tribune* (18 May 1876): 4–5.

Flaubert, Gustave. *Flaubert in Egypt: A Sensibility on Tour.* Trans. and intr. Francis Steegmuller. London: Bodley Head, 1972.

Flechia, Giovanni. *Storia delle Indie Orientali.* Turin: Sebastiano Franco, 1862.

'Le fontane luminose.' *L'esposizione nazionale del 1898.* Turin: Roux e Frassati, 1898. 226–7.

Forrest, G.W. *A History of the Indian Mutiny.* 2 vols. Edinburgh and London: Blackwood, 1904.

Foucault, Michel. *The Order of Things.* New York: Vintage, 1973.

– 'Panopticism.' *Discipline and Punish: The Birth of the Prison.* Trans. Alan Sheridan. New York: Vintage, 1995. 195–228.

Frajese, Vittorio. *Dal Costanzi all'Opera.* Vol. 2. Rome: Capitolium, 1977.

Francis, David Rowland. *The Universal Exposition of 1904.* St Louis: Louisiana Purchase Exposition Co., 1913.

Freyre, Gilberto. *The Portuguese and the Tropics: Suggestions Inspired by the Portuguese Methods of Integrating Autochthonous Peoples and Cultures Differing from the European in a New, or Luso–tropical, Complex of Civilisation.* Trans. Helen M. D'O. Matthew and F. de Mello Moser. Lisbon: Executive Committee for the Commemoration of the Vth Centenary of the Death of Prince Henry the Navigator, 1961.

Fryer, John. *A New Account of East India and Persia.* Vol. 2. London: Hakluyt Society, 1909.

Gautier, Théophile. *Caprices et zigzags.* Paris: Hachette, 1856.

– 'Melancholia': *Poésies complètes.* Ed. René Jasinski. Vol. 2. Paris: Nizet, 1970.

Genette, Gérard. *Palimpsests: Literature in the Second Degree.* Trans. Channa Newman and Claude Doubinsky. Lincoln and London: U of Nebraska P, 1997.

Giacosa, Giuseppe. 'Ai lettori.' *La Lettura* 1 (1901): 1–5.

Gilbert, James B. 'World's Fairs as Historical Events.' *Fair Representations: World's Fairs and the Modern World.* Eds. Robert Rydell and Nancy Gwinn. Amsterdam: VU UP 1994. 13–27.

'Gli italiani all'estero: La mostra dell'Eritrea e della Somalia italiana.' *L'esposizione di Torino 1911: Giornale ufficiale illustrato dell'esposizione internazionale delle industrie del lavoro.* Vol. 2. Turin: Momo, 1910–11. 524–532.

Goethe, Johann Wolfgang von. *Faust.* Ed. and Trans. Stuart Atkins. Cambridge, MA: Suhrkamp/Insel, 1984.

Gonzato, Silvino. *Emilio Salgari: Demoni, amori e tragedie di un capitano che navigò solo con la fantasia.* Vicenza: Pozza, 1995.

Gozzano, Guido. 'A Candida Bolognino.' Appendice II, *Verso la cuna del mondo: Lettere dall'India.* Ed. Giorgio De Rienzo. Milan: Mondadori, 1983. 169.

– 'Agra: L'immacolata.' *Verso la cuna del mondo: Lettere dall'India.* Ed. Alida D'Aquino Creazzo. Florence: Olschki, 1984. 82–7.

– *Cara Torino: Poesie e prose scelte.* Turin: Viglongo, 1975.

– 'Le caste infrangibili.' *Verso la cuna del mondo: Lettere dall'India.* Ed. Alida D'Aquino Creazzo. Florence: Olschki, 1984. 59–63.

– 'La città moritura.' *Cara Torino: Poesie e prose scelte.* Turin: Viglongo, 1975. 207–9.

- 'I crisantemi alla mostra dei fiori.' *Cara Torino: Poesie e prose scelte.* Turin: Viglongo, 1975. 205–6.
- 'Da Ceylon a Madura.' *Verso la cuna del mondo: Lettere dall'India.* Ed. Alida D'Aquino Creazzo. Florence: Olschki, 1984. 40–9.
- 'La danza d'una Devadasis.' *Verso la cuna del mondo: Lettere dall'India.* Ed. Alida D'Aquino Creazzo. Florence: Olschki, 1984. 50–8.
- 'Il dono della meraviglia.' *Cara Torino: Poesie e prose scelte.* Turin: Viglongo, 1975. 195–7.
- 'Il fiume dei roghi.' *Verso la cuna del mondo: Lettere dall'India.* Ed. Alida D'Aquino Creazzo. Florence: Olschki, 1984. 111–7.
- 'Fachiri e ciurmadori.' *Verso la cuna del mondo: Lettere dall'India.* Ed. Alida D'Aquino Creazzo. Florence: Olschki, 1984. 88–93.
- 'Glorie italiane all'estero: Gli orrori del Paradiso.' *Verso la cuna del mondo: Lettere dall'India.* Ed. Alida D'Aquino Creazzo. Florence: Olschki, 1984. 135–43.
- 'Goa: "La Dourada."' *Verso la cuna del mondo: Lettere dall'India.* Ed. Alida D'Aquino Creazzo. Florence: Olschki, 1984. 19–31.
- 'Le grotte della Trimurti.' *Verso la cuna del mondo: Lettere dall'India.* Ed. Alida D'Aquino Creazzo. Florence: Olschki, 1984. 3–11.
- 'L'impero del Gran Mogol.' *Verso la cuna del mondo: Lettere dall'India.* Ed. Alida D'Aquino Creazzo. Florence: Olschki, 1984. 71–81.
- 'Un Natale a Ceylon.' *Verso la cuna del mondo: Lettere dall'India.* Ed. Alida D'Aquino Creazzo. Florence: Olschki, 1984. 32–9.
- 'L'Olocausto di Cawnepore.' *Verso la cuna del mondo: Lettere dall'India.* Ed. Alida D'Aquino Creazzo. Florence: Olschki, 1984. 103–10.
- 'Il Padiglione della città di Torino.' *Cara Torino: Poesie e prose scelte.* Turin: Viglongo, 1975. 198–201.
- 'Rosolie di stagione.' *Cara Torino: Poesie e prose scelte.* Turin: Viglongo, 1975. 187–90.
- 'I tesori di Golconda.' *Verso la cuna del mondo: Lettere dall'India.* Ed. Alida D'Aquino Creazzo. Florence: Olschki, 1984. 64–70.
- 'Torino d'altri tempi.' *Cara Torino: Poesie e prose scelte.* Turin: Viglongo, 1975. 140–54.
- 'Le Torri del silenzio.' *Verso la cuna del mondo: Lettere dall'India.* Ed. Alida D'Aquino Creazzo. Florence: Olschki, 1984. 12–18.
- 'Un vergiliato sotto la neve.' *Cara Torino: Poesie e prose scelte.* Turin: Viglongo, 1975. 175–86.
- *Verso la cuna del mondo: Lettere dall'India.* Ed. Alida D'Aquino Creazzo. Florence: Olschki, 1984.
- 'Un voto alla dea Tharata-Ku-Wha.' *Verso la cuna del mondo: Lettere dall'India.* Ed. Alida D'Aquino Creazzo. Florence: Olschki, 1984. 127–34.

Gramsci, Antonio. *Quaderni del carcere*, Ed. Valentino Gerratana. Turin: Einaudi, 1975.

La grande esposizione di Londra. Turin: Tipografia Subalpina, 1851.

Graydon, William Murray. *The Butcher of Cawnpore*. Philadelphia: McKay, 1896.

Green, Martin. *Seven Types of Adventure Tale: An Etiology of a Major Genre*. University Park: Pennsylvania State UP, 1991.

Greenhalgh, Paul. *Ephemeral Vistas: The Expositions Universelles, Great Exhibitions and World's Fairs 1851–1939*. Manchester: Manchester UP, 1988.

Grillo, Elena. 'The World in the Days of Excelsior.' *Excelsior: Documenti e saggi / Documents and Essays*. Ed. Flavia Pappacena. Rome: Di Giacomo, 1998. 203–8.

Grisay, Aletta. 'L'India di Guido Gozzano e quella di Pierre Loti.' *La rassegna della letteratura italiana* (Sept.–Dec. 1967): 427–30.

Guest, Ivor. *The Divine Virginia*. New York: Marcel Dekker, 1977.

Guglielminetti, Marziano, ed. *I colloqui e le prose: I Crepuscolari*. Milan: Mondadori, 1974.

Guida illustrata del visitatore alla esposizione generale in Torino del 1884. Milan: Sonzogno, 1884.

Gupta, Pratul Chandra. *Nana Sahib and the Rising at Cawnpore*. Oxford: Clarendon, 1963.

Hamon, Philippe. *Expositions: Literature and Architecture in Nineteenth-Century France*. Trans. Katia Sainson-Frank and Lisa Maguire. Intr. Richard Sieburth. Berkeley: U of California P, 1992.

Harris, Neil. 'Museums, Merchandising, and Popular Taste: The Struggle for Influence.' *Material Culture and the Study of American Life*. Ed. Ian M. G. Quimby. New York: Norton, 1978. 140–74.

Haeckel, Ernst Heinrich. *Lettere di un viaggiatore nell'India*. Trans. Michele Lessona. Turin: UTET, 1892.

Hautecoeur, Louis. *Histoire de l'architecture classique en France*. Vol. 7. *La Fin de l'architecture classique*. Paris: Picard, 1957.

Hay, Denys. *Europe: The Emergence of an Idea*. 2nd ed. Edinburgh: Edinburgh UP, 1968.

Hegel, G.W.F. *The Philosophy of Fine Art*. Trans. F.B.P. Osmaston. London: Bell, 1920.

Heidegger, Martin. 'The Age of the World Picture.' *The Question Concerning Technology and Other Essays*.' Trans. and intr. William Lovitt. New York : Garland, 1977. 115–54.

Henty, G.A. *Rujub, the Juggler*. London: Chatto & Windus, 1893.

Heredia, José-Maria de. *Les Trophées*. Paris: Les Belles Lettres, 1984.

Holmes, T. Rice. *A History of the Indian Mutiny*. 5th rev. ed. London: Macmillan, 1898.

Horkheimer, Max. *Eclipse of Reason.* New York: Continuum, 1974.

Huizinga, Johan. *Homo Ludens: A Study of the Play Element in Culture.* Boston: Beacon P, 1955.

Hunter, William W. *A History of British India.* Vol. 1. London: Longmans, 1899.

Hutchins, Francis, G. *The Illusion of Permanence: British Imperialism in India.* Princeton, NJ: Princeton UP, 1967.

'L'illuminazione.' *Torino e l'esposizione italiana del 1884: Cronaca illustrata della esposizione nazionale-industriale ed artistica del 1884.* Turin/Milan: Roux & Favale/Treves, 1884. 66.

L'Isle-Adam, Villers de. *L'Ève future.* Paris: P.O.L. Éditeur, 1992.

'L'Italia ha dichiarato la guerra alla Turchia: La squadra italiana intima la resa alla piazza di Tripoli.' *La Stampa* 30 September 1911.

James, Henry. Preface to *The Princess Casamassima. Theory of Fiction.* Ed. and intr. James E. Miller. Lincoln: U of Nebraska P, 1972.

Kaye, John. *History of the Indian Mutiny of 1857–58.* 6 vols. Ed. G. B. Malleson. London: Longmans, Green, 1897–8. Reprint Westport, CT: Greenwood, 1971.

Kayser, Wolfgang. *The Grotesque in Art and Literature.* Trans. Urlich Weisstein. New York: Columbia UP, 1981.

Kant, Immanuel. *The Critique of Judgment.* Trans. James Creed Meredith. Oxford: Oxford UP, 1969.

Keats, John. 'Ode to a Grecian Urn.' *Selected Poems.* Ed. Nicholas Roe. London: Dent, 1995.

Kelly, M. Harding. *Dick's Love, or the Shadow of Cawnpore.* London: Simpkin, Marshakk, Hamilton, Kent & Co., 1914.

Klibansky, Raymond, Erwin Panofsky, and Fritz Saxl. *Saturn and Melancholy. Studies in the History of Natural Philosophy, Religion and Art.* Nendeln/Liechtenstein: Kraus, 1979.

Klotz, Volker. *Abenteuer-Romane: Sue, Dumas, Ferry, Retcliffe, May, Verne.* Munich: Hanser, 1979.

Kopytoff, Igor. 'The Cultural Biography of Things: Commoditization as Process.' *The Social Life of Things: Commodities in Cultural Perspective.* Ed. Arjun Appadurai. Cambridge: Cambridge UP, 1986. 64–91.

Kubler, George. *Portuguese Plane Architecture between Spices and Diamonds, 1521–1706.* Middletown, CT: Wesleyan UP, 1972.

Kyriazi, Gary. *The Great American Amusement Parks: A Pictorial History.* Secaucus, NJ: Citadel, 1976.

'In che cosa la mostra di Palermo differirà da quella di Milano e di Torino.' *Palermo e l'esposizione nazionale del 1891–92. Cronaca illustrata.* Milan: Treves, 1892. 10.

L.N. 'The International Exhibition – No. XVIII. The United States Exhibit.' *Nation* (19 October 1876): 238–9.

Lancellotti, Arturo. *Le mostre romane del cinquantenario.* Rome: Palombi, 1931.

Lang, John. *Wanderings in India and Other Sketches of Life in Hindostan.* London: Routledge, 1859.

Lanoye, Ferdinand. *L'Inde contemporaine.* Paris: Hachette, 1858.

Lanza, Domenico. 'L'Esposizione.' *L'esposizione nazionale del 1898.* Turin: Roux e Frassati, 1898. 3–6

Lavini, Giulio. 'L'architettura nazionale.' *L'architettura italiana* 7 (November 1911): 13–14.

Lecocq Charles. *La figlia di Madama Angot. Opera comica in 3 atti.* Turin: Guidici e Strada. 18–.

Levin, Harry. 'Literature as an Institution.' *Accents* 6 (1946): 159–68.

Levra, Umberto. *Fare gli Italiani: Memoria e celebrazione del Risorgimento.* Turin: Comitato di Torino dell'Istituto per la Storia del Risorgimento, 1992.

Lévi-Strauss, Claude. *Tristes tropiques.* Paris: Plon, 1955.

Lombroso, Cesare. *L'uomo delinquente in rapporto all'antropologia, giurisprudenza ed alle discipline carcerarie.* Turin: Bocca, 1884.

López-Rey, José. *Velázquez: Catalogue raisonné.* Vol. 1: *Painters of Painters.* Cologne: Taschen, 1999.

Loti Pierre. *L'Inde (sans les Anglais).* Paris and Pondicherry: Kailash, 1992.

Luti, Giorgio. *Critici, movimenti e riviste del Novecento letterario Italiano.* Rome: La Nuova Italia Scientifica, 1986.

Mack Smith, Denis. *Modern Italy: A Political History.* Ann Arbor: U of Michigan P, 1997.

Magris, Claudio. 'L'avventura di carta ci segna per la vita.' *L'isola non–trovata. Il libro d'avventure nel grande e piccolo Ottocento.* Milan: Emme, 1982. 151–6.

Mainardi, Patricia. *Art and Politics of the Second Empire: The Universal Expositions of 1855 and 1867.* New Haven, CT: Yale UP, 1987.

Majumdar, R. C. *The Sepoy Mutiny and the Revolt of 1857.* Calcutta: Firma K. L. Mukhopadhyay, 1963.

Mantegazza, Paolo. *India.* Milan: Treves, 1884.

Manzoni, Alessandro. 'Marzo 1821.' *Tutte le opere.* Florence: Giunti, 1967. 19–20.

Manzotti, Luigi. *Excelsior: Azione coreografica, storica, allegorica e fantastica in sei parti e undici quadri.* Turin: Edizioni del Teatro Regio, 2000.

Marchis, Vittorio. '"Per dare un più vivo movimento all'industria." Esposizioni e innovazione tecnologica nel Piemonte dell'Ottocento.' *Tra scienza e tecnica: Le esposizioni torinesi nei documenti dell'archivio Amma: 1829–1898.* Ed. Pier Luigi Bassignana. Turin: Allemandi, 1992. 83–102.

Marcora, G. 'Relazione alla Camera.' *Palermo e l'esposizione nazionale del 1891–92. Cronaca illustrata.* Milan: Treves, 1892.

Martin, Robert Montgomery. *The Indian Empire.* 8 vols. London and New York: London Printing and Publishing Co., 1858.

Marvin, Carolyn. *When Old Technologies Were New: Thinking about Electric Communication in the Late Nineteenth Century.* New York: Oxford UP, 1988.

Marx, Leo. *The Machine in the Garden: Technology and the Pastoral Ideal in America.* Oxford: Oxford UP, 1964.

'Melancholy Tragedy at Cawnpore.' *Bombay Times* 20 July 1857.

Mendoza, Eduardo. *La Ciudad de los prodigios.* Barcelona: Seix Barral, 1986.

Merli, Stefano. *Proletariato di fabbrica e capitalismo industriale. Il caso italiano: 1880–1890.* Florence: La Nuova Italia, 1972.

Mendelson, Edward, ed. *Pynchon: A Collection of Critical Essays.* Englewood Cliffs, NJ: Prentice Hall, 1978.

Milano e l'esposizione italiana del 1881: Cronaca illustrata della esposizione nazionale–industriale ed artistica del 1881. Milan: Treves, 1881.

Miller, Perry. *The Life of the Mind in America, from the Revolution to the Civil War.* New York: Harcourt, 1965.

Misra, Anand Swarup. *Nana Saheb and the Fight for Freedom.* Lucknow: Information Dept., 1961.

Mitchell, Timothy. 'The World as Exhibition.' *Comparative Studies in Society and History* 31.2 (April 1989): 217–36.

Monaldi, Gino. *Le regine della danza nel secolo XIX.* Turin: Bocca, 1910.

Mondo, Lorenzo. *Natura e storia in Guido Gozzano.* Rome: Silva, 1969.

Money, Edward. *The Wife and the Ward, or a Life's Error.* London: Routledge, 1859. Reprint: *Woman's Fortitude: A Tale of the Cawnpore Tragedy.* London: Whittingham, 1881.

Mor, Antonio. 'Introduzione.' *Verso la cuna del mondo: Lettere dall'India.* By Guido Gozzano. Milan: Marzorati, 1970. 5–21.

Moretti, Franco. *Modern Epic: The World–System from Goethe to García Màrquez.* Trans. Quintin Hoare. London: Verso, 1996.

Moriondo, Carlo. *Torino 1911: La favolosa esposizione.* Turin: Daniela Piazza, 1981.

Le mostre coloniali all'esposizione internazionale di Torino del 1911: Relazione generale. Rome: Bertero, 1913.

Muddock, J.E. *The Great White Hand or the Tiger of Cawnpore: A Story of the Indian Mutiny.* London: Hutchinson, 1896.

Mumford, Lewis. *The City in History: Its Origins, Its Transformations, and Its Prospects.* New York: Harcourt, 1961.

Musumeci, Mario 'Un restauro a tempo di danza.' *Excelsior: Documenti e saggi / Documents and Essays.* Ed. Flavia Pappacena. Rome: Di Giacomo, 1998. 145–52.

Naitza, Giovanni Bosco. *Il colonialismo nella storia d'Italia, 1182–1949.* Florence: La Nuova Italia, 1975.

Nathan, Ernesto and Secondo Frola. 'Proclama.' *Le esposizioni del 1911 a Roma, Torino, Firenze: Rassegna illustrata delle mostre indette nelle tre capitali per solennizzare il cinquantenario del Regno d'Italia.* Ed. Guido Treves. Milan: Treves, 1911. 4.

Neuschäfer, Hans–Jörg. 'Eugène Sue e il romanzo d'appendice. Sulla storia di un genere letterario "triviale."' *Trivilalliteratur? Letteratura di massa e di consumo.* Trieste: Lint, 1979. 211–34.

Nicoletti, Manfredi. *L'architettura Liberty in Italia.* Bari: Laterza 1978.

Nietzsche, Friedrich. *Human, All Too Human.* Trans. R. J. Hollingdale. Intr. Richard Schacht. Cambridge: Cambridge UP, 1996.

Nisbet, Hume. *The Queen's Desire: A Romance of the Indian Mutiny.* London: White, 1895.

North, Charles N. *Journal of an English Officer in India.* London: Hurst and Blackett, 1858.

Nye, David E. *American Technological Sublime.* Cambridge, MA: MIT, 1994.

O.G.B. 'La vita orientale e la grande *Kermesse* all'Esposizione di Torino.' *Le esposizioni del 1911 a Roma, Torino, Firenze: Rassegna illustrata delle mostre indette nelle tre capitali per solennizzare il cinquantenario del Regno d'Italia.* Ed. Guido Treves. Milan: Treves, 1911. 107.

O'Hara, John M., trans. *The Trophies.* By José–Maria de Heredia. Westport, CT: Hyperion, 1978.

Olmo, Carlo. 'L'ingegneria contesa: La formazione del Museo Industriale.' *Tra scienza e tecnica: Le esposizioni torinesi nei documenti dell'archivio Amma: 1829–1898.* Ed. Pier Luigi Bassignana. Turin: Allemandi, 1992. 103–22.

Oppenheim, James. *The Olympian.* New York: Harper, 1912.

Oswell, G.D. *Sketches of Rulers of India.* Vol. 1. Delhi: ResearchCo Publications, 1972.

Pagliasco, Valeria. 'Se il buon giorno si vede da *Sieba.*' *Excelsior: Azione coreografica, storica, allegorica e fantastica in sei parti e undici quadri.* By Luigi Manzotti. Turin: Edizioni del Teatro Regio, 2000. 59–64.

Pappacena, Flavia. 'L'*Excelsior* di Luigi Manzotti.' *Excelsior: Azione coreografica, storica, allegorica e fantastica in sei parti e undici quadri.* By Luigi Manzotti. Turin: Edizioni del Teatro Regio, 2000. 9–17.

– 'From Giovanni Cammarano's Notebook: The Choreographic Score of the Ballet' *Excelsior: Documenti e saggi/Documents and Essays.* Ed. Flavia Pappacena. Rome: Di Giacomo Ed., 1998. 285–312.

– 'The New *Excelsior* by Caramba.' *Excelsior: Documenti e saggi/Documents and Essays.* Ed. Flavia Pappacena. Rome: Di Giacomo Ed., 1998. 313–26.

– 'The Transcription of the Ballet *Excelsior.*' *Excelsior: Documenti e saggi/Documents and Essays.* Ed. Flavia Pappacena. Rome: Di Giacomo, 1998. 249–68.

Pareto, Raffaele, and Giovanni Sacheri. *Enciclopedia delle arti e industrie compilata colla direzione degli ing. R. Pareto e G. Sacheri.* Turin: UTET, 1878–98.

Parisella, Antonio. 'Fuori dalla scena: Le classi popolari e l'esposizione del 1911.' *Roma 1911.* Ed. Gianna Piantoni. Rome: De Luca, 1980. 53–66.

Pasolini, Pier Paolo. *Il caos.* Ed. Gian Carlo Ferretti. Rome: Editori Riuniti, 1979.

Pater, Walter. *Appreciations. With an Essay on Style.* London: Macmillan, 1920.

Patetta, Luciano. *L'architettura dell'eclettismo: Fonti, teorie, modelli 1750–1900.* Milan: Mazzotta, 1975.

Pavoni, Rosanna, and Ornella Selvafolta. 'Milano 1894: Le Esposizioni Riunite.' *Milano 1894: Le Esposizioni Riunite.* Milan: Silvana, 1994. 7–20.

Pearce, Charles E. *Red Revenge: A Romance of Cawnpore.* London: Stanley Paul, 1909.

Pearson, Michael N. *The Portuguese in India.* Cambridge: Cambridge UP, 1987.

Petronio, Giuseppe. 'Dieci tesi sulla letteratura di consumo e la letteratura di massa.' *Trivialliteratur? Letteratura di massa e di consumo.* Trieste: Lint, 1979. 17–19.

Pettinati, Nino. 'La ferrovia di Superga.' *Torino e l'esposizione italiana del 1884: Cronaca illustrata della esposizione nazionale–industriale ed artistica del 1884.* Turin/Milan: Roux & Favale/Treves, 1884. 70.

Pichetto, Giuseppe, and Francesco Devalle. 'Prefazione.' *Tra scienza e tecnica: Le esposizioni torinesi nei documenti dell'archivio Amma: 1829–1898.* Ed. Pier Luigi Bassignana. Turin: Allemandi, 1992. 9.

Picone Petrusa, Mariantonietta, Maria Raffaella Pessolano, and Assunta Bianco. *Le grandi esposizioni in Italia: 1861–1911. La competizione culturale con L'Europa e la ricerca di uno stile nazionale.* Naples: Liguori, 1988.

Piromalli, Antonio. *Ideologia e arte in Guido Gozzano.* Florence: La Nuova Italia, 1972.

Pizzi, Italo. *L'Islamismo.* Milan: Hoepli, 1903.

Plum, Werner. *World Exhibitions in the 19th Century: Pageants of Social and Cultural Change.* Bonn: Friedrich-Ebert-Stiftung, 1977.

Poesio, Giannandrea. 'Galop, Gender and Politics in the Italian *Ballo Grande.*' *Proceedings of the 20th Conference of the Society of Dance History Scholars.* Riverside: Society of Dance History Scholars, 1997. 151–6.

Porcelli, Bruno. *Gozzano: Originalità e plagi.* Bologna: Patron, 1974.

Portigliatti Barbos, Mario. 'Cesare Lombroso e il museo di antropologia criminale.' *Torino nell'Italia Unita.* Vol. 5. *Storia illustrata di Torino.* Ed. Valerio Castronovo. Milan: Sellino, 1993. 1441–60.

Pozzo, Felice. 'Bibliografia.' Giovanni Arpino and Roberto Antonetto. *Emilio Salgari il padre degli eroi*. Milan: Mondadori, 1991. 185–99.

– 'Io terrei assaissimo che questo volume fosse una glorificazione del valore italiano. *La Stella Polare e il suo viaggio avventuroso*. Turin: Viglongo, 2001. xxxv–lvi.

Prezzolini, Giuseppe. *La coltura italiana*. Florence: La Voce, 1923.

Propp, Vladimir. *Morphology of the Folktale*. Trans. Laurence Scott. Austin: U of Texas P, 1975.

Pynchon, Thomas. 'Entropy.' *Slow Learner: Early Stories*. Boston: Little, Brown, 1985. 79–88.

– *V: A Novel*. Philadelphia: Lippincott, 1963.

Ragone, Giovanni. 'La letteratura e il consumo: Un profilo dei generi e dei modelli nell'editoria italiana (1845–1925).' *Letteratura italiana*. Vol. 2. *Produzione e consumo*. Turin: Einaudi, 1982. 687–772.

Raikes, Charles. *Notes on the Revolt in North–Western Province of India*. London: Longman, 1858.

Rapport sur l'Exposition universelle de 1855 présenté à l'Empereur par S.A.R. le prince Napoléon. Paris: Imprimerie Impériale, 1857.

Relation officielle du voyage et des réceptions des délégués de la ville de Turin à Paris et des délégués du Conseil Municipal de Paris à Rome, Florence et Turin. Paris: Imprimerie Nationale, 1913.

Richepin, Jean. *Nana Saheb: Théatre en vers*. Paris: Fammarion, 1883.

Ritter Santini, Lea. *Le immagini incrociate*. Bologna: Il Mulino, 1986.

Riva, Massimo. *Malinconie del moderno: Critica dell'incivilimento e disagio della nazionalità nella letteratura italiana del XIX secolo*. Ravenna: Longo, 2001.

Robustelli, Giovanni. *Album–ricordo dell'esposizione del 1884 in Torino*. Vol. 2. *L'esposizione industriale*. Milan: Treves, 1884.

Roccia, Rosanna. 'Il tempo e le occasioni.' *Torino città di loisir: Viali, parchi e giardini tra Otto e Novecento*. Ed. Vera Comoli Mandracci and Rosanna Roccia. Turin: Archivio storico della città di Torino, 1996. 11–42.

Romano, Roberto. 'Le esposizioni industriali italiane: Linee di metodologia interpretativa.' *Società e storia* 3 (1980): 215–28.

Rousselet, Louis. *L'Inde des Rajahs: Voyage dans l'Inde centrale et dans les presidences de Bombay et du Bengale*. Paris: Hachette, 1875.

Russell, William Howard. My *Diary in India in the Year 1858–9*. 2 vols. London: Routledge, 1860.

Rydell, Robert W., and Nancy Gwinn, eds. *Fair Representations: World's Fairs and the Modern World*. Amsterdam: VU UP, 1994.

– *World of Fairs: The Century-of-Progress Expositions*. Chicago: U of Chicago P, 1993.

Sacerdote, Gustavo. *La vita di Giuseppe Garibaldi, secondo i risultati delle più recenti indagini storiche con numerosi documenti inediti.* Milan: Rizzoli, 1933.

Said, Edward W. *Culture and Imperialism.* New York: Vintage, 1994.

– *Orientalism.* New York: Vintage, 1979.

Salgari, Emilio. *Il corsaro nero.* Genoa: Donath, 1898.

– *Le due tigri. Emilio Salgari: Edizione annotata – Il primo ciclo della jungla.* Ed. Mario Spagnol and Pietro Citati. Milan: Mondadori, 1969.

– *Le meraviglie del Duemila: Avventure.* Turin: Viglongo, 1995.

– *I misteri della jungla nera. Emilio Salgari: Edizione annotata – Il primo ciclo della jungla.* Ed. Mario Spagnol and Pietro Citati. Milan: Mondadori, 1969.

– *Le pantere di Algeri.* Milan: Vallardi, 1972.

– *I pirati della Malesia. Emilio Salgari: Edizione annotata – Il primo ciclo della jungla.* Ed. Mario Spagnol and Pietro Citati. Milan: Mondadori, 1969.

– *I predoni del Sahara.* Milan: Mondadori, 1973.

– *Il re del mare: Edizione integrale annotata.* Ed. Mario Spagnol and Giuseppe Turcato. Milan: Mondadori, 1971.

– *I Robinson italiani.* Genoa: Donath, 1896.

– *La* Stella Polare *e il suo viaggio avventuroso.* Turin: Viglongo, 2001.

– *Le tigri di Mompracem. Emilio Salgari: Edizione annotata – Il primo ciclo della jungla.* Ed. Mario Spagnol and Pietro Citati. Milan: Mondadori, 1969.

– *Una tigre in redazione: Le pagine sconosciute di un cronista sempre in viaggio con la fantasia.* Ed. Silvino Gonzato. Venice, Marsilio, 1994.

Sangiorgio, Gaetano. 'La mostra dei costumi.' *Milano e l'Esposizione nazionale del 1881: Cronaca illustrata della esposizione nazionale–industriale ed artistica del 1881.* Milan: Treves, 1881. 194.

Sanguineti, Edoardo. *Guido Gozzano: Indagini e letture.* Turin: Einaudi. 1966.

Saragat, Giovanni. 'I chioschi all'Esposizione.' *Torino e l'esposizione italiana del 1884: Cronaca illustrata della esposizione nazionale–industriale ed artistica del 1884.* Turin/Milan: Roux & Favale/Treves, 1884. 346; 378–82.

– 'Tipi umani: Operai all'esposizione.' *Torino e l'esposizione italiana del 1884: Cronaca illustrata della esposizione nazionale–industriale ed artistica del 1884.* Turin/Milan: Roux & Favale/Treves, 1884. 219.

Sarti, Vittorio. *Nuova bibliografia salgariana.* Turin: Pignatore, 1994.

Savarkar, V.D. *The Indian War of Independence, 1857.* Delhi: Ram Tirath Bhatia, 1970.

Savoia, Luigi Amedeo. *La* Stella Polare *nel Mare Artico.* Milan: Hoepli, 1902.

– *Osservazioni scientifiche eseguite durante la spedizione polare di s. a. r. Luigi Amedeo di Savoia duca degli Abruzzi: 1899–1900.* Milan: Hoepli, 1903.

Scammell, Geoffrey V. *The World Encompassed: The First European Maritime Empires, c. 800–1650.* London: Methuen, 1981.

Schroeder–Gudehus, Brigitte, and Anne Rasmussen. *Les fastes du progrès: Le guide des expositions universelles: 1851–1992.* Paris: Flammarion, 1992.

Scobey, David. 'What Shall We Do With Our Walls? The Philadelphia Centennial and the Meaning of Household Design.' *Fair Representations: World's Fairs and the Modern World.* Ed. Robert W. Rydell and Nancy Gwinn. Amsterdam: VU UP, 1994. 87–120.

Segalen, Victor. *Essai sur l'exotisme: Une esthétique du Divers.* Paris: Fata Morgana, 1978.

Selvafolta, Ornella. 'I chioschi nel parco.' *Milano 1894: Le Esposizioni Riunite.* Ed. Rosanna Pavoni and Ornella Selvafolta. Milan: Silvana, 1994. 35–40.

Selvatico, Pietro. *Le condizioni dell'odierna pittura storica e sacra in Italia rintracciate nella Esposizione Nazionale seguita in Firenze nel 1861.* Padua: Antonelli, 1862.

Sen, Surendra Nath. *Eighteen Fifty–Seven.* Calcutta: Government of India P, 1957.

Serra, Renato. *Le Lettere.* Ed. M. Biondi. Milan: Longanesi, 1974.

Sheperd, W.J. *A Personal Narrative of the Outbreak and Massacre at Cawnpore During the Sepoy Revolt of 1857.* 1st Indian ed. New Delhi: Academic Books Corporation, 1980.

Shepp, James W, and Daniel B. Shepp. *Shepp's World's Fair Photographed.* Chicago: Globe Bible Publishing, 1893.

Sherer, John Walter, and Francis Cornwallis Maude. *Memories of the Mutiny.* London: Remington, 1894.

Sieburth, Richard. 'Introduction.' *Expositions: Literature and Architecture in Nineteenth–Century France.* By Philippe Hamon. Berkeley: U of California P, 1992. vii–xv.

Sinclair, Bruce. 'Technology on Its Toes: Late Victorian Ballets, Pageants, and Industrial Exhibitions.' *Context: History and the History of Technology. Essays in Honor of Melvin Kranzberg.* Ed. Stephen H. Cutliffe and Robert C. Post. Bethlehem, PA: Lehigh UP; London and Toronto: Associated University Presses, 1989. 71–87.

Singh, Shailendra Dhari. *Novels on the Indian Mutiny.* Delhi: Arnold–Heinemann India, 1973.

Sistri, Augusto. 'L'Esposizione internazionale del 1911.' *Storia illustrata di Torino.* Ed. Valerio Castronovo. Vol. 6. *Torino nell'età giolittiana.* Milan: Sellerio, 1993. 1621–40.

Slade, Joseph. W. 'Entropy and Other Calamities.' *Pynchon: A Collection of Critical Essays.* Ed. Edward Mendelson. Englewood Cliffs, NJ: Prentice Hall, 1978. 69–86.

Sobrero, Mario. 'Impressioni notturne all'Esposizione di Torino: Serate elettriche.' *Le esposizioni del 1911 a Roma, Torino, Firenze: Rassegna illustrata delle mostre indette nelle tre capitali per solennizzare il cinquantenario del Regno d'Italia.* Ed. Guido Treves. Milan: Treves, 1911. 258–9.

Sonnino, Sidney. 'Torniamo allo Statuto.' *Scritti e discorsi extraparlamentari 1870–1902.* Vol. 1. Ed. Benjamin F. Brown. Bari: Laterza, 1972. 575–97.

Spadolini, Giovanni. *L'autunno del Risorgimento.* Florence: Le Monnier, 1972.

Steinmetz, Horst. 'Genres and Literary History.' *General Problems in Literary History: Proceedings of the 10th Congress of the International Comparative Literature Association, New York 1982.* Ed. Anna Balakian et al. Vol. 1. New York: Garland, 1985. 251–5.

Strafforello, Gustavo. *Storia popolare del progresso materiale negli ultimi cento anni.* Turin: UTET, 1871.

Tamburini, Luciano. 'Diario di un diario: L'anno scolastico di *Cuore* nei giornali cittadini.' *Cent'anni di Cuore: Contributi per la rilettura del libro.* Ed. Mario Ricciardi and Luciano Tamburini. Turin: Allemandi, 1986. 1–42.

'Il tempio di Vesta.' *Torino e l'esposizione italiana del 1884: Cronaca illustrata della esposizione nazionale industriale ed artistica del 1884.* Turin/Milan: Roux & Favale/Treves, 1884. 81–2.

Tenkotte, Paul A. 'Kaleidoscopes of the World: International Exhibitions and the Concept of Culture–Place, 1851–1915. *American Studies* 28 (1987): 5–29.

Terruggia, Amabile. 'Da un'Esposizione all'altra: Risultati e speranze.' *Torino e l'esposizione italiana del 1884: Cronaca illustrata della esposizione nazionale industriale ed artistica del 1884.* Turin/Milan: Roux & Favale/Treves, 1884. 26–7.

Thapliyal, Hari Prasad. *The Life and Works of Peshwa Nana Saheb.* Delhi: Sahitya Kendra Prakashan, 1985.

Thomson, Mowbray. *The Story of Cawnpore.* London: Bentley, 1859.

Todorov, Tzvetan. *On Human Diversity: Nationalism, Racism, and Exoticism in French Thought.* Trans. Catherine Porter. Cambridge, MA: Harvard UP, 1993.

Toga-Rasa. 'I moretti all'esposizione di Torino.' *Le esposizioni del 1911 a Roma, Torino, Firenze: Rassegna illustrata delle mostre indette nelle tre capitali per solennizzare il cinquantenario del Regno d'Italia.* Ed. Guido Treves. Milan: Treves, 1911. 302–3.

Tomasi di Lampedusa, Giuseppe. *Il gattopardo.* Milan: Feltrinelli, 1991.

– *The Leopard.* Trans. Archibald Colquhoun. New York: Avon, 1975.

Torino e l'esposizione italiana del 1884: Cronaca illustrata della esposizione nazionale industriale ed artistica del 1884. Turin/Milan: Roux & Favale/Treves, 1884.

Torino esposizione 1911. Monografia illustrata edita dalla direzione generale del Touring Club Italiano col concorso della Commissione Esecutiva dell'Esposizione di Torino 1911. Milan: Touring Club Italiano, 1911.

Torino, i suoi dintorni e l'esposizione nazionale del 1884. Guida pratica di Luigi Filippo Bolaffio. Milan: Treves, 1884.

Trevelyan, George. *Cawnpore*. New ed. London: Macmillan, 1886.

Turletti, Vittorio. 'Il castello del Valentino.' *Torino e l'esposizione italiana del 1884: Cronaca illustrata della esposizione nazionale–industriale ed artistica del 1884.* Turin/Milan: Roux & Favale/Treves, 1884. 23–24.

Verga, Giovanni. 'L'amante di Gramigna.' *Novelle.* Milan: Rizzoli, 1981.

Verne, Jules. *The Steam House.* Ed. Charles F. Horne. New York: Parke, 1911. Vol. 12 of *Works of Jules Verne.* 15 vols. 1911.

Vernizzi, Cristina. 'Echi del Risorgimento dopo l'Unità.' *Cent'anni di Cuore: Contributi per la rilettura del libro.* Ed. Mario Ricciardi and Luciano Tamburini. Turin: Allemandi, 1897. 48–53.

Viglongo, Giovanna. 'L'editore ai lettori: *Le meraviglie del Duemila.*' *Le meraviglie del Duemila.* Turin: Viglongo, 1995. v–xxiii.

– 'L'editore ai lettori: *La* Stella Polare *e il suo viaggio avventuroso.*' La Stella Polare *e il suo viaggio avventuroso.* Turin: Viglongo, 2001. v–xxiv.

'Il villaggio eritreo all'Esposizione di Torino.' *L'esposizione di Torino 1911: Giornale ufficiale illustrato dell'esposizione internazionale delle industrie del lavoro.* Vol. 2. Turin: Momo, 1910–11. 293.

'Villaggio somalico all'Esposizione.' *L'esposizione di Torino 1911: Giornale ufficiale illustrato dell'esposizione internazionale delle industrie del lavoro.* Vol. 2. Turin: Momo, 1910–11. 340.

Villa, Tommaso. 'Discorso in occasione dell'assemblea del 5–11–1895.' *Guida ufficiale della esposizione nazionale e della mostra di arte sacra.* Turin: Roux e Frassati, 1898. 19–22.

Wade, Stuart C. *A Week at the Fair, Illustrating the Exhibits and Wonders of the World's Columbian Exposition.* Chicago: Rand, McNally, 1893.

Wahlen, Auguste. *Moeurs, usages et costumes de tous les peuples du monde, d'après des documents authentiques et les voyages les plus récents.* Brussels: Librairie historique–artistique, 1843–44.

Ward, Andrew. *Our Bones Are Scattered.* London: John Murray, 1996.

Warshow, Robert. *The Immediate Experience.* Garden City, NY: Anchor, 1964.

White, Hyden. 'The Historical Text as Literary Artifact.' *The Writing of History: Literary Form and Historical Understanding.* Ed. Robert H. Canary and Henry Kozicki. Madison: U of Wisconsin P, 1978. 41–62.

White Mario, Jessie. *Garibaldi e i suoi tempi.* Naples: De Dominicis, 1982.

Whitman, Walt. *Leaves of Grass: Selected Poems and Prose.* New York: Doubleday, 1977.

Wilde, Oscar. *Epigraphs and Aphorisms.* Boston: John W. Luce, 1905.

– *The Soul of Man under Socialism: The Complete Works of Oscar Wilde.* Vol. 10. New York: Doubleday, 1923.

Williams, Carlos William. 'To Elsie.' *The Collected Poems of William Carlos Williams.*

Vol. 1. Ed. A. Walton Litz and Christopher MacGowan. New York: New Directions, 1986. 217–19.

Williams, Raymond. *Culture and Society*. New York: Columbia UP, 1983.

Wilson, Joseph M. *Masterpieces of the Centennial International Exhibition*. Vol. 3. *History, Mechanics, Science*. New York: Garland, 1977.

Wolpert, Stanley. *A New History of India*. 5th ed. New York: Oxford UP, 1997.

Wornum, Ralph N. 'The Exhibition as a Lesson in Taste.' *The Crystal Palace Exhibition: Illustrated Catalogue. London 1851*. Intr. John Gloag. New York: Dover, 1970. i–xxii.

Yates, Frances A. *The Occult Philosophy in the Elizabethan Age*. London: Routledge, 1979.

Yengoyan, Aram. 'Culture, Ideology and World's Fairs: Colonizer and Colonized in Comparative Perspectives.' *Fair Representations: World's Fairs and the Modern World*. Ed. Robert Rydell and Nancy Gwinn. Amsterdam: VU UP 1994. 62–86.

Zachman, Jon B. 'The Legacy and Meaning of the World's Fair Souvenirs.' *Fair Representations: World's Fairs and the Modern World*. Eds. Robert Rydell and Nancy Gwinn. Amsterdam: VU UP 1994. 199–217.

Zini, Zino. 'Appunti di vita torinese.' *Belfagor* 28 (1973): 326–50.

Index

Abba, Giulio Cesare, 150
Abruzzese, Alberto, 82–3, 116
Abyssinia, 94
Adams, Henry, 171
Adorno, Theodor, 43, 44
Adowa, 94, 117, 226
Agamben, Giorgio, 253
Aganoor Pompilj, Vittoria, 305n15
Aimone, Linda, 21, 65, 273n2, 274n8,
    278n22, 289n3
Albertazzi, Adolfo, 182
Albertini, Luigi, 305n15
Albuquerque, Alfonso de, 229, 237
Aleardi, Aleardo, 151
Alfieri, Vittorio, 16
Alhambra Theatre, 76
Allwood, John, 44, 50, 273n2, 279n25,
    288n66, 292n17, 294n25, 299n52
Altick, Richard D., 218, 279n28,
    306n20, 312n49
Anderson, Benedict, 125, 295n34
Antona-Traversi, Giannino, 183
Antonetto, Roberto, 300n13
Antonini, Maria Cristina, 26, 115
Appadurai, Arjun, 206
Arabian Nights, 299n7
Arcari, Paolo, 99, 100, 116

Architettura italiana, 79, 84
Aristotle, 209, 253, 307n27
Arnaudon, Giacomo, 24
Arnold, Matthew, 6
Arpino, Giovanni, 300n13
Atkinson, William C., 246
Audisio, Aldo, 118, 119
Automobile races, 110–14. *See also*
    Barzini, Luigi; Borgese, Scipione

Baculo, Adriana, 24, 273n2, 289n5
Bakhtin, Mikhail, 208, 230, 231, 232,
    233, 234, 235, 236
Baldissone, Giusi, 303n8
Ball, Charles, 215, 218, 219, 308n33,
    312n46
Balzac, Honoré de, 140, 312n47
Bandi, Giuseppe, 150
Baricco, Pietro, 24
Barnes, Susan J., 315n69
Barthes, Roland, 35, 63, 208, 282n42,
    284n48
Barucchi, Luigi, 167
Barzini, Luigi, 182, 183; *Da Pechino a
    Parigi in sessanta giorni: La metà del
    mondo vista da un'automobile*, 112–4,
Basile, Ernesto, 291n14

Bassett, Ronald, 308n34
Bassignana, Pier Luigi, 20, 21, 65, 95, 273n3, 274n5, 274n8, 275n6, 278n20
Basso, Alberto, 66
Bataille, Henry, 304n12
Bava-Beccaris, General Fiorenzo, 32, 117
Beaumont, Cyril, 66
Bellamy, Edward, 167
Benadir, 91, 97, 99
Benedict, Burton, 172
Benjamin, Walter, 3, 39, 43, 44, 63, 229, 262, 279–80n29, 315n62
Berta, Augusto E., 292n16
Bertani, Agostino, 152
Bersezio, Vittorio, 18
Bhabha, Homi, 125
Bianchi, Nicolmede, 18
Bianco rosso e verde, 180, 183, 184, 302n2, 303n8, 304n9, 305n13
Bixio, Nino, 301n19
Blasetti, Alessandro, 286n55
Boissay, Charles, 44
Boito, Camillo, 40–1, 183, 280n30
Bollettino ufficiale dell'Esposizione Internazionale di Torino, 304n10
Bolognino, Candida, 178
Bolzoni, Giovanni, 292n16
Bombay Times, 212, 220
Bongie, Chris, 280n33
Bontempelli, Massimo, 7
Borgese, Giuseppe Antonio, 13–14, 176–80, 193, 201, 205, 301n1, 302–3n8, 305n15, 306n25
Borghese, Scipione, 110–15
Bortoluzzi, Paolo, 285n55
Boselli, Paolo, 291n13
Boxer, C.R., 315n66
Bragaglia, Anton Giulio, 183

Breckenridge, Carol A., 19, 103–4, 283n45
Brennan, Timothy, 125
Bresci, Gaetano, 119
Brooke, James, 12, 141, 145, 147, 155, 165
Buchan, John, 145
Buel, J.W., 116, 280n32
Buffalo Bill, 294n26
Buffon, Georges-Louis Leclerc, Comte de, 134
Burton, Richard, 237–8, 277n18
Burton, Robert, 251

Cagni, Umberto, 117, 297n44
Calani, Aristide, 212, 216–17, 308n33, 315n60
Calcaterra, Carlo, 8, 176–7, 302n3, 302n8
Camerlo, Elisabetta, 181, 182
Cammarano, Giovanni, 287n61
Camoëns, Luis de, 226–7, 230, 232–4, 243, 246; Lusiads, 246, 315n61
Cantù, Cesare, 74–6, 114, 289n68; Storia universale di tutti i popoli, dal principio del mondo fino ai giorni nostri, 74
Caramba (Luigi Sapelli), 285n55
Carducci, Giosuè, 151, 251–2, 253
Caricature, 234–8
Carita, Helder, 240
Casella, Angela, 302n7
Castronovo, Valerio, 15, 16, 17, 89, 305n15
Catalogue, as stylistic device, 131, 184–8, 231, 265
Cattaneo, Carlo, 222
Cavour, Camillo Benso, 18, 265
Cawelti, John, 136–7, 147, 149
Cawnpore (Kanpur), 205, 206, 207, 208, 211, 212, 213, 216, 217, 218,

219, 220, 221, 223, 225, 226, 306n24, 306n25, 307n30, 308n33, 308n34, 310n40, 311n46, 312n49, 313n51, 314n55, 314n57, 314n59. *See also* Gozzano, Guido, 'L'Olocausto di Cawnepore'

Chandra, Bholanatha, 223

Chaudhuri, Sashi Bhusan, 311n43

Chevrillon, André, *Dans l'Inde*, 179

Chiaves, Carlo, 305n15

Cinema, 38, 119

Collector, the, 60–1, 96, 106

Colonialism, 43, 96, 97, 100, 145, 147, 226. *See also* Italian (National, International/Universal) Exhibitions; Universal Exhibitions/Expositions (World's Fairs)

Comandini, Alfredo, 294n29

Comerio, Luca, 286n55

Cornalba, Elena, 73

Corriere della Sera, Il, 112, 118, 301n1, 305n15

Corte, Clemente, 215, 221–3, 226, 309n39

Corti, Maria, 299n4

Covino, Andrea, 24

Crepuscolarismo (Twilight School of Poetry), 8

Criminal anthropology, 104, 105

Crispi, Francesco, 94, 278n21, 305n15

Crivelli, Filippo, 285n55

Crystal Palace, 19, 24, 48, 63, 166, 269, 275–6n12, 276n13

Cudini, Pietro, 303n8

D'Andrade, Alfredo, 39–41

D'Annunzio, Gabriele, 151, 250, 259, 260, 316n72; *Il fuoco*, 256–7

Dante Alighieri, 100, 250, 254, 316n70

D'Aquino Creazzo, Alida, 302n3, 302n4, 302n6, 303n8, 306n25

Darwin, Charles, 104

Darwinism, 100, 134, 177

D'Azeglio, Massimo, 8, 11, 273n7

De Amicis, Edmondo, 9, 21–2, 96, 182, 183; *Cuore*, 18, 150; *Torino 1880*, 52–65

De Anna, Luigi, 298n47

Debord, Guy, 298n50

De Cesare, Raffaele, 87

De Gubernatis, Angelo, 179

De Lanoye, Ferdinand: *L'Inde contemporaine*, 179, 210, 308n33, 309n37, 313n53

Defoe, Daniel: *Robinson Crusoe*, 143–4

Deledda, Grazia, 182, 305n15

De Lesseps, Ferdinand Marie, 69, 70, 277n18

Deleuze, Gilles, 274n10

Dell'Ara, Ugo, 285n55

Della Sala-Spada, Agostino, 167

De Luca, Pasquale, 37, 102–3, 117

De Marchi, Alberto, 302n8

Depretis, Agostino, 19, 94

De Roberto, Federico, 182

De Warren, Edouard, 219, 235–6, 309n39, 315n63

De Rienzo, Giorgio, 178, 179–80, 302n4, 302n6, 303n8

Derrida, Jacques, 238

Diderot, Denis, 23

Di Fazio Alberti, Margherita, 299n3

Di Giacomo, Salvatore, 183

Dioramas, 33, 115, 190, 191, 218, 279n28. *See also* Panoramas

Dogali, 92, 94, 226

Domenica del corriere, La, 118, 183

Domény De Rienzi, Louis-Grégoire, *Océanie, ou cinquième partie du*

*monde. Revue géographique et ethno-
graphique de la Malaisie, de la Micronésie, de la Polynésie et de la Mélanésie*,
126
Donath, Antonio, 118, 126, 273n5,
297n45
Donna, La, 180, 182, 184, 301–2n2,
305n15, 306n25
Doria, Giorgio, 242
D'Ormeville, Carlo, 78, 285n54
Duff, Alexander, 309n37
Dumas, Alexandre, 13, 138, 149, 150,
151–6, 159, 161–2, 300n11; *Le comte
de Monte-Cristo*, 149, 150, 152; *Les
Garibaldiens: Révolution de Sicile et de
Naples*, 152; *Les mémoirs de Garibaldi*
(The Memoirs of Garibaldi), 13,
151, 152–62, 165, 301n18; *Les trois
mousquetaires* (The Three Muske-
teers), 138, 152, 161; *On Board the
Emma*, 152; *Robin Hood le proscrit*,
300n11
Durkheim, Émile, 305n13
Dürer, Albrecht, 248, 250–9,
316n61

East India Company, 222, 224
Eastman, John C., 97, 281n35,
293n22
Eco, Umberto, 51, 125, 190
Edison, Thomas Alva, 73
Egri, Susanna, 286n55
Eiffel Tower, 29, 35, 278–9n23, 282–
3n42
Ekphrasis, 6, 241, 256, 261–2
Electricity, 28–30, 73, 276–7nn16–17,
288–9nn65–7, 289n4
Eliot, T.S., 176
Emerson, Ralph Waldo, 170
Empire Theatre, 76

Entropy, 13, 171–3, 175, 280n33
Epps, Brad, 45, 275n11, 291n11
Eritrea, 95, 99, 101, 297n44
Esploratore, L', 126
*Esposizione internazionale di Milano
Aprile–Novembre 1906*, 117, 279n27,
292–3n20
*Esposizione di Milano 1906: Guida uffi-
ciale*, 67
*Esposizione del 1884 in Torino. Illustrata,
L'*, 46
Esposizione nazionale del 1898, L', 50,
277n18, 279n27
*Esposizione di Torino 1911: Giornale uffi-
ciale illustrato dell'esposizione interna-
zionale delle industrie del lavoro, L'*,
103, 107, 183, 279n28, 282n41,
304n10
Ethiopia, 297n44
Exoticism, 69–70, 280n33, 287–8n62.
See also Italian (National, Interna-
tional/Universal) Exhibitions, and
exoticism; Salgari, Universal exhi-
bitions, and exoticism
Exposition, meanings of, 5–7
Expositions. *See* Italian (National,
International/Universal) Exhibitions; Universal Exhibitions/Expo-
sitions (World's Fairs)
Exposition magazines (catalogues), 5,
37, 102, 107, 182–3
Exposition narratives: definition of,
5–6. *See also* De Amicis, Edmondo;
Gozzano, Guido; Manzotti, Luigi;
Salgari, Emilio

Faldella, Giuseppe, 183
Farina, Salvatore, 183
Faruffini, Federico, 151
Fattori, Giovanni, 151

Ferrario, Giulio: *Il costume antico e moderno*, 126
Ferrettini, Ernesto, 101, 186
Feuerbach, Ludwig: *The Essence of Christianity*, 41
Feuilleton, 8, 13, 152
Ficino, Marsilio, 253
Figuier, Louis, 278n23
Findling, John, 273n2
Flaubert, Gustave: *Flaubert in Egypt*, 192; *Salammbô*, 199
Flechia, Giovanni, 311n46, *Storia delle Indie Orientali*, 216
Fleming, Ian, 145
Florence (Firenze), 10, 15, 21, 54, 79, 86, 103, 242. *See also* Italian (National, International/Universal) Exhibitions
Fontana, Riccardo, 66
Forrest, G.W., 308n33, 314n57–58
Fortunato, Giustino, 88
Foscolo, Ugo, 54, *Ultime lettere di Jacopo Ortis*, 205
Foucault, Michel, 14, 57, 59–60; epistemic break, definition of, 14; panopticism, definition of, 55–6
Fourier, Charles, 63
Fracci, Carla, 285n55
Frajese, Vittorio, 66, 71
Francis, David Rowland, 96, 281n36, 293n24, 296n41
Frassati, Luigi, 305n15
Freyre, Gilberto, 315n66
Frola, Secondo, 86
Fryer, John, 237

Gallo, Stefano, 273n2
Gama, Vasco da, 228–9, 232, 233
Garibaldi, Giuseppe, 13, 15, 18, 19, 150–66, 265, 300nn13–16, 301nn17–

19, *Le mie memorie*, 300n14. *See also* Dumas, Alexandre, *Memoirs of Garibaldi*; Sandokan
Gautier, Théophile, 179, 253
Genette, Gérard, 206, 226, 233, 234
Giacosa, Giuseppe, 181–2
Gibbs, William, 171
Gilbert, James, 52, 294n30
Giolitti, Giovanni, 19, 88, 292n18, 305n15
Giornale illustrato dei viaggi e delle avventure di terra e di mare, 126
Giro del mondo, Il, 126
Goa, 177, 227, 228, 229, 230, 237, 239–48
Gobineau, Joseph-Arthur, comte de, 134
Goethe, Johann Wolfgang von, 232
Golconda, 315–16n70
Goode, George Brown, 38
Gotta, Salvator, 7–8
Gozzano, Guido, 7–8, 13–14, 103, 127, 302nn3–6, 302–3n8, 304n10, 305nn13, 305–6n17, 306n18, 308n33, 311nn44–45, 315–6n70; 'Un addio,' 180; 'Agra: L'immacolata,' 259–63, 302n2; 'La belva bionda,' 180; 'Le caste infrangibili,' 301n2, 311n45, 315n64; 'Da Ceylon a Madura,' 187, 190, 193–7, 301–2n2; 'La città moritura,' 192, 254–5, 258, 304n10; and contemporary journalism 179–84, 304nn11–12, 305nn13–15; 'I crisantemi alla mostra dei fiori,' 254, 304n10; 'La danza d'una Devadasis,' 197–200, 301n2; 'Dittico della pace e della guerra,' 305n13; 'Il dono della meraviglia,' 191–2, 304n10; 'All'esposizione del lavoro:

l'Acquarium,' 304n10; 'Fachiri e ciurmadori,' 91, 301–2n2, 315n64; 'Il fiume dei roghi,' 301n2; 'Glorie italiane all'estero: Gli orrori del Paradiso,' 187, 304n9; 'Goa: "La Dourada,"' 205–6, 226–48, 259, 301–2n2; 'Le grotte della Trimurti,' 184–5, 187–9, 193, 202, 301n2; 'Guerra di spetri,' 180; 'L'impero del Gran Mogol,' 187, 301–2n2; 'Un Natale a Ceylon,' 254, 301n2; 'Gli occhi dell'anima,' 180; 'L'Olocausto di Cawnepore,' 205–26, 311n45, 301n2; 'Il Padiglione della città di Torino,' 254, 304n10; and race, 188–9, 235–8; 'Rosolie di stagione,' 265–6, 304n10; 'La scelta migliore,' 180; 'Sull'oceano di brace,' 304n9; 'Superga,' 304n10; 'I tesori di Golconda,' 264, 266, 267, 301n2; 'Torino suburbana: la gran cuoca,' 304n10; 'Le Torri del silenzio,' 186, 187, 202–5, 301n2; 'Un vergiliato sotto la neve,' 186, 248–59 304n10; *Verso la cuna del mondo: Lettere dall'India*, 13, 176–80, 301–2n2, 302n3, 302n7, 302–3n8, 305–6n17, 306n25; *La via del rifugio*, 8; 'Un voto alla dea Tharata-Ku-Wha,' 194, 304n9. See also Exoticism; Imperialism; India
Graf, Arturo, 7
Gramsci, Antonio, 5
Green, Martin, 143, 149, 150, 300n12
Greenhalgh, Paul, 273n2
Grillo, Elena, 74
Grimoin-Sanson, Raoul, 298n52
Grisay, Aletta, 302n4, 302n7, 306n25
Grotesque, the, 196–7, 200, 218, 232, 234, 235, 239

Guadalupi, Gianni, 303n8
Guattari, Félix, 274n10
Guerzoni, Giuseppe, 150
Guest, Ivor, 73
Guglielminetti, Amalia, 305n15
Guglielminetti, Marziano, 177, 303n8
Gupta, Pratul Chandra, 218, 306n24, 308n33, 309n38, 312n50, 312–13n51

Haeckel, Ernst, 179
Hamon, Philippe, 53, 191, 194–6, 208, 212
Haussmann, Georges-Eugène, 35, 59
Hautecoeur, Louis, 81
Hawthorne, Nathaniel, 175
Hay, Denys, 4
Hegel, Georg Wilhelm Friedrich, 247, 307n28
Hegemony, definition of, 5
Heidegger, Martin, 37
Henty, G.A., 312–13n52
Herder, Johann Gottfried von, 75
Heredia, José Maria de, 227, 246–8, 254
Holmes, T. Rice, 212, 216, 308, 309n38
Horkheimer, Max, 43
Huizinga, Johan: *Homo Ludens*, 265
Hunter, W.W., 237
Hutchins, Francis G., 206
Huysmans, J.K., 260

Illustrazione italiana, L', 48, 151, 286n56
Illustrazione popolare, L', 151
Imperial paradigm, definition of, 103
Imperialism, 3–4, 6, 10–11, 124, 143–4, 202; 270–1; British, 147, 205–26; Italian, 10–11, 74, 88, 147, 166,

226; Portuguese, 226–48. *See also* Italian (National, International/Universal) Exhibitions

India, 13, 297n44; 315n66; represented by Gozzano, 176–9, 184–248, 259–68; represented by Salgari, 126, 135, 137, 141–2; represented in Universal Exhibitions, 103, 276–7n17, 293n22, 295n35

Indian Rebellion (Mutiny), 142, 205–26

Induno, Domenico, 151

Instant books, 117, 118

International expositions. *See* Universal Exhibitions/Expositions (World's Fairs)

Intorno al mondo, 126

Irony, 138, 234, 236, 246, 258

Irving, Washington, 167

Italian (National, International/Universal) Exhibitions, 3; architecture of 10, 39–44, 79, 80–6, 280n31; attendance at, 21; and collective (national) identity, 3, 8–9, 10–11, 27–8, 45–9 51–2, 80, 103–4, 281n36; colonialism and colonial exhibits 10–11, 89–101; compared to expositions abroad, 3–4, 9; contradictions of, 5, 10, 14, 85–86, 106–07; ethnic displays in, 281n36; and exoticism, 26–7, 40–1; history of, 19–23, 273–4n8; ideology of 5, 31–2, 80; and imperialism, 3–4, 10–11, 89–101, 102–9; international recognition of 102–4; North vs South in, 86–8; and the picturesque, 24–5; as places of amusement and leisure, 9, 23–31, 273n3, 278n19; and politics, 47–51; and progress, 22, 51–2, 80, 88–9; and

science and technology, 21–3, 26–7, 80; spectacle (the spectacular), in, 28–9, 37–9, 48–51, 280n32; strikes, during, 32–3, 89, 278n21; topography (location) of, 23–4, 33–5, 100–1; totalizing (universalizing/globalizing) ambitions of, 22–3, 35–7, 43–4, 51–2, 80, 281nn34–5; and travel, 11, 110–22; and war, 89; and Western civilization, 45–6, 51–2, 80, 103–4

Italy, 3, 7; process of nation formation in, 8–9; industrialization, in, 9; and national identity, 15–9. *See also* Italian (National, International/Universal) Exhibitions

James, Henry, 53, 140

Juvarra, Filippo, 55, 82–3, 290n9

Kant, Immanuel, 169, 175

Kaye, John, 216, 220, 224–5, 307n27, 308n33, 309nn37–8, 314n55

Kayser, Wolfgang, 196–7, 306n19

Kelly, M. Harding: *Dick's Love, or the Shadow of Cawnpore,* 219

Klibanski, Raymond, 251, 316n71

Klotz, Volker, 137

Kopytoff, Igor, 266

Kubler, George, 315n68

Kyriazi, Gary, 293n23

Lampedusa, Giuseppe Tomasi di, 142, *Il gattopardo,* 106–7

Lancellotti, Arturo, 85

Lang, John, 308n33

Lanza, Domenico, 37

Lavini, Giulio, 84–5

Lazzeri, Gerolamo, 305n13

Leatherstocking Tales, 143

Le Bon, Gustave, 134
Lecocq, Charles, 315–6n70
Lejeune, Philippe, 227
Le Play, Frédéric, 31–2
Lessona, Michele, 283n44
Lettura, La, 180
Lévi-Strauss, Claude, 43
Levin, Harry, 299n4
Libya, 74, 89, 102
L'Isle-Adam, Villers de, 73
Livingstone, David, 296n43
Loescher, Hermann, 283n44
Lombroso, Cesare, 104–5, 277n18
Loti, Pierre, 227, 305n17, L'Inde (sans les Anglais), 179, 228
Luigi Amedeo, Duke of the Abruzzi, 117–19, 296n42, 297nn44–6, 298n48
Lumière, Auguste and Louis, 287–8n62
Lupati, Cesarina, 305n14
Luti, Giorgio, 301n1

Mack Smith, Denis, 18, 88
Maggi, Luigi: Gli ultimi giorni di Pompeii, 67
Magrini, Luciano, 182
Magris, Claudio, 138–9, 230
Mahzar, Fahreda (Little Egypt), 293n23
Mainardi, Patricia, 273n2
Majumdar, R.C., 216, 306nn23–4, 308n33, 311n43
Mangone, Mario, 273n2
Mantovani, Roberto, 118, 119
Mantegazza, Paolo, 167, 179, India, 126
Mantegazza, Vico, 182
Manzoni, Alessandro, 142, 165, 166
Manzotti, Luigi: Excelsior, 9, 65–78,

114, 168, 285nn52–5, 286nn56–7, 287n60–1, 288n63–4; Amor, 287n60; Sport, 287n60
Marcora, G., 87
Mare, Il, 126
Marenco, Romualdo, 67
Marinetti, Filippo Tommaso, 185
Marradi, Giovanni, 151
Martin, Robert Montgomery, 312n50
Marvin, Carolyn, 73
Marx, Leo, 170
Massaua, 92
Maude, Francis Cornwallis, 312n47
Mazzini, Giuseppe, 15, 18, 19, 163, 265
Mazzoni, Guido, 183
May, Karl, 126, Der Verlorene Sohn, 149
Medici, Giacomo, 152
Mendoza, Eduardo, La ciudad de los prodigios, 4
Menelik, Emperor of Abyssinia, 94
Miceli, Luigi, 22
Midway Plaisance, 293nn22–3
Milan, 9, 20, 28, 32, 33, 35, 66, 73, 79, 87, 102, 110, 112, 116–17, 123, 167, 273–4n8, 274n9, 276n17, 277n18, 282n40, 284n47, 284n51, 285–6n55, 287n60, 288n67, 289n68, 292n20, 296n41, 301n1
Milano e l'esposizione nazionale del 1881: Cronaca illustrate della esposizione nazionale-industriale ed artistica del 1881, 49, 102, 120, 276–7n17, 282n40, 288n66, 295n37
Miller, Perry, 170
Misra, Anand Swarup, 311n43, 315n60
Mitchell, Timothy, 194
Momento, Il, 304n10
Momigliano, Attilio, 7

Mondo, Lorenzo, 302n7
Money, Edward, 312–13n51
Montalembert, Count of, 222
Mor, Antonio, 177, 302n7
Moretti, Marino, 305n15
Moriondo, Carlo, 24, 79, 80–1, 88–9, 92
Muddock, J.E., 308n33
Mumford, Lewis, 290n8

Naitza, Giovanni Bosco, 226
Napoleon I (Bonaparte), 149
Napoleon, Prince Joseph, 35–6
Napoleon III, 50
Nathan, Ernesto, 86
Nationalism. *See* Italian (National, International/Universal) Exhibitions, and nationalism; Universal Exhibitions/Expositions (World's Fairs), and nationalism
Negri, Ada, 305n15
Neuschäfer, Hans-Jörg, 299n1
Nicoletti, Manfredi, 291n14
Nietzsche, Friedrich: *Human, All Too Human*, 264
Nisbet, Hume, 312–13n51
North, Charles, 212
North Pole, expeditions and narratives, 117–19, 171, 296n41, 297n44, 297–8nn46–7
Nuova arena, La, 123–4
Nye, David E., 37, 73, 170, 276n16, 301n21

Oceano, L', 126
Odyssey, 233, 299n7
Olmo, Carlo, 273n2, 274n4
Olympic Games, 22, 65, 284n50
Oppenheim, James, 276n16
Orengo, Nico, 303n8

Oswell, G.D., 209–10, 224
Ottino, Giuseppe, 28, 276n17

Padiglione del Giornale, 107
Padiglione della Moda, 119, 192
Padiglione del Risorgimento, 281n38
Pagliasco, Valeria, 72
Palermo, National Exposition of 1891–2, 32, 35, 87–8, 94, 96, 291n14
Panofsky, Erwin, 196, 251, 316n71
Panopticon, 55–6, 76. *See also* Foucault, Michel
Panoramas, 33, 190, 279n28, 312n49
Panzini, Alfredo, 182
Papin, Denis, 68
Pappacena, Flavia, 69, 71, 284n51, 285nn52–3, 285n55, 287n61
Parks, as exhibition settings, 24–6, 275n10
Parody, 206, 226–7, 234, 238, 247
Pascarella, Cesare, 151
Pascoli, Giovanni, 151
Pasolini, Pier Paolo, 43, 280n33
Pastonchi, Francesco, 7
Pastrone, Giovanni, *Cabiria*, 67
Pater, Walter, 260
Pavoni, Rosanna, 115, 284n47
Paxton, Joseph, 24, 63, 276n13
Pearce, Charles E., 312–13n51
Pearson, Michael N., 229, 237, 315n66
Per terra e per mare: Avventure e viaggi illustrati, scienza popolare e letture amene, 126
Pettinati, Nino, 28
Picone Petrusa, Mariantonietta, 21, 27, 28, 105, 290–1n10
Piedmont, 16, 19, 20, 21, 57, 74, 86
Piemontesismo, definition of, 19

Piromalli, Antonio, 178
Pizzi, Italo: *L'Islamismo,* 179
Plum, Werner, 273n2
Pomba, Giuseppe, 283n44
Popular literature/fiction, 124, 127, 136; vs high literature, 8, 124–5
Porcelli, Bruno, 302
Portigliatti-Barbos, Mario, 104
Pourtauborde, Ernest, 100–2
Pozzo, Felice, 118, 297n45, 298n48, 299n2
Pratesi, Giovanni, 285n55
Prezzolini, Giuseppe, 181
Propp, Vladimir: *Morphology of the Folktale,* 300
Proudhon, Pierre-Joseph: *Projet d'une exposition perpétuelle,* 122
Pynchon, Thomas, 171, 173; 'Entropy,' 172

Quest, theme of the, 177, 238, 243

Rabelais, François, 131
Ragone, Giovanni, 182
Raikes, Charles, 308–9n36
Renan, Ernest, 134
Richepin, Jean: *Nana Saheb,* 217–18
Risorgimento, 9, 13, 15, 16, 18–19, 46, 68, 80, 118, 151, 155, 164, 216, 281n36
Ritter Santini, Lea, 257, 316nn71–2
Riva, Massimo, 253, 257, 316n72
Robida, Albert, 119, 167
Robinsonaden, 144, 300n9
Robustelli, Giovanni, 22, 23, 84, 279n27, 281n38, 294n28
Roccia, Rosanna, 23–4, 275–6n12, 276n14
Rohmer, Sax, 145
Romani, Claudio, 281–2n39

Rome, 9, 10, 15, 16, 17, 18, 33, 40, 46–7, 48, 66, 79, 85, 86–7, 111–12, 229, 239, 287n60, 289n1, 292n15, 301n1, 305n15
Rosselli, Amelia, 305n15
Rousselet, Louis: *L'Inde des Rajahs: Voyage dans l'Inde centrale et dans les présidences de Bombay et dans le Bengale,* 126
Rubens, Peter Paul, 242
Rue des Nations, 45
Russell, W.H., 216, 223, 314n56
Rydell, Robert, 99–100, 105, 295n35

Sacchi, Gaetano, 152
Sacy, Sylvestre de, 38
Sahib, Nana, 207, 213, 216, 217–18, 219, 223, 224, 308n33, 309n38, 310nn40–2, 311n43, 312n47–8, 51, 313n53, 314n55
Said, Edward, 4, *Culture and Imperialism,* 6–7, 11, 299n8; *Orientalism,* 114, 270, 306n21, 307n31
Salandra, Antonio, 180
Salgari, Emilio, 7, 8, 11–12, 14; and the adventure novel, 125–6, 136–50; *Sull'Atlante* 124; *Le avventure del padre Crespel nel Labrador,* 297–8n47; *Il bramino dell'Assam* 124; and British imperialism, 147, 165–6; *I cacciatore di foche nella baia di Baffin,* 124; *La capitana dello Yucatan,* 124; *Ciclo della jungle* (jungle cycle), 12, 146; *Il corsaro nero,* 299n3; *I corsari delle Bermude,* 124; *Le due tigri,* 12, 134, 141, 142, 134, 141, 142; epic code, in, 138–40; estrangement of Western models, in, 143–7; and ethnocentrism, 144–5; exoticism, in, 130–3, 140–1, 144–5, 148; *Sulle fron-*

tiere del Far West, 124; *Le grandi pesche nei mari australi*, 297–8n47; influence of Dumas on, 150–66; and the Italian Risorgimento, 155, 164; *Il leone di Damasco*, 124; *Le meraviglie del Duemila*, 13; *I minatori dell'Alaska*, 124; *I misteri della jungla nera*, 12, 130, 133, 134, 141; *I naufragatori dell'Oregon*, 124; *Gli orrori della Siberia*, 124; *Nel paese dei ghiacci*, 297–8n47; *Le pantere di Algeri*, 124, 131–2; *I pescatori di balene*, 297–98n47; *I pirati della Malesia*, 12, 124, 128, 129, 134, 141; *Al Polo australe in velocipede*, 297–8n47; *Al Polo Nord*, 297–8n47; and popular fiction, 124–5, 127–8, 136–7; *I predoni del Sahara*, 124, 133; *Il re del mare*, 161; *La regina dei Caraibi*, 124; *I Robinson italiani*, 144; *I selvaggi della Papuasia*, 126; *Una sfida al Polo*, 297–8n47; *La stella Polare e il suo viaggio avventuroso*, 118–19; *Le stragi delle Filippine*, 124; *Gli strangolatori del Gange*, 124; *Le tigri di Mompracem (La tigre della Malesia)*, 12, 124, 130, 134, 135, 141, 142–3, 146–7, 148, 151, 156, 160, 161, 163. *See also* Sandokan

Sandokan, 12–13, 123, 131, 134, 145; and the adventure hero, 135–50; Garibaldi, as model for, 150–66. *See also* Salgari, Emilio

Sangiorgio, Gaetano, 295n37
Sanguineti, Edoardo, 302n7, 305n16
San Secondo, Rosso di, 183
Saragat, Giovanni, 26, 94, 278n19
Sarti, Vittorio, 299n2
Savarkar, V.D., 311n43
Savoy, House of, 16–17, 25, 27–8, 29, 48–9, 50, 55, 59, 82, 83, 117–18, 297n44

Saxl, Fritz, 251, 316n71
Scammel, Geoffrey V., 229
Schroeder-Gudehus, Brigitte, 273nn1–2
Schwartz, Maria Speranza, von, 151
Science fiction, 13, 167, 168
Scobey, David, 49–50
Scott, Walter: *Ivanhoe*, 300n11
Segalen, Victor, 178, 188, 191
Selvafolta, Ornella, 296n40
Selvatico, Pietro: *Le condizioni dell'odierna pittura storica e sacra in Italia, rintracciate nella esposizione nazionale in Firenze nel 1861*, 292n15
Sen, Surendra Nath, 308n33, 311n43
Serao, Matilde, 305n15
Serpa Pinto, Alexandre Alberto, 277n18
Serra, Renato, 182
Shepp, James W.: *Shepp's World's Fair Photographed*, 295–6n39
Sheperd, W.J., 212, 308n33, 312–13n51, 314n55
Sherer, John Walter, 307n31, 312n47
Sieburth, Richard, 6, 33,
Sinclair, Bruce, 68, 70, 74, 278n19
Singh, Shailendra Dhari, 312–13n51
Sistri, Augusto, 22, 84, 85
Slade, Joseph W., 171
Sobrero, Mario, 289n4, 295n32
Somalia, 92, 95, 97, 99
Sonnino, Sidney, 51
Stampa, La, 89, 110, 118, 180, 301–2n2, 302–3n8, 304n9, 305n15
Stanley, Henry M., 296n43
Steinmetz, Horst, 299n4
Stigler Tower, 35, 279n24

Sublime ('natural' and 'technologi-
cal'), 13, 37, 135, 168–70, 173, 174,
175, 197, 279n26
Sue, Eugène: *Les Mystères de Paris,* 149
*Sul tetto del mondo: Viaggio di S.A.R. il
Duca degli Abruzzi al Karakoram,*
298n49
Superga, 27, 53–6

Taine, Hippolyte, 134
Tenkotte, Paul A., 293n22, 294n27
Terrail, Ponson du, 299n1
Thapliyal, Hari Prasad, 309n38,
311n43
Thomson, Mowbray, 308n33
Thovez, Enrico, 183
Times, The, 207, 208–9, 213, 308n35
Todorov, Tzvetan, 4, 128, 145
Toga-Rasa, 100
Tommaseo, Niccolò, 283n44
Tommaso di Savoia, Duke of Genoa,
297n44
Toqueville, Alexis de, 222
*Torino e l'esposizione italiana del 1884:
Cronaca illustrate della esposizione
nazionale-industriale ed artistica del
1884,* 21, 25, 182–3, 279n27,
281n38, 282n41
Trevelyan, George, 151, 212, 220,
222, 306n24, 308n33, 312n50,
313n52, 314n59
Treves, Fratelli, 20, 176
Tribuna, La, 305n15
Tripoli, 89, 297n44
Turin: and the baroque, 10, 83–6; as
Italy's capital, 8–10, 15–19; as mod-
ern metropolis, 52–3, 57, 63, 79–
80, 83, 86; 1884 National Exposi-
tion in, 21–31, 35, 39, 46, 94; 1898
National Exposition in, 32, 35, 50–

1, 94–5, 115; Teatro Regio, in, 66,
292n18; University of, 7, 104,
283n44, 295n36, 301n1. *See also* De
Amicis, Edmondo, *Torino 1880;*
Italian (National, International/
Universal) Exhibitions
Turkey, 89, 281n36, 292n18
Turletti, Vittorio, 25

Uccialli, treaty of, 94
Umberto I, King of Italy, 94, 117, 119,
274n2, 276–7n12
Universal Exhibitions/Expositions
(World's Fairs), 3–5, 273n1; and
architecture, 81, 291n11; attendance at, 289n5, 290–1n10; in Austria, 50; and the bourgeoisie, 4; and
collective identity, 45, 49; and colonialism, 43, 96–7; contradictions in
(antinomies in), 4–5, 14; and exoticism, 27, 293nn 22–3, 294n26; in
France, 9, 19, 29, 44–5, 50, 52, 95,
100, 102, 103, 119, 121–2, 279n25,
281n34; in Great Britain, 9, 19, 24,
45, 48, 52, 102, 121; ideology of, 31–
2; and imperialism, 4, 99–100, 103,
295n35; and leisure (freetime),
4, 26–7, 31–2, 273n2, 278n16; and
literature, 5; and mass culture, 4;
and nationalism, 44–5, 52, 84;
and politics, 47–8, 48, 49–50; and
science/technology, 4, 26–7, 80;
in Spain, 45–6, 275n11; spectacle
(the spectacular) in, 37–9, 41–3,
280n32, 298n50; topography of,
33–7; totalizing (universalizing/
globalizing) ambitions of, 4, 14,
37, 43, 44, 51–2, 80, 294n30; and
travel, 296n41, 297–8n47, 298n51;
in the United States, 24, 45, 47, 49,

52, 96, 102, 281n35, 281n36, 282n40, 292n17, 295–6n39; and Western civilization, 31, 45, 52, 80, 103, 104, 121–2; and workers' unions, 121–2. *See also* Italian (National, International/Universal) Exhibitions
Universal (providential) history, 51, 74, 76, 253
Universo pittoresco, L', 126

Valentino Castle, park of, 22, 23–6, 39, 82, 89, 91, 122, 254
Valigia, La, 126
Vallini, Carlo, 7–8
Van Dyck, Anthony, 241–2,
Vascello, Il, 126
Vecchi, Augusto, 152
Velázquez, Diego, 241–2
Venice, 126, 277n18
Verga, Giovanni, 209, 306n26
Verlaine, Paul, 260
Verne, Jules, 66, 124, 128; *Vingt mille lieues sous les mers* (*Twenty Thousand Leagues under the Sea*), 149, 300n11; *L'île mystérieuse* (*The Mysterious Island*), 144, 300n9; *La maison à vapeur* (*The Steam House*), 216, 310n41, 310–11n42; *In the year 2889* (*La journée d'un journaliste americain en 2889*), 167, 301n20
Vernizzi, Cristina, 15, 274n1
Victor Emmanuel II, King of Italy, 15, 18, 71, 274n3, 281–2n39
Victoria, Queen of Great Britain, 208, 220–1, 223–5, 276n13
Viglongo, Giovanna, 118, 168, 297n46
Villa, Tommaso, 32, 46–7, 50–1, 281n37

Villari, Pasquale, 88
Virgil, 229, *Aeneid*, 229, 233
Volta, Alessandro, 69
Voltaire (François–Marie Arouet), 75

Wagner, Richard, 88
Wahlen, Auguste: *Mœurs, usages et costumes de tous les peuples du monde, d'après des documents authentiques et les voyages les plus récents*, 126
Ward, Andrew, 307–8n32
Warren, Édouard de, 218–19, 235–6, 309n39, 315nn60, 63
Warshow, Robert, 136, 137
Weber, Max, 172
Wells, H.G., 167
White, Hayden, 209, 210, 213, 216
White Mario, Jessie, 151
Whitman, Walt, 64–5
Wilde, Oscar, 260
Williams, Carlos William, 236
Williams, Raymond, 166
Wilson, Joseph, 281n36; *The Masterpieces of the Centennial International Exhibition*, 45
Wolpert, Stanley, 223
World's Fairs. *See* Universal Exhibitions
Wornum, Ralph N., 84
Wyss, Johann David: *The Swiss Family Robinson*, 144

Yates, Frances, A., 253, 257, 316n71, 316n73
Yengoyan, Aram, 45

Zachman, Jon B., 292n19
Zini, Zino, 15